CONSPIRACY CULTURE

Conspiracy theories are everywhere in postwar American culture. From postmodern novels to *The X-Files*, and from gangsta rap to feminist polemic, there is a widespread suspicion that sinister forces are conspiring to take control of our national destiny, our minds, and even our bodies. Conspiracy explanations can no longer be dismissed as the paranoid delusions of far-right crackpots. Indeed, they have become a necessary response to a risky and increasingly globalized world, in which everything is connected but nothing adds up.

Through an engaging and cogent analysis of books such as Betty Friedan's *The Feminine Mystique*, Don DeLillo's *Underworld*, movies such as Oliver Stone's *JFK*, the internet, and other forms of popular culture, Peter Knight explores how conspiracy culture has developed, from the 1960's countercultural suspicions about the authorities to the 1990s, where a paranoid attitude is both routine and ironic. *Conspiracy Culture* analyses conspiracy narratives about familiar topics like the Kennedy assassination, alien abduction, body horror, AIDS, crack cocaine, the New World Order, as well as more unusual ones like the conspiracies of patriachy and white supremacy.

Conspiracy Culture shows how Americans have come to distrust not only the narratives of the authorities, but even the authority of narrative itself to explain What Is Really Going On. From the complexities of Thomas Pynchon's novels to the endless mysteries of *The X-Files*, Knight argues that contempory conspiracy culture is marked by an infinite regress of suspicion. Trust no one, because we have met the enemy and it is us.

Peter Knight is Lecturer in American Studies at the University of Manchester.

CONSPIRACY CULTURE

From the Kennedy Assassination to *The X-Files*

Peter Knight

London and New York

First published 2000
by Routledge
11 New Fetter Lane, London EC4P 4EE

Simultaneously published in the USA and Canada
by Routledge
29 West 35th Street, New York, NY 10001

Routledge is an imprint of the Taylor & Francis Group

© 2000 Peter Knight

Typeset in Garamond by Steven Gardiner Ltd
Printed and bound in Great Britain by Biddles Ltd, Guildford and King's Lynn

British Library Cataloguing in Publication Data
A catalogue record for this book is available
from the British Library

Library of Congress Cataloging in Publication Data
A catalogue record for this book has been requested

ISBN 0-415-18977-2 (hbk)
ISBN 0-415-18978-0 (pbk)

CONTENTS

List of figures   vii

Preface   ix

Introduction: Conspiracy/Theory   1

1   Conspiracy/Culture   23

2   Plotting the Kennedy Assassination   76

3   The Problem with No Name: Feminism and the Figuration
    of Conspiracy   117

4   Fear of a Black Planet: "Black Paranoia" and the Aesthetics
    of Conspiracy   143

5   Body Panic   168

6   Everything is Connected   204

    Afterword   242

    Notes   245
    Index   283

FIGURES

1.1 Gateway to the "dark side": www.disinfo.com   56

2.1 The many different images of Lee Harvey Oswald   92

3.1 "I'll just die if I don't get that recipe." Still from   126
     The Stepford Wives

5.1 Still from *The X-Files*   172

5.2 Still from *Outbreak*   192

PREFACE

Branch sits in his glove-leather chair looking at the paper hills around him. Paper is beginning to slide out of the room and across the doorway to the house proper. The floor is covered with books and papers. The closet is stuffed with material he has yet to read. He has to wedge new books into the shelves, force them in, insert them sideways, squeeze everything, keep everything. There is nothing in the room he can discard as irrelevant or out of date. It all matters on one level or another. This is the room of lonely facts. The stuff keeps coming.

(Don DeLillo, *Libra*)

Like the culture of conspiracy theory this book discusses, it has seemed at times that my investigations had entered an infinite regress of speculation and explanation, note-taking and revision. There is *always* one more clue to chase, one more theory to pursue, one more connection to make—not least when dealing with contemporary research materials. I first began thinking about conspiracy before *The X-Files* had aired. At first the television show seemed to have been deliberately planted for me as a clue that I had tapped into something significant (not, of course, that I would entertain such a paranoid suspicion). At times, however, trying to keep track of the endlessly proliferating plot lines of *The X-Files* and other recent cultural texts has produced a sense of vertigo, as I entered what (in connection with the operations of the CIA) has been described as a wilderness of mirrors. In the end I had to imagine a coherent totality behind the unfinished culture that was (and still is) unfolding as I was writing. There was always one more *X-Files* episode to watch; likewise, Thomas Pynchon and Don DeLillo both published enormous new novels after I thought I had finished with those sections. That sensation of vertigo, of both fearing and desiring a sense of coherence beneath the incomplete fragments, is not so far from the conspiracy culture this book describes.

This study began as the work of a lone gunman, mutated at one point into a conspiratorial collaboration, but has in the end reverted to being the pursuit of a lone agent. Finally, however, I've begun to realize that there was a conspiracy all along, a veritable cabal of scholars and media commentators all working—coincidentally, they say—around the same topic. I owe much to that shadowy syndicate of theorists of conspiracy theory whose ideas have helped shape my own.

My first thanks go to Hugh Haughton, Joe Bristow and colleagues at York University who helped me plot my way through the labyrinth of doctoral research, kindly funded by the British Academy. Steven Connor and Hermione Lee, as well as Rebecca Barden at Routledge, helped to suggest a further plot twist beyond the false ending of the dissertation, and a British Academy Postdoctoral Research Fellowship generously enabled me to expand my ideas from the self-contained system of post-modern literature to the distributed circuit of American culture. The School of American and Canadian Studies at Nottingham provided a supportive home for that transition, and in particular I would like to acknowledge the support of Douglas Tallack, Mark Jancovich, and Dave Murray. A year as a Fulbright Junior Research Fellow at New York University enabled me to immerse myself in the everyday culture of conspiracy. For this I am grateful to the Fulbright Commission, as well as to Andrew Ross and the other members of the American Studies Program at NYU, in particular Nikhil Pal Singh, Bridget Brown, and Alondra Nelson. Alasdair Spark, a long-time collaborator on matters conspiratorial and co-organizer of a conspiracy theory conference held at King Alfred's College in 1997, has been a generous Deep Throat informing many of the ideas contained here, and tirelessly passing on research materials and inside information. For their participation in that conspiracy conference, and in an ongoing international dialogue on conspiracy culture, I would also like to thank in particular Eithne Quinn, Ingrid Walker Fields, Pat O'Donnell, and Jodi Dean. Portions of Chapter 6 were first presented at the DeLillo Conference at Rutgers in 1998, and I am especially indebted to responses from John McClure and Skip Willman. Gratitude is also due to intellectual and social co-conspirators John Plotz, John Arnold, Paul Whitty, Heather Middleton, Mary-Ann Gallagher, Sophie Breese, Ed Morris and Susannah Sayler, as well as to my parents for their continual support over the years. Clues left at the scene of the crime point to the shadowy but undeniable influence of Lindsay Porter.

Portions of Chapter 1 appeared in a different guise as "'A Plague of Paranoia': Theories of Conspiracy Theory Since the 1960s," in *Fear Itself: Enemies Real and Imagined in American Culture*, ed. Nancy Schultz (West Lafayette, IN: Purdue University Press, 1999), 23–50. A version of Chapter 3 appeared as "Naming the Problem: Feminism and the Figuration of Conspiracy," *Cultural Studies* 11 (1997): 40–63, reprinted by permission of Taylor & Francis, (http://www.tandf.co.uk/journals). Sections of Chapter 6 were published as "Everything Is Connected: *Underworld*'s Secret History of Paranoia," *Modern Fiction Studies* 45 (1999): 811–36, © Purdue Research Foundation, reprinted by permission of The Johns Hopkins University Press.

Introduction

CONSPIRACY/THEORY

This is the age of conspiracy, the age of connections, links, secret relationships.

(Don DeLillo, *Running Dog*)

It remains for the future to decide whether there is more delusion in my theory than I should like to admit, or whether there is more truth in Schreber's delusion than other people are as yet prepared to believe.

(Sigmund Freud, "Psychoanalytical Notes on an Autobiographical Case of Paranoia")

No matter how paranoid you are, you can never be paranoid enough.

(*The X-Files*)

At the turn of the millennium in America it seems that conspiracy theories are everywhere. From *JFK* to *The X-Files*, from the Oklahoma bombing to TWA flight 800, and from rumors about the CIA distributing crack in the ghetto to suspicions about the origins of HIV/AIDS in a government laboratory, the language of conspiracy has become a familiar feature of the political and cultural landscape in the last couple of decades. Even the First Lady has intoned the word "conspiracy" on national television. During an interview on NBC's *Today* show, before her husband's public confession in the Monica Lewinsky scandal, Hillary Rodham Clinton attacked the President's accusers, claiming that there is a "vast right-wing conspiracy that has been conspiring against my husband since the day he announced for president."[1] Although her remark generated much comment and more than its share of mockery, not least on talk radio, it was nonetheless in keeping with the times.[2] The possibility of a conspiratorial explanation has come to be taken for granted (or at least cynically evoked), from the darkest recesses of the Internet, right up to the White House.

1

   Hillary Clinton's carefully planned off-the-cuff accusation is a headlining indication of how prominent conspiracy thinking has become in recent years. But conspiracy theories have a long history in the USA. It could even be argued that the Republic itself was founded amid fears and allegations on both sides, with the leaders of the American revolution well schooled in discerning political intrigue and deception, a lesson they had learned from British politics. "They saw about them," writes Bernard Bailyn, "with increasing clarity, not merely mistaken, or even evil, policies violating the principles upon which freedom rested, but what appeared to be evidence of nothing less than a deliberate assault launched surreptitiously by plotters against the liberty both in England and in America."[3] Introducing Bailyn's contribution to a wide-ranging anthology of American writings on conspiracy-minded countersubversion, David Brion Davis asks, "Is it possible that the circumstances of the Revolution conditioned Americans to think of resistance to a dark subversive force as the essential ingredient of their national identity?"[4] The identity of the emerging state was shaped by the continual fear of sinister enemies, both real and imagined, both external and internal. American history has seen more than its share of nativist demonology, as citizens have sounded the alarm about the threat to God's chosen nation, conjuring up tales about subversive forces ranging from Catholics to Communists, and from the Masons to the militias.[5]

   Traditionally these countersubversive fears have been regarded as little more than the delusional rantings of those on the fringes of society, a persistent but marginal feature of American political life. Since the 1960s, however, conspiracy theories have become far more prominent, no longer the favoured rhetoric of backwater scaremongers, but the lingua franca of many ordinary Americans. Following the assassination of President Kennedy in 1963 in particular, conspiracy theories have become a regular feature of everyday political and cultural life, not so much an occasional outburst of countersubversive invective as part and parcel of many people's normal way of thinking about who they are and how the world works. You now need, as the popular wisdom has it, to be a little paranoid to remain sane. A certain kind of world-weary paranoia has become the norm, in both entertainment culture and popular politics. It is always in danger of spiraling out of control, but it is also held in check by a paradoxical self-ironizing awareness of the diagnosis of paranoia. I may be paranoid, the thinking goes, but that doesn't mean that they're not out to get me. Conspiracy theories are now less a sign of mental delusion than an ironic stance towards knowledge and the possibility of truth, operating within the rhetorical terrain of the double negative. They are now presented self-consciously as a symptom that includes its own in-built diagnosis. The rhetoric of conspiracy takes itself seriously, but at the same time casts satiric suspicion on everything, even its own pronouncements. More often than not, recent conspiracy culture is marked by a routinized air of cynicism, as people are prepared to believe the worst about the world they live in—even if they also show a nostalgic gullibility in continually being shocked to find out that things are indeed as bad as they suspect. This book examines how and why a reconfigured culture of conspiracy has become so influential over the last quarter century or so.

The usual photofit picture of the conspiracy theorist is an obsessive, petty-minded right-wing paranoid nut, a proponent of extremist politics with a dangerous tendency to single out the usual suspects as scapegoats. In recent decades, however, the images and rhetoric of conspiracy are no longer the exclusive house-style of the terminally paranoid. Instead they circulate through both high and popular culture, and form part of everyday patterns of thought. The logic of conspiracy has become a ready source of scenarios for both entertainment and literary culture, from the gangsta rap songs of the Wu-Tang Clan to the novels of Don DeLillo. At the same time as the growth of a culture *about* conspiracy, it is arguable that a culture *of* conspiracy has become an implicit mode of operation in American politics, with the rise of the national security state over the last half-century. The pursuit of policy objectives through clandestine means has at various times over the last fifty years or so come to be taken for granted by the political establishment. A presumption towards conspiracy as both a mode of explanation and a mode of political operation have together formed what might be termed "conspiracy culture."

Conspiracy theories, this study will argue, are now less likely to give vent to alarmist fears about an occasional irruption of the normal order of things, than to express a not entirely unfounded suspicion that the normal order of things itself amounts to a conspiracy. The style of conspiracy culture has accordingly changed from a rigid conviction about a particular demonized enemy, to a cynical and generalized sense of the ubiquity—and even the necessity—of clandestine, conspiring forces in a world in which everything is connected. Certainty has given way to doubt, and conspiracy has become the default assumption in an age which has learned to distrust everything and everyone.

Conspiracy theories have traditionally functioned either to bolster a sense of an "us" threatened by a sinister "them," or to justify the scapegoating of often blameless victims.[6] More recently, however, the discourse of conspiracy has given expression to a far wider range of doubts, and has fulfilled far more diverse functions. Conspiracy theories have come to express doubt about the legitimacy of authority in an age when less than a quarter of Americans trust the government (in comparison with fifty years ago when three-quarters trusted the authorities).[7] Narratives of conspiracy now capture a sense of uncertainty about how historical events unfold, about who gets to tell the official version of events, and even about whether a causally coherent account is still possible. They speak to current doubts about who or what to blame for complex and interconnected events. In the era of transnational corporations and a globalized economy, conspiracy-minded stories and rumors in the USA also voice suspicions about who—if anyone—is in control of the national economic destiny, and what it means to be American. The rhetoric of conspiracy likewise expresses concern about whether we are in control of our own actions, and even whether we are in control of our own minds and bodies. Conspiracy talk involves working out not only where corporate responsibility begins and ends, but also, in times of viral confusion, where our corporeal identity has its limits. Popular conspiracism has mutated from an obsession with a fixed enemy to a generalized suspicion about conspiring forces. It has shifted, in effect, from a paradoxically secure form of paranoia that bolstered one's sense of identity, to a far more insecure version of conspiracy-infused anxiety which plunges everything into an infinite regress of suspicion. In short, there is now a permanent uncertainty about fundamental issues of causality, agency, responsibility and identity in an age when many Americans' sense of assured national and personal destiny has been cast into profound doubt. The various case studies of this book document how the function, style and significance of these conspiratorial fears have changed in significant ways since the 1960s.

After the first chapter, which presents a summary of the broad changes in the style and function of conspiracy thinking since the 1960s (through an analysis of Pynchon's *Vineland* [1990]), each of the chapters examines a different aspect of contemporary conspiracy culture. Chapter 2 deals with the Kennedy assassination, the mother-lode of this new conspiracy style, and explores why it functions as an inevitably ambiguous point of origin for a loss of faith in authority and coherent causality—the primal scene, as it were, of a postmodern sense of paranoia. The next two chapters explore how the logic of conspiracy has shaped two of the new social movements emerging from the 1960s, namely feminism and black activism. In each of these cases, images of conspiracy have helped develop the analysis of institutional oppression (sexism and racism respectively), but in doing so they have blurred the distinction between a literal allegation of conspiracy and a metaphorical allusion. The following chapter discusses how previous fears about invasion of the body politic have mutated into an everyday panic about the viral infiltration of the body itself, as people find themselves integrated into a globalized environment of risk. The final chapter assesses how conspiracy culture has given expression to fears and fantasies that everything is becoming connected. Far from being committed to an outdated and simplistic notion of causation, recent conspiracy theories have begun to give popular voice to cutting-edge ideas about causal connections inspired by chaos and complexity theory. A reading of DeLillo's *Underworld* (1998) brings all these issues together. The remainder of the introduction outlines various theories about conspiracy theory that have gained currency recently, and argues that a different approach is required to explain the new modes of conspiracy culture described in this study.

Academic Alarmism and Popular Paranoia

The prominence of conspiracy theories in American politics and culture has generated much anxious discussion in recent years, not least in the aftermath of the Oklahoma bombing and its panicked revelations about the rise of paranoia-promoting militias. In addition to a seemingly endless supply of television documentaries salaciously going over the same old theories and personalities in the name of concerned investigation, there have been numerous newspaper editorials and newsmagazine feature articles seeking to diagnose the zeitgeist, from *Newsweek* to *Z Magazine* on the Web.[8] Alongside these items of armchair sociology there have begun to appear a range of scholarly books dealing with different aspects of conspiracy culture. What many of these popular and academic studies have in common is their insistence on condemning and disproving the cultural logic of paranoia.

The most wide-ranging of the recent academic studies is Daniel Pipes's *Conspiracy: How the Paranoid Style Flourishes and Where It Comes From*. It provides an overview of fears in the West principally about Jewish and secret-society conspiracies from the time of the Crusades to the present. Building on Pipes's previous study of conspiracy theories in the Middle East, the book documents the many episodes of scapegoating that have shaped Western history, the majority of which, in Pipes's view, have been fueled by anti-Semitism. Pipes emphasizes that what he terms "conspiracism," whether on the left or the right, has been a force of unparalleled evil. "In the period between the two world wars," he explains, "leaders rode conspiracism to power in Russia and Germany, then used it to justify aggressive campaigns for territorial expansion."[9]

Pipes's study is in the tradition of the historian Richard Hofstadter's classic essay, "The Paranoid Style in American Politics." In this article, Hofstadter argues that the "paranoid style" has always been a recurrent feature of American politics. He outlines outbursts of demonological fervor in American history, from before the founding of the Republic, through the rise of movements such as anti-Masonism and anti-Catholicism in the nineteenth century, and onto the anti-Communism of the twentieth century. In each case it is assumed that conspiracy theories are dangerous and distorted—if not entirely false—accounts of historical events. There is, however, often a recognition that there might be a kernel of truth to at least some of the conspiracy theories. Hofstadter acknowledges that "paranoid writing begins with certain defensible judgements"; he admits there was, for example, "something to be said for the anti-Masons."[10] But what distinguishes the "paranoid style" from more orthodox scholarship,

Hofstadter continues, is the "rather curious leap in imagination that is always made at some critical point in the recital of events" (PS, 37). In the final analysis, then, the paranoid style is a sign of "distorted judgement," and Hofstadter confesses that his terminology inevitably is "pejorative" (PS, 5). Pipes likewise warns readers that he is dealing "not with the cultural elite but its rearguard, not with the finest mental creations but its dregs."[11]

In a similar fashion, Robert Robins and Jerrold Post's *Political Paranoia: The Psychopolitics of Hatred* tracks the influence of paranoia in a long series of case studies drawn from politics and public events. The book offers potted biographies and thumbnail historical sketches (ranging from Jim Jones to Pol Pot), revealing in each episode that paranoia is to blame for the worst excesses of history. Somewhat strangely, like Pipes they engage in a concerted discussion of whether Hitler's or Stalin's regime was the most paranoid and hence the most destructive (both books agree that it is the latter in terms of the ultimate body count).

Both *Conspiracy* and *Political Paranoia* conclude that when the paranoid style dominates politics we had better watch out. They insist that conspiracy thinking is no longer a real threat in the USA, and that its most dangerous excesses are to be found either in the past, or in other countries (Pipes, for example, singles out the Middle East as particularly attracted to the paranoid style). Other commentators, however, have argued that a culture of paranoia remains a serious political threat in America, even if it doesn't lead directly to the kind of genocide associated with Hitler and Stalin. Chip Berlet of the Political Research Associates, for example, is a prominent and tireless campaigner against the scapegoating of minorities by far-right organizations. Along with groups like the Southern Poverty Law Center, Berlet monitors the activities of militias and neo-Nazi movements, denouncing the seductive but harmful tendencies of conspiracism. "Conspiracist scapegoating," writes Berlet, "is woven deeply into US culture and the process appears not just on the political right but in center and left constituencies as well." It is not, he warns, a victimless crime.[12]

In contrast to most commentators, Elaine Showalter's *Hystories: Hysterical Epidemics and Modern Culture* taps into popular current events and trends which are for the most part not expressly political, but which are nevertheless fiercely contested within the public arena. Showalter presents a series of case studies of current "epidemics" of hysteria—from Gulf War Syndrome (GWS) to alien abduction scares—in which patients turn to conspiratorial explanations for what she insists are psychological disturbances. Though sympathetic to their very real psychological suffering, she nonetheless roundly castigates people's tendency to blame external conspiracies for personal problems. She states plainly that "contemporary hysterical patients blame external sources—a virus, chemical warfare, satanic conspiracy, alien infiltration—for psychic problems."[13] Like Pipes and Robins and Post, Showalter finds the willingness to believe in conspiratorial explanations an all-too-common mode of popular thought in an age of increasing public gullibility.

Together these investigations uncover traces of conspiracism in almost every era and in every aspect of American culture, and they warn of the unparalleled power of popular paranoia to foment hatred. However, it might be argued that the tendency to find evidence of conspiracism behind every major event in world history is itself in danger of producing a conspiracy theory of conspiracy theories. The more we learn about its sinister ubiquity, the more conspiracism becomes not merely a powerful ideology but a mysterious force with a hidden agenda that takes over individual minds and even whole societies. For Pipes and for Robins and Post, conspiracism is a malign force which emanates from the fiendishly seductive demagoguery of powerful leaders, and which the masses are hoodwinked into believing. In addition to this conspiracy-infused form of intellectual history, the figuration of the spread of paranoid thinking as an "epidemic" (Robins and Post) or a "plague" (Showalter) likewise renders it an inscrutable and virtually unstoppable force that infiltrates innocent minds.

With their attacks on the dangerous delusions of paranoid politicians, their followers, and the mind-numbing influence of mass culture, these commentators thus end up replicating the very mode of paranoid thinking they seek to condemn. In listing the tell-tale traits of the paranoid style, they duplicate the tendency of paranoid political tracts to provide an identikit picture of the demonized enemy (the "How-to-tell-if-your-neighbor-is-a-Communist" approach). What we should really be scared of, they suggest, is the spread of popular paranoia. By invoking the term "conspiracism," Pipes presents a picture of conspiracy theory as an ominous sounding ideology, something akin to Communism, and which likewise demands an ever-vigilant crusade against its creeping threat. "Conspiracism manages to insinuate itself in the most alert and intelligent minds," he warns us, "so excluding it amounts to a perpetual struggle, one in which the reader is invited to join."[14] In effect, conspiracism here becomes a demonized and reified entity on which most of the ills of history can be blamed. There is more than a hint of academic alarmism about the proliferation of popular paranoia.

Summing up this fear of the rising tide of public gullibility, Showalter writes in the preface to the paperback edition of *Hystories* that "we have a long way to go before credulity, superstition, and hysterical epidemics are on the wane."[15] Pipes, for instance, vents his spleen particularly on the World Wide Web as a current source of conspiracism, since the very technology, he argues, mesmerizes its viewers into credulity. These studies are in tune with the many recent works of popular science which engage in skeptical debunking of public misunderstandings, from Carl Sagan's *The*

Demon-Haunted World to Michael Shermer's *Why People Believe Weird Things.*[16] In many ways the vilifying of popular paranoid gullibility recalls intellectual attacks of the 1950s on the stultifying effects of "masscult," which amount to a virtual conspiracy theory of how the masses are duped not just by totalitarian leaders but also by the entertainment industry.[17] But the more recent assault on conspiracism is not just confined to condemning the dumbed-down masses and right-wing scaremongers. Pipes, for instance, is motivated by a sense that the left has escaped far too lightly from these critiques (hence his special concern to point out the evils of Stalin). Reviving the Culture Wars attacks on the secret infiltration of universities by tenured radicals since the 1960s, he suggests that academia and the liberal media have come to accept a certain conspiratorial, anti-authoritarian attitude as normal; indeed, Pipes considers the whole project of Marxism as essentially conspiracist in its account of the collaboration of owners against workers. Pipes takes issue with what he regards as woolly-headed political pieties from left-leaning critics who, in his view, should know better. In a return to another Culture Wars favourite, Robins and Post likewise mount an attack on the literary theory of deconstruction, for example, for tending (like Oliver Stone's *JFK*, in their view) to muddy the distinction between truth and falsity. The charge is that these cultural practices weaken the epistemological immune system of the audience, leaving them vulnerable to infection by paranoia. There is undoubtedly some justification to the claim that the left as well as the right have come to take a certain conspiratorial outlook for granted (though, as Chapter 1 discusses, the division of the political spectrum into left and right no longer makes much sense in the world of conspiracy culture). But instead of merely extending the reproof of conspiracy thinking to include not only the duped masses but the so-called tenured radicals, it would make more sense to investigate why a formerly extremist view has become so mainstream and popular.

All these writers suggest that conspiracy theories have been and will continue to be very harmful forms of belief. Together they suggest that it is the responsibility of the intellectual to condemn the paranoid style wherever and whenever it is discovered. Their ultimate concern is less to understand the exact cause or significance of the "plague of paranoia" than to help prevent an outbreak. In contrast, the present study starts from the position that contemporary conspiracy thinking can indeed be dangerous and deluded, but it can also be a necessary and sometimes even a creative response to the rapidly changing condition of America since the 1960s. Conspiracy culture, in short, provides an everyday epistemological quick-fix to often intractably complex problems. The task is therefore not to condemn but to understand why the logic of conspiracy has become attractive in so many different areas of American culture, and how it is reshaping how people think about questions of causality, agency, responsibility, and identity. Though they would strenuously deny that conspiracism can ever be counted as creative, Pipes and Robins and Post, for example, would agree that in the contemporary US it has ceased to be harmful. Both books argue that the paranoid style has now become a merely cultural phenomenon and hence insignificant, since, unless there is a body count that can be measured in thousands if not millions, outbursts of populist paranoia hardly register on their scales. This study, however, will argue that conspiracy thinking is becoming increasingly important in spite of—perhaps even because of—its cultural turn.

Refutations

Dismissals of the "epidemic of paranoia" seek not merely to condemn but also to refute and correct in order to cure this disease. Karl Popper's essays from the 1940s and 1950s on the "conspiracy theory of society" are merely the first in a long line of refutations of conspiracy thinking on theoretical grounds. Popper insists that, although there have undoubtedly been successful conspiracies from time to time, history operates more through chance and the combination of abstract forces than through the concerted actions of individual conspirators. He defines the conspiracy theory of society as "the view that whatever happens in society—including things which as a rule people dislike, such as war, unemployment, poverty, shortages—are the results of direct design by some powerful individuals or group."[18] Popper rejects this picture of historical causation, arguing that "the conspiracy theory of society cannot be true because it amounts to the assertion that all events, even those which at first sight do not seem to be intended by anybody, are the intended results of the people who are interested in these results."[19]

In an important article on the paranoid style in revolutionary America, Gordon Wood argues that eighteenth-century conspiracy theories (with their picture of small cabals covertly influencing public events) were very much in tune with wider assumptions about historical agency at the time. Wood nevertheless insists, like Popper, that conspiracy theorists in the twentieth century have got it all wrong. He argues that, with the rise in the nineteenth century of the social sciences which viewed history as the effect of abstract forces rather than individual conspiring agents, conspiratorial interpretations of events "now seemed increasingly primitive and quaint."[20] The persistence of conspiracy theories into the twentieth century, he continues, can indeed only be explained "as mental aberrations, as a paranoid style symptomatic of psychological disturbance" favored by the marginal and the powerless. Wood explains that, as "modern social science emerged," attributing events to conspiracy theories became "more and more simplistic":

In our post-industrial, scientifically saturated society, those who continue to attribute combinations of events to deliberate human design may well be peculiar sorts of persons—marginal people, perhaps, removed from the centers of power, unable to grasp the conceptions of complicated causal linkages offered by sophisticated social scientists, and unwilling to abandon the desire to make simple and clear moral judgements of events.[21]

In effect, Wood's conclusion is that conspiracy theorists just don't understand how history works, a view that has been reasserted in numerous magazine essays and scholarly articles. As the case studies in this book demonstrate, however, conspiracy theories now register a widespread loss of faith in the "sophisticated social scientists" themselves, as well as their model of historical causation. With their complex and often contradictory "conceptions of complicated causal linkages" in our "post-industrial, scientifically saturated society," conspiracy theories now participate, along with new sciences such as ecology and chaos theory, in a wider challenge to orthodox models of how history works. Conspiracy talk of recent decades has therefore tended to provide not simple moral certainties but increasing doubt and uncertainty about even the most fundamental assumptions of What Is Really Going On.

Definitions

Since the revelations during the mid-1970s in the wake of Watergate about the conspiratorial activities of government agencies, a priori dismissals of conspiracy theory have become less tenable for many Americans. Indeed, as Chapter 1 discusses in more detail, a quasi-paranoid hermeneutic of suspicion is now taken for granted by many Americans, including the scholarly community. Those intent on condemning the paranoid style are, however, seldom swayed by the argument that, since some conspiracy theories have turned out to be true, then conspiracy thinking is no longer necessarily delusional. They insist that the revelations about, say, Watergate or the Iran–Contra dealings are not the vindication of a crackpot conspiracy theory, but the product of proper investigative journalism. If a conspiracy theory turns out to be true, it is redescribed as astute historical analysis (and, conversely, if a historical speculation turns out to be unfounded, then it is often dismissed as a conspiracy theory). The point about conspiracy theories, of course, is that virtually no one claims to believe in a conspiracy theory as such. The people accused of holding conspiracy theories about the death of JFK, for example, are very insistent that they are assassination researchers and not conspiracy buffs. It's only other people who believe in conspiracy theories, the argument goes.

10

For many commentators, conspiracy theories are by definition deluded, simplistic and harmful, and anything that doesn't fit that rubric is not a conspiracy theory. It comes as no surprise, then, that on this view conspiracy theories are to be condemned, almost by definition. Robins and Post, for example, insist that, while suspiciousness in itself might have an adaptive utility (in their terminology drawn from evolutionary psychology), *paranoid* suspiciousness is bad.[22] Pipes is likewise extremely clear in defining a conspiracy theory (not least, as we have seen, because in doing so he provides the reader with a spotter's guide to the virus of paranoia that is to be eradicated from the immune system of the body politic). He classifies conspiracy theories into two groups: "petty conspiracy theories," which merely involve fears about people seeking to gain local advantage; and "world conspiracy theories," which include fears about a political take-over by a malign force with global aspirations.[23] Pipes here is echoing Hofstadter's definition of the paranoid style not so much as a tendency to "see conspiracies here or there in American history," as a belief in "a 'vast' or 'gigantic' conspiracy as *the motive force* in historical events" (PS, 29; emphasis in original). Because petty conspiracy theories (and even some world conspiracy theories) do not lead to measurable political atrocities, Pipes and other commentators rule out in advance the very kinds of conspiracy theory that might challenge their model of what a conspiracy theory is.

The term "conspiracy theory" often acts as an insult itself, an accusation of unsophisticated, wooly-headed thinking that verges on the mentally disturbed. Calling something a conspiracy theory is not infrequently enough to end discussion. Part of the task of the present inquiry, however, is to investigate how and why some forms of belief about historical events and daily life get labeled as conspiracy theories and diagnosed as paranoid, while others do not. Instead of measuring up conspiracy theories against a gold standard of rationality to which they will often be in deficit, it is more profitable to understand how they function as barely articulated suspicions about who is in control of things in an increasingly interconnected world. In contrast to the restrictive definitions of conspiracy theory that most commentators promote, this book considers a broad spectrum of conspiratorial representations, from fully elaborated theories to passing suspicions about hidden forces. Some of these forms of everyday conspiracy culture are barely recognizable as conspiracy theories by traditional definitions. There is no fixed set of inherent qualities that makes something a conspiracy theory, since in many cases a view becomes a conspiracy theory only because it has been dismissed as such. Indeed, one of the most significant shifts in the function and format of conspiracy thinking in recent decades is from the deliberate promotion of single-issue demonological doctrines to a more fluid and contradictory rhetoric of paranoia that suffuses everyday life and culture.[24]

Corrections

Many discussions of conspiracy theories condemn them not only by definition or for theoretical reasons, but also on factual grounds. They make
clear that paranoid thinking is so dangerously attractive because it has all
the trappings of proper academic work (not least the proliferation of footnotes), but with none of the scholarly rigor or integrity. Showalter, for
example, warns that the temptation of paranoid thinking undermines a
"respect for evidence and truth."[25] Pipes goes so far as to maintain a stead-
fast distinction between proper scholarship and the pseudoscholarship of
conspiracy theory by distinguishing all the latter items in his bibliography
with small capitals, sometimes with odd results. For example, in his view
Marxism is underpinned by a theory of capitalists in conspiracy against the
working class, or, in later versions, against the Third World. Immanuel
Wallerstein's work on world systems theory is therefore marked out by
the same type face that brands the "Protocols of the Elders of Zion."

Though Pipes's insistence on policing the boundary between the legitimate and the paranoid is taken to an extreme (some might even say to a
paranoid extreme), many other writers have likewise sought not merely to
analyze and condemn but also to correct the delusions of paranoid
thinking. In her analysis of outbursts of hysteria, Showalter takes pains to
point out misinterpretations of the medical literature promoted by
Chronic Fatigue Syndrome (CFS) sufferers, in addition to factual inaccura-
cies spread by proponents of Gulf War Syndrome (GWS)—dismissals
which were ill received by both groups. Pipes likewise dedicates a significant
portion of his book to recounting What Really Happened in, say, the
Russian revolution, in order to demonstrate that Marxism–Leninism is
based on a paranoid worldview. At times Pipes's *Conspiracy* and Robin and
Post's *Political Paranoia* begin to read like history primers, providing thumbnail overviews of events from the fourteenth century to the present. This
tendency to rewrite in beginner's guide fashion the history of the modern
world reaches a bizarre extreme in Gregory S. Camp's *Selling Fear: Conspiracy Theories and End-Times Paranoia*. The book is an attempt by a religious
scholar to provide both an anatomy and a refutation of contemporary
right-wing Christian conspiracy thinking, and much of its 288 pages are
taken up with potted accounts of the history of American affairs, from the
Revolution to President Bush's discussion of a "new world order."[26]

With their compulsion to correct and condemn it is hard to work out
whom these works are addressed to and intended for. Showalter, for
example, writes in the breezy populist tone of the public intellectual address-
ing the so-called generally educated reader, while Robins and Post adopt
the judicious measure of policy recommendation (the latter pair have
indeed served as consultants to several US administrations). Given that
these discussions of conspiracy theory on the whole arise from and address

a scholarly community, we might then wonder why their authors feel obliged to correct and condemn misconceptions that by their own admission are often inexcusable. Surely their presumed audience doesn't need reminding that Jews aren't about to take over the world, or that the US government is not in cahoots with little gray aliens? It would seem that the intended readers for these studies are the ones on the whole least likely to need such correction. Moreover, the real targets of their scorn—the seemingly gullible masses—are not likely to be cured of their delusions by a one-paragraph dismissal of their pet theories. *Hystories*, for example, was met by a barrage of abuse (including death threats) from CFS and GWS sufferers who weren't in the least convinced by Showalter's pithy dismissals of their allegations.[27]

These dismissive accounts of conspiracy thinking work from the premise that it is the responsibility of the public intellectual to dispel ignorance wherever and whenever it is found. Robins and Post, for example, take issue with Patricia Turner's book on the history and function of conspiracy rumors in African American communities.[28] She argues that conspiracy theories in black culture are a popular and strategically resistant way of understanding larger social processes such as economic, medical and environmental racism, as well as consumerism and the corporate control of scientific knowledge. Turner suggests that conspiratorial urban legends need to be understood less as factual accounts of events, than as homemade stories which have symbolic resonance with the conditions of everyday life for many people in black communities. Robins and Post take issue not so much with Turner's interpretation of these conspiracy narratives as with her refusal to "condemn them or suggest their potential for destructiveness."[29] They are scandalized that "a leading scholar" could acknowledge "the falsity of such rumors" and still insist that they form a protest against consumer culture, for instance. In their view the responsible intellectual must help rid the world of the "virus of paranoia" by all available means.[30] But unless we can tune in to exactly why conspiracy culture appeals to so many people, there is little chance of curbing its worst excesses (or even its creative ironies). Understanding why normal people believe weird things is harder but ultimately more fruitful than trying to disprove those weird beliefs by dogmatic insistence on the proper version of events. Robins and Post also warn that because there is often a "reluctance in some white elite media circles to criticize black leaders publicly, paranoid statements concerning blacks are legitimated—or go unchallenged—to a degree that other such charges are not."[31] Yet, if large numbers of African Americans do not trust officials and experts (not to mention their understandable distrust of "white elite media circles"), then no amount of condemnation by "a leading scholar" will make any difference. Instead of lamenting the fact that African Americans could be duped into believing such nonsense, it would be more to the point to ask why

13

other, more orthodox explanations should hold so little appeal. Recognizing the rhetorical function of conspiracy thinking—or merely omitting to condemn it—is not necessarily to recommend such views.

The Paranoid Style

If pointing out the error of conspiracism's ways is partly motivated by a general sense of intellectual responsibility, then it is also dictated by a more technical need to show that conspiratorial beliefs are delusional, before a symptomatic diagnosis can take place. Starting with Hofstadter's seminal article, the most common theory of conspiracy theory is that it is a sign of *paranoia*. Robins and Post's first chapter, for example, is on "The Mind of the Paranoid." In each case, a broadly psychological explanation is given for why people are attracted to conspiratorial accounts of how history works. To be fair, Hofstadter and those following in his footsteps are at pains to point out that they do not mean the term "paranoia" in any clinical sense.[32] Hofstadter, for example, argues instead that:

> there is a vital difference between the paranoid spokesman in politics and the clinical paranoiac: although they both tend to be overheated, oversuspicious, overaggressive, grandiose, and apocalyptic in expression, the clinical paranoid sees the hostile and conspiratorial world in which he feels himself to be living is directed specifically *against him*; whereas the spokesman of the paranoid style finds it directed against a nation, a culture, a way of life whose fate affects not himself alone but millions of others.
>
> (PS, 4)

In a similar fashion, Pipes acknowledges that like Hofstadter he does not mean the diagnosis of paranoia in any clinical sense. Yet he is nevertheless keen to point out that, in the case of many political leaders, a personal paranoia has often accompanied their conspiratorial politics. Robins and Post (the latter of whom is a medical psychologist) likewise get caught uneasily between literal and metaphorical ascriptions of paranoia. They provide psychobiographies of clinically paranoid leaders (complete with an absent domineering father and the need to purge inner demons in the case of Stalin), yet they also offer more general accounts of the spread of political paranoia into various groups and nations. Just how literally are these diagnoses meant to be taken? Are people who believe that conspiracies are the motive force of history and who believe that their group is being persecuted truly paranoid, or are they merely like genuine paranoid patients? If for paranoid individuals the inversion and projection of repressed desires functions to preserve the imperiled ego, then what in a group or nation corresponds to the ego? Which psychoanalytic theory of paranoia do these cultural diagnoses rely on? If it is implicitly Freudian (as their use of the model of projection would suggest), then what of Freud's claim that paranoia is the result of the inversion and externalization of repressed male homosexuality?

It is far from clear what analytical work the diagnosis of conspiracy culture as paranoid performs. It has become almost a cliché to describe as paranoid any person or any cultural artefact that gestures towards any kind of hidden agenda. It seems that labeling a view paranoid has now become an empty circular description with a gloss of scientific rigor: the paranoid is someone who (amongst other things) believes in conspiracy theories, and, conversely, the reason that people believe in conspiracy theories is that they are paranoid.

The notion of outbreaks of mass paranoia at least gives a name to people's tendency to blame scapegoats for their troubles, but, like Showalter, you could also call it hysteria and still be none the closer to explaining why and how these outbursts of conspiratorial thinking emerge at a particular historical moment. For Pipes as well as for Robins and Post, for example, the proliferation of conspiracy culture in American is merely "fashionable," a "modish" source of "titillation" for those who should know better—with the suggestion that as a fashion these things come and go of their own accord. "Recreational conspiracism," warns Pipes, "titillates sophisticates much as does recreational sex."[33] For her part, Showalter points towards some kind of fin-de-siècle or millennial fever, while other writers blame the spread of the Internet for exacerbating existing tendencies. But these explanations merely push the question further back: What makes this particular end of century so ripe for paranoia? And what causes the propensity for paranoia that cyberspace merely accelerates? For the majority of these commentators, popular paranoia is inscrutable in its origins and mystifying in its direction, merely a transhistorical psychic aberration. It acts like a plague virus which is persistent in society and which is liable to become epidemic at any moment, virtually without warning and without reason. It is the concern of the present study, however, to consider why conspiracy culture should emerge in such diverse forms at this particular time.

The diagnosis of paranoia—even if it is not individual but collective— still carries with it the suggestion that conspiracy theory is not simply misguided but a sign that society is suffering from an illness that should be pitied and, if possible, cured. For all Showalter's insistence that mental illness is not a moral failing, the bottom line is that people who believe in such things as alien abductions and satanic ritual abuse are not just deluded but actually sick and in need of help. While this diagnosis may be true of some conspiracy theorists, for many others inclined to conspiracy talk it is far from convincing. One reason is that for many people involvement in conspiracy culture is not a matter of fanatical belief to the point of maintaining a rigid delusional outlook, but a temporary and often contradictory attraction to unorthodox explanations about hidden forces. Moreover, even if it is sometimes applicable to some individuals, the diagnosis of an entire culture giving way to the paranoid style makes little sense. If the vast majority of Americans believe, for instance, in some form of conspiracy about the Kennedy assassination, what can it mean to regard as pathological a viewpoint that has become, if not a matter of society-wide faith, then certainly a far-from-abnormal assumption?

What makes the diagnosis of paranoia—whether literal or metaphorical—far more problematic in recent decades is that the supposed sufferers of this cultural sickness have themselves begun to appropriate the diagnostic language previously employed solely by scholarly commentators. Actual conspiracies of some stripe have undoubtedly existed at various times in the history of the United States. It would also be little exaggeration to claim that there have been conspiracy theories in some shape or other throughout American history. What is truly new and distinctive, however, is the emergence in the postwar years of the very concept of a "conspiracy theory" which is a sign of "paranoid" thinking. Although (according to the *OED*) the first recorded use of the phrase "conspiracy theory" dates back to an economics article from the 1920s, it only began to enter regular usage in the second half of the century. As we have seen, Karl Popper leant his considerable intellectual weight to honing a definition of conspiracy with which to condemn its assumptions all the more strongly. Since the 1960s, I want to suggest, the very notion of a conspiracy theory as a form of deluded historical explanation has been recognized, labeled, theorized, discussed, embraced, parodied, and finally incorporated into common usage. Indeed, the term "conspiracy theory" only entered the supplement to the *OED* for the first time in 1997, a somewhat overdue yet nonetheless timely indicator of its currency.

Conspiracy culture has become a surprisingly self-conscious phenomenon, building into itself the very terminology with which it had been diagnosed in the past. This process reached its logical conclusion with the 1997 Mel Gibson/Julia Roberts film *Conspiracy Theory*. Although many previous Hollywood films have featured conspiracy scenarios and even conspiracy theories, this film deemed it necessary and profitable to self-consciously advertise the content with neon-lit literal-mindedness—not "Conspiracy" but "Conspiracy *Theory*." As a film title, *Conspiracy Theory* takes to new heights the self-reflexive wisdom (in Golda Meir's version) that even paranoids have enemies.[34] In wearing the accusatory label on its sleeve, the film seems to deflect in advance any criticisms that might be made of it for unthinkingly giving in to the logic of paranoia. The title seems to promise both an example of a conspiracy theory, and a commentary on the very logic of conspiracy thinking.

If in the past the political charge of a conspiracy allegation could be defused in advance by diagnosing its proponents as paranoid, then in more recent decades there has been an increasing familiarity with the language of symptomology *within* popular conspiracy culture. The increasingly self-reflexive "paranoid" narratives have thus begun to internalize the modes of reading traditionally brought to bear upon them, to anticipate and disarm the authority of expert criticism. If *The X-Files*, as many pundits have claimed, is a symptom of a recent turn to paranoia in American society, then it is also a sophisticated and ironic diagnosis of that infliction. Likewise, William Burroughs's fictions of body horror need to be understood not as an inverted projection of repressed homosexual desire (as the classic Freudian diagnosis of paranoia would argue), but as a series of strategic and fantastical materializations of straight society's worst fears about same-sex desire, drug addiction and disease. In effect, like other popular forms of conspiracy culture since the 1960s, they reverse the emphasis from a psychology of conspiracy to a conspiracy theory of the institutions of psychology.

The final round of this hermeneutic one-upmanship comes when those accused of being paranoid turn the spotlight back on their accusers by asking whose interests are served by such symptomatic interpretations. Showalter, for example, is keen to point out that a belief in conspiracy theories about the Oklahoma bombing only serves to prolong the suffering of bereaved relatives whose relief is to be found not in inquiries into the possibility of a conspiracy but in counseling. Those inclined to conspiracy theories about the event, however, would contend that Showalter's analysis might itself play into the hands of those keen to cover up secret malfeasance by forces from the government or otherwise. What better way (the conspiracy theorist imagines a high-level military official musing) to divert attention from the awkward details of incompetence or concerted wrong-doing in the Gulf War than a well-respected academic telling everyone that none of it is true, and, what's more, that you're a touch hysterical if you believe it? A passage in Pynchon's monumental conspiracy classic *Gravity's Rainbow* (1973) captures this possibility nicely. Towards the end of this novel that reads as a catalog of postwar conspiracy theories, the narrator begins to discuss the famous urban legend about the conspiratorial suppression (in the novel by a tycoon called Lyle Bland) of an energy-saving carburetor in the 1930s:

> By way of the Bland institute and the Bland Foundation, the man has had his meathooks well into the American day-to-day since 1919. Who do you think sat on top of that 100-miles-per-gallon carburetor, eh? Sure you've heard that story—maybe even snickered along with paid anthropologists who called it the Automotive Age Myth or some shit—well, turns out the item was real, all right, and it was Lyle Bland who sprang for those

academic hookers doing the snickering and the credentialed lying.[35]

Even if—shock! horror!—respected academics like Hofstadter and Showalter are not working either knowingly or unwittingly for the CIA (though, the determined conspiracy theorist will point out, many *were* in the 1950s), the incorporation of such theories into conspiracy lore can be seen as part of an attempt to reconfigure the balance of power between the expert critic and the naïve exponent of the paranoid style.

A psychological explanation for the proliferation of conspiracy culture usually assumes that people blame external causes for what are essentially internal, psychic problems, sometimes of a sexual nature. Hofstadter, for example, claims that "the sexual freedom attributed to him [the enemy], his lack of moral inhibition, his possession of especially effective techniques for fulfilling his desires, give exponents of the paranoid style an opportunity to project and freely express unacceptable aspects of their own minds" (PS, 34). In the case of alien-abduction narratives, Showalter similarly concludes that "women are seeking external explanations for their own sexual dreams, unconscious fantasies, sensations."[36] While the claim that conspiracy-minded fears are a hysterical manifestation of the believer's unconscious desires or shameful fantasies is at times plausible, it nevertheless masks the possibility that such fears are as much an internalization of social tensions as they are an externalization of private, unconscious anxieties. Far from being a projection onto the outside world of repressed inner conflicts, then, much conspiracy culture might instead be understood as an attempt to make sense, albeit in a distorted fashion, of the deeper conflicts which reside not in the psyche but in society. It might sometimes be more useful to look for inner demons in the Pentagon than in people's minds.

Moral Panics

There is, however, an alternative theory of conspiracy theories which does not rely on a psychoanalytic premise of repressed desires. Beginning with the work of the Progressive historians in the first quarter of this century, this theory argues that many outbursts of what Hofstadter and others would later term the "paranoid style" were in fact deliberately orchestrated moral panics. On this view, these engineered eruptions of public anxiety enable those in power to pursue their own repressive policies. The red scares of the 1920s and 1930s, for example, were fueled by stories of Italian anarchists plotting to overthrow the government. According to this model, the demagoguery was not the natural expression of real (albeit greatly exaggerated) anxieties about vulnerable national identity in the face of increasing immigration from southern Europeans (baited as "socialists").

Rather, the public outbursts were conveniently manufactured and exacerbated by those in power to justify their own devious policies, such as anti-labor legislation. According to this model (which was revived by radical historians in the 1960s), the elite are not in the grip of a pathological delusion, but are ruthlessly rational in their manipulation of public sentiment.[37] Whereas Hofstadter, for example, viewed the rise of McCarthyism as a product of small-minded, backwater populist prejudice run riot, other historians would argue that he failed to take into account how elitist factions of the Republican Party latched onto McCarthyism to further their own political ends.[38]

Theories about moral panics fomented by the elite have the advantage that they do not rely on unprovable assertions about the psychological makeup of those inclined to conspiracy theories. With their frequently compelling accounts of the economic and political interests that are served by the promotion of conspiratorial beliefs, this approach can also offer the kind of detailed historical explanations that psychological theories often lack. But this theory suffers from several limitations of its own. Like the paranoid style analysis, it must assume that conspiracy theories are necessarily false, an increasingly untenable working assumption in the face of the catalog of revelations about the intelligence agencies that have emerged since the end of the 1960s. With its account of malevolent leaders hatching sinister plots to dupe the masses into believing demonological rhetoric (while cynically discounting that rhetoric in private themselves), this theory is also in danger of producing something akin to a conspiracy theory about the provenance of the masses' conspiracy theories. Finally, with its emphasis on the ruthlessly efficient manipulation of mass belief, it leaves no room for understanding why so many people come to believe conspiratorial theories. Nor can it recognize the uses that people make of the scaremongering stories they have had cynically forced upon them, and the sometimes surprising cultural and psychological work that these conspiracy-minded theories perform in people's everyday lives.

Poor Person's Cognitive Mapping

Although most discussions of conspiracy culture have sought to refute and condemn it, some commentators have begun to analyze why the discourse of paranoia has become so popular in recent years. In two of his essays on postmodernism, Fredric Jameson offers—almost in passing—a useful formulation of the relationship between conspiracy narratives and the contemporary social and economic situation. "Conspiracy," writes Jameson, "is the poor person's cognitive mapping in the postmodern age; it is a degraded figure of the total logic of late capital, a desperate attempt to represent the latter's system, whose failure is marked by its slippage into sheer theme and content." He finds "the omnipresence of the theme of paranoia" in a "seemingly inexhaustible production of conspiracy plots of the most elaborate kind in the postmodern age," from thrillers to cyberpunk.[39] This overproduction of "high-tech paranoia" is a sign that many people are no longer able to make sense of their lives within the larger historical and socioeconomic context. With its discovery of a hidden agenda behind the surface chaos of contemporary history, conspiracy theory attempts to provide a compensatory sense of historical location—"cognitive mapping" in Jameson's terms—that is missing from everyday life.

Jameson's formulation opens up the possibility of a materialist analysis of why people turn to conspiratorial explanations that doesn't rely on untenable psychoanalytic insights into believers' minds. It also provides a powerful historical explanation for the rise of conspiracy talk in the era of globalization. But in many ways the theory is too powerful. For Jameson contemporary conspiracy theory is always an attempt to "think the impossible totality of the contemporary world system."[40] Where theorists of the paranoid style find repressed sexuality as the fundamental source of fears and fantasies, Jameson's notion of the "poor person's cognitive mapping" always finds a repressed understanding of economics. The case studies in the present book, however, suggest that conspiracy culture fulfills diverse functions in different arenas.

Extrapolating from Jameson's previous work, it would seem that there is indeed a plot—in the narrative sense—to be uncovered in contemporary society. It is not the story of the secret machinations of a powerful cabal, but the "single vast unfinished plot" of class struggle.[41] Jameson's approach is predicated on the conviction that the economic mode of production is (in Althusser's phrase) the ultimately determining instance. Although Jameson rebukes the culture of paranoia for failing to accurately plot the "impossible totality of the contemporary world system," it might be argued that his faith in a monolithic and ultimately determined totality itself has strong conspiratorial overtones. And, as Chapter 6 suggests, some versions of recent conspiracy culture give voice to an increasing skepticism that there is any way to coherently plot the unpredictable causal links in an increasingly connected world. With their creation of a permanent free fall of suspicion, sophisticated forms of conspiracy culture from *The Crying of Lot 49* to *The X-Files* suggest that a final totalizing map can never be reached, and, moreover, that the obsessive desire to locate such an ultimate solution is illusory and dangerous—paranoid, even.

In contrast to Jameson's curt dismissal of the cultural logic of paranoia, Mark Fenster's richly detailed analysis bends over backwards to find the glimmerings of utopian political desires buried in the products of conspiracy theory. In conspiracy theorists' ceaseless quest to make public the dirty secrets of a corrupt government, Fenster discovers a commendable democratic impulse towards openness and justice. Yet, like Jameson's insistence that the cultural logic of paranoia is at the end of the day a degraded and desperate failure, Fenster finds conspiracy theory at fault. "Beyond its shortcomings as a universal theory of power and an approach to historical and political research," Fenster warns, "conspiracy theory ultimately fails as a political and cultural practice," mainly because it doesn't offer a plan for effective political action once the plot has been uncovered.[42] He also convincingly takes issue, for example, with the way conspiracy theory traditionally relies on an all-American ideology of ruggedly individual agency. Fenster likewise correctly dismisses the notion that conspiracy theorists necessarily form some kind of protopolitical radical community that is to be championed. Although these critiques are well founded, they nevertheless judge conspiracy theory by unreasonably strict standards of proper political thought and action which it will never live up to. Some conspiracy theorists do make claims for their radical politics, but most forms of everyday paranoia are rarely so grandiose or programmatic. The problem with Fenster's approach is that he implicitly requires conspiracy theory to fulfill a political function which it is always going to fail at. The cultural studies wager is that there are hidden utopian yearnings buried deep within popular culture, and which can be rearticulated to more productive political projects. Although this is an extremely important task for cultural analysis, it can end up insisting that other (usually less sophisticated) people's everyday cultural practices fulfill one's own political agenda—and then chastising them for failing at what they never intended in the first place.

The desire to find the hidden radical agenda in conspiracy culture is to be found in an extreme form in Jodi Dean's *Aliens in America*. For Dean stories of alien abduction and government conspiracy offer people a way of thinking about and registering an unfocused protest against the collusion of the military–industrial–scientific complex. *Aliens in America* received a harsh reception by reviewers who took issue with its refusal to condemn point-blank the delusions of alien abduction believers. These attacks on Dean's laudable attempt to take seriously people's everyday culture instead of instantly dismissing it were at times unhelpful and narrow minded. Yet there remains something unsettling about Dean's argument that the proliferation of paranoia is part of a wider erosion of the boundaries between the rational and the irrational that will lead to a greater democratic freedom liberated from the slavish reliance on experts.

Though Dean's account of the radically destabilizing potential of everyday paranoia is undoubtedly exaggerated, it is still an enticing notion. But the price that some people have to pay for that better future is too high. Conspiratorial accounts of having been abducted by aliens might yield a sense of empowerment and excitement in otherwise downtrodden lives, but in doing so they can lock the individual believer into a narrative of being a pawn in someone else's game, systematically dispossessed of both mind and body. They also commit the believer to views about the way the world works that can make functioning in the everyday world difficult. Furthermore, in welcoming the acceleration of skepticism into paranoia as a sign of healthy populist dissent, Dean, though deeply sympathetic to her subjects, is in danger of championing their misery and confusion for her political agenda.

Some conspiracy culture is hopelessly deluded and spiteful, but some of it is undoubtedly ironic and subversive. Much of it is somewhere in between. While a sympathetic approach to popular culture is indispensable for generating insightful symptomatic readings, it is surely a mistake to cast other people at whatever cost as the principal actors in one's own revolutionary drama. Instead of measuring the culture of paranoia against a political yardstick it will always fall short of, the remaining chapters explore the meaning of conspiracy culture for both those who produce and those who consume it.

1

CONSPIRACY/CULTURE

Everything is some kind of plot, man.
(Pynchon, *Gravity's Rainbow*)

AGENT SCULLY: What makes you think that this a
conspiracy? That the government's involved?
KURT CRAWFORD: What makes you think it isn't?
(*The X-Files*)

The paranoid is the person in possession of all the facts.
(William Burroughs)

At first sight there is a remarkable continuity in the discourse of American conspiracy over the centuries. The obsessions that Richard Hofstadter documented in his snapshot portrait of the "paranoid style" can still be found at the turn of the millennium. Conspiracy theories about the malign influence of Jewish bankers, the Illuminati and the Masons persist today, from the pages of the Liberty Lobby's *Spotlight* magazine, to Pat Robertson's best-selling *The New World Order* (1991). Indeed, Daniel Pipes argues that a frighteningly resilient anti-Semitism continues to be at the heart of most conspiracy theorizing.[1] Yet alongside these familiar demonologies there have emerged significant new forms of conspiracy culture, which operate in very different ways to more traditional modes of the paranoid style. Moreover, even those traditional forms of right-wing extremist conspiracy thinking take on new meanings and serve new purposes. This chapter will outline and explain the major changes in the scope and function of conspiracy culture since the 1960s. The first part summarizes each element in this shift, and the second part examines as a case study the career of Thomas Pynchon, and his novel *Vineland* (1990) in particular. As Chapter 2 makes clear, however, plotting the trajectory of popular paranoia over the last few decades is far from straightforward. The basic story is of a loss of innocence, which is often seen as a direct consequence of the Kennedy assassination in November 1963. Yet that tale of a widespread fall into conspiracy-minded suspicion and self-perpetuating doubt is itself usually a product of a later need to backdate the causal origin of present woes to the early 1960s. The causally coherent narrative about a growing skepticism towards the authority of experts and the government is undermined by a more general distrust in the authority of narrative to tell such a causally coherent story.

Despite these in-built difficulties, it is nevertheless possible to sketch out in broad terms changes in the shape and function of conspiracy culture over the last few decades. The traditional portrait of the conspiracy theorist is as a marginal, paranoid crackpot, usually located on the far right of the political spectrum, and, in the American context, in a decided minority. Hofstadter, as we have seen, identifies the paranoid style as an "old and recurrent mode of expression in our public life," but one which is the "preferred style only of *minority* movements."[2] The following sections show how this model is in need of revision, since conspiracy theories are no longer necessarily the mark of—in order—a delusional, right-wing, marginal, political, dogmatic mindset.

I. THE CHANGING STYLE OF PARANOIA

(Un)deniable Plausibility

As the Introduction argued, conspiracy talk cannot be understood any more as straightforward evidence of a delusional, quasi-paranoid mentality. A growing self-consciousness in the rhetoric of paranoia ensures that conspiracy theories are rarely the naïve and unmediated symptoms of a deranged mind. Many conspiratorial pronouncements are now prefaced with a self-aware disclaimer along the lines of, "I may sound paranoid, but ..." It has also become harder to dismiss conspiracy theories as proof of a collective propensity to paranoia quite simply because in many people's eyes they have become far more plausible. Since the 1960s more and more Americans have taken the idea of conspiracy, if not for granted, then certainly as a possibility always to be considered. The catalog of prominent conspiratorial events and revelations has produced a climate in which further rumors are more likely to be entertained than immediately dismissed.

If the operating principle in the clandestine world of the intelligence agencies is "plausible deniability," a policy which ensures that those higher up the chain of command are never connected to the dirty work of agents in the field, then for many in the normal world there is an air of what might be termed undeniable plausibility about rumors of government conspiracy. With hotly contended issues like Gulf War syndrome, the assumption for many Americans is that the government is not only responsible for whatever caused the illnesses originally, but is also covering up its culpability. In the light of the revelations about episodes such as the Tuskegee Institute syphilis studies, and the testing of nuclear radiation, LSD and Agent Orange on unsuspecting army personnel and civilians, it would come as no surprise, the argument goes, that the government would have conducted similarly callous experiments on servicemen and women during the Gulf War. Even if a particular conspiracy theory turns out to be wildly unfounded, for many people it is nevertheless a reasonable assumption that a conspiracy theory is an initially viable explanation for strange events and coincidences.

The rhetoric of conspiracy is thus no longer the hate-filled lingua franca of extremists, but has become part of the American vernacular. Since the 1960s conspiracy culture has produced an accumulative litany of acronyms, code names and trebled names, less a credo of fixed belief than a shorthand of routinized suspicion. The evocative roll call includes: JFK, RFK, MLK, Malcolm X, Marilyn Monroe, MK-ULTRA, Operation Paperclip, Phoenix, Mongoose, Majestic-12, COINTELPRO, Lee Harvey Oswald, James Earl Ray, Sirhan Sirhan, Arthur Herman Bremer, Mark David Chapman, John Hinckley Jr, LSD, MIA, CIA, FBI, NSA, Secret Service, Octopus, Gemstone, Roswell, Area 51, Tuskegee, Jonestown, Chappaquiddick, Waco, Oklahoma, Watergate, Iraqgate, Iran-Contra, October Surprise, Savings & Loan, Whitewater, Lockerbie, TWA flight 800, O. J., Ebola, AIDS, crack cocaine, military–industrial complex, black helicopters, gray aliens, grassy knoll, magic bullet, lone nut. This mantra of popular paranoia ranges from the undeniably plausible to the wildly spec-ulative. But the logic is that the few cases of actually proven conspiratorial misdealings (e.g. COINTELPRO, the FBI's much abused program of domestic spying on and infiltration of black activist groups, amongst others) warrant at least an initial skepticism about official denials in all sub-sequent cases.

What is more significant, however, is that it is becoming increasingly hard to be certain of the difference between the plausible and the paranoid. With both a restricted access to real information (despite the Freedom of Information Act) and an overload of data (particularly on the Internet) it is proving more difficult to distinguish between false rumors and actual revelations. As far as the conspiracy theorist is concerned (and to some extent we are all conspiracy theorists now), the possibility of deliberately planted false clues—"disinformation"—means that we can never rest in our interpretative endeavors. Take the example of the now notorious rumor about the crash landing of an alien UFO at Roswell, New Mexico in 1947.[3] On 8 July 1947 the Roswell Army Air Field issued a press release announcing that the wreckage of a "flying disk" had been found, a story quickly picked up by the local and then the national media, which began to link the crash to recent talk and sightings of "flying saucers." The story was then denied by the Army Air Force, who announced that the sighting of an unidentified flying object and its metallic debris was merely a weather balloon falling to earth. In the half-century since the crash (and most intensely since the rediscovery in the late 1970s of the case), many people have revisited those early rumors, insisting that the weather balloon story was a cover-up for a far more disturbing truth, the most popular of which is that aliens had landed, and (in more elaborate versions), that the government and the military knew this, and became involved with the aliens in one way or another, and have been covering both elements up ever since.[4] According to many conspiracy theorists, President Eisenhower created Majestic-12 (MJ-12), a top secret committee of military, intelligence and academic personnel to orchestrate the concealment of the truth behind the crash, namely that four "extra-terrestrial biological entities" (EBEs) had been found near the crash site.

Although the much reprinted MJ-12 documents are undoubtedly a hoax, the military and the intelligence agencies have indeed returned to investigate the case (and other sightings) several times. The Air Force's long-running Project Blue Book investigation into UFO phenomena concluded that all the sightings could be explained away in terms of natural phenomena. The Robertson Panel, a classified committee of scientists convened by the CIA in 1953, likewise came to the conclusion that there was no good evidence that UFOs were of alien origin. But a 1997 article in the CIA journal *Studies in Intelligence* admitted that the weather balloon story was a cover-up, and even that the National Security Council had been instructed (on the advice of the Robertson panel, who were apparently worried about the public succumbing to mass hysteria) to debunk UFO rumors, through such means as Project Blue Book.[5] According to this article, the truth that had to be kept quiet was the existence of high-altitude spy planes and other experimental craft. In the wake of a string of sensational books on Roswell, New Mexico Representative Steven Schiff urged the General Accounting Office to hunt for any documents on the case. The Air Force was prompted by this move to begin a six-month investigation of its own, which reported in July 1994 that the crash was not of a weather balloon but a balloon that was part of Project Mogul, a top secret mission to track Soviet nuclear tests. In response to criticism by ufologists about the first (and supposedly definitive) report's silence on the question of alien bodies reputedly found at the site, the Air Force launched a further inquiry. This explained that in the 1950s the USAF had used crash-test dummies in experiments on high-altitude parachutes, and therefore local eyewitnesses may have retrospectively combined the two elements to form the Roswell myth of recovered alien bodies.[6]

Here at last was supposedly the ultimate answer to what the UFO community dubs a "cosmic Watergate," given in a spirit of post-Cold War glasnost. Yet the repeated pattern of denial, concealment and false revelation casts a shadow of suspicion on any official pronouncement in this—and many other—cases. It is not so much that everyone believes that the government is inevitably lying (though many Americans take that as read). Rather, even if the story of covert weapons research is true, there is no certain way of knowing for sure that it is true. For many, a lingering suspicion always remains; nothing is ever quite what it seems; no "final report" ever ensures that the case is truly closed. According to a *Time/* Yankelovich poll, 80 percent of Americans believe the US government knows more about extraterrestrials than it chooses to let on.[7]

In addition to never quite being able to fully believe in official pro-nouncements by experts and authorities, there is the mounting difficulty of not knowing which experts to trust. The trial of O. J. Simpson, in which the defense alleged that there had a been a police conspiracy to frame the former football star, heard from a phenomenal number of expert scientific witnesses, not just on the evidence but on the nature of DNA testing itself, adding a level of complexity most people were content to ignore.[8] For most amateur inquirers, when the various experts are in dis-agreement, there is no obvious and agreed-upon criteria for working out which expert to believe, other than to call in a further expert, and so on, potentially for ever. Obviously conspiracy theorists do come to conclusions, but the specter of uncertainty always haunts their seemingly solid convictions.

In the eyes of many Americans, the only safe bet is that there *might well be* a conspiracy, for all the public at large know are likely to ever know. The burden of proof is now reversed, such that the authorities must strenuously provide conclusive evidence that there has been no initial conspiracy or sub-sequent cover-up. Of course, with the default mode of reception set to battle-weary paranoia, any denial of a conspiracy is itself often taken as evidence of a desire to cover something up. Contemporary conspiracy culture is therefore always poised on the edge of an infinite abyss of sus-picion. The prime-time conspiracy show, *The X-Files*, stylishly captures the possibility that we have entered what David Martin's book on the CIA and the Cold War termed a "wilderness of mirrors."[9] Looking back over his five years of investigating the paranormal and unexplained events chronicled in the FBI's X-Files, a disillusioned Special Agent Mulder con-fesses sadly at a UFO conference that his all-too-gullible belief in alien life has been exploited by the conspiracy he has begun to uncover. He an-nounces that his ready belief in a government plot to hide the existence of extraterrestrial life was cynically used by the higher ranks of power in order to mask their sinister medical experiments on unwitting victims, who in turn were fed abduction stories to lead them off the trail. "The con-spiracy is not to hide the existence of extraterrestrials," he explains, "it's to make people believe in it so completely that they question nothing."[10] By the next series, however, Mulder has once again found what he thinks is conclusive evidence of alien visitations, and now believes that the official denial was a carefully coordinated lie to conceal the fact that the government has all along been involved with alien–human hybrid DNA experiments. With its endless reversal and re-evaluation of all certainties, *The X-Files* (as Chapter 6 discusses in more detail) dramatizes in a condensed and stylized form the perpetual motion of suspicion that marks out recent conspiracy thinking. Far from offering a paradoxically comforting and fixed paranoid interpretation of the last half-century of American history, it revels in an infinite hermeneutic of suspicion which undermines every stable conclusion the Special Agents reach. Rather than dwelling on any particular fixed *product* of conspiracy theorizing, *The X-Files* concentrates, in line with other examples, on the *process* of repeatedly discovering that everything you thought you knew is wrong.

Invisible Government

The rise of a cultural fascination with conspiracy as an undeniably plausible working assumption in the last few decades cannot be separated from the emergence of what might be termed a culture *of* conspiracy. It is not just that conspiracy thinking has become more legitimate as a popular mode of historical explanation because a few conspiracies have been unmasked in a very public fashion. An internalized fantasy of conspiracy and counter-conspiracy also seems to captivate those on the inside of the power game. During the twentieth century, and since the foundation of the CIA in 1947 in particular, American politics has increasingly relied on clandestine means to pursue its goals, and a bureaucratic culture of secrecy has come to be taken for granted. A year after the Kennedy assassination, David Wise and Thomas Ross argued in their ground-breaking study that there is an "invisible government" at work in the United States, forming "an interlocking, hidden machinery" that gathers intelligence and carries out its own policies. An informed citizen, they suggest, "might come to suspect that the foreign policy of the United States often works publicly in one direction and secretly through the Invisible Government in just the opposite direction."[11] This doppelgänger government dates primarily from the National Security Act of 1947 and the development of the Cold War, and is comprised in the main by the sprawling intelligence community, which includes the CIA, the National Security Council, the Defense Intelligence Agency, the National Security Agency, Army Intelligence, Navy Intelligence, Air Force Intelligence, the State Department's Bureau of Intelligence and Research, the Atomic Energy Commission and the FBI.

The investigations into political assassinations during the 1970s (particularly the Rockefeller Commission and the Church Committee of 1975), in addition to the Watergate and the Iran-Contra hearings, exposed the extent of so-called black budget operations that were not publicly accountable. The intelligence agencies were revealed to operate as a permanent, covert political force, both in foreign policy and—just as illegally—within the USA. The loose, and sometimes conflicting, collection of intelligence interests, supported by a network of business and government contacts both inside the United States and abroad, together constitute what has been termed a national security state. Each agency automatically classified ever-increasing numbers of documents, a process which has continued since the end of the Cold War. The mere existence of this factory of secrets led citizens to believe that the government really did have something to hide, even if the routine classification of documents hid nothing more than government embarrassment or its assumption that the public were not to be trusted with knowing what its representatives were really thinking. Secrecy, as the historian Richard Gid Powers explains, "became the explanation for almost everything that ailed America." An official obsession with secrecy, in effect, helped fuel the popular fixation on conspiratorial secrets at the heart of government.[12]

The existence of this mirror world of secret power has fascinated as much as it has frightened the American public. Following Jürgen Habermas's analysis of the emergence of the public sphere in the eighteenth century, Jodi Dean has suggested that secrecy is the necessary flipside of there being a public realm at all, and that, in the present, "the very idea that the public has a right to know, that public rule depends on access to information, on full disclosure, puts the secret at the heart of the public."[13] This argument has a neat structural logic, but it tells us little about the particular conditions under which a hyperbolic fascination with, and resigned acceptance of, secrecy emerges in the last quarter of the twentieth century. We might instead turn to Michael Rogin, who suggests that in the postmodern turn of American politics since Kennedy's presidency, secrecy has paradoxically become a spectacle.[14] Rogin argues that covert action has become both a practical necessity and a compensatory, symbolic fantasy of successful American macho heroism in the face of the comparative decline of US influence in the roulette game of the global economy in which it is merely one more player vulnerable to its vicissitudes. The classic example is the extravagant Hollywood spectacle of Rambo's single-handed covert operation which serves belatedly to win the war in Vietnam that had caused so much damage to America's sense of imperial destiny. In the figure of President Reagan, the spectacle of Hollywood and the theater of politics became notoriously confused. But even all-too-literal cases of covert action, once uncovered, work to promote a form of national politics that is very much for show. In the world at large, the revelation via the Iran–Contra hearings of illegal, clandestine US involvement in Nicaragua served as a self-inflating promotion of American military muscle power, alongside other vanity actions like the invasion of Grenada. On the domestic scene, the uncovered spectacle of secrecy likewise tries to recruit an increasingly skeptical public—by vicarious participation in the drama—into the fantasy that America could still get its own way in the world through heroic outlaw actions.

The dialectic of fear and fantasy about this clandestine other world has permeated American fiction and films. In addition to the phenomenal success of the thriller in the postwar period, more literary novels such as Don DeLillo's *Libra* (1988), Norman Mailer's *Harlot's Ghost* (1991), and James Ellroy's *American Tabloid* (1995) exude a deep attraction to the generic conventions of the thriller and the clandestine romance of the intelligence agencies. Mailer confesses that he wrote *Harlot's Ghost* not out of any special inside knowledge of the workings of the CIA, but through a deep imaginative affinity with the subject, using, he explains, "the part of my mind that has lived in the CIA for forty years."[15] Mailer even claims (somewhat ironically) that, if he had come from a different background and had been of a different political persuasion, "it would not have been impossible for me to have spent my life in the CIA."[16]

Perhaps more intriguing than the postwar novelist's fascination with the world of spooks is the tendency for former intelligence agents to write novels themselves. For example, G. Gordon Liddy, the Watergate burglar and CIA operative (and, according to several accounts, possible Kennedy assassination suspect), has become a talk radio host and the author of thrillers such as *Out of Control* (1979). Likewise, in the "Musings of a Cigarette Smoking Man" episode of *The X-Files*, the notorious arch-conspirator is apparently revealed to be the ruthless orchestrator of just about every event since the war, from the assassination of JFK to the exclusion of the Buffalo Bills from the Superbowl. We also learn that he was prepared to give it all up, but has been repeatedly rejected in his attempts to publish a detective fiction novel. When one of his stories is finally accepted by a magazine, he is disgusted to find that it has interfered with the original ending, and therefore tears up his resignation letter.[17] In a similar fashion, *Three Days of the Condor*, a stylish 1970s conspiracy thriller, features Robert Redford as a CIA employee whose task is to process popular novels to see if Agency plans have accidentally leaked out, and to scour their pages for future ideas.[18] These examples suggest how a mutual feedback loop between the fictional and the factual world emerges, with the real spies learning the discourse of conspiracy from novelists, and vice versa. More generally, a fascination with conspiracy in entertainment merges with and reinforces the atmosphere of secrecy which structures American politics, and together they form what might be termed a "conspiracy culture." The development of this force field of conspiracy over the last few decades has radically changed the way both ordinary people and policy makers represent the operation of history to themselves. A hidden agenda is often the only agenda.

With the rise of the national security state since World War Two, conspiracy theories have therefore become more widespread and acceptable not least because conspiracy has become more widespread and acceptable. If the plans of the governing elite are now less likely to inspire popular and congressional consensus (for reasons explored in more detail below), then behind-the-scenes black budget operations become increasingly important. As 1960s radical and Kennedy assassination investigator Carl Oglesby comments, "conspiracy is the normal continuation of normal politics by normal means."[19] Though not everyone would go so far as Oglesby, for many Americans the Watergate hearings brought home just how deeply ingrained the everyday procedure of conspiracy has become in government. In the last decade, moreover, the Oliver North hearings only served to confirm what many felt they already knew. Though the hearings failed to connect President Reagan to the complex tangle of drugs and arms trading (skeptics saw it merely as a case of "plausible deniability" that was not very plausible), they did reveal how ready middle-ranking functionaries were to assume that barely stated ends are to be achieved by clandestine means. The undeniable plausibility of conspiracy theories that the American public has learnt to read over the last quarter century has enabled it—sometimes—to reconnect the buried causal links that the policy of plausible deniability is designed to sever. The response to the official injunction to "Deny Everything," as the tag line of one *X-Files* episode puts it, is the conspiracy theorist's conviction that "everything is connected."[20]

As we saw in the Introduction, for Hofstadter the paranoid style is not a belief in a conspiracy now and again, but in conspiracy as "*the motive force* in history" (PS, 29). Though a far cry from Hofstadter's diagnosis of a thoroughgoing paranoid delusion, the kind of default suspicion towards the authorities that has permeated American culture since the late 1960s nevertheless implicitly assumes something resembling conspiracy as the motive force, if not for the whole of history, then certainly in recent American politics. The difference, however, is that, whereas for Hofstadter the conspiracy theorist fundamentally misunderstood the structural workings of history, the amateur conspiracy theorizing of more recent decades is frequently in tune with an institutional analysis of a political system whose self-vaunted commitment to democratic openness is undermined by the repeated revelation of conspiracy-minded wrongdoing. At the end of the day such conspiracy theories might well turn out to be unfounded, but, given all that we have learned about the less than democratic operation of government in the United States, it is a not unreasonable working hypothesis that there exists a clandestine or tacit collusion of vested interests that verges on a conspiracy. People who see conspiracies everywhere may be paranoid, but they may also have latched—perhaps accidentally, but nevertheless acutely—onto the transformation of secrecy as the necessary spectacle of postmodern American politics.

31

Much of the rhetoric of paranoia explored in this study operates in a very different fashion to the typical portrait sketched in Hofstadter's essay. A rigid and detailed conspiracy theory about a small cabal of ruthless agents diverting the course of America's manifest destiny has given way to a more fluid and provisional sense of there being large, institutional forces controlling our everyday lives. In many ways a conspiracy-minded predilection towards suspicion now functions less as an outmoded humanist faith in rational—albeit malign—agency, and more as a quasi-structural analysis of sinister forces in the dawn of a posthumanist era. In this way, the contemporary discourse of conspiracy gives narrative expression to the possibility of conspiracy without conspiring, with the congruence of vested interests that can only be described as conspiratorial, even when we know there has probably been no deliberate plotting. The rhetoric of conspiracy thus offers a symbolic resolution to the problem of representing who is responsible for events that seem to be beyond anyone's control. It speaks to a time in which neither an older faith in individual agency nor an emergent understanding of complex causation is satisfactory. Conspiracy theories bridge the gap between the two by reintroducing the possibility of naming and blaming in an age of unthinkably complex global connections. As Chapters 5 and 6 discuss in more detail, the growing entanglement of industrial and financial processes creates a permanent environment of risk in which distant threats invade the body itself. If everything is becoming increasingly connected since there is no longer any possibility of total immunity, then paranoia becomes a default sensibility, an automatic response to the low-intensity but insidious infiltration of the last enclaves of privacy. Even the traditional conspiracy-minded separation of Them and Us comes unstuck as the well-policed boundaries of both the body politic and individual bodies become compromised through the logic of the virus. The earlier, more focused form of demonological paranoia ripe in the McCarthy years of the Cold War has increasingly given way since the 1960s to a more diffuse belief in conspiring forces which are everywhere but which can't be located anywhere in particular in a decentered global economy.

Wake Up America!

Conspiracy theories have become not just more popular because they are more plausible, but they have also shifted their political function and location. For Hofstadter and other commentators, the typical American conspiracy theorist is a right-wing misfit who is incapable of sophisticated political thought. In recent years, however, that profile has changed, as conspiracy thinking has emerged in all parts of the political spectrum.

The uncanny repetition of political assassinations in the 1960s—each of which was blamed on a lone gunman—provoked many Americans to question the official version of events. To many minds already disenchanted with the powers that be, it seemed improbable that the assassinations of John and Robert Kennedy, and Martin Luther King (as well as Malcolm X) could be merely isolated incidents of misguided violence. Only a generation before, a conspiracy theory might have been the mark of a right-wing fanatic, but by the end of the 1960s it became the identifying style and posture of significant numbers of those in tune with the New Left and the counterculture. An article from *Esquire* magazine in 1966, entitled "Wake up America! It Can Happen Here! A Post-McCarthy Guide to Twenty-three Conspiracies by Assorted Enemies Within," charts the brave new world of conspiracy theory in hip, humorous fashion. Wedged between the tail end of a discussion on "the calculus of sex" and adverts for the Relax-A-Cizor waistline reduction device, the guide adopts the dryly sophisticated tone of What Every Bachelor Needs To Know. It scarcely needs to provide any commentary in its outlines since, in a "post-McCarthy" age, the assorted conspiracy theories speak for themselves—the article ends snappily with the throw-away, "And that's what's happening, baby."[21]

In the more muted rhetoric of hindsight, several contributors to the collection *The 60s Without Apology* discuss the conspiratorial dimension of that decade. The authors of the ironic "Lexicon of Folk-Etymology" explain that, "in the practice of overt politics, the term 'paranoia' was applied when fear and anxiety analogous to that encountered in drug use were manifested intrapsychically."[22] Herb Blau, another contributor to the collection, concludes that "it was conspiracy theory which dominated perception in the 60s, for good reason or wrong, almost more on the left than on the right."[23] From a very different political perspective, John Carroll, a sociologist writing in the late 1970s, criticizes the 1960s youth movements as the prime site of emergence of "the paranoid personality." "This decade appears as peculiarly paranoid," he argues, "when one considers the accumulated diversity, intensity and persistence of the revolt against inherited authority."[24]

The presumption towards conspiracy fed into the wider countercultural challenge to the establishment that dominated the political scene of the late 1960s and early 1970s—and is still a driving force for Oliver Stone, a self-appointed spokesperson for the boomer generation. For many on the left (but also on the right), conspiracy theories about the "lone nut" assassinations of the 1960s became the cornerstone of a skepticism towards government that was firmly cemented into place by Watergate and the subsequent revelations during the 1970s about the activities of the security agencies. By the mid-1970s the sheen of conspiracy theory as a bright new political attitude (captured in the snappy prose of the *Esquire* article) had grown dull with frequent use. An article in *Harper's* magazine of 1974 documents the emergence of paranoia as a routinized countercultural sensibility. Hendrik Hertzberg and David McClelland's piece, "Paranoia: An Idée Fixe Whose Time Has Come," hedges its bets in suggesting that paranoia is both a "recent cultural disorder," and a "natural response to the confusion of modern life."[25] Their article understands paranoia as an important language which is spoken across the political spectrum, from the President to antiwar dropouts. The authors characterize the Nixon presidency as "a Golden Age of political paranoia," in which "the paranoid strategies of projection, denial, and the use of code language with private meanings ... have been played out on a national scale."[26] They also discuss the appropriation and proliferation of the language by those who would be the targets of Nixon's countersubversion. "Hippies," they claim, "could no more communicate their thoughts without 'paranoia' and 'paranoid' than they could eschew 'like,' 'y'know,' and 'I mean.'"[27] Significantly, Hertzberg and McClelland turn to Thomas Pynchon for further elucidation of this "idée fixe," finding in his novels an extreme expression of a popular political mood. But, as the second half of this chapter explains, Pynchon's novels themselves provide an analysis of what happens when the concept of paranoia becomes the topic of color supplement sociology. Between postmodern fiction and popular magazines there emerges a feedback loop of symptomatic diagnosis, as the language of paranoia becomes increasingly self-conscious and ubiquitous. By the mid-1970s, then, conspiracy thinking had spread into diverse cultural arenas, becoming less the mark of irrational extremism than the default world view for a countercultural generation.

A sense of the pervasiveness of complex conspiring forces has helped shape the new social movements arising from the New Left in the 1960s, namely the student protests, feminism, gay liberation and black activism. Whereas most previous conspiracy theories—not least with McCarthyism—posited a threat to the American way of life and politics by subversive minorities, since the 1960s these new forms of oppositional conspiracy culture have been based on the assumption that the American way of life is itself a threat to those marginalized by it. Most of the conspiracy theories presented in Hofstadter's essay decry occasional irruptions by alleged subversives in the normal workings of American politics. More recently, however, many conspiracy theories suggest not so much a particular, invasive threat to the natural order of American life, as that the natural order of things itself presents a pervasive threat to its citizens. Right-wing libertarians have long complained that the presence of "big government" constitutes a conspiratorial threat to regular Americans, but their working assumption is that the truly American values of life, liberty and the pursuit of happiness never harmed anyone. What is new is an increasingly widespread suspicion that true American values might well be the problem—that society, as David Thoreau warned enigmatically in the mid-nineteenth century, is "in conspiracy against the manhood of every one of its members."[28]

The novels of William Burroughs, for example, provide a sexualized, literal-minded endorsement of Thoreau's aphorism. Burroughs's exuberantly paranoid novels suggest that fears of persecution are not something to be explained away or read as symptoms of neurosis, but are fully warranted responses to state control of private pleasures through what the mad doctor in *Naked Lunch* calls "forms of disciplinary procedure."[29] The Foucauldian vocabulary is appropriate, since Burroughs's novels highlight in particular the institutional mechanisms of surveillance and disciplinary control of illicit sexuality and drug use. With the criminalization of identity in place of individual acts, a kind of low-level paranoia becomes a permanent condition in Burroughs's Nova trilogy of the 1960s, a result of a constant self-policing. This routinized sense of paranoia emerges from the internalization of the panoptical gaze of the state in connection with homosexuality. This is a far cry from the usual, Freudian model of how paranoia works, namely a projection onto the external world of repressed internal fantasies.[30] "This enemy," declares Hofstadter, for example, "seems to be on many counts a projection of the self: both the ideal and the unacceptable aspects of the self are attributed to him" (PS, 32). In particular (though no more precisely), the "sexual freedom" attributed to the enemy gives "exponents of the paranoid style an opportunity to project and freely express unacceptable aspects of their own minds" (PS, 34). In contrast, in Burroughs's novels paranoia is not so much a consequence of repressed homosexuality, as a justifiable reaction to the State's desire to exercise its power in order to "cure" and control what it labeled as deviance, whether homosexuality or drug use. In the world of Burroughs's novels (as in Foucault's theories of the disciplinary society), the State's panicked insistence on surveilling individual bodily desires manifests itself as a caring but claustrophobic concern for citizens. It is, however, the proscription of certain activities as forbidden pleasures that produces in citizens the paranoid fear that the State will discover their guilty secret. A form of popular paranoia emerges, then, not as a result of a pathological condition, but as a necessary reaction to the mundane operation of everyday bureaucracy. It is less an isolated reaction to an occasional abuse of power than the logical by-product of a routinized state of affairs. And in recent years the extension of surveillance has come about not through the apocalyptic achievement of Orwellian state control, but through seemingly benign corporate processes such as the gathering of consumer profiles via credit card purchases, website visits, workplace monitoring supposedly for the employees' own safety, and so on. In the "era of the massive codification and storage of data," Don DeLillo suggests, "we are all keepers and yielders of secrets."[31]

35

Bargain and Compromise

The new forms of conspiracy culture explored in this study are not merely the result of a shift amongst the disaffected in American politics towards a more radical, left-leaning stance. They also reflect and feed into a more fundamental restructuring of the very nature of American politics. Hofstadter's pioneering work on the paranoid style is within the tradition of political science studies on the politics of intolerance and right-wing extremism.[32] His conviction, that only the fringe (especially on the right) of American politics suffers from a conspiratorial imagination, needs to be understood partly as a reaction to the excesses of McCarthyism that were still vivid—and, as a footnote in the essay suggests, to the perceived excesses of the conspiracy-obsessed reaction to the Kennedy assassination by European writers (PS, 7, note 5). Hofstadter's stance is that of a cosmopolitan intellectual denouncing the small-minded backwater politics of right-wing hate groups.[33] Trying to reassure himself that the fundamental stability of the American political system will remain unharmed by these isolated episodes of extremist scaremongering, he asserts that the paranoid spokesman (and in Hofstadter's account it is usually a man) fails to see "social conflict as something to be mediated and compromised" (PS, 31). The "paranoid style" is the last resort of those who are marginal to the centers of power and whose "ultimate schemes of values" cannot be accommodated by "normal political process of bargain and compromise" (PS, 39). Hofstadter thus reads countersubversive literature as a failure by various minorities to solve class conflict through "the usual methods of political give-and-take" (PS, 29). On this line of thinking, aggrieved fringe groups in effect fail to understand the exceptionalist doctrine of American politics, that the social and economic mobility of American society provides immunity from European epidemics of violent upheaval spread by fundamental conflicts of class, race, gender, and sexuality.

Although Hofstadter's insistence on the "paranoid style" as a minority phenomenon makes some political sense in the tense atmosphere in America before the publication of the Warren Commission Report into the assassination of President Kennedy, such a claim is no longer plausible. Taking the Kennedy assassination as an example, opinion polls indicate that the vast majority of the American public now believe that there was some form of a conspiracy involved (though, as Chapter 2 explains, the story of public opinion surrounding the case is far from straightforward). Likewise, before the 1960s opinion polls indicated that three-quarters of Americans trusted their government. The same poll in 1994 revealed that only a quarter trust the powers that be.[34] More important than the mere increase in the amount of conspiracy belief in circulation is the shift of conspiracy theory from the fringe to the mainstream of American political and cultural life since the time of Hofstadter's essay. Conspiracy talk has not only become pervasive in American culture, but it is also now concerned with the major conflicts in American society—albeit sometimes in displaced form. Chapters 3 and 4, for example, outline how the rhetoric of conspiracy has shaped everyday discussion of racism and sexism.

Some commentators have argued that in recent years a form of "fusion paranoia" has emerged, in which the traditional left and right wing fringes bond together, with, for example, militia websites quoting Noam Chomsky.[35] However, the problem is not so much that a new and even more dangerous cluster of fringe politics is emerging which redraws the map of normal political science, joining the far left and far right into a scary coalition. It is, rather, that the political language and style of the fringe is often the most instantly appealing form of popular dissent, and it is a discourse which spills over from the explicitly political fringe world of the militias and the Patriot movement to more mainstream expressions of conspiratorial uneasiness. In a world in which the triumph of laissez-faire global capitalism has come to be taken for granted, for many people there is no way of framing an analysis of what is happening or registering their dissatisfaction other than in the "crackpot" rhetoric of the conspiracy theorist.

At first sight the theories of the militias and Patriot movement indeed seem far-fetched. Their websites and pamphlets put forward the idea that there is a conspiracy of international institutions—including the Council on Foreign Relations (CFR), the Trilateral Commission, and even the United Nations itself—which aims to establish a "New World Order." The claim is that this will involve the creation of a sinister global government, which will take over the sovereign powers of the United States. There are, for example, regular reports of unmarked black helicopters, which are thought to be either involved in alien visitations or are the advanced guard of a UN invasion. The Little Black Helicopter web page, for example, asserts that "Little Black Helicopters are aircraft used by the United Nations to prepare for a total Take-over of the United States. The privately held property inside the United States would be inter-nationalized, the citizens' weapons confiscated, and children gang-raped if we allow them to continue their covert operations."[36] These sightings and accusations have become quite common, causing Boutros Boutros-Ghali, former Secretary-General of the UN, to once remark ironically: "It's great to be back from vacation. Frankly I get bored on vacation. It's much more fun to be at work here, blocking reform, flying my black helicopters, imposing global taxes."[37] There are also accusations that personal information is being secretly stored in the magnetic strip on driving licenses, and a rumor that the cryptic markings on the back of road signs have been put there to guide the invading United Nations forces massing just over the border.

These sightings and discoveries are taken as proof that the citizens of America are in imminent danger of having their freedom taken away by powerful and unaccountable international forces. An editorial in *The New American*, the John Birch Society's magazine, acknowledges that "the CFR itself is not *the* conspiracy." Yet, it continues, "behind the CFR and other powerful internationalist groupings such as the Trilateral Commission, behind the giant tax-exempt foundations, behind the Wall Street and Federal Reserve financial and banking interests, behind presidents and prime ministers, behind the NAFTA/GATT/IMF/NATO/UN axis, behind even the communist menace itself—is the conspiracy for global control."[38] In the more mainstream political arena, Pat Robertson and Pat Buchanan have both put forward the idea that there is a conspiracy of international financiers and organizations like the World Bank seeking to slowly and surreptitiously take control of the economy, and then the political sovereignty, of the United States. Robertson, for example, argues in his best-selling book, *The New World Order*, that the "Establishment" is planning to create a "world system in which enlightened monopolistic capitalism can bring all diverse currencies, banking systems, credit, manufacturing, and raw materials into one government-supervised whole, policed of course by their own world army."[39] Buchanan likewise insists that "real power in America belongs to the Manhattan money power."[40]

These fears of a New World Order conspiracy can easily shade into tedious and vicious scapegoating, which often contains a barely concealed anti-Semitic strain.[41] At its most violent extreme, the militia and Patriot movement ideology of suspecting federal authorities of planning to remove citizen rights has led to horrifying incidents like the Oklahoma bombing. But there are many more attracted to this conspiratorial line of thinking who are not fully paid-up members of a militia.[42] Though sometimes farfetched, stories about the US government knowingly collaborating with "alien" powers or about the sinister influence of unelected, shadowy internationalist organizations make sense in the current age of rapid globalization. Many governments are indeed finding themselves increasingly vulnerable to global economic forces and organizations over which they have little control. In their study of globalization, Richard Barnet and John Cavanagh discuss how "the formidable power and mobility of global corporations are undermining the effectiveness of national governments to carry out essential policies on behalf of their people." In particular, "tax laws intended for another age, traditional ways to control capital flows and interest rates, full-employment policies, and old approaches to resource development and environmental protection are become obsolete, unenforceable, or irrelevant."[43]

With their ideological insistence that the American Republic was founded to promote the liberty of individuals against the power of intrusive government, many on the far right find themselves asking what role the government now plays. If, they wonder, after the end of the Cold War there is no longer a role for the government as protector of its citizens against an

"evil empire," and if the federal government is betraying its role as protector of its citizens' freedom by signing up to global trade agreements
(viewed as selling out their interests to global institutions and megacorpora-
tions), then what is government for?[44] Despite what might seem like
slash-and-burn privatization and deregulation during the last two decades,
many on the right insist that the octopus-like tentacles of "big government"
have extended everywhere, forming part of a creeping conspiracy to deny
the people of their rights. Conspiracy theories about the jack-booted activities of government agencies—from the incineration by the BATF of the
Branch Davidian compound at Waco, to the shooting by the FBI of Vicki
Weaver and her son at their hut in Ruby Ridge (Idaho)—express the
growing sense of the illegitimacy of federal powers. The government can
only justify its existence, the reasoning continues, by making its daily
presence more noticeable (and supposedly more necessary) by intrusive surveillance and interference. On the one hand, then, there are stories like the
implanted surveillance chips and driving licenses which speak of fears
about increased government control. Conspiracy theories about a United
Nations or alien takeover, on the other hand, express fears about a *lack* of
national sovereignty in the face of aggressive world—or other-worldly—
competition.

Whether for good or ill, the Keynesian promise of the State controlling
the economy in order to cushion its citizens from the ruthless logic of the
market is becoming a far less feasible option for many governments. Far-
right conspiracy theorists are not alone in worrying that even the
American government is handing over its proper sovereignty to global organizations and corporations. Many on the left, and in the broad rainbow
coalition of non-government organizations that in December 1999 fought
the "Battle in Seattle" in protest against the World Trade Organization
negotiations, have also expressed alarm that individual governments are
no longer in control of their own economic destinies—though they reach
very different conclusions about why that is significant and what action
should be taken. In a distant echo of right-wing alarmism, one left-leaning
commentator warns, for example, that "with massive budget cuts in the
UN agencies for social and economic development and increases for 'peace-
keeping,' the United Nations itself threatens to become a military instru-
ment of corporate power."[45]

One thing that both sides agree on is that globalization has brought much
anxiety into the formerly safe heartlands of middle America. "The
American Dream of the middle class has all but disappeared," one commentator has noted, "substituted with people struggling just to buy next
week's groceries." He continues:

What is it going to take to open the eyes of our elected officials?
AMERICA IS IN SERIOUS DECLINE. We have no proverbial

tea to dump; should we instead sink a ship full of Japanese imports? Is a civil war imminent? Do we have to shed blood to reform the current system? I hope it doesn't come to that, but it might.[46]

That commentator was Timothy McVeigh. Although in hindsight his musings contain an ominous chill, they are in tune with a popular sense of betrayal and disillusionment. With the rolling back of the New Deal compromise between labor and capital since the mid-1970s, and the increasing privatization of public responsibility, insecurity and resentment have become an everyday reality for many ordinary Americans, especially those left out of the current economic boom. Under the pressures of globalization, the security of a corporate job for life and all its attendant benefits have eroded: whereas in the 1950s GM was the nation's largest employer, by the mid-1990s Manpower Inc. occupied that symbolic slot. Facing international competition, transnational corporations—whose loyalty is no longer to the nation but to the global constituency of shareholders—downsize, outsource and relocate without warning. The advertising slogan of the 1950s doesn't ring true any more: what is good for GM is no longer necessarily good for America.

The suburban ideal of the safe and stable nuclear family has gradually faded since the 1950s, with the increasing Thirdworldization of the domestic economy, producing a narrowing of economic horizons for the many, and the fantasy of a "postindustrial" lifestyle for the few. The long period of economic growth has seen a widening of the gap between rich and poor, accompanied by an increasing polarization of American society, with a decline in wages in real terms for those in the eroding middle ground. Many in this formerly secure mainstream have turned to the language and logic of extremist politics. This attitude of routine hostility manifests itself in areas ranging from renewed anxieties about immigration, to the much-discussed crisis of masculinity. Deregulation may encourage flexibility, but flexibility for corporations often means insecurity for workers (and increasingly for the middle class who had traditionally been exempt from the job insecurity of blue collar workers). Furthermore, the tacit acceptance of structural underemployment, coupled with the erosion of some basic parts of the welfare state, has contributed to an increasing feeling of alienation from the political process and the American ideal.[47]

William Pierce's *The Turner Diaries* (1978) is perhaps the most notorious cultural expression of this mentality taken to its most bloody and dangerous extreme. Its scenario of a fertilizer-bomb attack on a federal building is supposed to have directly influenced McVeigh. The novel describes a populist revolution by disgruntled whites to form a breakaway "Aryan" republic, accompanied by the killing of blacks and Jews. It also exultantly describes how the "Day of the Rope" brought the mass hangings of white "race traitors" who before the revolution had shown liberal tolerance to Jews, immigration, affirmative action or the gun control lobby.

In the wake of the Oklahoma bombing much was written in the mainstream media about *The Turner Diaries'* incendiary racist plot. But in the haste to condemn the novel's heavy-handed message, however, few if any considered what makes up the bulk of the book. In many places the overarching story of violent revolution is almost forgotten amid the welter of mechanical details. More than anything, Earl Turner's diaries are taken up with accounts of planning, sourcing and making things. As well as being responsible for the secret communication equipment of the "Organization" (the white supremacist revolutionary movement), Turner is involved in bomb-making with Bill, who is a "machinist, a mechanic, and a printer."[48] Together they build mortar-bombs which are then used in an attack on the Capitol in which "only 61 persons were killed" (*TD*, 62):

> Bill and I finished our special-ordnance job together yesterday. We modified a 4.2 inch mortar to handle 81 mm projectiles. The modification was necessary because we have so far been unable to pick up an 81 mm mortar for the projectiles which we grabbed in the raid on the Aberdeen Proving Ground last month. One of our gun-buff members, however, had a serviceable 4.2 mortar which he had kept hidden away since the late 1940s.
>
> (*TD*, 56)

At one point Turner goes to sort out a problem with a radio transmitter at another clandestine unit. He is amazed to find that they have messed up what should have been a simple task:

> The reason for their difficulty became obvious as soon as they ushered me into their kitchen, where their transmitter, an automobile storage battery, and some odds and ends were spread out on a table. Despite the explicit instructions I had prepared to go with each transmitter, and despite the plainly visible markings beside the terminals on the transmitter case, they had managed to connect the battery to the transmitter with the wrong polarity.
>
> (*TD*, 25)

Turner soon discovers why the men are so inept (with more than a hint that their "polarity" is wrong): they are a bunch of writers and thinkers, unused to solving problems with their hands and home-spun ingenuity. He soon manages to sort the problem out, with a detailed account of diodes, signals, and transistors.

As much as it is a conspiratorial blueprint for racial warfare and an attack on multiculturalism, *The Turner Diaries* is also a homage to the value of skilled labour. Its meticulous accounts of all the resourcefulness of its protagonist (trained as an electrical engineer) is in many ways a lament for the way those skills have begun to be redundant in postwar America. It is significant that Pierce's fantasy of a "rank-and-file" member of the Organization taking control of his destiny through technical competence should be written in the mid-1970s. It is very much a symbolic product of the retreat from Vietnam and the OPEC oil crisis which together spelled the beginning of the end of America's dominant global destiny on the international scene, and of the preeminence of the all-American worker (read: straight white men) on the domestic front. It therefore also comes as little surprise that the novel should have returned with a vengeance in the mid-1990s, when the full force of a new phase of globalization was beginning to erode the last vestiges of security for that group.

For many on the conspiracy-minded right, it is neither ironic nor coincidental that the achievement of America's manifest destiny with the final triumph of US-style free market capitalism across the globe has brought with it the fragmentation and decline of a traditional American sense of identity in the heartlands. No wonder many people are worried about what it means to be American when "American" jobs are exported south of the border, and when they are forced to compete with immigrants, minorities and women for the social privileges and the financial rewards that had previously seemed an inalienable right. (In *The Turner Diaries*, the white women in the Organization are occupied as helpmates to the men in their more glamorous and heroic roles.) By this logic, globalization and multiculturalism are twin components of a conspiracy against the normal man. From the other side of the fence, however, in a postfordist economy that has neither the financial leeway nor the political will to maintain affirmative action programs, the increasing competition for diminishing social resources amongst so-called minority groups leads to mutual suspicions between the disinherited. In an ironic reversal of fortunes, even the white Anglo male establishment now seeks to redefine itself as an embattled minority interest group in the face of a larger conspiracy.[49]

As we have seen, Hofstadter reassured himself and his readers that the paranoid style was a last resort of those on the fringes of American politics unable or unwilling to participate in the process of "bargain and compromise" of liberal democratic politics. But "the usual political methods of give-and-take" can only work in a climate of public welfare and widespread prosperity needed to cushion the real clash of interests, coupled with a popular faith that the political process works for everybody. Hofstadter offered reassurance that, since the paranoid style was confined to the fringes of American politics, the mainstream was therefore immune. It is now arguable, however, that the traditional public sphere has eroded into an arena of competing and mutually suspicious interest groups, many of whom voice their claim in the rhetoric of conspiracy (Chapter 4 discusses arguably the most notorious example of this, namely the escalation of conspiracy rhetoric between militant black and Jewish organizations). We might conclude that, whereas the emergence of the paranoid style once indicated a failure to understand the workings of American consensus politics, conspiracy culture now manifests an implicit understanding of the failure of an idealized consensus. In a nation increasingly fragmented into minorities each of which feels itself to be besieged, paranoia becomes the default political style.

The Cultural Logic of Paranoia

For many Americans, then, paranoia has come to be taken for granted in recent decades. But contemporary conspiracy culture functions in a very different mode to the paranoid style of politics that Hofstadter described. There has been an important transformation in what counts as an example of the paranoid style. Hofstadter downplays the significance of his choice of examples, explaining that he had chosen American case studies simply because he happened to be an Americanist (though he does go on to suggest that there might be a connection between the paranoid style and the formation of a sense of national identity in the nascent Republic). What he also takes for granted, yet doesn't comment on, is that all the instances are more or less explicitly *political*. For Hofstadter and those writing later in the same tradition, the paranoid style is a mode of political activity, and it is a feature of explicitly political events, regimes, parties, and movements. It is to be found in pamphlets, speeches, manifestos, newspaper editorials, and other orthodox forms of political expression. It only becomes significant when it becomes a danger on the national scene, from the anti-Masonic party of the nineteenth century to the McCarthyite red scares of the twentieth. As we have seen, in keeping with Hofstadter's political focus Pipes and Robert Robins and Jerrold Post argue that, while the paranoid style is currently to be found in virulent form elsewhere in the world, in the USA it has largely disappeared in recent decades, since it has no influence on national politics. The latter pair, for example, dismiss Lyndon LaRouche's brand of right-wing anti-Semitism as "pure cultural paranoia."[50] Indeed, Pipes insists that in the West the paranoid style may now have a "widespread presence," particularly in popular culture, but that cultural turn entails that it is no longer able to change the course of history.

Even if we disagree with the conclusion that "cultural paranoia" is insignificant, what is undeniable is that the paranoid style is no longer confined to the narrowly political realm. An updated survey of the paranoid style since the time Hofstadter was writing in the early 1960s would have to feature a much wider range of examples.[51] It would still include some examples from the political sphere, but these would be from new social movements such as feminism and African American activism—and even then there would be a mixture of explicitly political pronouncements and more off-the-cuff expressions of underlying attitudes. Drawing on examples from the Internet and alternative media, it would have to document the kinds of amateur everyday politics that rarely show signs of coalescing into recognizable political movements, but which nevertheless involve engagements with major issues of the day. Such a revision would also have to include many examples of conspiracy thinking that permeate the cultural scene. American pop culture, from the Hollywood thriller to gangsta rap and from supermarket tabloids to *The X-Files*, has become saturated with the rhetoric of conspiracy. Likewise, the map of postmodern fiction usually locates at its center the novelists of paranoia such as Thomas Pynchon, William Burroughs, Joseph Heller, William Gaddis and Ishmael Reed.

In recent decades, then, paranoia has become the stuff of entertainment and philosophical reflection, part of everyday American culture. The popularization of the paranoid style is no doubt part of the much lamented general cultural turn in US politics, in which substance is replaced by style. The impeachment trial of President Clinton provides perhaps the most telling example of this turn, in a case that was not without its own accusation and countercharges of vast conspiracies, and which ultimately had less to do with electoral politics than with media appearance. But the spread of the paranoid style into the cultural realm also reflects a change in the style and function of conspiracy thinking. Hofstadter's examples are mainly single-issue nativist movements—such as anti-Masonry and anti-Catholicism—for whom a particular demonological view helped forge a definite sense of group, and even national, identity. By contrast, many people today engage with conspiracy theories in an eclectic and often contradictory manner, as part entertainment, part speculation, and part accusation, without necessarily being a signed-up member of a militia or political movement. Though there are still examples of paranoid politics structured by a single, rigid doctrine of scapegoating, for many Americans conspiratorial explanations are less an item of inflexible faith than an often uncoordinated expression of doubt and distrust. Refutations of conspiracy theorizing often accuse it of dogmatically blaming social ills on scapegoated minorities, but in recent decades the paranoid style is more likely to involve an imprecise sense that forces beyond one's individual control are conspiring to shape historical events, but without ever specifying the exact mechanism. If a precise picture of the imagined enemy ensured a tight-knit entrenchment of community identity in the past, then in the present a somewhat vague sense of the conspiring enemy—often no more than a conviction that

"They" are to blame—hinders the formation of a coherent in-group. Isolated outbreaks of countersubversive movements and theories have thus given way to an everyday low-intensity paranoia that operates at the level of image and rhetoric rather than political credo. The paid-up member of the National Silver Party during the conspiracy-infused bimetallism debates of the 1890s has become an armchair consumer of *The X-Files* in the 1990s.

Conspiracy theory becomes something that people buy into—often quite literally—on a non-committed basis. There are, for example, numerous conspiracy websites which function not so much as shrines to particular nativist doctrines as supermarkets of alternative beliefs. A good example is disinfo.com, a popular search engine and gateway to a range of "dark side" and conspiratorial ideas. The brainchild of Richard Metzger, disinfo.com was established in 1996 through a million-dollar deal with the global media company TCI. Like many other media corporations, TCI wanted to buy some cutting-edge content for its web traffic, but (according to Metzger), when the parent company found out how radical the content was to be, it pulled the plug. The site then moved under the wing of razorfish.com, a hip Internet service provider based in Manhattan. In addition to information on counterculture heroes like Aleister Crowley, disinfo.com provides annotated background and links to "alternative" news stories ranging from the plausible to the fantastic. It also links to the Infinity Factory, a web-based local cable TV interview show based in New York, and to Metzger's latest venture, "Disinfo Nation," a late-night conspiracy/tales of the weird magazine program airing in the UK on Channel 4. Like many other start-up Internet businesses, disinfo.com has attracted high-level investment and interest, but has been slow to turn a profit. Though a labor of love on the part of its writers and designers, with no small measure of countercultural commitment to all things radical, the site is also a business, selling books and paraphernalia, as well as generating revenue through advertising.

In the e-commerce revolution, conspiracy theories are a product like any other, part of a self-sustaining cottage industry of alternative America, from small publishers like Feral House to mail-order book firms on assassinology like the Last Hurrah Bookshop, and from 'zine-style' publications like *Paranoia* to the purveyors of *X-Files*-related memorabilia. Indeed, many people's participation in the world of conspiracy theory is less likely to be as a paid-up member of a dedicated organization, than as a casual browser of the Web, checking out the spoof alien abduction prevention kits at schwa.com, or posting stories about the Montauk Project on alt.conspiracy. Whatever else it might have become, conspiracy theory is an integral part of the infotainment culture at the turn of the millennium, hovering somewhere between committed belief and the culture of consumption.

As If

It is not just that people's interest in conspiracy has begun to waver between the serious and the spoof. Many conspiracy theories themselves have come to fluctuate between the two poles. Unlike Hofstadter's concern only for serious political manifestations of the paranoid style, the present study brings together factual and self-consciously fictional examples, not least because the two often blur into one another. At its most extreme, hoax theories have been taken seriously, and, conversely, straight-up allegations have been treated as material for fictional elaborations. A good example of the former case is Leonard C. Lewin's *Report from Iron Mountain*, which is an anonymous, satirical, and fictional exposé of supposed secret US government plans to maintain the nation on a permanent war economy even during peacetime.[52] The first irony is that just four years later Daniel Ellsburg leaked to the *New York Times* the all-too-real Pentagon Papers, the military's own secret history of America's involvement in Vietnam.[53] The second irony is that, by the 1990s, Lewin's original spoof had come to be taken seriously by the right-wing militia and Patriot movement, who were circulating pirate editions, convinced that the report was indeed a government document that had been accidentally released. Lewin was forced to assert his authorship and copyright, and Simon & Schuster issued a reprint in 1996.

There is also, for instance, the "Nomenclature of an Assassination Cabal," a photocopied manuscript by the pseudonymous William Torbitt, which has circulated among conspiracy researchers since the early 1970s. The Torbitt Document offers an astounding exposé of the Kennedy assassination as a Nazi coup d'état, involving Lyndon Johnson, J. Edgar Hoover, John Connally, and the former German rocket scientist Werner von Braun. The document makes links between the Mafia, NASA, the ultrasecret Defense Industrial Security Command (DISC), the FBI, and corporate interests. Some parts of the enormously detailed text are plausible, not least the discussion of Operation Paperclip, the American plan to rescue Nazi intelligence officers and rocket scientists at the close of the war. Other parts seem to fade off into more fanciful territory, with allegations about NASA's UFO program headquartered in the notorious Area 51 in the Nevada desert. The document taps into many of the major conspiracy theories of the last half-century, and its samizdat circulation has lent it cult status. Yet its mysterious origins have led some people to wonder if it is a hoax. Len Bracken, in an afterword to the first published edition of the Torbitt Document, wonders if it is not a piece of Soviet disinformation. Indeed, documents smuggled out of Russia by the former KGB archivist Vasily Mitrokhin purportedly reveal that some conspiracy theories about the JFK shooting were constructed as deliberately inflammatory propaganda by the Soviets—as far as these revelations can even now be believed.[54] But (as Chapter 2 makes clear) some conspiracy theories about the Kennedy assassination uncover more than they perhaps intend, even if they turn out to be false. As Bracken puts it, "just as there is disinformation in all information, there is information in all good disinformation."[55]

Some conspiratorial hoaxes have thus come to be taken seriously. A made-up story can sometimes take on a life of its own, as the metaphorical becomes materialized. This possibility is adroitly dramatized in Umberto Eco's *Foucault's Pendulum* (1989).* The novel features idle employees at a publishing house who for fun make up the most elaborate conspiracy theory imaginable. However, the last laugh is on them as the conspiracy they fabricated seems to materialize before their eyes. Indeed, the blurring of the factual and fictional is now often sent into spiraling free fall with conspiracy theorists' suspicion that false leads have been deliberately planted by the powers that be in order to divert them from uncovering an even more sinister truth, a story line which *The X-Files* trades on repeatedly. On the other hand, more than a few *X-Files* viewers have come to take the show's conspiracy and fringe-science revelations as fact, perhaps convinced by the knowledge that the background to each episode is often meticulously researched. The show, for example, has gradually developed a complicated account of extraterrestrial invasion and collusion. But many of its details of small gray aliens, prehistoric aliens and hybrid DNA experiments are taken from the Krill Report, an account of fierce battles between special forces and threatening space invaders that was posted by John Lear on the Paranet UFO bulletin board in 1987, and has circulated on the Net ever since. Supposedly written by O. H. Krill (O. H. stands for Original Hostage), it tells the history of alien–human contact. It describes how aliens had reneged on their original agreement with the US government merely to conduct research experiments on cattle and humans, and are now abducting large numbers of humans, as well as implanting electronic control devices, in order to create a genetically hybrid race in pursuit of their goal of colonization. Although the Krill Document has the rhetoric and trappings of an official document, it is nevertheless a fabulously inventive fake whose details have taken on a life of their own.

For many skeptical commentators, the popularity of *The X-Files* and its clones demonstrate that the American public has become increasingly gullible in recent years, no longer able to tell the difference between reputable sources and fake documents. But they might better be understood as part of a more general shift in the way people encounter conspiracy theories at the turn of the millennium. Everyday paranoia now functions

*Umberto Eco, *Foucault's Pendulum*, trans. William Weaver (London: Secker & Warburg, 1989).

less as a firm conviction in certain revealed facts than as a default skepticism that it is always plausible that there is a hidden agenda to public events. The conspiracy culture explored in the following chapters oscillates between the hoax and the accurate revelation, between the serious and the ironic, between the factual and the fictional, and between the literal and the metaphorical. In many instances consumers of conspiracy don't really believe what they buy, but neither do they really disbelieve it either. Often people believe rumors with a provisional commitment, believing them *as if* they were true.

More than any other item of contemporary conspiracy culture, *The X-Files* operates in the key of "as if," with its continual explorations of the epistemological quicksand between certainty and suspicion, in a dramatic style that wavers between the spoof and the deadly serious. Again and again, a provisional, mundane explanation is reframed by a more sinister hypothesis, and vice versa. For example, a USDA scientist with the improbable name of Dr Bambi puts forward to Agent Mulder her theory that sightings of Unidentified Flying Objects are in fact prompted by light reflecting off swarms of airborne cockroaches. By the end of that episode, however, Mulder has uncovered clues which suggest not that aliens are cockroaches, but that the miniature mechanical roaches causing the unexplained fatal swarms are in fact aliens—or, at the very least, government-engineered robots utilizing alien technology.[56] Many episodes float different kinds of explanation—some mundane, some paranormal—for a strange phenomenon without ever really offering an ultimate solution. "I don't know how else to explain what's happening here," Agent Scully announces, faced with a range of equally implausible theories. In "Small Potatoes," for example, babies in a local hospital are being born with vestigial tails. Scully at first puts the exaggerated reports down to the inhabitants' susceptibility to supermarket tabloid stories about alien–human couplings, but then concedes that there might be a physiological rather than a psychological explanation. In turn the audience is led to believe that it is a statistical anomaly involving a rare but possible medical condition, then that the deformities are due to medical malpractice, and finally that a local freak with strange powers is involved. The man appears to be able to seduce women easily, which Scully at first attributes to a date-rape drug, or an identical twin. But it begins to seem that he can change shape and appearance at will, a paranormal ability that in other episodes has been associated with top-secret alien–human hybrid creatures.[57]

In this way, *The X-Files* continually offers up plausible explanations, only to undermine them with highly improbable (and frequently conspiratorial) ones, and vice versa. In the wildly parodic "The Post-Modern Prometheus," for example, Scully dismisses rumors of a monster in a small-town community as a product of the population's addiction to Jerry Springer shows (deliciously spoofed in a cameo performance by Springer himself). "What we're seeing here," Scully explains, "is an example of a culture for whom daytime talk shows and tabloid headlines have become a reality against which they measure their lives." For his part, Mulder confesses that he is "alarmed that you'd reduce these people to a cultural stereotype."[58] She then puts forward the classic psychoanalytical explanation that monsters are a projection of unacceptable parts of the self or group, only then for the monster to materialize in full gory detail. Scully then offers a medical explanation, which in turn is undermined by further revelation about the complicated history of the "monster." The audience is left in hermeneutic limbo, with the plausible explanations left hovering, neither fully disproved nor entirely confirmed. The show has likewise examined tricky contemporary phenomena such as satanic ritual abuse and false memory syndrome.[59] Instead of presenting a stern rebuttal or eager endorsement of either side of the debate, the episodes complicate the issues further, suggesting that the truth of the issue cannot be reduced to a physical certainty or psychological formula. As Chapter 6 discusses in more detail, the central ongoing interpretative dilemma of *The X-Files* is whether there really are aliens or alien–human hybrids (as Mulder at first believes), or, as Scully comes to suspect, all the evidence they uncover is "just a smokescreen" to hide the government's clandestine and illegal medical experiments on its citizens, possibly in search of a biowarfare weapon.[60] Again and again the personal faith of each agent is placed in doubt, with each explanatory framework remaining plausible but not conclusive. There is always the possibility that the evidence will be reframed in a larger, more paranoia-inducing scenario, or that another interpretation will emerge. The piecemeal unfolding of the convoluted conspiracy arc over seven series ensures thus that there is an endless deferral of revelation, producing an infinite regress of interpretation. In a comic episode written by the show's star, David Duchovny, Agent Mulder is told by an ageing Roswell cop that Babe Ruth and a (fictional) black baseball star of the 1940s were aliens. Mulder summarizes the interpretative possibilities succinctly and sarcastically: "Was Ex an alien who was metaphorically a man or a man who was metaphorically an alien, or something in between that was literally an alien–human hybrid?"[61] As formerly figurative explanations are given a new and dramatic lease of life, the distinction between the literal and the metaphorical becomes blurred. Psychological explanations undermine physiological ones, and vice versa.

Not only does *The X-Files* leave its central characters and its viewers in a hermeneutic limbo, then, it also enters into a game of bluff and double-bluff with expectations of both its audience and the alarmist critics of popular paranoia. In "Wetwired," for example, the clichéd idea of television infiltrating and controlling the minds of its viewers is turned on its head. The stock 1950s paranoia about subliminal ideological indoctrination via the airwaves is revealed in the case under investigation to be quite literal, with viewers' minds quite literally scrambled by secret signals buried in normal broadcasts. Scully puts forward the more mundane, sociological explanation that repeated exposure to simulated violence on television could prompt ordinary small town folk into a murderous frenzy. But there are strong clues, needless to say, that the technology is being developed by the intelligence agencies and tested on unwitting civilians in the search for a remote-triggered mind-controlled assassin.[62] *The X-Files* often deliberately and wittily exploits a self-ironizing aesthetic that comes ready equipped with the tools and rhetoric of symptomatic cultural diagnosis.

Again and again the show humorously includes exactly the kind of accusation that is levelled against most crackpot conspiracy culture. "One more anal-probing, gyro-pyro, levitating ectoplasm alien anti-matter story, I'm gonna take out my gun and shoot somebody," an exasperated and disillusioned Agent Mulder announces to Scully in Season Five.[63] A self-mocking sociological critique of the show's excesses is thus hardwired into the drama itself, in effect shortcircuiting the more normal relationship between the "pathology" of popular paranoia and the legitimate diagnosis of it. Learning that Mulder has been watching a video of a "guaranteed authentic" alien autopsy he purchased by mail order, Scully exasperatedly informs her partner, in a moment that blurs the boundaries between the fictional world the show creates and real world in which it participates, that "this is even hokier than the one they aired on the Fox network."[64] The first irony is that the Fox network ran trailers for a repeated showing of the infamous alien autopsy footage during that episode. The second irony is that the autopsy footage in "Nisei" indeed turns out to be real. The third, far more disturbing irony, is that the film, though of a real autopsy, turns out to be evidence not so much of the existence of aliens as a clue to the government's clandestine program of medical experiment—a revelation that is itself later cast into doubt.

The show feeds off and feeds into its audience's sophisticated and world-weary familiarity with sociological and psychological accounts of conspiracy-minded beliefs, by holding out the promise of such symptomatic readings, only then to revert, half-ironically, to a far more literal-minded faith in the conspiratorial explanation. In "Drive," for example, Mulder is hijacked in his car by a crazed man who spouts off about an International Jewish Conspiracy in league with the government, declaring that: "You see it every day on the TV: they're droppin' Agent Orange, they're putting radiation in little retarded kids' gonads. Yeah, I've watched you sonsabitches, sneakin' around my woods at night. You think I don't know?" "Well," Mulder replies sardonically, "on behalf of the International Jewish Conspiracy, I have to inform you that we're almost out of gas."[65] It turns out, needless to say, that the man's crazed behavior seems to be linked to classified US Navy experiments involving extremely low frequency radio near his home.

Not infrequently *The X-Files* plays self-consciously upon its dangerously close relationship to the outré world of supermarket tabloids. In "Small Potatoes," for example, Scully finds Mulder reading a supermarket tabloid for background information on their way to investigate the monkey-tail baby case, and neither she nor the audience know how seriously to take Mulder's sardonic promotion of tabloids as a vital source of uncensored information. In "Pusher," a man (who turns out to have strange psychic powers) is apprehended by an FBI team in a supermarket. At the checkout the sharp-sighted viewer can catch a glimpse of a mocked-up tabloid, the front cover of which in a blink-and-you'll-miss-it moment of self-referentiality features the Flukeman, a monster found inhabiting the Jersey sewer in a previous *X-Files* episode.[66] A member of a committee convened at the beginning of Season Six to decide whether the X-Files should be closed down declares that "I'm reading here a very pie-in-the-sky report [based on the events shown in *The X-Files: Fight the Future*, the 1998 feature film] about global domination plans by vicious, long-clawed spacelings." In a moment of self-reflexive cross-referencing, another panel member quizzes Mulder whether the spacelings he claims to have seen were from the film *Men in Black*. Mulder admits that he didn't see the film, but his inquisitor mutters that it was a "damn good movie."[67]

In a similar (but less complex) fashion *Men in Black* (1997) itself plays with the idea that the outlandish stories in supermarket tabloids might actually be the plain truth. Newly recruited by the government as an alien protection agent, Will Smith stares in disbelief as his more experienced colleague (played by Tommy Lee Jones) buys a "hot sheet" to find new leads in the case they are working on. In the film's comically matter-of-fact world of regular alien visitation, the paper turns out to provide a thoroughly factual explanation for the seemingly unbelievable story of a man waking from a thirty-five year coma—he was an alien. Moreover, *Men in Black* plays with a common symptomatic analysis of ufological lore, namely that the space aliens crudely stand in for the repressed knowledge of the all-too-real traffic in undocumented immigrant aliens. In a witty reversal of this interpretation, the opening scene reveals not that the ETs are symbolic substitutes for illegal immigrants from Mexico, but that the wetbacks are quite literally aliens from another planet.[68] With their ironic endorsement of supermarket tabloids and their satiric reversal of stock cultural analysis, *Men in Black* and *The X-Files* are less a cause or even a celebration of dumbing down, than an attack on the earnestness of skeptical critics, and an investigation into the incommensurabilities of different forms of explanation. High-minded dismissals of conspiracy-minded publications like the *Weekly World News* as the thin end of the wedge of public stupidity fail to appreciate how the magazines themselves contain a complicated pose of approval and ridicule of both their own audience and their own material.[69]

The Routinization of Paranoia

In the conspiracy culture typified by *The X-Files*, belief in a conspiracy is no longer necessarily a sign of gullible paranoia, as it was for Hofstadter, and as it still is for many stern critics. This half-ironic, half-serious mode of conspiracy thinking is also in a different league to the committed political stance found in some countercultural reworkings of demonology that emerged in the 1960s and 1970s, typified, for example, by the pious insistence on solving the Kennedy case as a tribute to the dead President's sacred memory. We can measure the shift between the earlier, more earnest mode and the later, more ambivalent style with two definitive conspiracy films of their respective eras. Alan J. Pakula's *Parallax View* (1975) is a sombre and portentous meditation on the collusion between corporate and government covert interests. Its reworking of the two Kennedy assassinations features Warren Beatty as a radical journalist who becomes caught up investigating the ominous death of witnesses to the shooting of a presidential candidate. The film holds out the rapidly diminishing hope of a lone detective fighting against the corrupt and ruthless plans of sinister corporations to alter the course of history. The film is bleak in its mood, styling and outcome, with the suggestion that the monolithic, faceless Parallax Corporation—the interior of whose headquarters is shot in heavy, dreary tones—has got away with another political assassination.

By contrast *Conspiracy Theory* (1997) operates less as a political thriller and more as a romantic comedy. The main interest is the will-they-won't-they love story involving Mel Gibson and Julia Roberts. A far cry from Beatty's moody portrayal of a reluctantly heroic investigative reporter with anti-establishment attitude, Gibson's taxi driver is a cartoon version of a paranoid misfit, a kind of lovable and hapless Travis Bickle who keeps his coffee locked in a chained fridge. Unlike *Parallax View*'s gesture towards the real drama of state-of-the-art investigative journalism in the Watergate case, *Conspiracy Theory*'s hero anachronistically mimeographs a half-dozen copies of a conspiracy newsletter, forming a strange denial of the media-savvy saturation of much contemporary conspiracy culture which the film itself in no small way enacts. The irony in the world of the film, of course, is that some of Fletcher's conspiracy rantings turn out to be true, but that irony never really becomes a political call to arms. The film hovers somewhere between a self-conscious parody of conspiracy culture and a half-serious engagement with it. A quarter of a century earlier, the film's clinching revelation (that Fletcher is a victim of a government mind-control assassin program gone wrong) might have been shocking. But by 1997 it is on the one hand merely the plot device that brings him closer to Julia Roberts, and, on the other, something that is exposed with little comment because it is more or less to be expected, merely a conventional part of the thriller's scenery.

The film's literal-minded, self-reflexive title is, as I have noted, curiously disconcerting. It seems to promise that the film will provide a thorough-going parody of crackpot paranoia, but within the logic of the film all the revelations turn out to be true—even Fletcher's fanciful fears about a plot to induce an earthquake to kill the president. The film seems strangely uncertain whether it is endorsing or condoning conspiracy thinking—or merely putting it on view. Joel Silver, the film's producer, was far from convinced by the subject matter: "What a weird idea to believe that there might be bar codes on the back of Federal road signs that are secret instructions for the UN army planning a takeover. It shows," he opines, "the persistence of paranoia." Though hamming up his character's paranoia for comic effect, Mel Gibson nevertheless suggested a more open-minded approach to the issue: "I have no doubt that there's a covert force at work somewhere, keeping things undercover and admitting only certain things to the public." In a similar vein, Richard Donner, the director, acknowledges that halfway through the film there is a shift of faith as Fletcher's fears are seen to be warranted. "Even paranoids really have people following them sometimes," he declares.[70] The ambivalence felt by the film's makers is evident in the final product: it confirms all Fletcher's worst fears, yet its dominant mood is comic, with the love plot providing an emotional resolution that the conspiracy plot never can.

In a similar fashion, Chris Carter, the creative force behind *The X-Files*, shows signs of a faith in a 1960s-style countercultural faith in the oppositional necessity of conspiracy theory, yet at the same time he revels in the camp aesthetic of aliens and spooky goings-on in the woods. Carter admits to being a "thirty-eight year old surfer" who credits cult classic television hits from the 1960s such as *The Twilight Zone* and *The Night Stalker* as his source of inspiration for *The X-Files*.[71] In each series there are episodes which hold the basic premise of *The X-Files* at a comic distance. In "José Chung's *From Outer Space*," for example, Mulder and Scully's investigation of an alien corpse is told through several layers of humorously exaggerated and self-reflexive narrative framing devices, the mainstay of which is José Chung's "science fiction nonfiction novel" about the events. The front cover of the latter's book on the events features the image of a gray alien's enigmatic face taken from Whitley Strieber's classic account of alien abduction, with the difference that this one is smoking a cigarette (as an eyewitness swears during the episode). Likewise, in a piece of witty casting, the sinister agent, who informs Mulder that the alien body he thought he had discovered is a hoax, is played by the television show *Jeopardy*'s Alex Trebek.[72] Although the episode includes glimpses of earth-shattering proof that aliens have crash-landed (or, at the very least that the government is covering up the evidence), the story is given full ironic treatment.

Despite the temptations of all-out spoof, *The X-Files'* approach remains ambiguous. Carter admits that the coverage of the Watergate hearings and President Nixon's resignation were "the most formative event of my youth," and that his basic left-libertarian political outlook is summed up by the show's slogan, "Trust No One."[73] It comes as little surprise, therefore, that the series returns repeatedly to the fact and symbolism of Watergate. In one version of the abduction by aliens of Agent Mulder's sister that lies at the heart of the show's mythology, a news item about Watergate is playing on the television in the background as the events unfold. Likewise, in a direct homage to Watergate, Mulder's initial inside informer is named Deep Throat, and, after the X-Files unit has been officially shut down, Agents Mulder and Scully arrange to meet one another clandestinely in the underground garage in the Watergate hotel complex.[74] Displaying its debt to a post-1960s political sensibility, the series returns again and again to the idea that the government is not only keeping secrets from the American public, but is actively betraying it, principally through unauthorized medical experiments on unwitting citizens. Carter recognizes that "the show's original spirit has become kind of the spirit of the country—if not the world," fuelled by a complex and "growing paranoia," not helped by the fact that "there are no easy villains any more" in a post-Cold War world.[75] Although Carter seems to take it for granted that many of the show's revelations (or at least the basic premise of government malfeasance) are in some form or other true, at the same time he holds that conviction at arm's length.

This double-think is a feature not just of conspiracy entertainment, but also of less explicitly fictional forms. We might compare anthologies of conspiracy materials, one from the 1970s, the others from the 1990s. Following Hofstadter's outline analysis of the "paranoid style," the historian David Brion Davis put together in 1971 an anthology of countersubversive literature. It presents a wide survey of the kind of nativist demonology studied by Hofstadter, presumably with the assumption that historians and students would use the primary material as the basis for an investigation into the scope and causes of political extremism in the USA, an obviously troubling issue at the tail end of the 1960s. To find a comparable collection in the 1990s, however, we would have to turn to trade paperback anthologies of fringe culture that are very far from Davis's university press research tool. Examples would include *Popular Alienation* and *Cyberspace Counterconspiracy*, editor Kenn Thomas's selection of articles from the conspiracy magazine *Steamshovel Press*; *It's a Conspiracy!*, a semi-spoof roundup of the usual conspiracy theories by the self-styled National Insecurity Council; *Conspiranoia!*, a meticulously cross-referenced handbook of matters conspiratorial by former *Details* magazine editor, Devon Jackson; *The Seventy Greatest Conspiracies of All Time*, the ever-expanding book and website by journalists Jonathan

Vankin and John Whalen; *Everything Is Under Control*, a similar encyclo-
pedia of conspiracy theories by Robert Anton Wilson, former *Playboy*
editor and author of the cult conspiracy trilogy, *Illuminatus!*; and *The Big
Book of Conspiracies*, Doug Moensch's cartoon guide to popular paranoia.
What these collections have in common is their uneasy stance between
critical distance and enthusiastic familiarity. Unlike Davis's scholarly
approach, most of these editors and writers seem neither to fully
endorse the conspiracy theories they are describing, nor to wholeheartedly
hold them up for ridicule. "Is it fact? Is it fiction?" Jackson asks in the
introduction to *Conspiranoia!*, "creative nonfiction? Rumor and urban
myth, or suppressed secrets finally brought to light?" It is "all of the
above and more," Jackson concludes, remaining firmly agnostic till the
last. [76]

It is also hard to work out who the audience of these volumes is meant
to be and what purpose they are meant to serve—other than as a cash
cow for their publishers. (One suspects that, like the bifocal readership
of the *Weekly World News*, there are more amateur cultural critics seeking
the frisson of intellectual slumming than there are "real" readers.)
Though varying in style and format, the governing tone of these
volumes (and their equivalents on the Web) is a complex one involving
a relish of the weird, and a half-ironic detachment from some of the
more implausible theories. They also contain an earnest, vaguely countercultural desire to teach citizens the truth about what their government is
doing to them, as well as a wearied air of resignation that too many bad
things have happened in American history in recent decades to make
change possible. All this is suffused through a commercial sense that
though all this once underground stuff is now common knowledge,
people still want to read about it. Richard Metzger of the disinfo.com
website, for example, exudes an amalgam of committed countercultural
preaching, ironic interest in fringe beliefs, and cynical weariness that
most things have turned out to be true but their revelation has made
little difference (Figure 1.1). In interviews with conspiracy community
luminaries for his fortnightly webcast and in conversations with this
author, he reveals both a sincere wannabe 1960s radical ambition to
educate his audience and expose injustice, and also a very 1990s digital
hipster cynicism about making money on the Web from the niche marketing of public gullibility. In a review of the unamerican.com website for
the "Disinfo Nation" show, for example, Metzger found it guilty of
"commodifying rebellion for mass-market consumption," but went on
to acknowledge ironically that it was "like this programme, for instance."[77] Conspiracy culture is thus no longer a symptom of a naïve
and fervent demonology, but a very knowing acceptance of suspicion as
a default mode—including even a cynical and self-reflexive skepticism
about that suspicion itself.

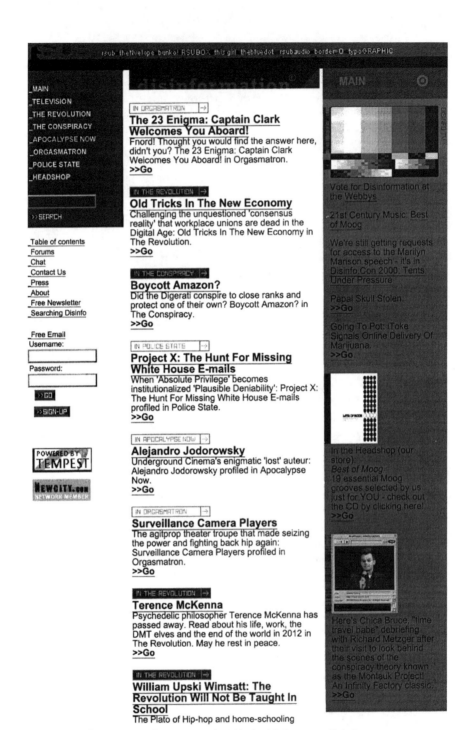

Figure 1.1. Gateway to the "dark side": www.disinfo.com.

56

II. *VINELAND* AND VISIBILITY

"They accuse *us* of being paranoids"

The career of Thomas Pynchon, America's foremost novelist of paranoia, encapsulates the changing style and function of conspiracy thinking outlined so far. Pynchon has been identified as one of a handful of novelists who captured—if not inspired—the mood of the generation. For example, Morris Dickstein's sympathetic commentary on the cultural experiments of the 1960s, *Gates of Eden*, argues that "Pynchon's sensibility, like that of some earlier Beat figures ... strikingly foreshadowed the mood of young people in the late sixties." For them, according to Dickstein, "paranoia, like radicalism, drug-taking, and communal life, was both a rejection of the official culture and a form of group solidarity, promising a more fully authentic life-possibility."[78] As much as they are a commentary on the emergence of a popular culture of conspiracy, Pynchon's first three novels also played a not insignificant role in the formation of that culture. His fourth novel, however, marks a revision, if not a major rethinking, of the paranoid style of fiction. The remainder of this chapter explores how Pynchon's earlier, more countercultural novels of paranoia as a proto-political possibility give way to the paradoxical stance of cynical gullibility dramatized in *Vineland*.

Published in the same year as Hofstadter gave his "Paranoid Style" lecture, Pynchon's first novel, *V.* (1963), likewise revolves around a series of historical snapshots of popular paranoia, ranging from fears about anar-chists in fin-de-siècle Florence to rumors about alligators in the sewers of New York in the 1950s. The only thing these diverse events seem to have in common is that Herbert Stencil, son of a diplomat and the very embodi-ment of the paranoid style in public officials, believes they provide evidence of "The Big One, the century's master cabal ... the ultimate Plot Which Has No Name."[79] Each of these seemingly strategic moments of social and economic crisis also represents a significant moment in the buried history of the paranoid style. *V.* becomes both a test case of the possibilities of reading between the lines of history, and an examination of the historical emergence of that mode of paranoid reading. Like Hofstadter's essay, Pynchon's first novel gestures towards a psychohistorical reading of the paranoid style. Significantly, it is Eigenvalue, Stencil's dentist and substitute psychoanalyst, who gives the clearest—and clearly satirical—diagnosis of Stencil's condition:

> Cavities in the teeth occur for good reason ... But even if there are several per tooth, there's no conscious organization there against the life of the pulp, no conspiracy. Yet we have men like Stencil,

who must go about grouping the world's random caries into cabals.[80]

V. toys with the possibility that there is a "conscious organization" to the seemingly random appearances of people whose only common link is the letter V in their names. It tempts the reader into the paranoid style, so as to make its lesson all the more vivid, that "grouping the world's random caries into cabals" is a mistake. Both Pynchon's first novel and Hofstadter's "Paranoid Style" essay—albeit from different perspectives—thus participate in a wider attack by 1960s intellectuals on the institutionalized culture of paranoia that dominated Cold War politics.

The 1960s, I have been arguing, witnessed a broad shift from conspiracy theories leveled against already victimized people on the charge of counter-subversion of the status quo, to conspiracy theories proposed by the people about abuses of power by those in authority. Pynchon's second novel, *The Crying of Lot 49* (1966), marks the midpoint of this transition. It reads as a journalistic survey of the LA scene in the summer of 1964, and portions of the novel were in fact published in *Esquire* magazine in 1965. The book is a sharply humorous sampling of the rapidly changing zeitgeist, and one of the new fashions it identifies is the emergence of paranoia as a popular, but zany, cultural language. The novel is full of self-conscious references to paranoia, not least with a would-be Beatles-style pop group called The Paranoids. At the same time, there are still some quick satires on the kind of political fanatics studied by Hofstadter and his colleagues. The Peter Pinguid Society, for instance, distance themselves from "our more left-leaning friends over in the Birch Society."[81] In the time of flux the novel depicts, it is comically unclear whether "We" or "They" are the more prone to paranoia. In the following exchange, Oedipa and her lawyer, Metzger, meet up with Mike Fallopian of the Peter Pinguid society:

> "You one of these right-wing nut outfits?" inquired the diplomatic
>   Metzger.
> Fallopian twinkled. "They accuse *us* of being paranoids."
> "They?" inquired Metzger, twinkling also.
> "Us?" asked Oedipa.
>
> (*CL*, 32)

With its wry commentary on the translation of paranoia as a 1950s political style into the affected anxieties of a 1960s Californian housewife, *The Crying of Lot 49* at times speaks in the same idiom as "Wake up America! It Can Happen Here!," the article from *Esquire* magazine of the same year discussed above. Included in the list and garish cartoon illustration of the twenty-three "enemies within" there are several that are familiar from the world of *The Crying of Lot 49*. There is for example the Zip-Code Plot, in which the Jewish-controlled "Post office or the Commissar ... will know exactly where you are, what you are doing and who is with you because you have been branded on ... the right hand" (note in *Lot 49* the old sailor with a tattooed sign of WASTE, the alternative postal system [*CL*, 87]). Then there is the Flag-Stamp Intrigue, which finds extremely suspicious a 1963 US stamp that omits the words "U.S. Postage" (think of the discovery by Oedipa and Genghis Cohen the philatelist of anomalous US stamps [*CL*, 66–68]). The *Esquire* article even lists the threat of Hypno-Subversive music from groups like the Beatles (compare Pynchon's British Invasion-style combo, The Paranoids).

For all its satire on the paranoid style, Pynchon's novella does begin to consider, however tentatively, the possibility that Oedipa's quest for some transcendent but arcane revelation is an enormous red herring, such that she fails to notice the obvious social ills around her which need no con-spiracy theories to explain them.[82] In addition to its various vignettes on traditional right-wing conspiracy theories, the novel floats the possibility that paranoia might provide a model for plotting together as an alternative counterconspiracy all those left out of mainstream American society. As much as Oedipa's paranoia sidetracks her from the obvious, it also leads her to discover the existence—even if still imaginary—of a counter-conspiracy, a "calculated withdrawal, from the life of the Republic, from its machinery" (*CL*, 86).

Whereas *The Crying of Lot 49* only briefly introduces the potential of a counterconspiracy into its post-McCarthy satires on Cold War paranoia, *Gravity's Rainbow* produces a full-blown exploration of this possibility. *Lot 49* portrays the summer of 1964, and marks the beginnings of the student-led counterculture, describing demonstrations in Berkeley's Sproul Plaza and experiments with LSD. At the end of the novel Oedipa wonders if "perhaps she'd be hounded someday as far as joining Tristero itself," which suggests either that she'll be pressurized into joining the counterconspiracy of alternative America, if the Tristero turns out to be a benign and progressive conspiracy, or, if the Tristero reveals itself in the end to be the forces of reaction, that she'll end up throwing in her lot with the forces of conformity (*CL*, 150). By the time *Gravity's Rainbow* was published in 1973 the real identity of the Tristero had become irrelevant, since the adventure of the counterculture was nearly over. In the final section of the novel, "The Counterforce," Pirate Prentice, eccentric SOE officer and chaser of V-2 rockets, outlines what holds this Counterforce together. "Creative paranoia," Prentice explains, "means developing at least as thorough a We-system as a They-system."[83]

As many commentators have observed, paranoia became as integral to the counterculture as the use of drugs, and *Gravity's Rainbow* fully recog-nizes that the two are intimately connected. Reefer "papyromancy" (*GR*, 442), along with "dreams, psychic flashes, omens, cryptographies, drug-epistemologies," becomes part of the Counterforce's armory of creative paranoia (*GR*, 582). If the discourse of paranoia in *The Crying of Lot 49* is occasionally surrounded by a "ritual reluctance" to name things directly, then in *Gravity's Rainbow* it becomes omnipresent, transformed, for example, into a brash Broadway tune: "Pa—ra—nooooiiiia, Pa-ra-noia! / Ain't it grand ta see, that good-time face, again!" (*GR*, 657). Paranoia is endlessly and outrageously discussed, theorized, and utilized, from the five "Proverbs for Paranoids," to the many narratorial working definitions ("If there is something comforting—religious, if you want—about paranoia, there is still also anti-paranoia, where nothing is connected to anything, a condition not many of us can bear for long" [*GR*, 434], and so on). Just about every character is paranoid in one way or another, which is hardly surprising since the novel is overflowing with the intricate conspiratorial details of the interwar cartels involved in rocket development.[84] The significance is that in the decade between Pynchon's first novel and his third, conspiracy theories had mutated from a political style in need of explanation, to a self-conscious and necessary working assumption for the counterculture.

Mindless Pleasures

Towards the end of 1989 rumors began to circulate in academic and literary circles that Pynchon's long-awaited new novel was about to be published. In the nearly two decades since his last novel, *Gravity's Rainbow*, Pynchon had come to be regarded by many critics as one of the most important novelists in postwar America—and one whose name was synonymous with paranoid conspiracies. Whatever this new novel was ostensibly about, it would inevitably amount to a symbolic story about the legacy of the 1960s, and about the fortune of the paranoid style, even if by default. As it turned out, the novel was explicitly a story about the fate of various paranoid ex-hippies struggling to survive in the dark years of the Reagan era. *Vineland* became one more contribution—albeit an extremely ambiguous one—to the by then familiar thirtysomething (now fiftysomething) genre, one more plotting of the lives of 1960s radicals who in various ways sold out or were betrayed. Yet it was also a novel in which Pynchon's trademark focus on paranoia was apparently missing.

The critical reception of Pynchon's fourth novel was divided, and the key issue seemed to be *Vineland*'s substitution of joking references to mass culture for the notoriously erudite conspiratorial allusions in the earlier novels. On the one hand, *Vineland* was favorably reviewed by the majority of newspaper critics, and the novel became Pynchon's first real commercial success, staying on the *New York Times* bestseller list for nearly four months in 1990. Its popularity with readers and some newspaper critics was probably due to its straightforwardness in comparison with the reclusive author's earlier, highly intricate and allusive conspiracy fictions. Terrence Rafferty in the *New Yorker* found it "the clearest novel Thomas Pynchon has written to date," and Christopher Walker in a letter to the *London Review of Books* characterized it as "Pynchon's most user-friendly novel."[85] Designating it a Main Selection, the American Book-of-the-Month Club emphasized that *Vineland* was "eminently scrutable, richly accessible, enormously readable," in an attempt to reassure readers for whom Pynchon had become a byword for convoluted obscurity—a specialist in what one reviewer labeled the "highbrow conspiracy thriller."[86]

But for others the novel was an anticlimax after 17 years of waiting and false rumors. Wendy Steiner thought *Vineland* a "parody of Pynchon's genius," with "inventiveness reduced to gimmickry, high comedy become wisecracking, emotional power shrunk to sentimentality." The book, she concluded, "is a great disappointment."[87] Christopher Lehman-Haupt in the *New York Times* commented that "it's a little as if Upton Sinclair had been captured by ninja warriors and lived to tell the tale to an R. Crumb high on acid."[88] Disappointment with the novel seemed to go hand-in-hand with the perception, as Lehman-Haupt put it, that "Mr Pynchon's paranoia seems to have eased." Although some critics (for example, Salman Rushdie, and Paul Gray in *Time* magazine) still found Pynchon to be promoting paranoid plots, most were struck by the comparative absence of "that nexus of ideas with which he is most frequently associated—namely the linkage of plot, quest, knowledge and apocalypse."[89]

Frank Kermode's article in the *London Review of Books* commented at length on Pynchon's trademark theme of paranoia, a feature which Kermode himself had analyzed years previously in an article which was influential in establishing Pynchon in the canon (and thereby making *The Crying of Lot 49* one of the most frequently taught books on English degree courses in the States).[90] In his review Kermode reminds us that Pynchon "explores, more intensively maybe than anyone else has ever done, the relation between fictional plot and paranoid fantasy." *Vineland*, however, came as a disappointment to Kermode, not so much because it dropped these concerns altogether, but because it merely repeated them "in a manner even more bitter but also less guarded by irony, less cogent." Yet what disappointed Kermode more than anything about *Vineland* was its endless references to popular culture and the detritus of everyday life. He wished the novel had contained a glossary, since he found it frustrating that so many of the references were lost on him. What made it worse, he complained, there was no reference volume in which he could look up the brand names, the slang and the television trivia. This is a significant comment, because Pynchon's previous novels have generated an entire academic industry devoted to explicating the arcane and improbably learned allusions (there are, for example, exegetical companion volumes to both *Gravity's Rainbow* and *Lot 49*).[91] "It will be remembered,"

Kermode warned, "that the paranoia of the earlier books always sought sign-systems, not only interesting in their extraordinary complexity and extent but also menacing." For Kermode, *Vineland* proved a letdown precisely because it replaced the complex and wide-ranging focus in the earlier novels on semiological paranoia with (in the title originally proposed for *Gravity's Rainbow*) the "mindless pleasures" of mass culture.[92] In the critical reception of *Vineland*, both sides agreed, then, that highbrow paranoia had given way to a schizophrenic immersion in pop culture. Yet it can be argued that the apparent absence of conspiracy from *Vineland* is part of a meaningful continuation of Pynchon's dialogue with paranoia. More importantly, the easing of "Mr Pynchon's paranoia" is directly connected with the story *Vineland* tells about the increasing saturation of mass culture.

Endless Tangled Scenarios

Unlike Pynchon's previous novels, the plot of *Vineland* is not itself a conspiracy plot. *V.* sets on collision course its two main stories, namely the development of "the plot that has no name" and the beat scene of 1950s New York. *The Crying of Lot 49* has the shape of a detective story which uncovers clues towards the Tristero conspiracy. *Gravity's Rainbow*, though it disperses its narratives amid a welter of discourses and endless derailings of the plot, pieces together the story of The Firm's conspiratorial control of prewar industries in general and Tyrone Slothrop in particular. By contrast, *Vineland* consists of a series of interrelated stories that reach back from the present into the past but refuse to coalesce into a single conspiracy theory.

The present action of the novel, which takes place in the summer of 1984, sees 1960s survivors Zoyd, Frenesi, and their daughter Prairie being chased by their longtime enemies, drug enforcement agents Brock Vond and Hector Zuñiga. As this story proceeds, we gradually learn about events at the People's Republic of Rock and Roll at the tail end of the 1960s, as well as an account of DL Chastain's ninja training in postwar Japan, stories of Frenesi's parents in McCarthyite Hollywood, and her grandparents' time in the labor unions of the 1930s. The novel does feature a few "Pynchonesque" moments, like the mysterious giant footprint which wipes out the labs of "shadowy world conglomerate Chipco," or the sinister midflight raid by unnamed forces on Zoyd's night crossing to Hawaii—though these episodes are closer to Godzilla and sci-fi movies than the John Buchan or Raymond Chandler scenarios of the first three novels.[93] But the narrative events are never totally overshadowed by the pervasive presence of conspiracy which would link together all characters and events of the novel into a coherent plot. Whereas Pynchon's first three novels were shaped—however satirically—by the generic conventions of detective fiction and the thriller, his fourth turned for its structure to romance. Where Oedipa Maas's detective mission promises to expand outwards to involve the legacy of the whole of America, for example, Prairie Wheeler's quest is for her mother. Oedipa leaves the domestic scene in search of the political; by contrast, Prairie must uncover the political story of Frenesi's activities at the end of the 1960s in order to recover the domestic. The classic denouement of the romance—the revelation of the protagonist's true parentage—is in *Vineland* played out as farce.[94] In what should be the final, cataclysmic tableau, Brock Vond descends from the sky in his new guise as "Death from Slightly Above" and reveals his true identity to his "daughter" in the clearing, only for him to be yanked back up into the helicopter. The revelation leaves Prairie nonplussed, as she coolly retorts that "you can't be my father, Mr Vond, my blood is type A. Yours is Preparation H" (*VL*, 376). The only secret revealed at the end of the novel is that there are no secrets left.

Unlike a conspiracy theory which aims to untangle the clues so as to reveal a single plot, the narrative of *Vineland* operates in line with DL and Takeshi's principle of Karmic Adjustment, which tries to avoid the "danger of collapsing [everything] into a single issue" (*VL*, 365). Pynchon's aesthetic principle in this novel is a process of *entanglement*. The novel shows DL, Zoyd and Prairie as they each, at different times, "clumsily piec[e] the story together" (*VL*, 282)—and this is what the reader also has to do. There are many pieces to this jumbled jigsaw, not least the countless mini-narratives about what happened to each of the characters after the 1960s were over. To tell the story of one character's life, the narrator has to tell the story of them all. In place of a series of clues which promise to lead towards a grand revelation, *Vineland* relies on a series of "endless tangled scenarios" (*VL*, 284). We learn, for example, how Frenesi and her new husband Flash become "tangled in an infinite series of increasingly squalid minor sting operations" (*VL*, 72). In the computer files at the Sisterhood of Kunoichi Attentives headquarters digital versions of Frenesi and DL exist, "woven together in an intricacy of backs covered, promises made and renegotiated" (*VL*, 115). DL's old teacher Inoshiro Sensei prepares her "to inherit his own entanglement in the world" (*VL*, 180). Likewise the story of the finances of Vato and Blood, the tow merchants, is connected with "Specter's tangled financial saga" (*VL*, 182). At the Thanatoid Roast '84, "Thanatoid wives bravely did their part to complicate further already tangled marriage histories" (*VL*, 219). In Hollywood, Frenesi's mother, Sasha, became "entangled in the fine details of the politics in the town at the time" (*VL*, 289). And when DL and Takeshi finally get it together in a penthouse high over Amarillo the moment is framed by "a fractal halo of complications that might go on forever" (*VL*, 381).

Entanglement has always been a distinctive characteristic of Pynchon's work. In *The Crying of Lot 49*, for example, Metzger explains that "our beauty lies in this extended capacity for convolution" (*CL*, 21), and the first page of *Gravity's Rainbow* announces that "this is not a disentanglement from, but a progressive *knotting into*" (*GR*, 3). But whereas the narrative threads in the first three novels were—however improbably and satirically—all knotted into the workings of a "master cabal," in *Vineland* there is only an increasing complication. Likewise Pynchon has consistently manifested a talent for complexity in his sentence construction. We might compare, however, the much-quoted ending of *Lot 49* with the closing scenes of *Vineland*. In the former the sentences, like the choices they outline, arrange themselves like a computer language into the semblance of binary clarity: "Either Oedipa in the orbiting ecstasy of a true paranoia, or a real Tristero," and so on (*CL*, 126). By contrast in *Vineland* the rambling, convoluted syntax remains till the end:

> A tour bus, perhaps only lost in the night, swept in with a wake of diesel exhaust and waited idling for its passengers, some of whom would discover that they were already Thanatoids without knowing it, and decide not to reboard after all. There were free though small-sized eats for everyone, such as mini-enchiladas and shrimp teriyaki, and well drinks at happy-hour prices. And the band, Holocaust Pixels, found a groove, or attractor, that would've been good for the entire trans-night crossing and beyond, even if Billy Barf and the Vomitones hadn't shown up later to sit in, bringing with them Alexei, who turned out to be a Russian Johnny B. Goode, able even unamplified to outwail both bands at once.
>
> (*VL*, 384)

In *Vineland* subclauses proliferate, intervening in the flow of the sentence; brand names and pop references pile up like so much prosaic lumber to be fitted in; and phrasal verbs are separated from their prepositions, producing only a sense of anticlimax when they are finally reached. In short, the yearning towards a revelation of the previous novels is replaced by a perpetual cluttering up in this one.

Entanglement makes sense as the structuring principle of *Vineland* because it has become impossible to maintain the kind of Manichaean oppositions between Them and Us which structure traditional conspiracy thinking. The prospect that the We of the counterculture might end up working for Them had already been raised towards the end of *Gravity's Rainbow*, but in *Vineland* betrayal becomes a key theme.[95] The paranoid divisions between Them and Us blur and re-emerge and become confused once more through three generations of political compromise and betrayal. As well as the main stories of Frenesi's and others' co-option into the snitch system which mark the demise of the paranoid certainties of the counterculture versus the government, *Vineland* also establishes a series of narrative parallels and echoes which reinforce this point, without connecting the stories into a single conspiratorial plot. So, for example, many of the men in the novel—Zoyd, Hector, Brock, Takeshi, Weed Atman, Hub Gates—are separated from their wives/lovers, whichever side they are on. The domestic realm makes symbolic links beneath the political, with marriages, friendships, and even long-standing antagonisms establishing complex networks of indebtedness and complicity. In a similar vein, as much as Brock Vond is the embodiment of Their collapsing surveillance system, he himself is under surveillance by his superiors. It is ironically Vond's participation in the economy of paranoia that contributes to the devaluation of its political currency. The political landscape of *Vineland* produces many unlikely alliances and temporary rapprochements which work against the grain of the clear loyalties of the paranoid generation of the 1960s. The simple countercultural form of paranoia which appropriated and inverted the language of countersubversion for its own ends has thus outgrown its use in a world in which the opposing sides have become inextricably fused.

Not Much of a Secret

In *Vineland*, time for paranoid illumination is definitely past, in a novel that is marked out by its sense of belatedness. *The Crying of Lot 49*, for example, leaves its readers in suspense at the end of the novel, as Oedipa—and perhaps the 1960s more generally—wait in the auction room for a grand and conspiratorial revelation that will radically transform the mundanity of suburban America. By the time of *Vineland*, the final years of the 1960s and whatever "transcendent meaning" (*CL*, 125) they brought with them are long since passed. Whatever Oedipa was waiting for has already happened. *Vineland*'s opening word is "later," and its starting point is "later" in all senses: after the auctioneer's crying of lot 49, after the nuclear apocalypse hovering over the final scene of *Gravity's Rainbow*, and, in a novel published some five years after the present of its action, beyond even the apocalyptic year of 1984 and fears about the Federal Emergency Management Agency's (FEMA) alleged Rex 84 plan to intern all dissidents in concentration camps with the imposition of martial law.

We can gain a vivid sense of how the promise of paranoia has paradoxically become both outdated and routinized by comparing the opening paragraphs of *Lot 49* and *Vineland*. The former novel begins in the following way:

> One summer afternoon Mrs Oedipa Maas came home from a Tupperware party whose hostess had put perhaps too much kirsch in the fondue to find that she, Oedipa, had been named

executor, or she supposed executrix, of the estate of one Pierce Inverarity, a California real estate mogul who had once lost two million dollars in his spare time but still had assets numerous and tangled enough to make the job of sorting it all out more than honorary. Oedipa stood in the living-room, stared at by the greenish dead eye of the TV tube, spoke the name of God, tried to feel as drunk as possible.

(*CL*, 5)

The news that Oedipa is to sort out Pierce Inverarity's legacy arrives as a mysterious and anonymous intrusion into the mundanity of her life as a Californian housewife. Significantly, it remains unclear whether she finds out from a telephone call, a normal letter, or via some more secretive mode of communication. The enigmatic arrival of the announcement is perhaps an example of what Jesús Arrabal (an anarchist Oedipa meets on her nocturnal wandering) calls a "miracle," one of the "intrusions into this world from another" (*CL*, 86). Chasing up the clues in Pierce's will affords Oedipa glimpses of worlds and words unknown to her in the hermetically sealed world of Kinneret-Among-The-Pines. Her life of Tupperware parties up till this point is marked by an absence of paranoid significance, an "absence of an intensity" (*CL*, 12). As yet there are nothing like the "flinders of luminescent gods glimpsed among the wallpaper's stained foliage" (*CL*, 87) which she will strain to see with the old sailor once she has become "sensitized." Oedipa turns to the three possible comforts in her life—the TV, religion, and alcohol—but each remains mute. Paranoia will come to offer Oedipa some form of consolation, however compromised, for the loss of the "direct, epileptic Word" (*CL*, 81), in the shape of the Tristero conspiracy's "promise of hierophany" (*CL*, 20).

Vineland likewise begins with the arrival of a communication on a Californian summer's day, some twenty years later:

Later than usual one summer morning in 1984, Zoyd Wheeler drifted awake in sunlight through a creeping fig that hung in the window, with a squadron of blue jays stomping around on the roof. In his dream these had been carrier pigeons from some place far across the ocean, landing and taking off again one by one, each bearing a message for him, but none of whom, light pulsing in their wings, he could ever quite get to in time. He understood it to be another deep nudge from forces unseen, almost surely connected with the letter that had come along with his latest mental-disability check, reminding him that unless he did something publicly crazy before a date now less than a week away, he would no longer qualify for benefits. He groaned out of bed.

(*VL*, 3)

Hippie no-hoper Zoyd Wheeler struggles towards some kind of revelation in his dream about the message-bearing carrier pigeons, perhaps suffering from the same inability as his tripping companion Van Meter, who "had been searching all his life for transcendent chances exactly like this one the kids [whose dreams are like magic realist tales] took so for granted, but whenever he got close it was like, can't shit, can't get a hardon, the more he worried the less likely it was to happen" (*VL*, 223). The "light pulsing" in the message-bearers' wings might refer us back to the "pulsing stelliferous Meaning" (*CL*, 56) that Oedipa feels on the threshold of unveiling, but for Zoyd the paranoid's moment of illumination has always remained just out of focus. He describes how he "keep[s] tryin' to find out" through psychokinesis where Frenesi is, through "try[ing] to read signs, locate landmarks, anything that'll give a clue, but—well the signs are there on street corners and store windows—but [he] can't read" (*VL*, 40). For Oedipa the announcement of Pierce's death opens up the promise of discovering a "secret richness and concealed density of dream" (*CL*, 117), even if that quest turns out to be a red herring. By contrast, for Zoyd the "deep nudge from forces unseen" comes to him in a dream, which he automatically takes to be prophetic in a vague way. But it turns out to be nothing more mysterious than the arrival of his disability check, which acts as the annual guarantee of compliance with Drug Enforcement Agent Brock Vond's contract to keep him away from his former wife, Frenesi.

Whereas the announcement at the start of *The Crying of Lot 49* signals Oedipa's induction into the world of paranoia and surveillance, for Zoyd this is only "another nudge" in what has become a routinized and mundane surveillance operation over the last dozen or so years. He merely groans his way out of bed to start one more day. When the Tubal Detox doctor asks whether Zoyd has had the paranoid feeling of being persecuted for some time, Zoyd replies that "in Hector's case fifteen or twenty years" (*VL*, 43). From its promise of sudden illumination in *Lot 49*, paranoia in *Vineland* has become like background radiation, a permanent but inactive presence in Zoyd's daily life. The "Nixonian Reaction" ensured that "betrayal became routine," with "money from the CIA, FBI, and others circulating everywhere, leaving the merciless spores of paranoia wherever it flowed" (*VL*, 239). Likewise surveillance has become automated and anonymous and corporate; as Flash, informer and Frenesi's new husband, complains: "we're in th'Info Revolution here. Anytime you use a credit card you're tellin' the Man more than you meant to" (*VL*, 74). Even worse, paranoia seems to have become an irrelevance in a land whose TV shows turn "agents of government repression into sympathetic heroes," made worse by the fact that "nobody thought it was peculiar anymore, no more than the routine violations of constitutional rights these characters performed week after week, now absorbed into the vernacular of American expectations" (*VL*, 345). The forces of evil have not disappeared, but the discovery of their existence no longer inevitably comes as a moment of sudden insight. On the penultimate page, in the midst of the final buildup towards the seemingly happy ending with the return of Desmond the lovable mutt, the narrator presents a picture of the implacable forces of evil fixed into a classical tableau: "the unrelenting forces that leaned ever after the partners into Time's wind, impassive in pursuit, usually gaining, the faceless predators who'd once boarded Takeshi's airplane in the sky, the one's who'd had the Chipco lab stomped on, who despite every Karmic Adjustment brought to bear so far had simply persisted, stone-humorless, beyond cause and effect, rejecting all attempts to bargain or accommodate," and so on (*VL*, 383). Instead of becoming the focus of attention, these "unrelenting forces" form a stone frieze, a permanent carved backdrop against which the "endless tangled scenarios" of *Vineland* are told.

Because the "faceless predators" have become routine, the critical edge of paranoia as a countercultural weapon has been dulled. *Vineland* affords glimpses of a time when paranoia was as much a sign of fashion as "miniskirts, wire-rim glasses, and love beads" (*VL*, 198). For example, on a Hawaii-bound flight in the early 1970s Zoyd is nonplussed when a sinister craft docks alongside in mid-Pacific, helmeted officials board the plane and someone with a "blond hippie haircut" takes refuge in Zoyd's in-flight band, welcoming him "smoothly" with "Man's after you, eh" (*VL*, 65). In *The Crying of Lot 49* The Paranoids are a novice band hoping for a recording contract; in *Vineland* we learn incidentally that at the highpoint of the "Nixonian Reaction" they were playing the Fillmore Stadium (*VL*, 308)! As the novel frequently stresses, fashions and musical tastes are expendable, and by 1984 The Paranoids have been replaced by the "sonic apocalypse" (*VL*, 55) of Fascist Toejam, along with the novel's resident band, Billy Barf and the Vomitones. For Zoyd's teenage daughter, Prairie, paranoia is just one more antiquated accessory of her "hippie-freak parents" (*VL*, 16) and their friends. It is merely another item which signifies the 1960s, "an America of the olden days she'd mostly never seen, except in fast clips on the Tube meant to suggest the era, or distantly implied in reruns like 'Bewitched' or 'The Brady Bunch'" (*VL*, 198). She is "leery as always of anything that might mean unfinished business from the old hippie times" (*VL*, 56), and when her father expresses excessive concern for her safety on that summer day in 1984, she asks him, "Sure this ain't pothead paranoia?" (*VL*, 46).

Paranoia has become passé, however, not merely because it is part of a now outdated drug scene, but because everything turns out to be true.[96] In a version of Oedipa's long night of paranoia in San Francisco when signs of the Tristero appear wherever she goes, Zoyd has the feeling that on every one of his errands in Vineland that summer's day everyone else is out to get him. He insists that "it wasn't pothead paranoia—but neither was Zoyd about to step inside this bank" where "colleagues at desks could be seen making long arms for the telephone" (*VL*, 46). In *The Crying of Lot 49* there is hesitation and suspense surrounding Oedipa's moments of paranoia—is there really a conspiracy, or is she suffering from mental delusions? In *Vineland*, on the other hand, the moment of doubt has passed, and fears of conspiracy are shown to have been always already justified. In the later novel the fictive collapses into the factual, as *The Crying of Lot 49*'s striptease of history gives way to an endless visibility. Zoyd, Flash, Frenesi, DL and the other members of the former 24fps film collective now all live their lives after the feared and desired moment of revelation in the 1960s, in a world in which everything has endlessly been exposed.

This is not to say, however, that the need for paranoia has entirely disappeared. On the contrary, the endless confirmation of the clandestine ruses of state of power merely reconfirms the need for a resigned vigilance, an attitude that, like a pair of Levi's, is no longer a mark of student radicalism but the ubiquitous and neutral uniform for an entire generation. The fateful year 1984 indeed sees a revival of paranoia in Vineland, but this time round all their suspicions are matter-of-factly shown to be justified in the context of the novel: Zoyd, Frenesi and Flash have been cut off from the witness protection payments; the film archives are publicly burnt; and Brock is putting the heat not only on Prairie, but also on the Vineland cannabis growers in a personal offshoot of Reagan's War on Drugs, testing the "personal paranoia thresholds" (*VL*, 221) of the Holytail planters. Whereas in *The Crying of Lot 49* the syntax often hovers between certainty and doubt (it's *as if* there is a conspiracy, the logic goes), in *Vineland* it collapses before too long into dull actuality, only for the "merciless spores of paranoia" to take seed once more. Thus Frenesi jokes with a neighbor that the freezing of her bank account must be just a computer error, "but then, paranoid, decided not to repeat what she'd heard from Flash" (*VL*, 86). Likewise, in a return to the old days of the 24fps film collective, Ditzah tells her sister Zipi that "we all have to be extra paranoid" (*VL*, 262) when they find out that various members of their old group have gone missing. And under DL's guidance, Prairie must quickly revive the paranoid style as a retro 1960s fashion that is at one and the same time hopelessly out of date and very now.

Vineland speaks to a time when paranoid speculation has been replaced by a curious mixture of redoubled fear and epistemological resignation. In this novel, the paranoid suspicions held by the counterculture have all been confirmed, and conspiracies theories about the government conspiring against its citizens are taken for granted. Thus we find that Watergate has lost its aura of revelation, with its translation into *The G. Gordon Liddy Story* (*VL*, 339), just another late-night made-for-TV movie (starring Sean Connery), about the life of the CIA operative turned talk radio host. Likewise the government's campaign of surveillance against its own citizens has become so visible that the Bureau is obliged to place a Wide Load sign on the back of the lorry when they move Weed Atman's COINTELPRO file around. Special Agent Ribble of the Witness Protection Program asks Flash if he's "notice[d] how cheap coke has been since 1981" (*VL*, 353), insinuating a conspiracy theory which even as well versed a paranoid as Flash is still naïve enough to find incredible: "Roy! Is you're sayin' the President himself is duked into some deal? Quit foolin'! Next you'll be tellin' me George Bush" (*VL*, 353). The joke, of course, is that by the time of the publication of the novel the story about the connections between Reagan, Bush, the CIA, drugs, arms, the Contras and Iraq (not to mention Reagan's plans for FEMA to round up dissidents in an emergency) had all been endlessly displayed on TV with the Oliver North hearings. The novel suggests that there is no longer any excuse for believing that the government doesn't operate secret policies. "In those days," the narrator of *Vineland* comments sardonically about the 1960s, "it was still unthinkable that any North American agency would kill its own citizens and then lie about it" (*VL*, 248). The irony is that where conspiracy theories might have been a critical mode of narrative for an emergent counterculture in the 1960s, by the time of *Vineland* so much has been exposed that they are more believable than ever, but also no longer quite so necessary.

What makes it worse in *Vineland* is that power no longer feels the need to hide itself, or work through secret agencies. The film archive of 24fps, for example, is burned publicly in a suburban neighborhood. Reagan's War on Drugs becomes heavy handed, with Brock's troops "terrorizing the neighborhood for weeks, running up and down dirt lanes in formation chanting 'War-on-drugs! War-on-drugs!' strip-searching folks in public . . . acting, indeed, as several neighbors observed, as if they had invaded some helpless land far away, instead of a short plane ride from San Francisco" (*VL*, 357). The action takes on cartoon proportions with the Campaign Against Marijuana Production (CAMP), led by the neo-Nazi Count Kommandant Bopp, who requisitions the whole of Vineland airport in an increasingly visible operation. It begins to look like a national-emergency operation (coordinated with the invasion of Nicaragua) is being prepared, but even these plans are not kept hidden: "copies of these contingency plans had been circulating all summer, it wasn't much of a secret" (*VL*, 340). As we have seen, many critics balked at the obviousness of the paranoid politics in *Vineland*, convinced not even Pynchon could actually take seriously the rumors about FEMA being on the verge of implementing martial law.[97] But that obviousness forms an aesthetic response to a situation in which the hidden agendas of politics are no longer "much of a secret." Just when the paranoid strategy of always reading between the lines comes to be taken for granted, it is also ironically no longer so vital, because what had previously been hidden has now been made manifest. In *Vineland* there is an emptying out of paranoid allusions, since its signs of pop culture only point to other signs and images, locked in their own claustrophobic world of TV listings. This semiological dead end produces a flattening out—perhaps even a reversal—of a hermeneutic structured by surface and depth, by clues and hidden meanings. In many ways there is not much left for a critic like Frank Kermode to do, since the decoded interpretations are all there on the surface. In *Vineland*, mass-produced objects speak for themselves and the secret machinations of state power form the kind of postmodern political spectacle that Michael Rogin identifies. In order to read for the "unconscious" of *Vineland*, it now becomes necessary to focus on precisely the notions of obviousness, surface, and visibility.[98]

Whereas *The Crying of Lot 49* holds out the possibility of "another mode of meaning behind the obvious," a form of secret, revelatory understanding which promises, however mistakenly, to yield up the final truth about America, in *Vineland* there is only the obvious. *Lot 49* considers the possibility of a "transcendent meaning" that will be found "behind the hieroglyphic streets" (*CL*, 125), a concern that manifests itself in the repeated figurations of uncovering, revelation, and striptease. Even if the hope of a countercultural hidden "underground" of outsiders connected by a secret tradition proves illusory, the novel itself nevertheless manages to introduce a "ritual reluctance" into the mundane language of suburban California. In "The Courier's Tragedy," for example, when "things get really peculiar," a "gentle chill, an ambiguity, begins to creep in among the words" (*CL*, 48). *The Crying of Lot 49* opens out the glossy present of 1964 through its intertextual references to literature, art, science, history, and science, into the endlessly expanding labyrinth of a Borgesian library, clues pointing endlessly to other clues in a narrative prototype of hypertext, forming a chain reaction of paranoid interpretation.[99] Even if, as Oedipa worries, there is after all "only the earth" and not "another set of possibilities" (*CL*, 125), the Californian landscape has been transformed and illuminated in the course of the novel. But in *Vineland* it begins to seem that after all there might be "only the earth." When Ralph Wayvone, Sr, the San Franciscan Mafia boss, stands daydreaming in his coastal-view garden one foggy morning, "the fog now began to lift to reveal not the borderlands of the eternal after all, but only quotidian California again, looking no different than it had when he left" (*VL*, 94).

At times *Vineland* seems to hold out the hope of some hidden enclave in Vineland County—"about the last refuge for pot growers in North California" (*VL*, 220)—which would escape the legal and financial constraints of the outside world. The hinterlands consist of "regions unmapped" (*VL*, 173), a fact which temporarily delays the otherwise inexorable clampdown led by Kommandant Bopp's army. For the Yuroks, the indigenous people of this land, Shade Creek had always signified "the realm behind the immediate" (*VL*, 186). But this echo of the aspirations towards otherworldliness in *The Crying of Lot 49* is long since gone, as are

71

the native Indians: the "invisible boundary" which concealed "another intention" (*VL*, 317) has been dug up and paved over by cable TV developers. There are—or soon will be—no spaces left for secrets, mysteries, or any other form of resistance to the technorationalization of "the spilled, the broken world" (*VL*, 267) of the Californian landscape. Throughout *Vineland* there runs a subplot about the disenchantment of California (and, as the title of the novel suggests, of the original "legacy" of America itself), an ongoing tale of development, encroachment, yuppification and commodification. So, for example, the former hardcore union enclave has vanished—we learn about the transformation of a logger's bar into a New Age haven where "dangerous men with coarsened attitudes . . . were perched around lightly on designer barstools, sipping kiwi mimosas" (*VL*, 5).[100] Even spiritual secrets have been turned into commodities: the Buddhist mandalas of *Gravity's Rainbow* become translated into the "pizza mandala" at the Bhodi Dharma Pizza Temple in downtown Vineland (*VL*, 45); the lifelong training in oriental techniques undergone by DL Chastain has been made redundant by the fact that "today, of course, you can pick up a dedicated hand-held Ninja Death Touch calculator in any drugstore" (*VL*, 141); and the Sister Attentive of the Kunoichi retreat is more concerned with "cash flow" than spiritual matters (*VL*, 153). Not only do 1960s fashions like the miniskirt make a return, but the "big Nostalgia Wave" (*VL*, 51) sweeps up the 1960s themselves, turning the political ambitions of the decade into nothing more than a fashion, "as revolution went blending into commerce" (*VL*, 308). In the same way that spirituality and politics are doomed to eternal return as commodities, so too are the hidden recesses of Vineland's topography finally marked out for development. We learn, for instance, about "valleys still in those days unknown except to a few real-estate visionaries, little crossroads places where one day houses'd sprawl" (*VL*, 37); we hear "an industrious roar that could as well have been another patch of developer condos going up" (*VL*, 191), and the sound of birds battles against the "distant wash of freeway sound, the concrete surf" (*VL*, 194). When Zoyd and Prairie first arrive in "Vineland the Good" they find a world "not much different from what early visitors in Spanish and Russian ships had seen," but "someday this would all be part of a Eureka-Crescent City-Vineland metropolis" (*VL*, 317), because "developers in and out of state had also discovered this shoreline" (*VL*, 319).

The hidden depths and concealed realms which might encourage countercultural fantasies of a conspiratorial "We-system" (as *Gravity's Rainbow* termed it) have thus all but disappeared in the world of *Vineland*. Everything has become exposed (to use a film metaphor to which the novel itself is highly attuned), and it is in this light that we can make sense of the resurfacing of those characters like Frenesi and Flash who had gone underground at the end of the 1960s. When Frenesi hears of names being deleted from the computer list of informers she hypothesizes first that they have either died or been made to disappear, but then she speculates that "maybe they went the other way, surfaced, went up in the world again" (*VL*, 88). More frightening than the possibility that various of their friends have vanished down into the repressive depths of the state machine is the knowledge that they might have had the perversely comforting cloak of surveillance removed, returning them to the total visibility—and indifference—of the "upper world" (*VL*, 90). On this reading, then, the final failure of the 1960s underground culture comes about not through any of the conspiratorial fantasies of apocalypse which the counterculture predicted, but because there is nowhere left to hide. Everything is visible, and everything is connected, producing a situation in which a routine sense of paranoia is paradoxically both no longer necessary, and more vital than ever. *Vineland*'s cartoon take on the Reagan years is as distorted as the version of the 1960s its characters screen within their heads, and already seemed curiously nostalgic even by the time of its publication. But the novel is also presciently in step with the wider reconfiguration of the culture of conspiracy in the last decade or so. The final chapter of the present study explores in more detail the consequences for the paranoid style when everything becomes connected (a possibility that *Vineland* begins to hint at), but the conclusion of this one examines several theorizations of the era in which everything becomes visible.

Hermeneutic of Suspicion

Though wildly exaggerated, even by Pynchon's standards, *Vineland*'s simultaneous emptying out of paranoia into obviousness and its renewed anxiety about state oppression offers an insightful parable into the changing fortunes of conspiracy culture since the 1960s. Its portrayal of the routinization of paranoia among ex-1960s radicals resonates with larger cultural patterns. Eve Kosofsky Sedgwick, for example, comments on how a certain hermeneutic of suspicion has become the standard operating procedure across the humanities in recent years. The task of this Foucauldian method of analysis is to uncover the hidden textual ruses and traces of violence in discourse. "In a world where no one need be delusional to find evidence of systematic oppression," Sedgwick warns, "to theorize out of anything but a paranoid critical stance has come to seem naïve or complaisant."[101] In effect, she suggests, a routinized paranoia has become the default mode of contemporary cultural criticism. She begins to wonder, however, if a style of analysis for which she is in no small measure responsible has gone beyond its utility. You don't have to employ a sophisticated form of ideological detective work, Sedgwick points out, to uncover abuses of power which scarcely have to conceal themselves any longer, and many of which—such as the move to reinstate chain gangs in some Southern states—are explicitly for show. As the characters in *Vineland* discover, in this climate of saturated visibility, paranoia becomes both indispensable and unnecessary, so much taken for granted that it is in danger of collapsing in on itself.[102]

Peter Sloterdijk has argued that cynical reason has become one of the defining characteristics of the age, the favored mode of post-1968 intellectuals living in permanent, irony-laden bad faith, who realize that "the times of naïveté have gone." He describes this form of mass cynicism as the condition of "enlightened false consciousness," the way in which "enlightened people see to it that they are not taken for suckers."[103] In an age of cynical reasoning, we might add, any conceivable revelation about the realm of secrecy has already been anticipated in advance by a public which has become accustomed to always suspect the worst—but also to suspect anything that is revealed. Nothing comes as a surprise anymore, since every secret has been endlessly displayed and relayed through the media, yet the desire for discovery continues unabated. The truth is probably out there somewhere, as the *X-Files* enlightenment-yearning catchphrase insists, but (in the show's other trademarked slogan) we have also learned cynically to trust no one.

We might go further and argue that a form of cynical paranoia is an understandable reaction to what Fredric Jameson has famously called the cultural logic of late capitalism. Jameson claims that it is "the purest form of capitalism yet to have emerged, a prodigious expansion of capital into hitherto uncommodified areas." This "purer capitalism of our own time," he continues, "thus eliminates the enclaves of precapitalist organization it had hitherto tolerated."[104] Jameson goes on to argue that the final saturation of the logic of the commodity has penetrated the last sites of modernist resistance located in Nature and the Unconscious. In the world of *Vineland*, from the backwoods of Northern California to the clandestine underground, the last enclaves of secrecy are disappearing. Paranoia paradoxically becomes both ubiquitous and redundant when everything finally is connected, tied up into the global capitalist market.

A hyperbolic hermeneutic of suspicion is no longer an extremist posture when everything—even secrets—becomes available and visible as a commodity. Jean Baudrillard adds a further twist to this story, with his claim that the total saturation of the commodity-as-sign empties it of any depth of meaning it might once have had. The result is that "we no longer partake of the drama of alienation, but are in the ecstasy of communication." This ecstasy turns conspiracy thinking inside out. We are no longer dealing with "the obscenity of the hidden, the repressed, the obscure," Baudrillard declares, "but that of the visible, the all-too-visible, the more-than-visible; it is the obscenity of that which no longer contains a secret and is entirely soluble in information and communication."[105] Lamenting the seeming triumphal acceptance of this version of postmodernism, Terry Eagleton observes that the logic of late capitalism is just a sick joke at the expense of modernism. "Reification," he warns, "once it has extended its empire across the whole of social reality, effaces the very criteria by which it can be recognized for what it is and so triumphantly abolishes itself, returning everything to normality."[106] In effect, "postmodernism persuades us to relinquish our epistemological paranoia," because it becomes unnecessary when the distinction between figure and ground, original and copy, or secrecy and visibility has been erased.[107]

These apocalyptic accounts of postmodernism are in their own way as exaggerated as *Vineland*'s version of 1984. Yet they share the same paradoxical approach to the logic of paranoia that is at the heart of *Vineland*, and which structures the culture of conspiracy which has taken shape since the 1960s. A postmodern form of paranoid skepticism has become routine in a world in which the conspiratorial netherworld has become hypervisible, its secrets just one more commodity. Paranoia is therefore no longer necessarily the mark of right-wing demonological extremism (though that form of conspiracy thinking still undoubtedly exists, even if its functions are, as I have suggested, somewhat different). Rather, it is has become a default attitude for the post-1960s generation, more an expression of inexhaustible suspicion and uncertainty than a dogmatic form of scaremongering. This reconfigured form of popular paranoia is in effect one of the defining characteristics of what has come to be known as postmodern culture. The next chapter examines the connection between paranoia and the postmodernization of America in more detail, showing how conspiracy theories about the Kennedy assassination are central to accounts of the "legitimation crisis" of authority.

2

PLOTTING THE KENNEDY ASSASSINATION

> The Oswald shadings, the multiple images, the split
> perceptions—eye color, weapons caliber—these seem a
> foreboding of what is to come. The endless fact-rubble of
> the investigations. How many shots, how many gunmen,
> how many directions? Powerful events breed their network
> of inconsistencies. The simple facts elude authentication.
> How many wounds on the President's body? What is the
> size and shape of the wounds? The multiple Oswald
> reappears. Isn't that *him* in a photograph of a crowd of
> people on the front steps of the Book Depository just before
> the shooting begins? A startling likeness, Branch concedes.
> He concedes everything. He questions everything, including
> the basic suppositions we make about our world of light and
> shadow, solid objects and ordinary sounds, and our ability
> to measure such things, to determine weight, mass and
> direction, to see things as they are, recall them clearly, be
> able to say what happened.
>
> (Don DeLillo, *Libra*)

The assassination of President Kennedy in Dallas in 1963 has inspired more
conspiracy thinking in America than any other event in the twentieth
century. From official government enquiries to amateur websites, and
from Hollywood films to literary novels, those seven seconds of mayhem
in Dealey Plaza have been relentlessly examined for clues not just to a plot
to kill the President, but to the hidden agenda of the last four decades of
American history. In the collection of the unofficial Assassination
Archives and Research Center in Washington, DC there are more than
two thousand books on the JFK shooting and related topics. In the wake
of Oliver Stone's film *JFK* (1991), nearly half the books on the *New York
Times* top-ten bestseller list in early 1992 were about the case, and,
significantly, all of them promoted conspiracy theories of one kind or
another.[1]

The Kennedy assassination has become synonymous with conspiracy theory, weaving its way into the cultural fabric of everyday life in the postwar United States. In phrases like "magic bullet" and "grassy knoll" the lexicon of conspiracy research has entered the public vocabulary. The assassination and its accompanying culture of conspiracy never seem to be far from the headlines, nor from popular culture. JFK assassination theories make a cameo appearance in dramas as diverse as *Annie Hall* and *The Simpsons*. In Richard Linklater's cult film *Slacker* (1991), for example, the nerdy character running the local used book store confesses that studying the minutiae of the assassination is pretty much all he has done since graduating from college, the culmination of which is a manuscript he is working on that the publisher wants to call "Conspiracy A-Go-Go." It might be not much of an exaggeration to claim, as a Dallas psychologist asserts in the opening paragraph of D. M. Thomas's 1992 assassination novel *Flying in to Love*, that "Ten thousand dreams a night ... are dreamt about Kennedy's assassination."[2] Even when not directly there, the assassination seems to be an absent presence in many fictional and factual treatments of recent American history, a ghostly and unspoken moment of hidden causality. For example, in Thomas Pynchon's classic conspiracy text *The Crying of Lot 49* (1966), the assassination of President Kennedy is never mentioned, yet always seems to be hovering just out of reach—much like the sinister Tristero conspiracy that the novel outlines. Written in the year after the assassination, Pynchon's novella chronicles the attempts by a regular California housewife to investigate the mysterious death of a wealthy and important man with an Irish-sounding name (Pierce Inverarity) whose legacy seems to extend to the whole of America. Once Oedipa Maas starts looking, it appears that there are ominous signs everywhere, as the whole of America becomes a tantalizing clue to a mystery that remains just beyond her grasp. For many Americans since Pynchon's pioneering journey into the abyss of infinite suspicion, the Kennedy assassination has become an inexhaustible motherlode of conspiracy theory, the primal episode from which all subsequent events, clandestine or otherwise, seem to emerge. Many contemporary conspiracy theories wager that the whole of recent American history is somehow linked to those seven seconds in Dealey Plaza, and that by understanding the details of the shooting, the larger political picture will eventually be revealed.

In the immediate aftermath of the assassination, however, it seemed far from obvious that a conspiratorial take on the shooting would become dominant. In a footnote added to the published version of his lecture on the "paranoid style" (originally delivered shortly before the assassination), Richard Hofstadter reassures himself and his readers that "conspiratorial explanations of Kennedy's assassination have a far wider currency in Europe than they do in the United States," and even then there were only a handful of presumably "un-American" writers hinting at alternative explanations.[3] It is almost as if the rugged individualism of the American dream demands that even assassins must be perceived as lone agents, with Machiavellian conspiracies and their subsequent conspiracy theories belonging to a European tradition. Once merely confined to marginal voices, however, belief in some kind of conspiracy or a cover-up in the JFK case has now come to be taken for granted by many Americans. By 1992 three-quarters of Americans—including, allegedly, even President Clinton and Vice-President Al Gore—believed that there was a conspiracy or an official cover-up involved in the assassination.[4]

Two explanations for this popularity have gained common currency. The first is that conspiracy theories provide a consoling sense of closure, gravity and coherence in the face of the seeming randomness of a disaffected loner killing the President. William Manchester, author of the classic elegy, *Death of a President*, summed up this position in a letter to the *New York Times* in 1993:

> if you put the murdered President of the United States on one side of a scale and that wretched waif Oswald on the other side, it doesn't balance. You want to add something weightier to Oswald. It would invest the President's death with meaning, endowing him with martyrdom. He would have died for *something*. A conspiracy would, of course, do the job nicely.[5]

The other common explanation for the prevalence of conspiracy theories is that the traumatic assassination led to a widespread loss of faith, not just in the goodness of America that Kennedy seemed to represent, but in the legitimacy of the authorities who investigated the murder. Everything began to go wrong after that moment, the argument runs, and the story of the last four decades is one of increasing willingness to believe the worst about America in general, and the government and official agencies in particular. While there is some measure of truth to these popular claims, this chapter will argue that the turn to conspiracy theory in the Kennedy case is far more complicated than these pop-psychological explanations suggest. In many ways, the very opposite is the case. Far from providing a compensatory sense of certainty and coherence, conspiracy theories have highlighted—and fed into—an anxiety about the irredeemable strangeness of reality in postmodern times. Moreover, it is only in the subsequent climate of conspiracy emerging from the tail end of the 1960s that a mythical loss of innocence is backdated to the assassination itself.

Where Were You ... ?

For many Americans recent history is divided into before and after the Kennedy assassination. The presentation of the early 1960s as an idyll of innocence before the fall into violence, fragmentation and cynicism has become a common feature of numerous Hollywood films and made-for-TV movies. In *Love Field* (1992), for instance, Michelle Pfeiffer plays a Southern blue-collar housewife, obsessed with the glamorous life of the Kennedys. Against her husband's prohibition, she feels compelled to travel all the way to Washington to pay her respects to the dead President on that fateful weekend. On this voyage of discovery, she learns to respect not only the black man who ends up helping her, but also to respect herself as an independent woman. In a similar fashion, the voice-over by the main protagonist at the beginning of *Dirty Dancing* (1987) anchors the time of her own lost innocence to that of the nation: "That was the summer of 1963, when everybody called me Baby, and it didn't occur to me to mind. That was before President Kennedy was shot, before the Beatles, when I couldn't wait to join the Peace Corps, and I thought I'd never find a guy as great as my dad. That was the summer we went to Kellerman's."

For a generation of Americans the flashbulb memory of where they were when the President was shot has famously become a defining moment.[6] Even for those too young to remember, the assassination is seen as the moment when the latent destiny of American history was knocked off its true course. In various time-travel sci-fi narratives the killing of JFK functions as the ultimate trope of irreversibility. In Gregory Benford's *Timescape*, for example, the narrative returns repeatedly to those seven seconds in Dallas in an attempt to avert the future course of history—an ecological catastrophe, in the fictional present of the novel.[7] Even without the time-warping plots of such novels, the shooting is frequently inserted into a narrative of regret, nostalgia and loss. This tale of lost innocence manifests itself, for example, in the 1993 thriller *In the Line of Fire*, in which—for the first time in his career—Hollywood hard-man Clint Eastwood cries on screen. Eastwood plays Frank Horrigan, an ageing Secret Service agent, whose duty in the Kennedy motorcade 30 years ago in Dallas should have been to throw himself in front of the President and to "take the bullet." Horrigan's tears are occasioned not only by his eternal regret that he hesitated at the fatal moment, but also by his sense of nostalgia, a feeling that the current President is just not worth taking the bullet for. The obvious moral of the film is that despite the contemporary incumbent's self-conscious promotion of the Kennedy parallels, Clint would never cry for Clinton.

In various sites of popular culture, then, the assassination comes to be represented as not just a particularly vivid encounter with history in the making, nor even a watershed between two historical periods, but the very cause of an irreversible historical decline. It can also serve as a loss of innocence in a peculiarly personal way, a loss that is inseparable from conspiracy. For example, the late, well-known West coast conspiracy broadcaster Mae Brussell was "just a housewife, interested in tennis courts and dancing lessons and orthodonture for my children," until the shooting of Lee Harvey Oswald live on television prompted her into investigating the assassination.[8] In a similar fashion, Robert J. Groden, a prominent producer of enhanced images of the assassination and the "technical consultant" to Stone's *JFK*, turned 18 on the day of the shooting and has been trying to come to terms with the event ever since. In his writings he explicitly links his own personal coming of age to the process of public enlightenment about the workings of power in America.[9] Stone's movie (which will be considered in more detail below) itself produces a powerful story of decline and fall, linking the trauma of Vietnam and the trauma of the assassination into a unified causal and conspiratorial narrative. As the former New Orleans District Attorney Jim Garrison (whose story forms the basis of Stone's film) comments: "It's impossible for anyone possessed of reasonable objectivity and a fair degree of intelligence to read those twenty-six volumes and not reach the conclusion that the Warren Commission was wrong in every one of its major conclusions pertaining to the assassination. For me, that was the end of innocence."[10]

Popular as the tale of lost innocence may be, it must be remembered, however, that the United States has a long history of such cataclysmic moments, which form a perpetual jeremiad of innocence repeatedly lost and miraculously regained. In the twentieth century, long before the seemingly irreparable damage of Vietnam and Watergate, before even the unnerving repeated trinity of political assassinations in the 1960s, there had been, for example, the shock uncovering of the systematic deception of quiz shows in the 1950s, and the revelations about the rigging of the World Series in 1919. Given the nation's tendency to be perpetually surprised and perpetually dismayed at the revelation of treachery, not only does the insistence on the Kennedy assassination as a unique and sinister turn for the worse wear thin, it also suggests that the positive social gains of the 1960s and after count for nothing. If the Kennedy assassination is the result of a conspiracy by reactionary forces to pervert the course of history, as self-professed liberals such as Oliver Stone claim, then what about civil rights, feminism, gay and lesbian rights, and the ecology movement? Conspiratorial accounts of the political shootings of the 1960s as the moment when everything went wrong thus require a certain blindness to the progressive landmarks of that decade and after.

The opinion polls cited above seem to outline a steady progression towards doubt about the official version of events, and, coupled with the public surveys about the loss of faith in government mentioned in the introduction, they suggest that the Kennedy assassination fostered a culture of conspiracy. Yet there is good reason to call into question this story of cause and effect, with its pattern of innocence giving way to experience, since the development of theories about the JFK case has been markedly uneven. In addition to the two polls cited above one might also point, for example, to a pair of surveys carried out in 1964. The first, conducted before the official Warren Commission's report was released, indicated that only 29 percent of Americans believed Oswald acted alone; after its findings became public in late 1964, 87 percent believed the Commission's version.[11] Or, according to two Gallup polls conducted twenty years apart, we learn that 11 percent of respondents in 1976 believed that Oswald acted alone, and that the figure was the same in 1996. There might well have been a gradual shift of public opinion towards conspiracy over the last four decades, but that opinion is often varied and volatile. This is far from the common picture of conspiracy theorists as rigidly set in their beliefs once and for all.

Lone Gunman Theories

As much as the lesson of these figures is that opinion polls are not to be trusted, it is also that the story of inquiry into the assassination is one of fluctuation and contradiction. The assassination means many things to many people, and there is no single clear and easy lesson to be learnt from it. For the researchers who meet at conferences in Dallas every year, it is not only a mystery to be solved and a rallying cry for public action, but also an excuse for a get-together like any other special interest group. As well as the assassination and its conspiracy culture forming the basis for a flourishing cottage industry of memorabilia sales at conventions and on the Web, it is also the stuff of avant-garde paintings and experimental video art, such as Andy Warhol's *Jackie (The Week That Was)* (1963), and Ant Farm and T. R. Uthco's *The Eternal Frame* (1975).[12] For all the variety of approaches, however, a large part of the discussion about the case revolves around the seemingly stark choice between seeing the shooting as the action of a lone disaffected gunman, or as the result of a conspiracy of one kind or another. It is virtually impossible to mention the assassination without becoming embroiled in a debate about the existence or not of a conspiracy, the details of which are common knowledge for a surprising number of Americans. The opposition between the two camps is frequently fierce, and often explicitly ideological, but the two choices have more in common than at first sight. How did these two positions become cemented into place? Why did a conspiracy (or its pointed absence) become virtually the only narrative logic in which to plot the event?

The official no-conspiracy "lone gunman" version of the assassination was very quickly established. Within an hour and a half of the assassination, Lee Harvey Oswald had been arrested by police at a Texas movie theater in connection with the murder of Police Officer J. D. Tippit which had taken place some thirty minutes earlier. Later that same evening Oswald was charged with the murder of the President.[13] Two days later, after Oswald had himself been shot by Jack Ruby, Dallas District Attorney

Henry Wade gave a press conference in which he outlined the progress of the investigation. Several witnesses had seen Oswald in the "sniper's lair" in the School Book Depository, Wade announced, and his palm print was found on the rifle which had been hidden there. The gun had been purchased in Oswald's name, and he was seen carrying a long package into work that morning.[14] Within forty-eight hours, then, the "official" version of the assassination as the work of a lone gunman, Lee Oswald, had been fixed. Indeed, there is now some evidence to suggest that J. Edgar Hoover insisted that the FBI should put pressure on the local Dallas police to conclude that Oswald acted alone, even before the evidence had been assembled, possibly from a fear that Oswald's connections with the intelligence agencies—nebulous according to some accounts, distinctly conspiratorial in others—would cast a bad light on the Bureau.

On 29 November President Johnson appointed a commission to investigate the assassination, chaired by Chief Justice Earl Warren. The FBI and the Secret Service each conducted enquiries and handed over their lengthy reports to the Warren Commission by the middle of December. The Commission began hearing testimony in February, and finally produced its 888-page report in September 1964, though the twenty-six accompanying volumes of evidence and testimony were not released until the following month. It concluded that Oswald had carried out the assassination alone. "The Commission has found no evidence," the Report announced, "that either Lee Harvey Oswald or Jack Ruby was part of any conspiracy, domestic or foreign, to assassinate President Kennedy."[15] The Report, and the lone gunman theory it detailed, gained enormous credence in the United States in the first years after its publication. The *New York Times* printed the entire Report in a special supplement, and went on to publish selections from the hearings in a paperback edition that sold over a million copies. In many ways the Warren Commission succeeded in allaying fears that the assassination was the work of Soviet or Cuban forces, which was perhaps one of Johnson's immediate concerns only a year after the Cuban missile crisis. In a period of intense Cold War paranoia, it was therefore expeditious to believe that political assassinations were not in the American tradition. But in its concern to reassure the American public, the Warren Commission Report demonstrated an almost paranoid concern to dispel any suggestion of conspiracy.

Having emphatically denied any conspiratorial involvement, the Commission argued that "to determine the motives for the assassination of President Kennedy, one must look to the assassin himself."[16] Having examined "his family history, his education or lack of it, his acts, his writings, and the recollections of those who had close contacts with him," it concluded that:

Oswald was motivated by an overriding hostility to his environment. He does not appear to have been able to establish meaningful relationships with other people. He was perpetually discontented with the world around him. Long before the assassination he expressed his hatred for American society and acted in protest against it ... He sought for himself a place in history ... His commitment to Marxism and communism appears to have been another important factor in his motivation. He also had demonstrated a capacity to act decisively and without regard to the consequences when such action would further his aims of the moment. Out of these and the many other factors which may have molded the character of Lee Harvey Oswald there emerged a man capable of assassinating President Kennedy.[17]

As one Commission staff lawyer reputedly complained, this list reads like a series of clichés from a television soap opera.[18] Although the Report reassures its readers that "the Commission does not believe that the relation between Oswald and his wife caused him to assassinate the President," it draws on a host of other pop psychology favourites in its portrait of Oswald as a disaffected loner. With its dual emphasis on Oswald's political sympathies and his maladjustment, the Commission was caught between, on the one hand, the need to make some sense of the assassination for the general public by ascribing to Oswald rational political motives, and, on the other hand, the conviction that the killing of an American president was an inexplicable and psychopathic act. They were forced, in effect, to conclude that the assassination was simultaneously the work of a dissatisfied but otherwise unremarkable American, and something no right-minded American would consider. The accusation leveled against conspiracy theories—that in trying to explain everything they explain nothing—could be turned back against lone gunman theories, which by contrast explain the assassination by declaring Oswald's motives inexplicable.

The Commission's attempt at amateur psychobiography was only the first of many. Dr Renatus Hartogs, who had conducted a psychiatric evaluation of Oswald as a teenage truant, argued in *The Two Assassins* that Oswald had assassinated the substitute father figure of Kennedy out of a repressed Oedipal desire for his own mother.[19] Priscilla McMillan, a journalist who had first met Oswald and his wife in Russia in the early 1960s and who conducted in-depth interviews with Marina after the assassination, concluded that Oswald was a disaffected misfit suffering from delusions of grandeur.[20] Even Gerald Ford, Commission member and future president, produced a biography of Oswald. *Portrait of the Assassin* was not much more than a recapitulation of the Warren Commission's findings, although it did offer some behind-the-scenes glimpses of the Commission struggling to make sense of the claims that Oswald had been an FBI undercover agent.[21]

The Warren Commission's concern to decipher Oswald's inner mysteries was likewise followed by numerous attempts to diagnose both him and the American culture he emerged from. The authors of a 1970 textbook on paranoia, for example, include an appendix which offers thumbnail case histories not only of Oswald, but of all those who had carried out or attempted assassinations on American presidents or presidential candidates.[22] Swanson et al. discuss how Oswald's childhood was "disrupted by the death of his father prior to the subject's birth," and how "his mother was suspicious, grandiose and had unrealistic beliefs." They proceed to reveal that Oswald was "a slight man, 5'7" in height," and that "he did not work but read many books, including John Kennedy's biography." Reviewing previous and subsequent presidential potshots, Swanson et al. find a similar pattern in each of the stories. We learn, for example, that Charles Guiteau, who killed President Garfield in 1881, was "of slight build and 5'5" tall. He had had an erratic work record and relied on swindling and theft to support himself." If this were not enough to diagnose him as paranoid, it also emerges that he "sulked and daydreamed, was litigious and had grandiose ideas of starting a newspaper." But perhaps his principal manifestation of paranoia was that he "dropped out of high school at age 18 [*sic*: only 18?] and spent the remainder of the year reading the Bible." This psychological blueprint is repeated for the majority of the ten "lone gunmen." All the assassins, according to Swanson et al., "were nationally displaced individuals"; furthermore, "all had an erratic work adjustment," "all were slim and between 5' and 5'8","" and "all had a paranoid diagnosis at the time of their homicidal act." The obvious conclusion must surely be that most of the assassins were poor immigrants on poor diets, with an understandable—and often explicitly articulated—grudge against a country that failed to live up to their expectations.[23] But for Swanson et al. the conclusion is that paranoia is not only the "predominant cause" of Oswald's action, but is also in retrospect the crucial factor in nearly all previous and subsequent attempts. For many cultural commentators, moreover, paranoia is also the predominant *effect* of the assassination, with the nation's desperate turn to conspiracy thinking.

It must be noted, therefore, that it was only in the self-conscious national climate of paranoia resulting from the repeated political assassinations towards the end of the 1960s that psychological commentators and historians also came to diagnose paranoia as one of the motive forces in American history.[24] For example, in a 1971 collection of essays by social scientists, *Assassinations and the Political Order*, three essays seek to explore, in the words of one of the titles, "the psychopathology of assassination."[25] But the volume also broadens the discussion into questions of social psychology and sociology, with articles on the culture of violence in America and other countries.[26] In both cases, assassination becomes slightly more explicable if regarded as the result of either a personal or social malaise. The hope is that, once identified and theorized, this pattern of violent "self-realization" can be prevented. The collection, it must be noted, developed out of the work of the editor, William J. Crotty, as co-director of the Task Force on Assassination and Political Violence of the National Commission on the Causes of and Prevention of Violence. With the emergence of psychologizing texts about the motives of the lone assassins as well as the nation's suspicious response to the official explanations, paranoia comes to be seen, then, as both the effect *and* the cause of the political assassinations of the 1960s. Paranoia, in other words, becomes identified as both the causal factor and the resulting symptom of what was felt to be a peculiarly American affliction and crisis.

The dilemma over Oswald's rationality and responsibility has continued throughout the four decades of research. Indeed, in many ways the case has become a litmus test in deciding how far we are ever in control of our own actions during an era in which everything is becoming increasingly connected and controlled. For example, Gerald Posner, author of the 1992 study *Case Closed* which offers a forceful reexamination of the single assassin version, asserts that "Lee Harvey Oswald, driven by his own twisted and impenetrable furies, was the only assassin at Dealey Plaza on November 22, 1963."[27] The suggestion is that, although he may have acted alone, he was in a psychological sense not entirely in control of his own actions. But conspiracy theories, whether of the left or the right, likewise discount Oswald's agency, seeing him as a victim of clandestine forces beyond his knowledge or control—"just a patsy," as Oswald famously shouted to news reporters in the Dallas Police Building. A few commentators, however, have tried to restore some coherence to Oswald's "impenetrable" action. Alexander Cockburn, for example, argues that, however misguided, Oswald acted out of "radical political motives," in a preemptive strike against the President whom some suspected even then of ordering CIA plots to kill Castro.[28]

In his long novel, *Oswald's Tale: An American Mystery* (1995), Norman Mailer likewise builds a fairly convincing picture of Oswald as a worthy—if somewhat inept—political thinker and agitator. Although in the final analysis this portrait of the assassin is little more than another of Mailer's discoveries of himself in unlikely biographical subjects, what is interesting about *Oswald's Tale* is the distance Mailer has traveled from his earlier pronouncements about the assassination. In a review of Mark Lane's *Rush to Judgement*, Mailer called for the establishment of a Writers' Commission to replace the Warren Commission. "One would propose one last new commission," Mailer writes, "one real commission—a literary commission supported by public subscription to spend a few years on the case." He goes on to declare that he "would trust a commission headed by Edmund Wilson before I trusted another by Earl Warren. Wouldn't you?"[29] Mailer's assumption, like most countercultural figures of the 1960s, was that the government was hiding something, and it was up to novelists and intellectuals as the conscience of the people to tell the real version of events, which inevitably seemed to involve a conspiracy theory. Indeed, Mailer has shown a lifelong fascination with the intelligence community as a source of existential secrecy, ritual and covert power, a fascination which culminated in *Harlot's Ghost* (1991), a monumental semi-fictional investigation of the CIA that circled obsessively around the black hole of the assassination without ever quite tackling it head on.

In one light, then, Mailer's adoption of a lone gunman theory in *Oswald's Tale* seems to mark a complete ideological turnaround for his one-man literary commission into the culture of conspiracy in American politics. Mailer's volte-face might suggest a turn to the conservative as he consolidates his position as the grand old man of American letters; or it might indicate little more than a commercial opportunism, as *Oswald's Tale* was quickly produced to exploit the access to KGB files secured by the author in the wake of glasnost in the former Soviet Union. Yet Mailer's restoration of the agency of the lone assassin can also be read as very much in line with his earlier self-consciously radical politics of opposition, as he endeavors to read Oswald not as a psychopath but as a political actor who struggles heroically to express himself despite the handicaps of poverty and dyslexia. Indeed, Mailer confesses that, if anything, he started with a "prejudice in favor of the conspiracy theorists," but by the end of his minute analysis of Oswald's "soul" came to the conclusion that "Oswald was a protagonist, a prime mover, a man who made things happen—in short, a figure larger than others would credit him for being."[30] In providing a painstakingly detailed account of a voluntary action completely circumscribed by the mass of social pressures surrounding the murderer, Mailer is following the pattern of Theodore Dreiser's *An American Tragedy* (1925), whose title Mailer would like to have used had not Dreiser beaten him to it. Dreiser's determinist fiction recounts the true-life story of a hapless and poor young man who ends up killing someone (his fiancée, in this case), and is put on trial. Yet, once again echoing Dreiser's novel, having accumulated a mass of mitigating and often contradictory evidence, *Oswald's Tale* nevertheless concludes that Oswald is still responsible for the shooting, having created his own historical action, though not under conditions of his own choosing.

The real significance, however, of Mailer's repeated returns to the assassination is that the political valency of any interpretation cannot be guaranteed in advance. Conspiracy theories, it might be concluded, are neither necessarily radical nor reactionary, despite the tendency of most commentators to see them as either unremittingly harmful or inevitably progressive. From the outset, the liberal and radical left was divided on what to think about the assassination. For some, belief in a conspiracy was part of the "paranoid" mentality which had dominated the McCarthyite years of the Cold War, and was therefore to be rejected. In his one-man newsletter, *I. F. Stone's Weekly*, independent political columnist I. F. Stone made clear that the left should have no truck with political demonology:

> All my adult life as a newspaperman I have been fighting in defense of the Left and of sane politics, against conspiracy theories of history, character assassination, guilt by association and demonology. Now I see elements of the Left using these same tactics in the controversy over the Kennedy assassination and the Warren Commission Report. I believe that the Commission has done a first-rate job, on a level that does our country proud and is worthy of so tragic an event.[31]

Other commentators on the liberal left, however, came to take a conspiracy theory for granted as the explanation behind most social ills—Oliver Stone is the most prominent example here. As the tergiversations of Mailer's own career suggest, however, it is far from clear whether a lone gunman or a conspiracy theory is a priori the more politically naïve view. This confusion in reading the ideological significance of the Oswald's agency complicates any easy narrative about the aftermath of the assassination as an instant wake-up call to cynical distrust.

Conspiracy Theories

In contrast to Mailer's preference for Edmund Wilson over Earl Warren, the establishment media, however, quickly pronounced the Warren Commission Report a success. *Time*, for example, announced that "the Report is amazing in its detail, remarkable in its judicial caution and restraint, yet utterly convincing in all of its major conclusions."[32] *Life* magazine likewise proclaimed that "the Report is a great public document that reflects credit on its author, and the nation it represents."[33] Yet with the publication of the full twenty-six volumes of evidence, a few writers began to find nagging inconsistencies between the evidence and the Commission's conclusions.[34] The investigation into the Warren Commission's actions and motives formed a critical mirror of the Commission's own investigation of the assassin. In addition to the articles by European correspondents, those in *The Nation* and a whole series in *The Minority of One* during 1964 and 1965, the first two major books criticizing the Commission's conclusions appeared in the summer of 1966. Both Edward Jay Epstein's *Inquest* and Mark Lane's *Rush to Judgement* examined the contradictions and inconsistencies in the "official" version.[35] Where Epstein concluded that the Commission was compromised by its need to maintain national security, Lane argued that it was dictated less by inherently contra-dictory conflicts of interest, than by an outright desire to cover up the truth. In his reexamination of aspects such as the "magic bullet" theory, the capability of Oswald as a marksman, and the eyewitness testimony which pointed to a second gunman on the grassy knoll, Lane developed not only a conspiracy theory about the assassination of President Kennedy, but also a second conspiracy about the subsequent cover-up by the various intelligence agencies.

The case for a conspiracy reached a new level of public exposure in 1967 with New Orleans District Attorney Jim Garrison's indictment of business-man Clay Shaw for conspiring with other anti-Castro activists to murder the President.[36] The case didn't reach court until 1969; the trial lasted five weeks and was thrown out by the jury after less than an hour's deliberation. Both Garrison and his conspiracy theories were widely discredited as the work of an egomaniac with political ambitions (a smear campaign not without its own conspiratorial interpretations), and the upper hand once again returned to the advocates of the lone gunman theory. So, for example, in 1967–68 Attorney General Ramsey Clark convened two panels to review the medical testimony of the Warren Commission which had ignored the autopsy X-rays and photographs, an omission which had prompted much criticism.[37] But the Clark Panels only reconfirmed the Warren Commission's conclusions that Kennedy and Connally had been shot from the rear and from a downwards angle, with no evidence of a second trajectory, and hence no second assassin.

The critics of the lone gunman version were relegated to the world of the tabloids and small press "crackpot" publications, until the emergence of revelations about the covert and illegal operations of the intelligence community in connection with Watergate. In response to pressure from the media, Congress formed the Rockefeller Commission in 1975 and then the Church Committee in 1976, to investigate the domestic and foreign activities of the FBI and CIA.[38] Amongst the many findings were disclosures about Operation Mongoose (the CIA's continuation of the supposedly defunct campaign to regain Cuba), along with its covert contract with various Mafia figures to assassinate Castro. Although both committees included denials that there was any involvement by the intelli-gence agencies in the assassination of President Kennedy, there was suffi-cient public concern for Congress to reopen the investigation with the formation of the House Select Committee on Assassinations (HSCA), which looked into the murder of President Kennedy, as well as the shooting of Robert Kennedy and Martin Luther King in 1968.[39] The Report (another large fourteen-volume effort) appeared in 1979, and con-cluded that, though Oswald had fired the fatal shots, there was a 95 percent probability that a second gunman had fired from the grassy knoll. Without producing conclusive evidence of a conspiracy, the

Committee recommended that the Justice Department look into the affairs of Mafia members Santos Trafficante and Johnny Roselli. Like many other potential witnesses in the Kennedy case, both these men died violent deaths before they could give testimony, a phenomenon which then spawned a whole new group of conspiracy theories about the silencing of witnesses.[40]

The congressional investigations of the 1970s, however, are not necessarily signs of an uncompromised political openness and official willingness to believe in conspiracy theories. The HSCA investigations were not the last word from the authorities on the Kennedy case; indeed, it might be argued that each administration seems to return to the trauma with its own take on events. The first government inquiry found no evidence of conspiracy, nor did the second or third. The House Select Committee in 1979, however, was prepared to admit some form of Mob involvement, but in 1982 the Justice Department asked the National Academy of Sciences to review the acoustical evidence. Having found what it took to be grave errors in the 1979 Report, the Justice Department once again formally closed the case in 1988.[41] Then in a spirit of post-Cold War openness partly fueled by a desire to "help restore government credibility," and in direct response to the public outcry and heavy lobbying following Oliver Stone's film, Congress passed the President John F. Kennedy Assassination Records Collection Act (1992) which ordered the release of all government files pertaining to the case, subject to a security vetting procedure. The resulting Assassination Records Review Board (ARRB) even initiated some further testing of fibers and tissue fragments found on bullet fragments from the assassination, but with inconclusive results. In its final report the panel also concluded, however, that they had not necessarily secured "all that was 'out there.'"[42]

In addition to official investigations into the intelligence agencies (and the use by private citizens and advocacy groups of the Freedom of Information Act to discover similar stories), conspiracy theories about the Kennedy assassination began to gain widespread publicity in 1975 with the screening of the Zapruder footage for the first time on television by the daytime chat show host Geraldo Rivera. The home movie, which seemed to show Kennedy's head snapping backwards with the fatal shot, suggested to many viewers that the Warren Commission's account of a single gunman firing from behind was wrong. It became for many Americans visible proof, if not of a conspiracy, then of evidence that their government had lied to them. The Zapruder footage became an instantly recognizable sequence, its ubiquity promoted by the release of digitally enhanced versions on video. The original footage continues to hold a powerful mystique, and became the subject of an ownership struggle following the ARRB's recommendation that it be acquired for the National Archives. After a long legal dispute, an arbitration panel finally decided in

1999 that the government should pay the Zapruder family $16 million for the footage (though the family retained the copyright).

Vertigo of Interpretation

The increasing visibility of the formerly unseen Zapruder footage matched the wider public interest in the case. In addition to the early studies mentioned above, bestsellers outlining new interpretations of the evidence and putting forward ever more complex conspiracy theories about the event began to accumulate from the late 1970s onwards. The inventory includes David Lifton's *Best Evidence* (1980), a detailed analysis of the medical evidence in the case which concluded that the President's body had been surgically altered (possibly even switched) before the autopsy; Anthony Summer's *The Kennedy Conspiracy* (1980), a long overview of most aspects of the case, focusing on CIA intrigue; Robert Groden and Harrison Livingstone's *High Treason* (1989), which claims that not only was JFK's body interfered with but also that the autopsy photos and X-rays were forged; and Jim Marrs's *Crossfire* (1989), another overview which Stone used for *JFK*, and which includes the infamous list of witnesses connected with the assassination who have allegedly died mysterious deaths. With the thirtieth anniversary of the assassination and following Oliver Stone's highly controversial film, there has been a prodigious outpouring of books, magazine articles and television specials on the subject.[43]

What is remarkable about this catalog of amateur inquiries into conspiracy is the variety of different approaches and conclusions. Some examine discrepancies in the medical evidence in painstaking detail; some concentrate on the photographic evidence; some create computer simulations of the shooting; some are historical inquiries into the complex associations between the intelligence agencies, Oswald, and Cuban exiles; some explore the political history of Kennedy and Johnson's administrations against the background of the United States' entry into Vietnam; some are written by eyewitnesses and participants; some are written by people claiming to know or even to be one of the hired assassins; some offer imagined versions of a court case against Oswald; and some are outright fictional treatments of conspiracies surrounding the assassination. Some claim to have discovered clues to a prime conspiracy, while others detail evidence of a subsequent cover-up; some concentrate solely on the Kennedy assassination, while others insert that event into the larger story of political assassinations. The list of theories and suspects is therefore seemingly endless: writers have blamed the CIA, the FBI, renegades from both agencies, the Secret Service (and there is even a suggestion that JFK was killed by one of their guns going off by mistake), Cuban exiles, the Mafia, Dallas oil millionaires, right-wing Texans, left-wing sympathizers, Corsican Mafia, President Johnson, J. Edgar Hoover, Jimmy Hoffa, the military–industrial complex, an international banking cartel, the three hobos picked up in Dealey Plaza right after the shooting, and just about every combination of these groups. The spoof newspaper *The Onion* captured the sense of a frenzied overproduction of theories in their headline: "Kennedy Slain by CIA, Mafia, Castro, LBJ, Teamsters, Freemasons: President Shot 129 Times from 43 Different Angles."[44]

There are, of course, more than a few offbeat theories. Contenders for the most farfetched theory include Southern Californian swimming pool engineer George C. Thomson's book which argues that twenty-two shots were fired at President Kennedy, and in the cross fire five people were killed, including Officer J. D. Tippit, who was in fact impersonating JFK. According to Thomson, Kennedy escaped, and was seen a year later attending a private birthday party for Truman Capote.[45] Or there is the work of R. B. Cutler, octogenarian millionaire and former Olympian, who established the *Grassy Knoll Gazette* magazine, as well as the idiosyncratic Conspiracy Museum in Dallas. The museum has exhibits on the whole range of other Presidential shootings, as well as series of huge Japanese brushstroke murals, including, for example, *Old Man Sitting Under a Plum Tree*, in which the "Old Man represents assassinologists who have studied, researched, or long contemplated the mystery of the assassinations."[46] It also puts forward Cutler's own theory that the JFK shooting involved nine shots from four different locations. Then there is Jack White's theory that there are multiple Oswalds—possibly as many as sixty—who were used to set up the original Oswald as a patsy (Figure 2.1). White has propounded his theory on the JFK assassination lecture circuit, using hundreds of images of Oswald which, in his view, demonstrate the impossible variety in the alleged assassin's appearance. Finally—and in a very different league—there are *Weekly World News* headlines such as "JFK Was Shot to Prevent Him from Revealing Truth About UFOs!"

Even if we leave aside such examples as the inevitable *reductio ad absurdum* of assassinology, it is significant that there has been no steady convergence of opinion about the case, not only between the lone gunman and conspiracy theory camps, but *within* the latter position. For example, in a press release trying to present a united front of assassination researchers at the "November in Dallas" convention on the thirty-fifth anniversary of the shooting, the participants could only agree on a statement that:

> We believe these basic facts in the assassination of President Kennedy and the wounding of Governor John Connally: there was more than one shooter; there has not been a true investigation of this crime by our government; the intelligence agencies did not give those investigations the information they should have; the assassination case is still open and research should be ongoing.[47]

Figure 2.1 Kennedy assassination researcher Jack White's poster of the many different images of Lee Harvey Oswald. Like John Armstrong, White argues that these photographs cannot all be the same person. Courtesy of Jack White.

All acceded that the official version is not correct, but there was little or no consensus when it came to presenting an alternative account, other than that there was some kind of conspiracy or other. Despite the desire for a common front, over the three days of the conference participants had presented a remarkably wide range of theories and speculations, many of which were mutually incompatible—and this is not to mention the rival conference organized by the Committee on Political Assassinations in Dallas at the same time. The critical community often seems to spend more time debating one another than challenging their supposed common enemy of the official view. As Harrison Edward Livingstone, a prominent critic, writes:

> The facts are that there is fraud and misrepresentation in the critical community: hoaxes, opportunism, territorialism, copyright violations, bootlegging, vendettas, misinformation, serious misdirection by critics of other critics, disruption, suppression of vital evidence for commercial purposes, slandermongering, and interference with other researchers and witnesses ... the critical community is a madhouse.[48]

Additional evidence likewise leads not to convergence but to further dispute. New data is emerging all the time, fueled in part by conspiracy researchers' insistence that all postwar assassinations and clandestine events are related. After its five-year term of inquiry, the Assassination Records Review Board had established a mind-boggling collection of some 4.5 million pages and items in the National Archives relating to the assassination, but there is no consensus in the research community as to what any of the new material means. With the presumption now that all files must be released even if they only have a tangential relation to the assassination, the resulting overwhelming amount of documents makes it hard to work out whether any part of it contains something vital. In many ways, the problem is not that there is too little evidence to solve the case. On the contrary, there is now far too much information to allow anyone, whether critic or apologist for the Warren Commission, to encompass and account for, with reasonable certainty, all the contradictory and varied pieces of the puzzle. It has become practically impossible to sort the trivial from the genuinely significant, not just for conspiracy buffs, but even for the government lawyers and intelligence agents entrusted with vetting the release of previously classified information under the JFK Act (according to an anecdote I heard on a research trip to Washington). For who could have a knowledge of the entire history of covert politics over the last half-century encyclopedic enough to guarantee that items being released do not inadvertently offer a clue via an accidental association of names and dates, if not to a smoking gun, then perhaps to operating procedures and clandestine connections that the intelligence chiefs would want to remain secret?

Moreover, the information relating to the case is so diverse that it is virtually impossible for any individual, whether amateur or official, to comprehend all the data from such a wide variety of disciplines. A crash course in assassinology (or "assassination science," as the title of one book on the case dubs it) would have to include law, forensic medicine, acoustics, ballistics, nuclear physics, image analysis, political history, biography, psychology, and so on. Assassination researchers, like the academic scholars whose protocols they emulate (often to excess), take pride in having a narrowly defined subspecialism. Jack White recounts an influential conversation with Penn Jones, a grandee of the assassination research community, who told him that "to do really good research, you need to *specialize!* Pick out one or two JFK subjects that really interest you, and *then research the hell out of them!*"[49]

The problem is not just that the range of expertise is too diverse to master, but that in each area there is often no agreement between experts. There has never been, for example, agreement on the number, timing or direction of bullets, a question which is fundamental to the case. Viewing the Zapruder footage frame by frame, the Warren Commission asserted that, judging by the reaction of the President when the limousine comes back into view after it had disappeared behind a freeway sign, the first shot came somewhere between Z-210 and Z-225 (as the frames from the Zapruder footage are conventionally labeled). The fatal head shot comes at Z-313, which gives a total time for the shooting (factoring in expert analyses of the speed Zapruder's camera was running at) of 5.62 seconds. Based on an assessment by expert FBI marksmen that it takes 2.3 seconds to reload and fire the type of rifle found in the "sniper's lair," this meant that no more than three shots could have been fired in the time frame given by the Zapruder footage. Taking into account eyewitness testimony and other evidence of a bullet that had missed the car altogether, the Warren Commission concluded that all of Governor Connally's wounds must have been caused by the same shot that had hit the President in the back, the bullet from which was discovered in near pristine condition on Connally's gurney at the hospital—dubbed the "magic bullet" by critics who disbelieved that it could have caused all the wounds and remained nearly intact.

This scenario obviously relies on a series of expert opinions at crucial junctures, many of which have been challenged. Employing a different set of expert marksmen, a CBS documentary, for example, determined in 1975 that the minimum time to operate the Mannlicher-Carcano rifle was only 5.6 seconds and as little as 4.1 seconds, while the HSCA in 1977 managed to push the time back as far as 3.3 seconds.[50] The crucial split-second timing seems to depend on which experts you ask. There is likewise little agreement about Commission Exhibit 399, the magic bullet. Neutron activation analyses carried out in 1964, trying to match the chemical compounds of the bullet to metallic fragments found in JFK, Connally and in the limousine, proved to be inconclusive; more accurate tests had been developed by 1974 when the HSCA ordered new analyses, but these also produced contradictory results.[51] Gerald Posner's *Case Closed* sought to revive the single bullet theory, and made extensive use of a computer simulation of its flight path made by Failure Analysis Associates for a mock trial held by the American Bar Association in 1992. The simulation, backed up by analysis from ballistics experts, produced a persuasive account of how the bullet had been deflected and had tumbled, thereby causing the seemingly unlikely collection of wounds while remaining intact. However, Posner downplayed the fact that FAA had also made a second simulation showing an equally plausible alternative scenario, leading to the conclusion that expert computer simulations based on incomplete data can "prove" more or less anything in a court case.

The problem for many students of the assassination has become which experts to trust. For example, a panel of acoustics experts were appointed by the HSCA to examine the Dictabelt recording from a police motorcycle rider that apparently included the assassination gunshots (and which would therefore allow not only accurate timing of the shots, but also some indication of the direction.) After conducting lengthy and highly sophisticated analysis of the recordings, the panel of scientists concluded that there had been four shots, and that (with a 95 percent certainty) one of the shots had come not from behind but from the Grassy Knoll (and hence that there must have been a conspiracy). It was only Steve Barber, a rock drummer from Ohio who, on repeatedly listening to a version of the recording that had come free with a magazine, noticed the words "hold everything secure," which further investigation revealed had been spoken by Sheriff Decker some minutes *after* the shooting, and hence the sound pulses the acoustic experts had discovered on the tape were not gunshots at all.

Given so many contradictory findings, the question becomes: which expert do you trust—and how do you decide whether someone is indeed an expert? Assassination critics are quick to point out that many scientists commenting on the case might well be experts in their own field, but that doesn't necessarily qualify them to comment on other aspects. For example, the physician John K. Lattimer was chosen by the Kennedy family in 1972 to study the X-rays and autopsy photos which had become the object of much dispute. Cyril Wecht, then the President of the American Academy of Forensic Sciences, insisted that Lattimer, a urologist, was "unbelievably unqualified." "I don't know what in the world possessed this fellow Lattimer to have the arrogance, the effrontery, to project himself into this. He's a urologist, a kidney-and-bladder man. By definition this is a guy who never moves above the belly button."[52] With the boot on the other foot, however, we might turn to the HSCA's quizzing of the competence of the self-proclaimed photographic expert Jack White, who has claimed, amongst other things, that the back yard photos of Oswald holding a rifle and leftist magazines are faked because the size of the magazines do not correspond with the size of Oswald. In one exchange, White is forced to admit that he has never even heard of photogrammetry, the scientific technique of calculating the size of objects from two-dimensional images. Perhaps the most interesting case of how expertise becomes authorized is the publication in 1992 by the prestigious *Journal of the American Medical Association* (*JAMA*) of the definitive answer to the assassination (that JFK had been shot from behind by two bullets from a lone assassin), based on an interview with two of the physicians attending the wounded President in Parklands Hospital. As various critics have pointed out, in a series of articles that didn't go through the usual peer-review process, *JAMA* was lending its considerable scientific and institutional authority not to reproducible experimental work, but to eyewitness testimony that itself has been disputed, most prominently by Charles Crenshaw, another of the doctors in the emergency room.[53] For most amateur inquirers, when the various experts are in disagreement, there is no obvious and agreed-upon criteria for working out which expert to believe, other than to call in a further expert, and so on, potentially for ever, with little concurrence about who is qualified to authorize the higher authorities.

Far from the assassination leading steadily and inexorably to a consensus of conspiracy theorists, then, it has produced a hermeneutic of suspicion that begins to doubt everything—even the fundamental ground rules of proof and evidence. Many conspiracy-minded investigations of the JFK case work by pointing out the inconsistencies and suggestive coincidences in the official record and in further evidence the authors unearth. They may go on to create a tight-knit and coherent conspiracy theory, but often the initial move is to pick holes in the official version, and to unravel the coherence of the accepted view. For example, in his presentation on puzzling details in the shooting of Officer J. D. Tippit, Bill Drenas began by remarking that "this discussion has no hidden agenda. It does not support," he continued, "anybody's pro-conspiracy or anti-conspiracy theories. I am just a regular guy who wants to find out the truth."[54] Some of the coincidences surrounding the case are merely humorous or strange. For example, there used to be on sale in the gift shop at the Lincoln memorial in Washington a list of coincidences between the Kennedy and Lincoln assassinations ("reproduced on antiqued parchment that looks and feels old"), which includes gems such as "Lincoln's secretary, whose name was Kennedy, advised him not to go to the theater; Kennedy's secretary, whose name was Lincoln, advised him not to go to Dallas." But what are we to do with suggestive facts and coincidences such as Nixon's attendance of a Pepsi convention in Dallas on the day of the assassination? Or an FBI memo dated 23 November 1963 that surfaced in 1988 reporting that "Mr George Bush of the CIA" had been debriefed about the event? Or (in an example Norman Mailer discusses in *Oswald's Tale*) the fact that the last person Kennedy phoned when he was in Dallas was a Mrs J. Lee Johnson III?

Investigations into the Kennedy assassination reveal an excess of uncanny coincidences and contradictions, sometimes in the most mundane of facts. For example, at the 1997 "November in Dallas" convention the researcher John Armstrong gave an enormously detailed two-and-a-half hour presentation on the multiple inconsistencies in the account of Lee Harvey Oswald's life. Armstrong produced documents which seemed to show Oswald enrolled in different high schools in different cities in the same period, and sightings of him in the months prior to the assassination in different states at the same time. He also pointed to the discrepancies in the differing official records and eyewitness accounts of Oswald's height, eye and hair color, and, strangest of all, the divergence between, on the one hand, photographic and personal accounts of Oswald losing a front tooth in a teenage brawl and, on the other, dental records and a photograph that seems to show all the teeth intact taken when Oswald's corpse was exhumed in 1981, following speculation that it wasn't him buried there after all.

Many—perhaps all—of these anomalies can be explained away. For example, the eyewitness testimony to the Warren Commission placing Oswald in North Dakota (a place he never visited, and therefore the sighting has been taken as possible proof of an Oswald double) is the result of a mixture of mistaken memories, in part fueled by a typographical error in a newspaper article on Oswald that confused NO (for New Orleans) with ND (North Dakota).[55] It nevertheless seems unnerving that the most humdrum of daily details could be the cause of so much dispute. How can this kind of basic factual evidence ever be condensed into a single coherent account? How can the inconsistencies ever fit together? One way that conspiracy theorists attempt to explain away these anomalies is, of course, by claiming that they are the accidental evidence of a conspiracy—or even evidence of a deliberate conspiracy to plant misleading clues. The bulk of Armstrong's work, for example, is concerned with documenting the anomalies, but he is also forced to put forward a hypothesis, at first somewhat tentatively and reluctantly, that the only explanation for the wide discrepancies and doublings in the Oswald evidence is that all along there were in fact two Oswalds, which he designates Harvey and Lee. "In the early 1950s," he argues, "an intelligence operation was underway that involved two teenage boys—Lee Oswald from Fort Worth, and a Russian-speaking boy named Harvey Oswald from New York." Beginning in 1952, Armstrong continues, "the boys lived parallel but separate lives—often in the same city. The ultimate goal was to switch their identities and send Harvey Oswald into Russia, which is exactly what happened seven years later."[56]

A frequent criticism of conspiracy theorists is that they reach too quickly for explanations that rely on conspiratorial agency, when Occam's razor would dictate other, less elaborate explanations. Indeed, the ramifications of Armstrong's provisional and provocative theory are mind-boggling in their potential complexity. In a moment of paranoid free fall (and without the immediate time or resources to check all of Armstrong's facts), the audience was left to wonder what kind of America they were living in if two identical but different Oswalds had been groomed from their infancy for future historical roles: How far back does the conspiracy go? Are "They" able to plan and control every last detail with sickening efficiency? Though undeniably farfetched and inaccurate, by pointing out the apparent bizarre contradictions in the common-sense account, Armstrong's presentation seems to open up an irreparable rent in the fabric of reality that only a preposterous theory of a separate Lee and Harvey could hope to close. Indeed, it was the very implausibility of Armstrong's reluctantly reached conclusion that kept his conspiracy theory from falling into a rigid and fixed belief (though he has since gone on to make bolder and more definitive claims). The audience—myself included—were left hovering in a hermeneutic limbo, having caught a glimpse of the infinite regress of doubt that could erode even the most mundane pieces of evidence, yet without having to hand a fully (or even a remotely) convincing alternative to make the pieces fit back together.

If conspiracy theorists sometimes try to resolve contradictions in the evidence by an appeal to hidden layers of intentional plotting, then in other cases they make the more extreme (and doubly paranoid) claim that any new piece of information which would undermine existing theories or confirm rival ones might itself be a deliberate plant by the powers that be to lead investigators astray. Likewise the lack of evidence of a conspiracy can itself be taken as evidence of conspiracy to deliberately withhold vital information. The infamous backyard photos of Oswald confirm that he was indeed the lone gunman? Then they must have been faked. According to the vast majority of participants the autopsy report is accurate? Then the President's body must have been switched on the way back to Washington. The President's brain is missing from the National Archives? Then "They" must have removed it to hide the evidence, and so on.

In this way, many conspiracy theories about the Kennedy assassination open up a space of doubt and suspicion without ever fully closing it down. Nothing is certain; everything can be reinterpreted. A supplementary theory is always needed to explain the gaps in the existing theory by positing an intentional plan to leave misleading clues, and so on ad infinitum. The exponential, all-consuming logic of paranoia—not to mention the sheer volume of Kennedy assassination materials—threatens to plunge the case into an infinite abyss of suspicion, into what Jean Baudrillard has termed "a vertigo of interpretations."[57] In a discussion of the multiple apparitions of Lee Harvey Oswald, Don DeLillo suggests, only half-ironically, that "it is though we have been examining the career of a renowned and exceptionally deep-textured writer. Every aspect of his life and work has its own team of assistant professors of English to pan for minutiae and assorted micron droppings, to work up new explications and directions, devise new shifts in emphasis."[58] Like literary research in the wake of poststructuralism, the process of interpretation threatens (or promises?) to become endless. What would constitute final and definitive proof of a conspiracy in this most scrutinized of cases? A deathbed confession by one of the hired hitmen on the grassy knoll—to put alongside all the other deathbed confessions already in existence?[59] A new eyewitness account, to refract all those other seemingly definitive but endlessly contradictory eyewitness accounts? A computer enhancement of a blur on the grassy knoll that seems to be the shape of a man with a rifle, to rival similar digital enhancements revealing other tendentiously discernible shapes? Indeed, as much as assassination researchers profess a determination to bring about closure and conviction, they also often have a personal investment in keeping research going—not to mention a financial investment in prolonging the process of inquiry, with the proliferation of convention speaking and web merchandising funding the amateur research network.

If the "vertigo of interpretation" threatens to engulf the Kennedy assassination at every point, then the interesting question is how investigators deal with—or seek to repress—that possibility. Some researchers, as we have seen, choose to close up the gap as soon as it opens, by positing ever more baroque explanations of conspiratorial intention. Others, however, dwell longer in the limbo of uncertainty, even if they ultimately make a leap of faith towards coherence and resolution.

Three assassination novels dramatize the range of possible responses. In *Oswald's Tale* Norman Mailer interviews those Russians (including KGB officers) who knew Oswald during his time in the Soviet Union. In one interview Mailer will uncover an important new piece of evidence, but then must conduct further interviews and recount more life histories in order to establish the veracity of the original interlocutor, and so potentially onwards and backwards ad infinitum. Mailer seems aware of this problem, yet can only stop the rot by a pragmatic appeal to the time constraints of his limited sojourn in the former Soviet Union. It comes as no surprise that the epigram for the novel is taken from Marguerite's response to the Warren Commission's question about why her son had defected to Russia: "I cannot answer that yes or no sir. I am going to go through the whole story or it is no good."[60]

Richard Condon's assassination novel, *Winter Kills* (1974), leads its readers further into the abyss. The dead President's brother spends the entire novel pursuing one conspiracy theory after another, each of which at first seems entirely convincing, both for the protagonist and the reader. First Nick learns from a deathbed confession that there was more than one rifleman involved, and hence that the police failed to uncover a conspiracy. He is then led to suspect that the man behind the conspiracy is Z. K. Dawson, an oil millionaire and arms manufacturer, who ordered the murder of the President for his apparent disarmament tendencies. But Dawson informs him that in fact the police themselves were to blame. When Nick speaks to an assistant to the former chief of police responsible for protecting the President, he is told that the police were indeed complicit, but that in fact the Mafia were responsible. Chasing up what turn out to be a series of red herrings from a fake Mafia boss, he is told that the Mafia in reality were taking revenge for a Hollywood studio's loss of earnings as a result of a Marilyn Monroe-like character committing suicide in connection with the President. But a real Mafia boss informs Nick that a Jimmy Hoffa character is to blame, only for Nick to learn from an adviser to his father that the Mafia were actually taking revenge on the Kegans (the novel's Kennedy substitutes) for reneging on a rigged election. Nick then finds out that the police chief he thought he had spoken to in fact died years ago, and that the chief's assistant was himself a fake, as indeed was Dawson—and even a female reporter for a newsmagazine whom he encounters. What's more, everyone he meets along the way seems to end up dead.

All the theories in turn prove to be red herrings, each clue turns out to be misleading, and the novel thus sets up the alarming possibility that the truth might never be reached, and that the sensation of hermeneutic vertigo will last indefinitely. But the plunge into the abyss of epistemological skepticism is halted in the last few pages of the novel when we learn that in fact all the false clues have been deliberately fabricated and planted for Nick by an all-too-real conspiracy of the secret ruling elite led by his father. In this way the novel toys with the idea of an endless deferral of ultimate revelation and an insuperable instability of knowledge, only for this unsettling experiment to be recuperated at the last minute in the name of realism, causality and agency.[61] The novel thus seems to pull out of its spiraling tailspin of paranoia, but only by an aesthetically unconvincing and contrived twist of the plot. In its jerry-built convenience, then, the hurriedly erected façade of the ending fails to paper over the cracks in the ideological wallpaper that have been opened up by the bulk of the novel.

The possibility of an endless hermeneutic spiral is most famously carried to its logical and aesthetic extreme in Pynchon's *Crying of Lot 49*. As we saw in Chapter 1, the novel tells of Oedipa Maas, a young Californian housewife called upon to sort out the infinitely complex will of a former lover whose business interests seem to involve the whole legacy of America. As she pieces together the estate, she comes across clues to a sinister, ancient conspiracy called the Tristero which threatens her with signs of its existence everywhere she turns. Oedipa finds clues to the elusive Tristero and its underground postal system in the unlikeliest of places, from a scrawled cryptic sign on the wall of a bathroom in a San Francisco bar, to minor textual variations in a Jacobean tragedy, and from rumors at the Yoyodyne weapons corporation, to legends about the bones of Allied soldiers buried at the bottom of an Italian lake. The novel famously ends with Oedipa waiting at an auction for the crying of lot number 49, a stamp collection which promises to finally reveal the existence of the Tristero's involvement not only in Oedipa's own life in particular but American history in general. The novel leaves its protagonist and its readers in endless suspension, however, uncertain whether there is indeed a conspiracy, or only Oedipa's paranoid delusions. It is not just the ending but the entire fabric of the novel which prolongs this moment of suspense. The whole of *The Crying of Lot 49* continuously teeters on the edge of metaphors which never quite solidify into literal statements. Clauses beginning "as if" multiply endlessly, leaving both Oedipa and the novel's syntax permanently on the cusp of revelation. Here, in a scene that brings together the uncovering of secrets with the uncovering of bodies (in a link that the Web exploits to the full), Oedipa's discovery of the Tristero conspiracy is described in a series of ever-expanding conditional subclauses:

> So began, for Oedipa, the languid, sinister blooming of The Tristero. Or rather, her attendance at some unique performance, prolonged as if it were the last of the night, something a little extra for whoever'd stayed this late. As if the breakaway gowns, net bras, jewelled garters and G-strings of historical figuration that would fall away were layered dense as Oedipa's own street-clothes in that game with Metzger in front of the Baby Igor movie; as if a plunge towards dawn indefinite black hours long would indeed be necessary before the Tristero could be revealed in its terrible nakedness.[62]

In *The Crying of Lot 49* the moment of waiting is indefinitely prolonged, as if—in the language of calculus which the novel itself explores—the "vanishingly small" increment between the literal and the metaphorical were endlessly subdivided without ever fully bridging the gap.[63] Whereas *Oswald's Tale* and *Winter Kills* ultimately shy away from the vertigo of interpretation they induce, *Lot 49*'s inconclusive quest and suspended ending confronts—and even celebrates—in a most spectacular fashion the prospect that the final recuperation will never come. With its narrative logic of endless deferral and perpetual supplementarity, Pynchon's novel anticipates in a stylized form how the assassination has become submerged into an abyss of infinite interpretation and suspicion over the ensuing decades.

Oliver Stone's Oedipal Drama

In order to consider in more detail how conspiracy theories about the Kennedy assassination can lead more to confusion and causal incoherence than resolution, I now want to consider in detail two assassination fictions, each of which attracted much public debate. Oliver Stone's *JFK* and Don DeLillo's *Libra* offer very different responses to the vertigo of interpretation, and they suggest two very different models for the causal role of the assassination in recent American history.

Unfavorable reviewers of *JFK* were incensed by the "mixing of fact and fiction" in the film's now infamous combination of authentic assassination footage with artfully reconstructed documentary clips.[64] The *Washington Post* and *Time* began a fierce assault on *JFK* whilst it was still in production, with a headline in the former proclaiming that *JFK* was a "Dallas in Wonderland."[65] Stone replied in numerous Op-Ed pieces to these charges, sometimes claiming that the film was presenting to the cinema-going public the true version of history for the first time, and at other times arguing that the film was a "counter myth" to what he perceived as the mythical version of history told in the Warren Commission Report.[66]

In many ways *JFK* operates with a dual narrative logic of both history and myth, which undermines the claims about the film that it presents a coherent and plausible version of events—reductively so in the eyes of its detractors, necessarily so in view of its supporters. On the one hand, in Stone's conspiracy theory of recent history, nothing happens by accident. The bulletproof bubble top of the presidential limousine, the film suggests, was left off on the treasonous orders of the conspiring Secret Service agents. The car likewise slowed to a virtual standstill after the first shot, and just before the fatal last shot, not because the Secret Service driver was stunned into confusion, but because it was part of the incredibly devious planning of the conspirators. *JFK*'s conspirators take care not only of the minor details, but they also have the grand sweep of history in their grasp. The argument of the film is that the conspirators planned to replace Kennedy with the more bellicose Johnson in order to promote their military–industrial interests through the escalation of the Vietnam War. In Stone's version of history there are no accidents, no coincidences, and no signs of incompetence in the assassination and its subsequent cover-up.

Stone relies on a model of causality that features individual action as the sufficient antecedent to subsequent effects. *JFK* presents the Vietnam War, the student and race riots, and the assassination of Robert Kennedy as part of (to use Senator McCarthy's famous formulation) an "unbroken series" of events which the assassination conspiracy set in motion.[67] For Stone, the Present Situation is not the result of a complex and overdetermined set of events, processes and representations, but the inexorable consequence of purposeful decisions by individual agents. The film documents (or forges, according to many commentators) numerous inconsistencies in the Warren Commission Report, but it immediately inserts those anomalies into a tale either of an original conspiracy or of a subsequent cover-up.

JFK's detective fiction structure limits it to a restrictive model of causality and agency. When Garrison first submitted to the publishers a draft of *On the Trail of the Assassins*, on which Stone's film is based, it was a "straightforward" presentation of the case. But he was persuaded to rewrite the book, making it into more of a detective story, into a "chronicle of the experiences of one man who tried to get to the truth about the murder."[68] Garrison takes eagerly to the genre, and his self-stylization as a real-life Philip Marlowe carries over into *JFK*, with its heroic portrayal of the rugged individualist detective. In both the book and the film the lone gunman theory is rigorously repudiated, only for its underlying assumption about agency to return in a displaced form as Garrison's Lone Detective. In keeping with its hard-boiled detective fiction fantasies of lone agency, the film contains many other noirish elements, not least in its lighting: Garrison (played by Kevin Costner) is frequently haloed by a glaring brightness, whose obvious connotations of moral and intellectual clarity are contrasted with the murky scenes of the New Orleans "gay underworld" and the shadowy glimpses of Pentagon meetings.

There is, however, a narrative countercurrent in *JFK* which works against this hard-boiled model of historical agency and causality. The detective fiction structure which gives the film its forward-moving pace and narrative drive towards the "resolution" of the case in the final courtroom scene also produces a backwards-spiraling movement which undermines and delays its narrative drive. In conventional detective fiction the episodes of the investigation lead on teleologically to the ending, set in motion and motivated by the desire to solve the initial crime.[69] But the ending is also a ghostly, anticipated presence at the beginning. It is the conclusion that allows the beginning of the sequence of events to be identified as such; only in a completed sequence can the significance of individual episodes be grasped as so many clues to the reconstruction of the underlying story. Once the ending has been reached, the presumption is that no incident or detail will appear arbitrary or accidental. The ending therefore seems to demand a return to the beginning, in order at last to insert all the confusing details into one coherent story.

In *JFK* there is indeed a gradual progression of discovery through the investigation to the revelations in the courtroom. The direction of the film, following the life of Garrison, seems to lead in a fairly obvious way from innocence to experience. But the final courtroom sequence pieces together and replays the fragments of the assassination with which the film began. The ending thus begins to revise and color the beginning—quite literally. The initial chaos of the opening scene's black and white camera montage of gunshots in Dealey Plaza retroactively transforms itself into the comparative narrative clarity and color of the Zapruder film, which Garrison shows to the jurors. What seem like unintelligible and meaningless fragments at the beginning are coalesced into significance by Garrison's narrative commentary at the end of the film. In effect the film operates a three hour long game of hide-and-seek with its viewers, since the opening sequence takes us up to the very moment before the climactic fatal head shot, which is then only shown in the film's climax in the courtroom. The ending thus spreads its influence backwards over the narrative, initiating a retrograde movement that undermines the strong end-orientation of classic narrative plotting. As much as the opening event of the assassination determines the chain of detection, those events are themselves replotted by the subsequent detection; the beginning determines the ending, but it is the ending that shapes the beginning as a necessary origin.

In this way, Stone's *JFK* operates on an Oedipal logic. In *Oedipus Rex*, the murder of the father-king is the episode that sets in motion future events, including the forward-moving process of detection. In *JFK* Kennedy's death likewise results in Garrison's investigation. It also is the unknown origin behind Garrison's current sexual and political dissatisfaction, becoming a necessary but hidden cause which works out its logic in the course of the film.

But in *JFK* there is another narrative drive in play whose influence seeps backwards from the ending. The original murder in both Stone's film and *Oedipus Rex* is not merely a causal origin, but also a symbolically and aesthetically necessary act, demanded by the narrative coherence of the plot. In Sophocles' drama, instead of a prior event being the cause of significance for subsequent happenings, it is as if the unbearable significance felt by Oedipus in the present of the play "causes" him to imaginatively posit the original event. Meaning, as Jonathan Culler explains, "is not the effect of a prior event but its cause."[70] Similarly in *JFK* we see how Garrison feels the need to posit a grand, tragic event, an origin for the decline of both Jim Garrison and America. The state of decline felt by Garrison is so pronounced that only a correspondingly momentous original murder can do justice to the grandeur of his feelings. In *JFK*, the rhetoric of treason and the references to Kennedy as Hamlet Senior are matched only by the John Williams score, whose bombastic, funereal title music underlines the way in which the film's rhetoric pointedly recreates JFK as the fallen warrior-king.

The Oedipal subtext of the assassination produces a disturbance not only in the causal logic of historical action, but also in the "proper" teleological path of Garrison's sexuality. In *JFK*, one effect of the assassination is Garrison's loss of heterosexual desire for his wife, played by Sissy Spacek. She complains that he cares more about Kennedy than herself, as he sits up all night, poring over the details of the Warren Commission Report with fetishistic interest. The homoerotic desire that Stone's Garrison seems to feel for Kennedy (but can't address directly) manifests itself in two ways. The first is in Garrison's Hamlet-like obsession for the figure whom he eulogizes in speech as the "slain father-leader," a retrospective idealization of the young, beautiful President. The second way in which a repressed homosexuality returns to haunt the case is the emphasis Garrison places on the perversion of the New Orleans conspirators. Although *On the Trail of the Assassins* hardly makes reference to the New Orleans gay underworld, Stone lavishes much visual attention—a parallel form of fetishism—on the scene of the confusedly intertwined and decadent bodies of Shaw, Ferrie (two of the principal conspirators) and a black servant, filmed in close-up and edited into a frenzied montage.[71] The strength of Garrison's case in the film seems to depend on proving the improper connections between Shaw and the CIA in Washington. But the film insinuates that the improper connections were not the complex association of military and industrial vested interests, but the "perverted" sexual coupling of the conspirators. The film thus presents homosexual association as both the *result* of the assassination (in Garrison's fixation on the fallen father-king, and his loss of desire for his wife), and also the *cause* of the assassination. For Stone, the assassination becomes the event that un-manned America. But the weight of repressed homosexual desire felt by Garrison in the present of the film also leads him to posit retrospectively the assassination as the slaying of a father-king by the primal (homosexual) horde. In summary, then, it might be said that the effects of the assassination "produces" this particular grand conspiracy theory of the assassination as its cause. As much as Stone's film tries to assert its coherence and teleological clarity, it is repeatedly undermined by a second narrative drive which inverts cause and effect. The more it tries to suppress this narrative counter-current, the more it disrupts the manifest story with moments of rhetorical and visual excess.

Third Line

In hindsight it might seem obvious that Stone's career as a film-maker was leading up to *JFK*. It features as both the logical culmination and the hidden origin of his conviction that Vietnam was the event that un-manned America. In *Born on the Fourth of July* (1989), for example, Vietnam is the episode that induces the impotence of the Ron Kovic character, a patriotic young soldier who returns from Vietnam physically, sexually and emotionally paralyzed. *JFK* thus acts as both a prequel and a postscript to

Born on the Fourth of July, in its insistence on Vietnam as both the result *and* a cause of homosexual plotting.

The Kennedy assassination plays a similar topsy-turvy role in the career of other major contemporary American storytellers, albeit in different guises. It comes as no surprise, for example, that James Ellroy's obsession with low-life violence and intrigue should eventually find its logical culmination in *American Tabloid*, his 1995 novel which segues neatly into the previous novels in his LA trilogy. Likewise, Norman Mailer's lifelong imaginative interest in the hidden existential power of the famous and infamous came to the surface, as we have seen, in *Harlot's Ghost*. Indeed, it is only with *Oswald's Tale* that Mailer finally manages to put his finger on the absent presence of the assassination that has been there all along. For Mailer the conspiracy-infused shooting of the President forms the unacknowledged origin but also the logical culmination of his fixation on masculine violence, responsibility and desire. It finally crystallizes thematic concerns which had been shaping his writing all along.

For more than any other writer, though, Don DeLillo's career is intimately entwined with the Kennedy assassination. The JFK shooting and its surrounding culture of conspiracy have haunted DeLillo's career as a writer, and it might be argued that its influence and iconography are present in one form or another throughout his work, from the drive through Dealey Plaza in the final scene of his first novel, *Americana*, to the underground screening of the Zapruder footage in *Underworld*, his latest novel. DeLillo first tackled the assassination directly, however, in an essay for *Rolling Stone* magazine on the twenty-fifth anniversary of the case. Like Ellroy and Mailer, DeLillo finds in the assassination the emblematic story of America itself, entitling his article "American Blood."

In interview DeLillo has discussed how the assassination played a key role in his formation as a writer:

DECURTIS: The Kennedy assassination seems perfectly in line with the concerns of your fiction. Do you feel you could have invented it if it hadn't happened?

DELILLO: Maybe it invented me ... As I was working on *Libra*, it occurred to me that a lot of tendencies in my first eight novels seemed to me to be collecting around the dark center of the assassination. So it's possible I wouldn't have become the kind of writer I am if it weren't for the assassination.[72]

While DeLillo claims the shooting invented him as a writer, he also suggests that it was something waiting to be invented by him as the teleological conclusion of the thematic momentum building throughout his œuvre. On the one hand, then, the Kennedy assassination acted as an initial spur to creativity whose true import remained obscure. On the other hand, it was only during the writing of *Libra* that the assassination belatedly emerged as a thematically necessary moment, around which DeLillo's career as a writer of postmodern paranoid thrillers coalesced.

It is the tension between these two positions that is vital to DeLillo's treatment of the assassination and its conspiracy theories. Whereas *JFK* tries to suppress its dual narrative logic of origin and culmination, *Libra* highlights the contradictory movement of rupture and continuity. And where Stone's film displaces the sense of strangeness into a psychosexual Oedipal drama, DeLillo's novel confronts the uncanniness in terms of causality, agency and identity head on. Like Stone, DeLillo received harsh criticisms for his novel about the assassination. George Will, for example, writing in *The Washington Post*, accused DeLillo of being a "bad citizen" and a "literary vandal" for creating a fictionalized and conspiratorial version of American history.[73] But, unlike *JFK*, *Libra* evokes the narrative style and coherent causality of a conspiracy theory, only to expressly undermine it with an attention to the coincidence and confusion surrounding the case.

The complex narrative structure of DeLillo's novel draws attention to the paradoxes of causality that we find in his account of the assassination's role in his career. *Libra* is structured by two main plot lines. On the one hand, there is the story of Lee Harvey Oswald, a confused yet passionate young man who, in order to get Cuba to take an interest in him, decides—with a little prompting from the "real" conspiracy—to take a potshot at the President. The second plot line features a conspiracy of renegade CIA operatives who want to get Cuba back on the agenda, and so decide to stage a (failed) assassination attempt whose deliberately planted clues will point back to pro-Castro interests. The two plot lines seem to converge inexorably, but in the final analysis they do not cohere. The even-numbered chapters of *Libra* feature the preparations of the conspirators, and carry as titles dates in the months leading up to 22 November: "26 April," "20 May," etc. The odd chapters, on the other hand, consist of episodes from Lee Oswald's life, and are headed by place-names: "In the Bronx," "In New Orleans," and so on. The conspiracy plot is marked by a chronological tightening, as the increment between dates becomes less and less in the approach to 22 November. But the Oswald chapters drift geographically, only hitting upon Dallas at the end, as if by accident.

In DeLillo's version the process by which Oswald ends up on the conspirators' doorstep is far from obvious. The hapless patsy drifts through life, and it is only through a long series of chance connections and events that he ends up in New Orleans in the office of Guy Banister, the lynchpin between the CIA conspirators and the Cuban exiles. The conspirators are then forced to realize that "it was no longer possible to hide from the fact that Lee Oswald existed independent of the plot."[74] Most of the conspirators refuse to dwell on the strangeness of this fact, but it is vitally important for David Ferrie, the manic, gay, ex-airline pilot and on–off associate of Banister, Cuban exiles and mobsters, and, in DeLillo's rendering, a believer in the all-pervasive power of coincidence. In *Libra* Ferrie comments on these subterranean connections between the two plot lines:

> "Think of two parallel lines," he said. "One is the life of Lee H. Oswald. One is the conspiracy to kill the President. What bridges the space between them? What makes a connection inevitable? There is a third line. It comes out of dreams, visions, intuitions, prayers, out of the deepest levels of the self. It's not generated by cause and effect like the other two lines. It's a line that cuts across causality, cuts across time. It has no history that we can recognize or understand, but it forces a connection."
>
> (*L*, 339)

Ferrie goes on to inform Oswald that "they" are interested in the "signs that you exist," or, in other words, "evidence that Lee Oswald matches the cardboard cutout they've been shaping all along" (*L*, 330). Instead of exclusively defending one side or the other, DeLillo's novel devotes significant attention to the "third line" that connects coincidence and conspiracy. It explores dreams, symbols, uncanny connections and doublings, and even the eerily suggestive and condensed "poetry" of Oswald's odd dyslexic misspellings and aliases. It suggests that, at a fundamental level, the conspiratorial has become inseparable from the coincidental, or, more accurately, that we need to read coincidences *as if* they were signs of a conspiracy, without necessarily equating the two.[75]

Yet *Libra* also offers a convincing, realistic explanation for the artificiality which hovers over much of the evidence, with its scenes of the CIA plotters fabricating clues to a fictional patsy. Much to the surprise of the conspirators who had been inventing him out of "pocket litter" (*L*, 145), it turns out that Oswald actually exists, matching his pre-scripted double. DeLillo's novel thus performs a complicated double bluff: having alerted the reader to the inherent fictionality of the case, and having provided a rational and causal explanation for that sense of uncanniness, it then turns out that Oswald's entrance into the conspiracy is after all the result of a series of inexplicable coincidences. The rational, causal explanation is left hovering, both necessary and redundant, placed, as it were, *sous rature*.

In addition to the two main plot lines of lone assassin and conspiracy, *Libra* contains another form of "third line," namely the scenes describing Nicholas Branch, a retired CIA researcher, commissioned by the Agency to write the secret history of the assassination. Branch in theory has unlimited access to every conceivable piece of evidence, no matter how classified, holding out the promise of the kind of epistemological certainty that can only remain a fantasy for many conspiracy buffs. But even after thirty years Branch has not got beyond the note-taking stage, and the evidence keeps pouring in to his little home office, threatening to "branch out" endlessly:

> This is the room of theories, the room of growing old. Branch wonders if he ought to despair of ever getting to the end … Branch must study everything. He is in too deep to be selective … The truth is he hasn't written all that much. He has extensive and overlapping notes—notes in three-foot drifts, all these years of notes. But of actual finished prose, there is precious little. It is impossible to stop assembling data. The stuff keeps coming in.
>
> (L, 59)

Branch's research is in limbo and seems destined to remain that way. Although he recognizes the need for certainty and closure, he refuses to give in prematurely to cheap coincidences and paranoia. "He is writing a history," we are told, "not a study of the ways in which people succumb to paranoia" (L, 59). Despite his insistence that "there is enough mystery in the facts as we know them, enough of conspiracy, coincidence, loose ends, dead ends, multiple interpretations" to make inventing a "grand and masterful scheme" unnecessary, Branch nevertheless concedes that there is "endless suggestiveness" in the details. Even if he stops short of a "plot that reaches flawlessly in a dozen directions," he is forced to admit that "the cases do resonate, don't they?" (L, 59).

In interview DeLillo has claimed—somewhat disingenuously—that fiction "rescues history from its confusions" in order to provide a form of "redemptive truth" and "a sense that we've arrived at a resolution."[76] But by also concentrating on the "rhythms and symmetries that we simply don't encounter elsewhere" (DeLillo's other claim for the function of the novel), *Libra* embraces the possibility that closure and certainty are no more than convenient fictions. In effect it makes Nicholas Branches of us all.

Aberration in the Heartland of the Real

As well as exploring the territory between causality and contingency, *Libra* also investigates forms of agency that lie between the opposite poles of lone gunman theories and conspiracy theories. With the constant displacing and reframing of agency and double agency in the novel, Oswald is both a lone agent in control of his actions (taking a potshot to help poor little Cuba), and a pawn of the larger conspiracy. In this way, *Libra* revives the "lone gunman" option, only to create an Oswald who is less "alone" than we would ever have imagined, as he is reinserted into the vast social and textual fabric of postmodern America.

In *Libra* the very moment of the shooting is presented as a rupture in the chain of both causality and agency. The scene is narrated through the eyes of Oswald, as he peers through the scope on his rifle in the sixth-floor window of the School Book Depository. In theory this should provide the ideal narrative vantage point from which to produce a conclusive interpretation of the case (Oswald is either guilty or he's not), but instead the text hovers somewhere between a lone gunman and a conspiracy theory. We see Oswald fire off the first two rounds, injuring both the President and Governor Connally, and just as he is squeezing the trigger for what should be the third and fatal shot, the President's head explodes in the viewfinder:

> Lee was about to squeeze off the third round, he was in the act, he was actually pressing the trigger.
> The light was so clear it was heartbreaking.
> There was a white burst in the middle of the frame. A terrible splash, a burst. Something came blazing off the President's head. He was slammed back, surrounded all in dust and haze. Then suddenly clear again, down and still in his seat. Oh he's dead he's dead.
> Lee raised his head from the scope, looking right.
>
> (*L*, 400)

At first neither the reader nor Oswald realize what has happened. There's no attribution of agency or causality in the time-stopping frame-by-frame sentences, but then we realize that someone else has fired the shot. The narrative emphasizes that Oswald is "in the act," even that he is "actually pressing the trigger," but the act is not what he intended. Between his intention and someone else's conspiracy an unclosable gap has opened up. In the infinitesimal moment it takes to pull a trigger, it turns out that Oswald is neither fully in control of his own actions, nor entirely a pawn in someone else's game. In *The X-Files*, after six years of discovering that there is often a convoluted and obscured connection between cause and effect, Agent Mulder is forced to recognize that ironies of agency have become permanent, with "the inextricable relationships in our lives that are neither accidental nor somehow within our control, either."[77]

In the larger scheme of American history, for DeLillo the assassination belatedly comes to function as not merely a warp in Oswald's sense of agency, but as "an aberration in the heartland of the real" (*L*, 15), in Branch's words. In the interview conducted during the twenty-fifth anniversary of the assassination, DeLillo explained that "we've all come to feel that what's been missing over these past twenty-five years is a sense of manageable reality. Much of that feeling can be traced to that one moment in Dallas."[78] Looked at one way, DeLillo's comment is merely another expression of a sense of bereavement and lack of direction that has plagued America in recent decades; in *Libra* the assassination is described as the "seven seconds that broke the back of the American century" (*L*, 181). But characterizing the death of the President as an aberration in the heartland of the real also suggests a far more complex reading of contemporary history. In short, the assassination paradoxically comes to represent the causal origin of a rupture of "manageable" causality.

In his preparatory essay in *Rolling Stone* magazine, DeLillo suggests that even for the conspiracy theorist (or perhaps, *especially* for the conspiracy theorist) the case is marked as much by inconsistency and coincidence as it is by coherence and causality. He even suggests that the elemental physics of the case is cast into doubt, such that we are "almost forced to question the basic suppositions we make about our world of light and shadow, solid objects and ordinary sounds"—though it is perhaps more a question of there being no higher level of authority to appeal to when scientific experts disagree about the fundamental "facts" of the case.[79] For DeLillo further investigation of the case leads not to increasing certainty, but to a spiraling skepticism. The more you look, the more the case reveals not the hidden connections of a conspiracy, but the uncanny compressions and the unfathomably complex subterranean connections of everyday America.

In many ways *Libra* is a reading not of the assassination events but their representation in the Warren Commission Report, which the narrator describes epigrammatically as "the megaton novel James Joyce would have written if he'd moved to Iowa City and lived to be a hundred" (*L*, 181). For DeLillo the true meaning of the Report is not its revelations or even its significant omissions about any conspiracy plot, but the accidental insight it affords into the trivia of everyday life and the otherwise invisible interconnections of America:

> There are endless aspects, endless connections, between Jack Ruby and organized crime and anti-Castro groups and on and on for ever. And these links and connections would have been totally unrevealed if there had not been an assassination. That's what the assassination did; it cast a strong light on a part of the culture that nobody was aware of.[80]

Libra's view of recent American history reverses the usual tendency of conspiracy theories to align every last detail into a coherent metanarrative of covert power. Significantly, DeLillo took issue with Stone's *JFK*, because it offered not much more than a "particular type of nostalgia: the nostalgia for a master plan, the conspiracy which explains everything."[81] In *Libra*, on the other hand, an inquiry into the assassination does reveal the hidden sources of power, but, as the narrator in Pynchon's *Gravity's Rainbow* puts it, "power sources ... and distribution networks we were never taught, routes of power our teachers never imagined, or were encouraged to avoid."[82]

What amazes Nicholas Branch about the Warren Commission Report is that "everything is here":

> Baptismal records, report cards, postcards, divorce petitions, canceled checks, daily timesheets, tax returns, property lists, postoperative x-rays, photos of knotted string, thousands of pages of testimony, of voices droning in hearing rooms in old courthouse buildings, an incredible haul of human utterance.
>
> (L, 181)

There is no easy division to be made between irrelevant foreground minutiae and the real underlying forces of history: whatever there is, it's all here on the surface, both intensely significant and impossibly trivial at the same time. Pulling on the thread of the assassination reveals not the last thirty years of American history, but the entirety of America, from photos of Oswald's pubic hair to old shoes and pyjama tops. The death of a President brings with it not only a disruption in manageable causality, but also the dissipation of the biographical subject, as the agency and identity of the assassin (and indeed all those involved) are dispersed amid the welter of trivial evidence.

The Primal Scene of Postmodernism

In *Libra* the profusion of evidence to the mystery that is America is not to be found buried in hidden clues, but is immanent in the everyday world of glossy surfaces—in what Frank Lentricchia has called "the environment of the image."[83] The novel is alive to both the endless mediation of the assassination after the event (with, for example, Beryl Parmenter watching the continuous reruns on television of Ruby shooting Oswald), and the saturation of images and representations in the environment in which the action takes place. Clichés and brand-names form part of the interior monologue of characters whose inner lives are saturated with the external world of television, films and books. Oswald carries out the shooting at the same time as imagining the event on TV, and he tries—unsuccessfully—to live his life through the narrative style of pulp thrillers and movies. For Oswald representation becomes the guarantor of a reality that is but a ghost of itself. He becomes a fictional character in his own life that is populated with cinematic representations: "Lee walked home ... past hundreds of tourists and conventioneers who thronged in the light rain like people in a newsreel" (L, 40); and later we learn that, "He watches John Wayne talk and laugh. It's remarkable to see the screen laugh repeated in life. The man is doubly real" (L, 93). Oswald becomes the ultimate simulacrum, a series of endless copies, doubles and aliases without a stable original. "In the end," as DeLillo explains, "citing names and name reversals and variants, citing the possibility that he worked for one agency while appearing to work for another (whether he knew it or not, and that is the final modern touch), we are compelled to say that Oswald was his own double."[84] The crowd at Love Field airport in Dallas, for example, is likewise thrilled to find that Kennedy is also his own double: he "looked like himself, like photographs" (*L*, 392).

In "American Blood" DeLillo argues that all the presidential assassination attempts since John Kennedy's have been thoroughly mediated. DeLillo looks in detail at the shooting of President Reagan by John Hinckley, a "self-created media event."[85] Hinckley, DeLillo points out, claims he was motivated by his obsessive watching of the film *Taxi Driver*, which was based on the case of Arthur Bremer, who, having watched *Clockwork Orange,* stalks first Richard Nixon then George Wallace. Caught up in a funhouse of representations, Hinckley shoots President Reagan, an event which was, as DeLillo describes it, "pure TV, a minicam improvization."[86]

In the world of presidential shootings since 1963 (an aberrational world which has become all too normal), things are only felt to be real if they resemble their representations. It might be argued that the Kennedy assassination ushered in the era of the simulacrum, in which reality becomes a cheap copy of an original that itself seems to have lost all solidity. The genuine Zapruder footage might still have some residual aura of authenticity and power of shock (if only for the arbitration panel deciding the price the National Archives must pay for the original), but the endless repetition and retailing of the authentic work of art in the age of digital reproduction have begun to undermine its status and its effect. The Sixth Floor Museum in Dallas, for example, carefully recreates out of fully authentic-looking period details the scene the police discovered at the south-east window minutes after the assassination, only to reassure visitors that none of the exhibits are originals. In a similar fashion, as well as *JFK*'s recreation of actual documentary footage such as the live television broadcast of Ruby gunning down Oswald, it also reshoots seemingly true-life footage for which no original exists—the shadowy, handheld scene of top-level generals plotting the assassination being the most notorious example. Perhaps the same could be said of the original assassination: with the proliferation of second-by-second accounts of what took place in Dealey Plaza, access to the brute event before or outside of its endless mediated versions proves to be an illusory goal. On the twenty-fifth anniversary of the assassination crowds gathered in Dealey Plaza, as they do every year, in a form of unofficial memorial ceremony. Some were taking photos of people taking photos, while others held up "original" photos from 1963 in order to see how the real thing lived up to its representations; everywhere tourists and sympathizers jostled with the TV cameras recording the "event."[87] For Fredric Jameson the assassination is significant less for the horror of the event itself or even for what it says about Kennedy's popularity, than for its role as the "inaugural event" of the 1960s and all that decade signifies. The really important outcome of that television-saturated weekend of the assassination is not so much a national loss of innocence as "a new collective experience of reception."[88] The assassination led to the "coming of age of the whole media culture" in a "prodigious new display of synchronicity and a communicational situation that amounted to a dialectical leap over anything hitherto suspected." For Jameson, as for DeLillo, subsequent television events such as the instant playbacks of the Reagan shooting or the *Challenger* disaster were mere copies of that defining moment of endless repetition.[89]

It is plausible to argue that with the Kennedy assassination America entered a new mode of being and perception. DeLillo sums up this argument about the causal origin of the end of coherent causality:

> What has become unraveled since that afternoon in Dallas is not the plot, of course, not the dense mass of characters and events, but the sense of a coherent reality most of us shared. We seem from that moment to have entered a world of randomness and ambiguity, a world totally modern in the way it shades into the century's "emptiest" literature, the study of what is uncertain and unresolved in our lives, the literature of estrangement and silence.[90]

This "totally modern" world with its "'emptiest'" of literature is perhaps more commonly labeled postmodern. And, according to DeLillo, it is the conspiracy theorists of the Kennedy and other assassinations who have forced us to recognize the strangeness of this new world order, to recognize the Warren Commission Report, in the words of one commentator, as one of "the seminal texts of the Postmodernist era"[91]:

> The valuable work of [conspiracy] theorists has shown us the dark possibilities, prodded us to admit to ourselves the difficult truths of the matter. No simple solution, no respite from mystery and chronic suspicion. Conspiracy is now the true faith.[92]

Conspiracy theories about the Kennedy assassination have contributed to the larger hermeneutic of suspicion characteristic of postmodern culture, but they have done so by accidentally drawing attention to the lack of coherence and coordination in the plot of history. "The assassination of John F. Kennedy in 1963," a contributor to the volume *Assassination Science* concludes weightily, "marks the beginning of the Post-Modern period in the United States ... The 'babble of tongues' that comprises the historiography on the assassination is only a symptom of this Post-Modern mindset."[93]

In many ways, then, the story of how this traumatic event and its attendant culture of conspiracy has reshaped American history is deeply paradoxical. As we have seen, the assassination comes to represent the causal origin of a rupture in the "manageable" logic of historical causality. In effect it inspires an endless proliferation of narratives about the impossibility of coherent narratives. The contradictory, dual narrative logic which structures both the careers and the narrative creations of Stone, DeLillo and others also structures the story of the wider significance of the case in recent American history. On the one hand the assassination functions as the actual inaugural event in the society of the spectacle which operates through an inexhaustible hermeneutic of suspicion. On the other hand, it is only in the light of subsequent de-realized "minicam" versions of presidential assassination attempts that we come to recognize the significance of the Kennedy assassination as the symbolic event that led to the post-modernization of American history. In other words, it is only with the hypervisibility of revelation that has gathered pace since Watergate that we can backdate the climate of suspicion to November 1963, just as conspiracy theorists try to "reverse engineer" all of recent history to those fatal seven seconds in Dallas.

It is in this light that we can understand Jean Baudrillard's paradoxical account of the translation of political power into its own simulation. For Baudrillard, the Kennedy assassination only comes to take on the contours of "originality" with the discovery of its fake copies:

> Power can stage its own murder to rediscover a glimmer of existence and legitimacy. Thus with the American presidents: the Kennedys are murdered because they still have a political dimension. Others—Johnson, Nixon, Ford—only had a right to puppet attempts, to simulated murders. But they nevertheless needed that aura of an artificial menace in order to conceal that they were nothing other than mannequins of power.[94]

There is a measure of despairing nostalgia in Baudrillard's attempt to reground a coherent narrative of political power in a version of the innocence-to-experience story. It is only in the vertigo of interpretations surrounding Watergate that Baudrillard can belatedly posit the Kennedy assassinations as the real deal, and yet that vertigo is itself partly an effect of the culture of conspiracy that emerged from the Kennedy assassination. Characterizing the Kennedy assassination as the last moment of solid ground before the hermeneutic abyss opens up is a convenient fiction, a fictional moment of origin that is needed to stabilize the subsequent account of political and epistemological instability. Like many conspiracy theories about the Kennedy case, Baudrillard's account of the simulacrum of power attempts to create a coherent causal narrative even as it draws attention to the impossibility of telling such stories any more.

In many ways, then, the assassination of President Kennedy has come to function as the primal scene of postmodernism. It is represented as an initial moment of trauma that ruptured the nation's more innocent years, and which in retrospect has come to be seen as the origin for present woes. The effects of a primal scene, Freud argued, might not necessarily be felt at the time, but it becomes a hidden source of motivation in subsequent psychic events. In his revised version of the Wolfman case history, however, Freud suggested that a primal scene is not so much an actual event that causes future troubles as it is a symbolically necessary fiction of origin summoned up in the present. We might say that in a similar fashion the Kennedy assassination was indeed a highly charged event at the time, but it is only in subsequent decades that it has come to be figured as the moment of cataclysmic rupture in the course of American history. Like a primal scene, then, the traumatic seven seconds in Dallas are not so much an originating cause as an effect of future effects, an event that would have had to be invented had it not actually happened.

As we have seen, in accounts of postmodernism from Baudrillard to Jameson the highly mediated death of JFK represents the limit case before things became (in DeLillo's term) unmanageable. In this way, the confusing and contradictory events in Dealey Plaza which have been reshot and retold in countless media repetitions come to serve as an appropriate primal scene for the cultural logic of late capitalism that is dominated by the simulated spectacle. The increasing sense of doubt about even the most basic of facts and causal connections also makes the Kennedy case a fitting myth of origin for a cultural logic marked by its skepticism about the authoritative power of narrative. The proliferation of narratives about the conspiratorial activities of the authorities have in effect helped undermine the authority of narrative. In this way, the accumulated conspiratorial focus on the case over the last four decades has contributed to an ineradicable sense of strangeness, mystery and skepticism, making the assassination a fitting fountainhead for a widespread sense of paranoia, albeit very different to the "paranoid style" outlined by Richard Hofstadter.

The culture of conspiracy surrounding the Kennedy case is therefore so enduring, not because it provides a compensatory sense of closure and coherence, nor even because it led to a loss of innocence, but because it is very much in tune with a postmodern distrust of final narrative solutions. Indeed, as theoretical accounts of postmodern literature and film suggest, the culture of paranoia is inseparable from the culture of postmodernism, not least because they share a paradoxical fiction of origin in the Kennedy assassination.

3

THE PROBLEM WITH NO NAME: FEMINISM AND THE FIGURATION OF CONSPIRACY

Since the Industrial Revolution, middle-class Western women have been controlled by ideals and stereotypes as much as by material constraints. This situation, unique to this group, means that analyses that trace "cultural conspiracies" are uniquely plausible in relation to them.

(Naomi Wolf, *The Beauty Myth*)

"There's *something*, there's *got* to be," she said. "Go take a look. Would you do that, please? She's got her bust shoved out to here, and her behind girdled down to practically nothing! The house is like a commercial. Like Carol's, and Donna's, and Kit Sundersen's!"

"She had to clean it sooner or later; it was a pigsty."

"She's *changed*, Walter! She doesn't *talk* the same, she doesn't *think* the same—and I'm not going to wait around for it to happen to me!"

(Ira Levin, *The Stepford Wives*)

Some of the conspiracy theories we have been dealing with so far end up multiplying into elaborate and highly detailed accounts. From the Kennedy assassination to *The X-Files*, these baroque speculations often threaten to engulf everything in their omnivorous drive to interpretation. Many Americans, however, use conspiratorial rhetoric without ever developing fully formed conspiracy theories, or fully subscribing to the theories they do develop. The figuration of conspiracy articulates otherwise uncoordinated suspicions that daily life is controlled by larger, unseen forces which cannot be the result of mere coincidence. These fears hover somewhere between the literal and the metaphorical, between the conviction that nothing short of a conspiracy theory could account for the present situation, and the doubt that there is actually a conspiracy at work. The question of just how literally these accusations are meant to be taken can sometimes become crucial in people's struggle to understand and give

117

expression to the world around them. In the struggle to give a name to—and find someone to blame for—what Betty Friedan famously called the "problem with no name," feminist writers have often turned to conspiratorial rhetoric.

In 1990 Naomi Wolf scored a popular hit with *The Beauty Myth*, an analysis of how women still suffered from oppression, despite decades of seeming progress with the women's movement. Having outlined in the introduction the wiles of the "now conscious market manipulation" of the diet, cosmetics, and pornography industries, Naomi Wolf insists that "this is not a conspiracy theory."[1] And, having described how the "ideology that makes women feel 'worth less' was urgently needed to counteract the way feminism had begun to make us feel worth more," she then announces that this view "does not require a conspiracy." Likewise, in the introduction to *Backlash*, the book that consolidated the analysis of contemporary antifeminism started in *The Beauty Myth*, Susan Faludi performs a similar rhetorical maneuver. Having just given a brief overview of the many elements of the backlash that her book is to deal with, she then warns the reader that "the backlash is not a conspiracy."[2]

Why should writers like Wolf and Faludi insist so strongly that their analysis does not amount to a conspiracy theory? Metaphors of conspiracy, I want to suggest, have played an important role within a certain trajectory of popular American feminist writing over the last thirty years in its struggle to come to terms with—and come up with terms for—the "problem with no name."[3] On the one hand, conspiracy tropes have been crucial not only in organizing questions of blame, responsibility and agency, but also in linking the personal and the political in one transcoding metaphor around which a women's movement might coalesce. On the other hand, some academic feminists of a poststructuralist bent have in recent years taken issue with popular feminism in general and so-called victim feminism in particular, precisely because they rely on a model of social causation which is unnecessarily conspiratorial. This chapter explores how the figuration of conspiracy has helped produce a coherent women's movement, before going on to look at how it has also become the source of division between feminist thinkers.

The Feminine Mystique

Betty Friedan's *The Feminine Mystique* was an immediate success on its publication in 1963, staying on the *New York Times* bestseller list for nearly two years. Its popularity was no doubt due in part to its lively style: in many places the book reads like a thriller, with Friedan as the lone detective chasing up the clues to the mysterious mystique.[4] She describes how she listened to middle-class housewives talking about their dissatisfactions with married life, until "gradually I came to realize that the problem that has no name was shared by countless women in America."[5] At the end of her first foray into suburbia, for example, she writes that:

> I reported back to my guide [a psychoanalyst] and said that while all four seemed "fulfilled" women, none were full-time housewives and one, after all, was a member of his own profession. "That's a coincidence with those four," he said. But I wondered if it *was* a coincidence.
>
> (FM, 205)

As the search continues, so the little voice of doubt—presumably the one which also speaks to Raymond Chandler's Marlowe—becomes more insistent, as the pieces of the puzzle fit together:

> These were fine, intelligent American women, to be envied for their homes, husbands, children, and for their personal gifts of mind and spirit. Why were so many of them driven women? Later, when I saw this same pattern repeated over and over again in similar suburbs, I knew it could hardly be a coincidence.
>
> (FM, 207)

Friedan reads coincidence as signs of a conspiracy. She finds "many clues by talking to suburban doctors, gynecologists, obstetricians, child-guidance clinicians, pediatricians, high-school guidance counsellors, college professors, marriage counselors, psychiatrists, and ministers" (FM, 28). What the clues reveal is a concerted effort by welfare, educational and media institutions to manipulate women in the postwar period into returning to a life of domesticity, despite the gains which Friedan attributes to the "first wave" of late Victorian and early twentieth-century feminism.

In trying to "fit together the puzzle of women's retreat to home" (FM, 181), Friedan develops the notion of the feminine mystique. It amounts to a devastating, tailor-made ideology, part of a cunning and ruthlessly efficient program to persuade women to forgo self-fulfilment through careers in favor of homemaking and childrearing. Friedan describes, for example, how "Freudian theories were used to brainwash two generations of educated American women" (FM, 109). Even more disturbing, the feminine mystique has brainwashed American educators (FM, 155), those very college professors who themselves brainwashed their women students into expecting no more than a home and a husband out of life.

In developing an account of a conspiracy to "brainwash" American women into domesticity, Friedan draws on a buzzword of Cold War politics. The word (which is a translation of a Chinese phrase) came into popular usage in the USA in the wake of the scandal that only Americans

119

among the Allied troops captured in Korea had apparently succumbed to the enemy program of propaganda and indoctrination. Although a U.S. Army report on the incident concluded that it was mainly poor morale that accounted for the disproportionate rate of collaboration in the American contingent, it was popularly believed that brainwashing must be a deadly efficient technique of psychological warfare.[6] The term conferred a scientific legitimacy on suspicions that no American soldier in his right mind would wittingly choose the alien ideology of Communism; the only thing that could account for the shocking sight of American servicemen co-operating with the enemy was the belief that their minds had been taken over by force. The concept of brainwashing became popularized in novels and films such as *The Manchurian Candidate* (1959/1962), which portrayed the assassination of a presidential candidate by a brainwashed U.S. army officer.

In *The Feminine Mystique* the idea of brainwashing creates a picture of women as innocent victims of a scientific process of mind manipulation by external forces. Friedan describes "American housewives around forty [who] have the same dull lifeless look" (*FM*, 222); similarly, she writes about the "vacant sleepwalking quality in a thirteen year-old girl in a Westchester suburb," a zombified child who acted "like a puppet with someone else pulling the strings" (*FM*, 246). These descriptions were familiar from accounts of the brainwashed soldiers in Korea. In the same way that accounts of brainwashing in Korea played down un-American leanings, so too does Friedan's book imply that any undesirable beliefs which would seem contrary to the best interests of women (as defined by Friedan) must have been planted into their brains by the feminine mystique. Although Friedan seems to open up the possibility that women might have treasonous desires, the notion of external infiltration in fact serves only to confirm her faith in the fundamental innocence and rationality of women. "It is easy to see the concrete details that trap the suburban housewife," Friedan writes. "But the chains that bind her in her trap are chains that are made up of mistaken ideas and misinterpreted facts, of incomplete truths and unreal choices" (*FM*, 28). The feminine mystique, on this view, is merely a set of false beliefs, which can easily be set straight once the relevant facts are produced. Not only is lengthier education conducive to more and better orgasms, Friedan claims, but it is the only thing that will really break these mind-forged manacles. Although she may be infiltrated by bad ideas, for which the media, the psychologists and the professors are to blame, the American housewife is still fundamentally her own woman: such is the hidden persuasion of *The Feminine Mystique*.

Yet at crucial moments in Friedan's text this conspiracy scenario—which relies on a clear separation of inside and outside, self and other, victim and perpetrator—becomes compromised. If a woman is brainwashed into the false ideals of the feminine mystique by external influence, Friedan suggests, then she could also be conditioned into accepting a "new identity." The concluding chapter of *The Feminine Mystique* adopts the paranoia-laden imagery of brainwashing in its proposals for the creation of the New Woman: "drastic steps must now be taken to re-educate the women who were deluded or cheated by the feminine mystique"; there is also talk of "a concentrated six-week summer course, a sort of intellectual 'shock-therapy'" (*FM*, 323–24). If positive images of femininity as much as negative ones are to be implanted from without, then there is precious little left that could constitute an essential core of authentic personality.[7] Despite the brisk optimism in Friedan's text, there remains an unacknowledged sense of a vague but pervasive conspiracy of malign forces hovering over women's lives.

Friedan goes on to acknowledge that "a mystique does not compel its own acceptance," suggesting that there must have been some form of collaboration:

> For the feminine mystique to have "brainwashed" American women of nonsexual human purposes for more than fifteen years, it must have filled real needs in those who seized on it for others and those who accepted it for themselves ... There were many needs, at this particular time in America, which made us pushovers for the mystique: needs so compelling that we suspended critical thought.
>
> (*FM*, 160)

The scare quotes around "brainwashed" signal an awareness that the idea of mind-manipulation is, after all, only a metaphor. The traditional, rigid conspiratorial division into Them and Us cannot be maintained, and Friedan must instead look to an account of the hegemonic orchestration of women's needs and desires. But these needs are "so compelling" that "critical thought" is suspended, making the acceptance of the feminine mystique a seduction scene in which a woman's desires are so intense that she is no longer able to think straight: she becomes a "pushover," an easy conquest. By implicitly reasserting a picture of women as victims of a male conspiracy, Friedan's rhetoric works as a containment strategy for the dangerous possibility that women might be cooperating with the enemy, that, in effect, women might be double agents rather than autonomous agents.

Though at times in danger of undermining itself, Friedan's appropriation of the Cold War language of a brainwashing conspiracy does succeed in producing a transcoding metaphor which conjoins the "personal" aspect of women's lives to the "political" realm of national issues. This strain of imagery forms an account of sexual politics which reinterprets all aspects of personal experience into a coherent causal story of patriarchal institutions conspiring to keep women trapped in domesticity. In many ways, then, Friedan's appropriation of Cold War scenarios formed a breakthrough for feminism in its recognition of the political dimension of personal experience.

What makes her use of these culturally available narratives even more problematic, however, is that at the same time *The Feminine Mystique* borrows from a Hollywood version of Cold War politics, it also develops an attack on the culture industry. Nowhere does Friedan revel more in the narrative technologies of the thriller than in the chapter in which she gains access to the secret files of an ad-agency boss. Friedan states clearly whom she holds responsible for the brainwashing of women. Contrary to what we might expect (given the vehemence of her attack on Freud), "the practice of psychoanalysis ... was not primarily responsible for the feminine mystique." It was, she declares, "the creation of writers and editors in the mass media, ad-agency motivation researchers, and behind them the popularizers and translators of Freudian thought" (*FM*, 111).

In seeking to lay the blame for social ills on a deliberate conspiracy by the practitioners and managers of the culture industry, Friedan participates in the line of analysis developed by the Frankfurt School and anti-Stalinist intellectuals such as Dwight MacDonald. More specifically, Friedan draws on *Hidden Persuaders*, Vance Packard's influential exposé of the advertising industry.[8] Like Packard, she is horrified at the potential power advertisers wield in shaping the hearts and minds of consumers. Where Packard emphasizes the clinical efficiency of the "ultra-modern techniques" of "Motivation Research" (which turn out to be no more than crass Freudian generalizations), so Friedan, as we have seen, lends a patina of scientific credibility to her argument with the adoption of the language of brainwashing. And just as Packard seems to believe every single claim about the efficacy of advertising made by the "admen" in their trade magazines, so too does Friedan repeat as fact the comments that are made to her "in confidence" by an anonymous source in the advertising industry. Both are in effect duped by the industry's own promotion of its influence.

Friedan emphasizes the gendered separation of agents and victims with her account, for example, of the systematic collaboration between the advertising industry and the editors of women's magazines. She is in no doubt as to the effectiveness of the advertising agency/women's magazine conspiracy to brainwash women:

> It all seems so ludicrous when you understand what they are up to. Perhaps the housewife has no one but herself to blame if she lets the manipulators flatter or threaten her into buying things that neither fill her family's needs nor her own. But if the ads and commercials are a clear case of *caveat emptor*, the same sexual sell disguised in the editorial content of a magazine or a television

program is both less ridiculous and more insidious. Here the
housewife is often an unaware victim.

(FM, 202)

Though tempted to blame women for (literally) buying into the feminine
mystique, Friedan is ultimately concerned to point out how the devious advertising campaigns are targeted specifically against women. The crowning
moment of realization in *The Feminine Mystique* comes with the discovery
that during the postwar period of rapid suburban expansion women spent
three-quarters of the household budget. Friedan therefore asks pointedly,
"why is it never said that the really crucial function, the really important
role that women serve as housewives is *to buy more things for the house*?"
(*FM*, 181). *The Feminine Mystique* works against the familiar disparagement
of mass culture as a feminizing force, with its argument that women are
not so much in league with the culture industry, as the victims of its brainwashing campaigns.

Despite the insistence with which this case is made, Friedan repudiates
the logic of conspiracy in a fashion similar to the disavowals by Wolf and
Faludi. Halfway through the book, Friedan finally fits the last piece of the
puzzle together, realizing that "somehow, somewhere, someone must have
figured out that women will buy more things if they are kept in the under-
used, nameless-yearning, energy-to-get-rid-of-state of being housewives"
(*FM*, 181). Just in case we might begin to expect a place, date, and face to
be fitted to that anonymous "figuring out," Friedan cautions us that "it
was not an economic conspiracy directed against women." Similarly,
having spelled out the insidious uses to which pseudo-Freudian theories
were put in 1950s America, Friedan disavows the possibility that they
amount to a conspiracy. "It would be ridiculous," she admonishes the
reader, "to suggest that the way the Freudian theories were used to brainwash two generations of educated American women was part of a psychoanalytical conspiracy" (*FM*, 109).

But why is Friedan so adamant in rejecting the notion of a conspiracy?
Her vehemence must be read in part as a rhetorical maneuver to bring
under control the figurative language through which her argument has proceeded. In other words, she must insist that it would be "ridiculous" to
believe in a conspiracy theory, precisely because her text has already
opened up that possibility. It must also be remembered that for left-liberal
intellectuals in the post-McCarthy—but pre-Kennedy assassination—context in which *The Feminine Mystique* was written, conspiracy theories were
still the mark of an unacceptable political demonology. Perhaps also moti-
vating Friedan's explicit rejection of conspiracy is an awareness that her
analysis of the political dimension of women's personal experience was in
danger of not being taken seriously as a work of scholarship. Not only
does Friedan excoriate the culture industry, but she also seeks to avoid

contamination by mass cultural forms and figures in her own text. The book opens up the possibility of a conspiracy theory of sexual politics, only for that conclusion to be denied. In summary, then, we might say that *The Feminine Mystique* offers an account of what would come to be known as patriarchy *as if* it were a conspiracy, without ever fully cashing out the metaphor into literal fact.

I'll Just Die if I Don't Get That Recipe

Following on from Friedan's pioneering analysis, a whole subgenre of so-called mad-housewife fiction emerged in the early 1960s.[9] From Sylvia Plath's *The Bell Jar* (1963) to Alix Kates Shulman's *Memoirs of an Ex-Prom Queen* (1969), these novels draw on a range of imagery to express the sense of claustrophobic confinement in the domestic sphere. Tropes of slavery and imprisonment had been common in feminist writing for over a century, but now they were given a particularly dramatic form. In *The Bell Jar*, for example, the young narrator Esther suffers a nervous breakdown when she tries to conform her desires for intellectual and sexual freedom to society's prescription of a gingham-checked future for her. Her boyfriend, Buddy Willard, announces in a "sinister, knowing way" that after she had children she wouldn't feel like writing poetry any more. "So I began to think maybe it was true," Esther concludes, with a turn to familiar Cold War metaphors, "that when you were married and had children it was like being brainwashed, and afterward you went about numb as a slave in some private, totalitarian state."[10] In these novels the sense of being entrapped is often expressed in personal and psychological terms, as the heroines repeat the received wisdom that it is their own psychological refusal to adjust to their destined social and sexual role that is the problem. In contrast, the occasional use of Cold War figurations of conspiracy begins to provide a suggestive analysis of the problem with no name that is resolutely social and political.

In her survey of "protofeminist" fiction of the 1960s, Paulina Palmer endeavors to account for the prevalence of conspiracy images in the writing of that period. She does this by confirming—in a tone which combines historical authority and confessional intimacy—the accuracy of those figurations of "what many women feel living in a phallocratic culture." "There can be few women," she asserts, "who, at some time or other in their lives, have not experienced the frightening sense of being trapped in a conspiracy of male domination."[11] But, in a similar fashion to Friedan's retractions, having asserted that most women in early 1960s suburbia had the experience of living in a conspiracy, Palmer goes on to acknowledge that "in material terms this notion of a 'conspiracy' may be a simplification and exaggeration." Potentially simple minded and exaggerated, the rhetoric of conspiracy in mad housewife fiction was, in Palmer's view, no more than "a projection of imaginative reality," a metaphor which merely gestured towards women's experience. Yet, having suggested that the trope of conspiracy was nothing more than a material expression of a psychological reality, she immediately performs a double take, suggesting that "it may not be, in fact, the exaggeration which it first appears." Palmer's tergiversations underline how difficult it is to finally decide whether there really is a patriarchal conspiracy against women or whether the current situation is "merely" *like* a conspiracy.

No one has explored the no-man's-land between literal and metaphorical conspiracy theories more dramatically than the novelist Ira Levin. With his three novels (all of which have been made into films) *Rosemary's Baby* (1967), *The Stepford Wives* (1972) and *Sliver* (1991), Levin seems to specialize in plotting female paranoia. *Rosemary's Baby* (film version 1969) tells the story of a young New York housewife who becomes convinced that her neighbors are spying on her and that people are trying to interfere with her unborn baby. The ironic twist, however, comes with the revelation that her paranoia turns out to be justified: her entire circle of friends, including her husband, is part of a Satanist cult who have succeeded in impregnating her with the anti-Christ.[12] *The Stepford Wives* (filmed in 1975) features a pleasant American suburb in which the women are all model housewives, belated epitomes of the feminine mystique. It eventually turns out (more ambiguously in the novel, less so in the film) that the women look and act like "fembots" precisely because they *are* female robots. At a garden party, the model housewife played by Nanette Newman begins to malfunction and repeats endlessly the refrain, "I'll just die if I don't get that recipe!" The game is given away when the protagonist proves her suspicions by stabbing her best friend who has turned into a fembot and doesn't bleed (Figure 3.1). The protagonist learns—too late to save herself—that the Men's Association has been running a program to trade in their real wives who had become too much of a handful when—horror of horrors—they had even invited Betty Friedan to speak. In replacement, the men manufacture mechanical dolls, who are Disneyfied versions of the diligent housewife, with larger breasts and smaller behinds, "too nicey-nice to be real." Only, they *are* real in the world of the novel. Once again the protagonist's paranoia is confirmed, and her metaphorical suspicions are materialized into literal fact: there really is a conspiracy to turn women into domestic slaves.[13] Yet (in the novel version at least) there remains the lingering possibility that it is all a case of paranoid fantasy: the protagonist agrees to undergo psychoanalysis. Levin plays on the difficulty of naming the problem in conspiratorial terms, continually crossing the border between the figurative and the factual. The novel leaves the reader with a virtually unanswerable conundrum: if, in the real world outside the novel, there is not literally a conspiracy against women by the Men's Association, then why does it look

Figure 3.1 "I'll just die if I don't get that recipe!" (*The Stepford Wives*, dir. Bryan Forbes). Courtesy of the Kobal Collection.

like there is? The novel does not so much offer a factual explanation for women's sense of claustrophobic paranoia in suburbia, as point to the inadequacy of more orthodox explanations.

The Language of Conspiracy

In writings such as *The Feminine Mystique* and the subsequent growth of "mad housewife" fiction, the rhetoric of conspiracy hovers somewhere between the literal and the metaphorical. In the years following these proto-feminist experiments, however, the figuration of conspiracy in popular feminist writing increasingly became statements of fact. In the late 1960s, some feminist thinkers were concerned not merely to express their psychological experience, but to present a coordinated account of What Was Really Going On. The task was not so much to name the problem as to name the oppressor. Conspiracy and its related tropes became a focus of debate between feminist groupings in the question of who or what was basically to blame for (in the newly politicized terminology) the oppression of women. The three most cited candidates were, as the analysis of the time framed it, individual men, women in complicity with male institutions, or "the system." In the late 1960s these possibilities were articulated, for example, with the formation, fragmentation and repositioning of various radical feminist groups, which defined their differences through their manifestos. Groups such as Cell 16 of Boston and The Feminists of New York favored talk of conditioning and internalized oppression, employing a vocabulary of brainwashing, self-surveillance, infiltration, complicity and double-agency to account for why women seemed to conform to stereotypes of their inferiority and submissiveness.

What became known as the "pro-woman" line, on the other hand, explicitly rejected such conspiracy-minded psychological talk in favor of "external" factors, thereby removing blame from individual women. For example, the Redstockings, a breakaway group from the New York Radical Women (NYRW), declared in their 1968 manifesto that "women's submission is not the result of brainwashing, stupidity or mental illness but of continual, daily pressure from men."[14] If women seem to collaborate with their oppression, "pro-woman" feminists like the Redstockings maintained, it is only because they are reluctantly forced through circumstance into making complicitous compromises in order to survive. In the manifesto they go on to argue that:

> Attempts have been made to shift the burden of responsibility from men to institutions or to women themselves. We condemn these arguments as evasions. Institutions alone do not oppress; they are merely tools of the oppressor.

In effect, then, the Redstockings aimed to replace the abstract and metaphorical language of brainwashing with a particularized and literal naming of the enemy. By this logic, believing anything less played into the oppressor's hands.

What made these debates about the figuration of patriarchy even more fraught, however, was the increasing suspicion that women's groups had been infiltrated by real double-agents. So, for example, when in the autumn of 1968 the NYRW began to disintegrate, some of the original members, feeling that their former tight-knit camaraderie had in fact been deliberately undermined, began to talk about the presence of *agents provocateurs* and double-agents. Patricia Mainardi, a member of the inner circle of NYRW who went on to form the Redstockings, looked back on those meetings in an interview during the late 1980s:

> As the movement grew, so did the number of women whose commitment to the women's liberation movement was more tenuous. Your feeling was that these were people who were there to stop anything from happening. I would not be the slightest bit surprised [to discover] that there were agents and reactionaries there.[15]

Radical feminists thus had to confront the possibility that the very meetings in which discussion of the seemingly metaphorical conspiracy of patriarchy was on the agenda were themselves subject to the all-too-literal conspiracies of the CIA and FBI. When the Redstockings reformed in 1973 (after an absence of several years), they devoted much of their energy to denouncing what they now saw as a liberal plot to take over the radical feminist movement. The desire to construct what had gone wrong in the 1960s in terms of a literal, personalized conspiracy reached its high point when the Redstockings began to accuse Gloria Steinem and *Ms.* magazine of being involved with the CIA.[16] Talk of the literal surveillance carried out under COINTELPRO (the government's conspiratorial counter-intelligence program) thus coexisted uneasily with a more metaphorical—one might even say a more Foucauldian—understanding of social domination as a form of complicitous self-surveillance.

Much feminist writing of this time finds itself caught between a desire to create a new set of terms, and a need to continue appropriating the language and ideas of an older, more literal, and more male-identified form of political activism. The problematic engagement with the language of conspiracy takes place within a wider struggle during the 1960s over an appropriate language for feminism. Where some women sought to expunge all traces of a male-identified political vocabulary, others enacted a satirical appropriation of that language. Injecting a measure of humor and anarchic confusion into an already tense situation was the formation in the late 1960s of groups like WITCH (Women's International Terrorist Conspiracy from Hell) and Lavender Menace. The formation of WITCH in the summer of 1968 by Robin Morgan and Florika of NYRW can be read partly in response to the success of the Yippies. One of WITCH's first actions, for example, was to put a "hex" on Wall Street, recalling Abbie Hoffman's throwing money at the Stock Exchange the previous year. WITCH's formation and choice of name was also an ironic-yet-serious allusion to The Conspiracy, aka the Chicago Seven, the group of activists who were at this time on trial before the House Un-American Activities Committee (HUAC) for allegedly inciting a riot at the 1968 Democratic Convention. The HUAC was brought back into the limelight for the first time since the McCarthy years as part of the government's heavy-handed attempt to break the power of the increasingly militant Movement. Referring to the fact that the HUAC had not included any women in the subpoenas to appear before the Committee—a list which included Abbie Hoffman and the founder of the Yippies, Jerry Rubin—Ros Baxandall of WITCH asked, "How come we, the real subversives, the real witches, aren't being indicted?"[17] Her question is both a demand to be taken seriously by the exclusive all-male club of "real subversives," and an insistence that the "metaphorical" conspiracy of feminism would in the long run be more subversive than the macho posturings of what Baxandall referred to as the "boy's movement." In this way, the rhetoric and rationale of WITCH provided both a mocking debasement of the conspiracy mania of the masculinist New Left, and an implicit recognition that repressive government policies were once again being mobilized under the justification of "counter-subversion" in cases like the trial of the Chicago Seven. Though most of their street actions consisted of merry pranksterism, WITCH were likewise quick to announce in a more serious vein that "WITCHes must name names, or rather we must name trademarks and brand-names."[18] Joking talk of conspiracy thus coexisted uneasily with a literal desire to name names.

The formation of Lavender Menace tells a similar story of the parodic appropriation of the rhetoric of conspiracy at the turn of the decade. A group of lesbian feminists staged a disruptive protest at the 1970 Congress to Unite Women, adopting the tactic of embracing many of the accusations made against lesbianism by liberal feminists and those outside the movement. They called themselves the Lavender Menace in response to a comment made by Betty Friedan at this time about the potential infiltration of lesbians—a "lavender menace"—within the women's movement. Satirically confirming the charges made against them, they declared in their first resolution that "Women's Liberation is a lesbian plot."[19] The formation of Lavender Menace served to materialize the demonological fears of feminists like Friedan, ensuring that, as one of their slogans put it, "I am your worst fears / I am your best fantasy." Within the feminist movement at the beginning of the 1970s, then, groups like WITCH and Lavender Menace turned the language of conspiracy back against its originators (both macho revolutionaries and liberal feminists), disrupting the distinction between the literal and the metaphorical.[20]

The Conspiracy of Language

If the breakup of radical feminism towards the end of the 1960s was in part marked by a parodic recycling and deflation of the language of conspiracy, the emergence of cultural feminism in the 1970s was caught up in an inflationary circuit of literalness. During this decade the notion of patriarchy as a conspiracy solidified into factual statement. Whereas some radical feminists had countenanced the possibility that women could be conditioned or brainwashed into collaboration with patriarchal institutions, cultural feminists edged towards the position that all men are entirely guilty of creating a conspiracy to control women, who are all innocent victims.

Probably the most influential proponent of this position is Mary Daly. In *Gyn/Ecology* Daly makes it clear that America—and perhaps the whole world—is organized by a male supremacist conspiracy. She insists that being logical "would require that we admit to ourselves that males and males only are the originators, planners, controllers, and legitimators of patriarchy."[21] For Daly, "the fact is that we live in a profoundly anti-female society, a misogynistic 'civilization' in which men collectively victimize women" (*GE*, 29). No detail of social arrangement is accidental, for, as Daly goes on to declare, "within this society it is men who rape, who sap women's energy, who deny economic and political power" (*GE*, 29). Patriarchy "appears to be 'everywhere.'" Not only have "outer space and the future ... been colonized," but patriarchal control "is also internalized, festering inside women's heads, even feminist heads" (*GE*, 1). In *Gyn/Ecology*, the conspiracy of male power is total.

Daly repeatedly insists on the brutal facts of patriarchal power. She explicitly counsels against collapsing a literal understanding of the male supremacists' plot back into metaphorical talk of abstract forces:

> women—even feminists—are intimidated into Self-deception, becoming the only Self-described oppressed who are unable to name their oppressor, referring instead to vague "forces," "roles," "stereotypes," "constraints," "attitudes," "influences." This list could go on. The point is that no agent is named—only abstractions.
>
> (*GE*, 29)

Despite her insistence on literal facts instead of euphemistic sociological abstractions, *Gyn/Ecology* is often densely metaphorical. The book forms a remarkable attempt to escape through linguistic creativity from what Daly considers to be the "mind-poisoning" of patriarchy, which has even infected the women's movement. "This book," states Daly, "can be heard as a Requiem for *that* 'women's movement,' which is male-designed, male-orchestrated, male-legitimated, male-assimilated" (*GE*, xvi). Daly endeavors to create not just a new form of woman-centered politics, but a new form of feminist language which is not designed, orchestrated or legitimated by men. Whereas earlier feminists like Friedan were concerned to identify the problem with no name, Daly comes to see naming itself as the problem. For Daly, then, what is significant is that women are "unable to *name* their oppressor" (*GE*, 29; emphasis added). The point is, Daly warns, "no agent is *named*"; and recognizing that patriarchy amounts to a conspiracy requires not only "the courage to be logical," but also "the courage to *name*" (*GE*, 29). Literally naming the agents of the patriarchal conspiracy therefore becomes an important act in itself.

The emphasis on finding the right words is crucial to Daly's project, for she portrays language itself as a patriarchal trap. In addition to her use of the language of conspiracy, Daly turns her attention to the conspiracy of language. She writes about the "hidden agendas concealed in the texture of language," going on to argue that "deception is embedded in the very texture of the words we use, and here is where our exorcism can begin" (*GE*, 3). Daly uses various strategies in her campaign to combat the conspiracy of patriarchal language. One method is to revalorize the very terms which have been used against women. Daly takes the figure of witches, for example, and turns the negative associations of the word into a positive model for feminist activity. Daly aims to rewrite the "deception plotted by the male-supremacist scriptwriters" by (re)creating a new mythology—a new plot—for "Lesbians/Spinsters/Amazons/Survivors" (*GE*, 20). Unlike the playfulness of WITCH, however, Daly always takes her reappropriation of the term seriously.

A second tactic is the creation of woman-centered counterparts for male terms and characteristics. In place of men's "own paranoid fears" (*GE*, 29), for example, Daly offers the notion of "pronoia," or positive paranoia, which she defines as "seeing/making new patterns of perception as preparation for the latter/deeper stages of Journeying" (*GE*, 401). "Pronoia" is just one of the countless new coinings Daly employs in *Gyn/Ecology*. Her prose is shot through with a series of neologisms, which aim to bring about in miniature a disassembly and recombination of the patriarchal conspiracy. As Meaghan Morris argues, Daly's emphasis on the individual sign forecloses discussion on the effects of discourse as a whole.[22] In addition to new words, Daly also concentrates on the etymology of key terms. Her analysis, however, is often directed less to the deep cultural histories embedded in certain words, than to the surface appearance and literal inclusion of particular syllables. "Manipulation," for example, reveals within itself the word "man." Daly's emphasis on particular signifiers signals a shift towards a "literal-minded" view of language in the 1970s, in which individual words can come to cause social effects.

This concern with the material and the literal effects of representation has been fundamental to the campaigns against rape and pornography which began to dominate popular American feminist activism from the late 1970s on through the 1980s. The logic of conspiracy became indispensable to the analysis of rape, in books such as Susan Brownmiller's *Against Our Will*. Brownmiller defined rape as the "conscious process of intimidation by which *all men* keep *all women* in a state of fear," establishing a Manichaean division of society into men who are all guilty and women who are all victims.[23] Feminist analyses of rape began to describe it as the "all-American crime," and as the principal fact of patriarchy which ensures "the perpetuation of male domination over women by force."[24] In addition, Cold War paranoia about bodily invasion, infiltration and contamination returned as literal descriptions, as the female body became not a displaced metaphor for the national body politic, but the very site of politics itself.[25] Whereas the rhetoric of conspiracy in feminist writings of the early 1960s slyly appropriated and reconfigured contemporary political buzzwords, its use by antipornography feminists in the 1980s produced disturbing echoes of right-wing sexual and national demonology which were long past their sell-by date.

Pornography became theorized not just as a representation of an act of violent sex, but as a violent act in itself. In this way the distinction between the literal and the metaphorical was strategically collapsed, thus producing an insistence that pornography is not just like rape, but is rape itself; and that rape is not just like violence, but is violence itself. Once again, naming becomes a political act. As Andrea Dworkin comments in the introduction to *Pornography*, a man "actively maintains the power of naming through force and he justifies force through the power of naming."[26] By the 1980s, then, the issue of naming the problem had been replaced by the problem of naming, an issue which has continued to be crucial, for example, in the discussions of whether "date rape" counts as "real" rape. These popular studies of rape and pornography produced what has become known as victim feminism, marked by its tendency to see sexual politics as a struggle against an all-pervasive, all-powerful and all-too-literal conspiracy of male domination.

Crying Wolf

The question of whether the conspiracy to victimize women is literal or metaphorical reaches a rhetorical crisis point by the time of Naomi Wolf's *The Beauty Myth*. Wolf tells a parallel story to Friedan's account of an ideological backlash against the previous gains of feminism. For Wolf, "the more legal and material hindrances women have broken through" in "the two decades of radical action that followed the rebirth of feminism in the early 1970s," the more "strictly and heavily and cruelly images of female beauty have come to weigh upon us" (*BM*, 9–10). And, like Friedan, Wolf often presents this not as a congruence of diverse historical forces, but the result of conscious planning, particularly by the advertisers and the very industries which stand most to gain from such a return to domestic virtues. At times Wolf is explicit about her rewriting of Friedan for a new generation, with, for example, a recapitulation of the scenario of women being duped into the stupefied condition of Stepford Wives, automata who have been programmed to spend money no longer on their homes but on their bodies. "To paraphrase Friedan," writes Wolf, "why is it never said that the really crucial function that women serve as aspiring beauties is *to buy more things for the body?*" (*BM*, 66). At other times, however, Wolf is less specific about her intellectual inheritances, with the result that *The Beauty Myth* reads more as a palimpsest of the last thirty years of feminism, in which the faint outlines of previous positions and figurations are still visible. The history of feminism's coming to terms remains sedimented within the body of Wolf's text, but keeps resurfacing at key moments.

The Beauty Myth is punctuated by moments of textual anxiety over what is to be understood metaphorically, and what is to be taken literally. Wolf frequently insists that many of the tropes she employs to describe women's oppression by the beauty myth are no such thing: she means them literally. "Electric shock therapy is not just a metaphor," she warns (*BM*, 250). Wolf presumably means that the manipulation of women's minds is not just comparable to ECT, but is sometimes actually instantiated by shock therapy. A similar hesitation between the literal and the metaphorical occurs in a comparison between the physical mutilation of slaves and the "employment demand for cosmetic surgery" (*BM*, 55). "The surgical economy is no slave economy, of course," explains Wolf. But she goes on to add that, "in its demand for permanent, painful and risky alteration of the body, it constitutes—as have tattooing, branding, and scarification in other times and places—a category that falls somewhere between a slave economy and the free market." Wolf seems caught "somewhere between" a desire to produce elaborate comparisons and figures, and an awareness of feminism's long history of making itself a distinct project that cannot be collapsed into other terms and other struggles, from civil rights to the class war.

As the book progresses, Wolf engages in an endless process of bolstering up her rhetorical claims. When the comparisons seem to fall short and lose their force, Wolf redoubles her insistence. Tellingly, the closer to her own personal experience she comes, the more this strategy intensifies. In her heartfelt discussion of eating disorders Wolf is less equivocal, more certain that women's oppression is not somewhere between the metaphorical and the literal, but constitutes instead a literalization of the metaphorical:

> Women must claim anorexia as political damage done to us by a social order that considers our destruction insignificant because of what we are—less. We should identify it as Jews identify the death camps, as homosexuals identify AIDS: as a disgrace that is not our own, but that of an inhumane social order. Anorexia is a prison camp. One fifth of well-educated American young women are inmates. Susie Orbach compared anorexia to the hunger strikes of political prisoners, particularly the suffragists. But the time for metaphors is behind us. To be anorexic or bulimic *is* to be a political prisoner.
>
> (*BM*, 208; emphasis in the original)

Wolf first advocates regarding anorexia *as* political damage. The fact that this observation must be claimed rather than merely stated suggests that such comparisons are made more for strategic reasons than from a mere desire to describe the situation of anorexic women in itself. Next she suggests making comparisons with other analogous groups. The movement is towards a more complete identification, but the figure still remains a simile, if only in form alone ("as Jews," "as homosexuals").

Finally, feeling herself to be beyond metaphor in an extreme situation for which Orbach's comparisons are no longer adequate ("the time for metaphors is behind us"), Wolf insists on a total identification between eating disorders and political imprisonment. The element of comparison in the original metaphor is canceled out.

The implications of Wolf's rhetorical insistence on full identification in her metaphors received much criticism—as did Friedan's comparisons of being a suburban housewife with living in the Nazi concentration camps. Reiterating the equivalence between the personal and the political leads to an erasure of any differences that might exist in the various cases she mentions. Can anorexia "be" a prison camp in the same way that Auschwitz was a prison camp? Could a PLWA or a concentration camp internee escape their "prison" through a recognition of the false images of homosexuality or Jewishness, in which, by Wolf's logic, they are trapped? The comparisons are surely ill conceived, but the passage is nevertheless revealing in its focus on the problem of figuration itself. The declaration that "the time for metaphors is behind us" cuts both ways. It draws attention to Wolf's sense of redoubled urgency in a time of backlash, in which rhetorical circumlocution is a luxury that feminism can no longer afford. History, as far as Wolf is concerned, has in effect played a sick joke on women, turning their once figural language into literal fact. But the assertion also manifests an anxiety about language itself, speaking of a thwarted desire to match description with experience, to reach an unmediated realm beyond representation. The implication is that language—metaphor in particular—has repeatedly failed to do justice to feminism's project to make people see how things really are. Figuration, it would seem, has become an enemy of feminism, conspiring against women, preventing them from being understood.

Wolf is weighed down by the last three decades of feminist writing, which have become littered with dead or absorbed metaphors, requiring an ongoing forging and strengthening of new comparisons. For example, in the second chapter, which forms an extended comparison between the Beauty Myth and the worst aspects of religious cults, Wolf points out that "what has not been recognized is that the comparison should be no metaphor" (*BM*, 88). She continues:

> The rituals of the beauty backlash do not simply echo traditional religions and cults but *functionally supplant them*. They are *literally* reconstituting out of old faiths a new one, *literally* drawing on traditional techniques of mystification and thought control, to alter women's minds as sweepingly as any past evangelical wave.
>
> (*BM*, 88; emphasis in original)

In such passages the author of *The Beauty Myth* finds herself in the position of crying wolf: this time, the frenetic italics seem to say, it's really real, no longer a false alarm, no longer a metaphor. The movement towards a literalization of the figurative has pushed the language of her feminism to a crisis point, in which the more Wolf insists on the nonfigural nature of her assertion, the more it draws attention to its rhetorical status. The more her words slip from control, the louder she must shout them.

It is therefore extremely significant that the one image which Wolf doesn't insist on is the figure of conspiracy. *The Beauty Myth* begins with the following epigraph from Ann Jones:

> I notice that it is the fashion ... to disclaim any notion of male conspiracy in the oppression of women ... "For my part," I must say with William Lloyd Garrison, "I am not prepared to respect that philosophy. I believe in sin, therefore in a sinner; in theft, therefore in a thief; in slavery, therefore in a slaveholder; in wrong, therefore in a wrongdoer."[27]
>
> (*BM*, 7)

If this passage is quoted approvingly—and Wolf's page of epigraphs would be a strange place to introduce such irony if the excerpt is not meant to set the tone for the coming analysis—then we might expect a book on "How Images of Beauty Are Used Against Women" to contain much denunciation of the "male conspiracy." Yet, as we saw at the beginning of this chapter, Wolf's work exhibits a self-conscious cautiousness in connection with the term "conspiracy." In the introduction Wolf does indeed use the phrase "cultural conspiracy," but places it in scare quotes. Though prepared to embrace many other extravagant characterizations of the beauty myth, she feels obliged to signal her distance from conspiracy theories.

Although conspiracy theories are expressly rejected in *The Beauty Myth*, the narrative structure of personification on which they tend to rely makes a return—even in the very passages in which the repudiations are made. As Ann Jones's use of the Garrison quote demonstrates, conspiracy theories traditionally allow the possibility of apportioning blame for what might otherwise appear a series of unconnected and overdetermined events, attitudes and practices. They betray an attraction to the notion of reading history personally, of seeking a hidden cause behind every event, and behind every cause an evil conspirator who deliberately plots those events; in short, of giving a name to the faceless "problem." Wolf begins by pointing out that it is the *idea* of repressive beauty, rather than any particular item in the list of guilty industries, that is doing the damage. What to call this "idea," however, emerges as a problem in her prose. Following Henrik Ibsen she sometimes calls it a "vital lie" told by society to itself. Using the work of psychologist Daniel Goleman, she talks about "necessary fictions" and "social fictions that masqueraded as natural components." The title of the book, in a modulation of Betty Friedan's famous title, calls it the beauty *myth*. And, in the least precise formulation of all, when she claims that the beauty backlash does not require a conspiracy, she qualifies it by adding, "merely an atmosphere" (*BM*, 18).

But having removed all trace of malicious conspiratorial agents in these careful circumlocutions of what—if this were not a book directed towards the American popular market—might be termed patriarchy, ideology or hegemony, Wolf then describes how "the resulting hallucination materializes" (*BM*, 18). At the very moment of insistence on materiality, then, literal conspirators give way to figurative ones, as the text becomes crowded with prosopopeia. "No longer just an idea," Wolf continues, "it becomes three-dimensional, incorporating within itself how women live and how they do not live." The verb forms once again are active, conjuring up the specter of a metaconspiracy, an ideology with a ghostly human face, as we hear how "it [the contemporary backlash] has grown stronger to take over the work of social coercion that myths about motherhood, domesticity, chastity, and passivity, no longer can manage."[28] In the tone of Senator McCarthy sounding the alarm about a personified version of the Communist peril infiltrating America, Wolf goes on to tell how "it is seeking right now to undo psychologically and covertly all the good things that feminism did for women materially and overtly." But right at the end of the introduction this rhetorical return of the disavowed trope of prosopopeia is itself inverted, in a move invoking what can now only be described as a meta-metaconspiracy. In a reversion to what now seems a sinisterly anonymous passive verb form, Wolf explains how, "after the success of the women's movement's second wave, the beauty myth was perfected to checkmate power at every level in individual women's lives." But by whom was it perfected? Just when we had a grip on the Beauty Myth (to capitalize it in the same way that Wolf capitalizes Friedan's phrase, the "Feminine Mystique") as a Frankenstein's monster, a fabricated mishmash of cultural attitudes and images at once grotesque and desirable, so now we need to be on the lookout for the shadowy scientist himself, malevolently fulfilling his conspiratorial projects through the cunning manipulation of the poor dumb monster of the Beauty Myth. In this way, each repudiation of a conspiratorial mode of analysis only seems to restore an even more paranoid formulation, as each abstraction of agency is refigured into an act of deliberate contrivance by shadowy agents.

The Conspiracy of Theory

The reason *The Beauty Myth* manifests such anxiety about figuration in general, and the figure of conspiracy in particular, is doubtless due in part to Wolf's self-conscious rewriting of *The Feminine Mystique* at a time when some commentators were triumphantly declaring the advent of "post-feminism." Given the three decades of feminist struggle with the problem of naming which intervenes between the two books, it is not surprising that Wolf should betray a redoubled cautiousness in acceding to an image which by the 1990s has a long and troubled history. Wolf's reluctance to characterize her strategy as a conspiracy theory must surely also be understood in the context of a post-Cold War skepticism about that apparently outdated political rhetoric, with the collapse of Eastern European communism at the end of the 1980s. In a similar fashion Friedan's downplaying of conspiracy takes place in the post-McCarthy intellectual backlash against political demonology. Moreover, there are surely strong parallels between the Eisenhower era which Friedan describes (her initial moment of revelation comes "one April morning in 1959"), and the Reagan/Bush years in which Wolf's analysis takes shape, not least in the way that the individual presidents gave institutional legitimation to a paranoid rhetoric of national security.

Yet these explanations do not fully make sense of Wolf's vehemence that, despite appearances, her argument is not structured as a conspiracy theory. What must also be taken into account is Wolf's implicit recognition that conspiracy theories are a mark of the unscholarly. When in her second book, *Fire with Fire*, Wolf declares that "it's time to say fuck you, I'm gonna have footnotes, I'm gonna have breasts," her anxiety seems as much about not being taken seriously by "academic" feminism as it is a challenge to the antifeminist backlash.[29] Although her message is obviously that in the 1990s there should be nothing remarkable about being a woman with ideas, she seems as keen to emphasize the presence of her footnotes as the fact that she is a glamorous 1990s feminist. Wolf seems implicitly aware that the language of conspiracy is usually associated with crackpot theorists and assassination buffs. She must also be aware that the very label of a "conspiracy theory" often functions as an accusation of unprofessional research and unsophisticated thinking. And here we must recall that Wolf, like Friedan, directs her most impassioned attacks on the culture industry; indeed, they both construct what amount to conspiracy theories of advertising and the media. At times, then, Wolf's anxious denial of conspiracy theories is motivated by—dare one say—a paranoid fear of being contaminated by this popular and unscholarly way of thinking.

What makes this situation more complicated is that academic feminists have positioned themselves precisely in opposition to the conspiracy theorizing of popular feminists like Wolf. Influenced by Foucauldian posthumanist accounts of social domination, recent forms of theoretical feminism have often been premised on an implicit rejection of the simplistic (and resolutely humanist) notions of agency and causality with which conspiracy theories are traditionally associated. For example, one of the "three insights" which conclude Lynne Segal's analysis of feminist strategies for the future is, quite simply, "the recognition that women's subordination is not a result of a conscious conspiracy by men."[30] If we can clear up this embarrassing tendency, Segal seems to imply, we will be well on our way to ridding feminism of its persistent attraction to such annoying and misleading patterns of analysis. "We" in this case refers to those who, like Segal, feel that the project of radical feminism begun in the 1960s has been hijacked by what has passed under the sign of victim or cultural feminism.

There are several reasons for the repudiation of conspiracy theories by feminists influenced by poststructuralism and cultural studies. In Mica Nava's reassessment of theories about advertising, she notes how "current theories of culture and subjectivity take much more seriously notions of personal agency, discrimination and resistance, as well as (drawing on psychoanalysis) the contradictory and fragmented nature of fantasy and desire." This "new, more nuanced understanding of subjectivity," Nava goes on to explain, is crucial to "recent critical refutations of the notion that the media and advertising have the power to manipulate in a coherent and unfractured fashion and represent a move away from the notion of mass man and woman as duped and passive recipients of conspiratorial messages designed to inhibit true consciousness."[31] Feminists like Nava operating within a cultural studies framework have begun to employ the language of desire, fantasy and identification in place of conspiracy theories of, say, mass culture or patriarchal oppression. Instead of a paranoid fear of infiltration, contamination, and indoctrination by external forces, emphasis is placed on the way that people use culture to create their own meanings, as much as those meanings are imposed on them conspiratorially from above by the culture industry. Indeed, the rejection of conspiracy thinking has been integral in shaping the kind of feminist cultural studies performed by critics such as Nava.

Furthermore, feminisms informed by psychoanalytic accounts of subjectivity and poststructuralist theories of language position themselves precisely in opposition to the notions of psychology, agency, and causality on which conspiracy theories rely. For example, in her reassessment of *Sexual Politics*, Cora Kaplan draws attention to the way that Kate Millet's analysis amounts to a conspiracy theory of Freudian analysis. Kaplan argues that "Millett ... had to reject the unconscious, the pivotal concept in Freud, and something common to both sexes, because she is committed to a view that patriarchal ideology is a conscious conspiratorial set of attitudes operated by men against all empirical evidence of women's equal status in order to support patriarchal power in office."[32] Kaplan's accusations are doubly significant because, in her view, what popular feminist conspiracy theories of patriarchy fail to provide is any account of the workings of the unconscious and desire in personal and public life. Conspiratorial thinking is accused—quite rightly, in its more traditional forms—of cashing out the unconscious into the rational and the deliberate, producing a deterministic and thoroughly efficacious portrait of social agency. "What distinguishes psychoanalysis from sociological accounts of gender," writes Jacqueline Rose, "is that whereas for the latter, the internalization of norms is assumed roughly to work, the basic premise and indeed starting-point of psychoanalysis is that it does not."[33] On this line of thinking, conspiracy theories of patriarchy will inevitably fall short. The concept of the unconscious will always implicitly call into question the picture of a conscious, coherent, and entirely efficacious conspiracy (though, as we have seen, many feminist conspiracy theories have themselves fallen short of sustaining such an unequivocal and literal-minded position). In this way, the accusation of using a conspiracy theory has joined that list of untenable theoretical feminist positions which includes essentialism and functionalism, marking a boundary between sophistication and vulgarity—indeed, the accusation of an interlocutor's view as a "conspiracy theory" is often enough to end discussion.

Viewed from the other side of the divide, however, it is theoretical feminism which is the problem. Some feminists have even characterized poststructuralism itself as a cunning conspiracy by male theorists and their female dupes. Just when women as subjects were beginning to receive attention from historians, the argument goes, along came poststructuralism which "conveniently" announced that the very idea of the human subject was a fiction anyway.[34] The accusation of a conspiracy of theory speaks of the divide between feminists who concentrate on the literal and material dimensions of male oppression in cases such as pornography and rape, and those theorists whose emphasis is on the figurative and the representational. In the introduction to *Bodies that Matter*, Judith Butler talks about "the exasperated debate which many of us have tired of hearing." Butler is referring to stock criticisms of poststructuralism—such as "If everything is discourse, what about the body?"[35] The literal-minded insistence on the incontestable evidence of brute reality (which we saw in Wolf, for example) prevents any discussion of the way in which the very notion of the "material" carries with it a lot of unexamined ideological baggage.

What really exasperates Butler, however, is "when construction is figuratively reduced to a verbal action which appears to presuppose a subject," a misunderstanding which she felt had unfairly plagued the reception of *Gender Trouble*, her book on the constructedness of gender categories. This misunderstanding leads "critics working within such presumptions ... to say, 'If gender is constructed, then who is doing the constructing?'" In other words, these misguided readers assume incorrectly that "where there is activity, there lurks behind it an initiating and wilful subject." With this way of thinking, Butler continues, "discourse or language or the social becomes personified."[36] In effect, Butler is taking issue with (amongst others) feminists like Wolf who find deliberate conspirators lurking behind any social processes.

139

Butler's focus on the tendency to personify is borne out in the case of a work like *The Beauty Myth*. Yet Wolf's text is, as we have seen, scarred by a continual rhetorical struggle, as she now denies and now embraces conspiracy formulations, making social agency anonymous here and reinserting hidden agents there. The endless shuttling back and forth between literal and metaphorical depictions of conspiracy in popular feminist writings points up the impossibility of naming the problem in an unproblematic way. It seems there is no language adequate to capture both the necessity of holding people responsible, and the knowledge that history is larger than the work of any group of individuals. As the misreadings of Butler's notoriously difficult and abstract prose suggest, finding the right words is not easy. For all its failings—perhaps precisely because of its contradictions—the work of populist writers like Wolf and Friedan does gesture towards the almost impossible-to-grasp notion of a conspiracy without conspiring, of social construction without some cabal doing the constructing, and of agency without hidden agents.

Cultural Dupes

Writers such as Friedan, Wolf and Faludi remain popular, not least because they draw on the pleasures of popular genres like conspiracy thrillers and detective fiction. A paradoxical situation arises, then, in which academic feminism leads the way in displaying a sympathetic and perceptive approach to popular culture, yet reserves an often unacknowledged antipathy towards popular feminism for its attraction to the popular charms of conspiracy theory. Conversely, popular feminists such as Wolf and Faludi repudiate the term "conspiracy" in their desire to be taken seriously, even as they succumb to the "simplifying" attractions of personification, and usher in a barely disguised version of the conspiracy theory of mass culture.

The language of conspiracy has led to rhetorical divisions and (often all-too-literal) silences, not just between academic and popular feminism, but also within popular feminist writings. Quite simply, it seems that it is always other women who are brainwashed and victims of the conspiracy. This sense of superiority—of having transcended the historical and intellectual forces in which others are still enslaved—comes across almost by accident in the very choice of words used to name the problem. The use of the collective pronoun in feminist writing answers an understandable desire to assert a solidarity, to forge a sisterhood to oppose patriarchy. Yet insisting on using "we" brings about an implicit polarization between those who are subjected to the conspiracy to brainwash women, and those who are strong and wise subjects, able to recognize, criticize, and even to overcome its powers. Friedan, for example, mainly discusses the brainwashing of American women in the third person plural, giving the impression that—as she openly admits—once she was brainwashed by the feminine mystique, but now she has escaped the conditioning. Occasionally, however, she does use the first person plural. For instance: "there were many needs, at this particular time in America, that made *us* pushovers for the mystique: needs so compelling that *we* suspended critical thought" (*BM*, 160; emphasis added). Friedan's momentary alignment with the duped majority sits uneasily with her self-promotion as the heroic lone detective who has managed to uncover the secret conspiracy.

By the time of *The Beauty Myth*, the problem of the collective pronoun has become pervasive. Sentence after sentence of Wolf's prose enacts a basic but contradictory division between those who are duped and those who are in the know. Usually in the first half of the sentence she quotes a fact or figure about the oppression of women, phrasing it in the objective third person plural, only in the second half to claim an identification with that oppression through her use of the collective pronoun. Sometimes this has a disconcerting poignancy, particularly in the chapter on anorexia when Wolf reveals that she had suffered from eating disorders as a teenager: "they" could indeed include "me." But in many other places the shift of pronominal stance midway through a sentence places Wolf uneasily both on the inside and the outside of the brainwashing conspiracy: "If *those* women who long to escape can believe that *they* have been subjected to a religious indoctrination that uses the proven techniques of brainwashing, *we* can begin to feel compassion for ourselves rather than self-loathing; *we* can begin to see where and how *our* minds were changed" (*BM*, 128; emphasis added). As Tania Modleski points out, however, the desire to position oneself clearly "outside" ideology is misleading. "Today," writes Modleski, "we are in danger of forgetting the crucial fact that like the rest of the world even the cultural analyst may sometimes be a 'cultural dupe'—which is, after all, only an ugly way of saying that we exist inside ideology, that we are all victims, down to the very depths of our psyches, of political and cultural domination (even though we are never *only* victims)."[37] The tension in Wolf's very syntax thus gestures towards her contradictory positioning as both duped and knowing, both victim and vanquisher of a conspiracy whose spectral form hovers over the text.

In the same way that *The Beauty Myth* almost inevitably constructs its own category of the culturally duped, so too is it very hard not to regard American feminists like Wolf—and, more worryingly, her large readership—as dupes of their zeitgeist, unthinkingly spouting the language of the day, victims of modes of thought to which "we" have now seen through. Not only is it easy to dismiss popular feminism of the present as the work of those immersed in various "ideologies" to which "we" are immune (including, no doubt, the "ideology" of popularity), but there is an equally common conviction of having gone beyond the primitive ideas of feminism's past. Jane Gallop, in her rereading of some of the now more ignominious collections of feminist theoretical essays from the 1970s, draws attention to the tendency of dismissing the writings of the past as embarrassing mistakes, the products of women who inevitably become characterized as "cultural dupes." She describes moments in her classes when discussion was foreclosed with the exchange of knowing grimaces, when her "audience assumed that [she] was describing an error of earlier days, a foolish ... stance, that we were comfortably beyond, thanks to the poststructuralist critique." What Gallop discovers in such moments is "a notion of our history as a simple progress from primitive criticism to ever better and more sophisticated."[38] It is tempting to dismiss the reliance on conspiracy theories in earlier or less "sophisticated" feminists such as Friedan or Wolf as hopelessly outdated and misguided. As this chapter has argued, however, the rhetorical circumnavigations around the idea of conspiracy in these works capture some of the complexities of representing whom to blame for how things got to be as they are.

4

FEAR OF A BLACK PLANET: "BLACK PARANOIA" AND THE AESTHETICS OF CONSPIRACY

> How do you think that the crack rock gets into the country?
> We don't own any planes. We don't own no ships. We are
> not the people who are flying and floating this shit in here . . .
> Why is it that there's a gunshop on every street corner in this
> community? I'll tell you why. For the same reason that
> there's a liquor store on almost every corner in the black
> community. Why? They want us to kill ourselves. You go
> out to Beverly Hills, you don't see that shit. But they want
> us to kill ourselves. Yeah. The best way you can destroy a
> people is if you take away their ability to reproduce
> themselves. Who is it that's dying out here on these streets
> every night? Young brothers like yourselves ... [By
> shooting one another,] you're doing exactly what they want
> you to do.
>
> (*Boyz 'N the Hood*)

> [There exists a] "cultural conspiracy," a seeping intolerance
> fed by white politicians' attacks on affirmative action and
> immigration.
>
> (Jesse Jackson)

Like the engagement with the rhetoric of conspiracy in feminist thinking,
the recent prominence of conspiracy theories in black communities in
America suggests an important departure from Richard Hofstadter's association of the "paranoid style" with mainly right-wing white men.[1] As
with the trajectory of American feminism since the 1960s, conspiracy
thinking has played an important role in constituting various forms of
African American political and cultural activism. Moreover, in broadly the
same way that the women's liberation movement used conspiratorial
rhetoric to help shape its notion of patriarchy as institutionalized sexism,
so too have various black communities employed the language of conspiracy to gesture towards theories about institutional racism.

143

Conspiracy theories in American society have traditionally served to cohere a sense of the mainstream ("we, the people") who are under threat from a sequence of "alien" dangers, from Catholicism in the nineteenth century to Communism in the twentieth. As David Brion Davis explains, "movements of countersubversion have thus been a primary means of restoring collective self-confidence, of defining American identity by contrast with alien 'others,' and of achieving unity through opposition to a common enemy."[2] But increasingly that mainstream consensus has disappeared. Especially since the emergence of new social movements such as radical feminism, gay liberation, and black power in the 1960s, some popular conspiracy theories have drawn attention not to threats to the so-called American way of life from outsiders and "others," but to how that idealized and ideologized normality is a constant and conspiratorial threat to those very groups.

There are other important similarities between the role of conspiracy theories in feminist and black protest movements. Unlike, say, the huge archive of heavily documented research into the Kennedy assassination that relies on the protocols of historical and scientific evidence even as it challenges them, for both feminist and black proponents of conspiracy theory usually the only evidence worth consulting is the authority of experience. Though conspiracy theories are now extremely influential amongst African Americans, there have been comparatively few detailed and sustained published works of allegation and investigation produced by the black community.[3] Instead theories circulate by word of mouth, on the street, in rumors and jokes, in magazines and rap songs, as well as from the pulpit and from community leaders. When citations are given, they tend to be to well-known works of conspiracy theory, often of a New World Order and/or white supremacist bent. For example, the hiphopmusic.com website refers viewers wanting to know more about the source of gangsta rap conspiracy theories to an online bookstore selection which includes William Cooper's all-encompassing conspiracy opus *Behold, A Pale Horse* and A. Ralph Epperson's *The Unseen Hand: An Introduction to the Conspiratorial View of History*. As we found with feminism, conspiracy theories in black America tend to circulate not so much as definitive and painstakingly documented allegations, but as commonly held conjectures which operate somewhere between the literal and the figurative. In doing so they challenge the possibility of there being a universal, common sense approach to the facts of the case that every right-minded American should believe in. For many African Americans, a half-knowing, half-doubting recycling of conspiracy rumors comes to seem like common sense.

The parallels between conspiracy thinking in feminist and black activism are striking, but there are also important differences. While both have concentrated on vulnerable bodies, particularly in the realm of sexuality and reproduction, African American conspiracy theories usually concentrate on attacks on black *men*. The title of one popular book series on African American education, for example, is *Countering the Conspiracy to Destroy Black Boys*.[4]

We, the People, Charge Genocide

Though African American conspiracy theories have taken on new functions and a new prominence at the end of the civil rights era, there is a long history of conspiratorial thought in black America. As Patricia Turner suggests in her study of rumor in black culture, racial difference has been conceived in conspiratorial rhetoric by both blacks and whites since the first encounters.[5] Fears of cannibalism arose on both sides of the divide, and the history of mutual suspicion has continued ever since, from slavery, through Reconstruction and the rise of the first and second Ku Klux Klan, and on to the race riots of the twentieth century. Turner shows how black rumors of coordinated white hostility are usually more than justified, if not in the specific instance, then certainly within the larger context of the ongoing story of racial injustice and sanctioned violence. The historical case studies of Turner's *I Heard It Through the Grapevine* demonstrate a remarkable continuity of suspicions in the tropes of contamination and conspiracy, many of which center on fears about sexual and medical interference.

It is also important to recognize, however, that there have been significant shifts in conspiracy culture in black America since the end of the 1960s. The civil rights era brought a heightened awareness of how jim crow laws of segregation and the tacit acceptance of violence against blacks in the South added up to a coordinated and semiofficial policy of white supremacy, a conspiracy in deed if not in name. In a provocative petition to the United Nations in 1951, Paul Robeson, W. E. B. DuBois and others of the Civil Rights Congress argued that the reign of terror in the South constituted an act of genocide according to a UN definition. The report contained detailed documentation of lynchings, abuses of power, and economic neglect, leading the petitioners to declare that "We, the people, charge genocide. We, Negro and white petitioners, declare that jimcrow and segregation are a genocidal policy of government against the Negro people." Although Robeson himself went on to assert in a Marxist vein that "the prime mover of the mammoth and deliberate conspiracy to commit genocide against the negro people in the United States is monopoly capital," the *We Charge Genocide* report—though untypical in the directness of its accusation—was very much within the civil rights tradition of calling for an end to public policies and practices of discrimination.[6] But by the end of the 1960s black power advocates began to insist that the civil rights project of changing laws and pointing out manifest injustice had in effect changed very little. Unlike the 1951

145

petition to the UN with its focus on legally and consciously mandated policies and actions, many post-civil rights commentators have been drawn to conspiratorial rhetoric to explain how the unconscious thoughts and behavior of whites (and complicit blacks) amount to a conspiracy to keep blacks oppressed. They claim that life in the ghetto is the same *as if* there had been a deliberate conspiracy; the suggestion is that things couldn't be any worse if "They" had planned it. For example, in *Black Power*, Black Panther spokesmen Stokeley Carmichael and Charles V. Hamilton argue that "the groups which have access to the necessary resources and the ability to effect change benefit politically and economically from the continued subordinate status of the black community." They go on to warn, however, that:

> This is not to say that every single white American consciously oppresses black people. He does not need to. Institutional racism has been maintained deliberately by the power structure and through indifference, inertia and the lack of courage on the part of white masses as well as petty officials. Whenever black demands for change become loud and strong, indifference is replaced by active oppositions based on fear and self-interest. The line between purposeful suppression and indifference blurs. One way or another, most whites participate in economic colonialism.[7]

Here Carmichael and Hamilton suggest that white supremacy does not need to operate on the lines of a deliberate conspiracy, yet nevertheless it amounts to the same thing, since intentional action and unconscious neglect produce the same result and carry the same moral responsibility. I will return later to how conspiracy-infused discussions in black America have increasingly revolved around just how literally one should take the notion of a conspiracy to commit genocide. But for the moment it is sufficient to note that whereas earlier black theorists identified the overt dynamic of discrimination as a virtual conspiracy against blacks, post-civil rights activists have claimed that there are many forms of behavior which fall short of a strict conspiracy, but which nevertheless amount to the same thing. Many of the conspiracy theories that circulate in black communities are in effect now more extensive, but also less specific: almost any aspect of everyday life in the ghetto can be taken as a sign of the ongoing conspiracy.

As well as the portrayal of institutional and unconscious racism *as if* it were a conspiracy, the rhetoric of paranoia has altered in a second important way in the last few decades. With the cycle of violence and poverty in the ghetto continuing despite the seeming success of civil rights demands and affirmative action policies, for many black Americans there must be something else to explain the situation. That something else, of course, is a conspiracy. Because mainstream white society can no longer keep blacks in the ghetto by officially sanctioned means or overt action by groups such as the KKK, the argument goes, it has turned to more nefarious methods to keep them in their place. Since the 1960s a series of increasingly popular conspiratorial rumors have claimed that white supremacy continues through clandestine means. There are stories, for example, that the KKK owns the Church's Chicken fast food chain which is popular in black neighborhoods, and that the recipe contains an ingredient which makes black men sterile. Since the KKK can no longer hold sway through night rides and lynching, the reasoning goes, they have turned to more covert, corporate means to pursue their white supremacist goals.[8] Likewise, by far the most popular conspiracy theory currently circulating in black America is that crack cocaine was deliberately introduced by "the powers that be" into inner-city neighborhoods to devastating effect, just when, it is suggested, blacks might have had a chance to benefit from affirmative action policies to improve their lives.

"Black Paranoia"

Though increasing the range and function of naming and blaming, these developments in African American conspiracy culture since the civil rights era are merely the latest chapter in a long history of racial suspicion and hostility. What is almost entirely new, however, is that "paranoia" in black America in the 1990s has come under intense scrutiny, a topic of newspaper headlines, academic studies and heated public debate.[9] Unlike feminism's fraught encounter with the figuration of conspiracy which takes place mainly within the movement (and then often only implicitly), the politics of black paranoia is a matter for fierce and explicit argument both within black communities and in the mythical mainstream of American society. In a series of prominent public incidents and high-profile pronouncements by black celebrities, African American conspiracy culture has generated intense reactions and—in an irony that we have seen again and again— a great deal of popular alarm that borders on the paranoid.

More than any other event, the trial of O. J. Simpson brought the issue of race and conspiracy into the living rooms of America. Opinion polls indicated that three-quarters of African Americans believed that O. J. was innocent, and hence probably the victim of a police conspiracy to frame him. Conversely, over three-quarters of white Americans felt he was guilty. The disparity between black and white assessments of the likelihood of a police conspiracy and cover-up generated a lot of public anguish. At its most extreme, the LAPD was put on full alert just before the verdict was announced, in expectation of a repeat of the riots following the Rodney King beating verdict. Leaving aside for the moment the depressing conclusion that the "mainstream" often only learn what African Americans are thinking with the publication of opinion polls, the differing statistics demonstrated the huge gulf between black and white ideas of institutional conspiracy in America. For many blacks, the Rodney King case and many other less reported incidents demonstrated that a racially motivated police conspiracy was only too likely, fueled by a barely concealed white supremacist mentality for which Officer Mark Fuhrman unwittingly supplied the public expression on tape.[10] But for many whites, the widespread belief by African Americans in a police cover-up was evidence of an almost pathological inability to face the overwhelming facts and accept that there could not always be someone else to blame for black crime.

In addition to the O. J. case, there have been a series of other episodes which have put the topic of "black paranoia" into the public arena. A 1990 opinion poll of black Americans, for example, was routinely cited by white commentators endeavoring to explain the unbridgeable gap in everyday beliefs across the color line. Sixty percent said that it was true or at least plausible that the authorities had deliberately introduced crack into the ghetto, while 29 percent expressed a conviction or a suspicion that AIDS was the result of a genocidal conspiracy against the black population.[11] The black magazine *Essence* ran a cover story in September 1991 entitled "AIDS: Is It Genocide?"[12] The comedian Bill Cosby, for instance, hinted in the same year that AIDS is "something that was started by human beings to get after certain people they didn't like," while Spike Lee pronounced that "AIDS is a government-engineered disease."[13] Lee also insisted that "it is no mistake that the majority of drugs in this country is being deposited in black and Hispanic neighborhoods," an accusation that has been frequently repeated, from rap records to Congresswoman Maxine Waters's comment that: "People in high places, knowing about it, winking, blinking, and in South Central Los Angeles, our children were dying."[14] John Singleton's 1993 film *Boyz 'N the Hood* offered an extended airing of these fears in the scene where Furious Styles drives his son and his friend out to a billboard in Compton in order to teach them—and a rapidly gathering crowd—what is really going on in South Central. Furious begins by explaining how gentrification works to force out the poor and then push up property values for the new owners; the only solution is to keep things black owned. An old man interrupts and says that the only thing that brings down the value of property in the neighborhood are the gangs with their guns and drugs. In reply Furious asks, "How do you think that the crack rock gets into the country? We don't own any planes. We don't own no ships. We are not the people who are flying and floating this shit in here." He goes on to say that crack only became a problem when it started being noticed in white areas.[15]

The accusations of a conspiracy to flood the ghettos with drugs reached a crescendo in 1996 with the publication in the *San Jose Mercury News* of a three-part series on the connections between the Contras, their CIA sponsors, and the development of the crack trade in Los Angeles.[16] Gary Webb's article told the complex story of Danilo Blandón, a Nicaraguan exile allegedly involved in the cocaine drug trade, and his contacts with, on the one hand, CIA and Drug Enforcement Agency (DEA) associates, and, on the other, a dealer from South Central named Ricky Ross. "Dark Alliance" claimed to offer the first concrete evidence of what had long been rumored, that the CIA had, at the very least, turned a blind eye to the Contras' use of the drug trade to generate substantial cash to subsidize their guerrilla war in Nicaragua. At first the piece received little attention in the mainstream press, but it was picked up very quickly by the black community. Webb appeared on radio and television talk shows hosted by Jesse Jackson and Montel Williams among others, and an extended version of the article on the *Mercury* website (under an illustration of a crack smoker superimposed over the CIA logo) received over 100,000 hits a day. Congresswoman Waters (who represents South Central Los Angeles) latched on to the story, and demanded an official inquiry, as well as inviting the then Director of the CIA, John Deutch, to answer questions at a heated town hall meeting in South Central.

When the mainstream media finally covered the story, they ran articles challenging what they (incorrectly) saw as the principal claim, that the CIA had deliberately flooded the ghetto with drugs to fund the Contras. Alongside these attacks on Webb's reporting, most of the major papers, newsmagazines and current affairs programs ran stories—many of which were written by black journalists—about the rise of what was termed "black paranoia," supposedly in order to help their readers understand why so many African Americans might believe the allegations.[17] Reporting for the *New York Times* from Compton, Los Angeles, on the spread of the rumors, Tim Golden returned to the 1990 poll as a benchmark of the "profound mistrust of government" to be found in black America. Golden also cited the black psychiatrist Dr Alvin Poussaint of Harvard Medical School on the nature of "black paranoia," as if the willingness to believe that the CIA could engage in criminal activity were the sign of a mental aberration—and not a reasonable starting assumption (even if it later turned out to be false), given what emerged from the Iran–Contra hearings about the willingness of the government agencies to exceed their lawful powers.[18]

Compounding this consternation about the black masses suffering from a collective delusion, there was a hand-wringing sense of alarm at the role of the Internet in spreading the conspiracy theory. The *Los Angeles Times*, for example, found in the "Dark Alliance" story a "case study in how information caroms around the country at whiplash speed in the information age."[19] The insinuation is that the black population is the duped victim of technological mind control. This conclusion ignores the rather more significant lesson of the "Dark Alliance" story, namely that African Americans could be the savvy users of a technology—seemingly the preserve of white computer nerds—to bypass the usual media channels.

After months of ignoring the story, the *Washington Post* went for overkill, offering five articles on the topic in a single day, including a front-page piece by Michael Fletcher on black paranoia, as well as an article in the Style section on the vagaries of African American storytelling. Fletcher offered an analysis of what he saw as a tendency to allow "myths—and, at times, outright paranoia—to flourish," despite the "shortage of factual substantiation."[20] With the content of the rumors quickly dismissed, "black paranoia" became the news event in itself. A *Post* editorial, for example, piously declared a few days later that "the biggest shock wasn't the story but the credibility the story seems to have generated when it reached some parts of the black community."[21] Looking back on his abortive attempt to calm black anger in his town hall meeting, ex-CIA Director Deutch argued that "the significance of the episode is the credibility that the inflammatory and inadequately substantiated allegation had among many African Americans, especially in South Central Los Angeles."[22]

For many commentators, then, the real story was not the complex connections between the CIA, crack, and the Contras, but the shocking discovery of the extent and rapid spread of "black paranoia." Like the O. J. trial, the story highlighted the fact that what some people considered to be common sense was no longer held in common in the USA. For many black Americans, it was obvious that the story was at least plausible if not entirely true, while for many whites it was equally obvious that blacks suffered from a near-pathological tendency to believe in such rumors. As Jesse Jackson explained, "What makes it so believable to me is that there is just abounding circumstantial evidence. There is," he continued, "the weight of a lot of experiences with our Government operating in adverse or conspiratorial ways against black people. The context is what's driving the story."[23]

The anecdotal and semisociological essays in the mainstream media trying to explain the phenomenon tended to argue that it should come as no surprise that so many African Americans believe in the rumors, given the history of oppression they have suffered. Many commentators rehearsed in a quite perfunctory way the by now familiar litany of justified complaints: slavery; the Klan; the Public Health Authority/Tuskegee Institute syphilis experiment (in which 400 poor black men were deliberately infected with the disease without being told in order to study its long-term effects if left untreated); the FBI surveillance and harassment of Martin Luther King; the infiltration of the Black Panther Party and other organizations as part of the FBI's COINTELPRO operation, and so on. The articles conceded—somewhat patronizingly—that there might indeed be good reasons in the past why many African Americans should turn to conspiracy explanations. But the presumption was that in the present case of a crack explosion in the ghetto the allegations were unfounded, and therefore that the beliefs were not simply wrong but delusional and distinctly paranoid. Though recognizing the validity of fears about racial injustice in the past, these accounts in effect refused to make that link in the present. What at first seemed like a convincing and sympathetic explanation for the popularity of conspiracy theories in black America ended up redoubling the insulting accusation of a community-wide pathology. The rhetorical maneuver was to insist that if paranoia is justified, it isn't paranoia at all. In this way the ranks of mainstream commentators glossed over the fact that the evidence was far from clear in a case that involved more than its share of double-dealing and corruption by the intelligence and law enforcement agencies, even if there hadn't been a widespread and premeditated conspiracy against the black community.

The point of recounting a history of official disdain and criminal interference with African American lives, however, should not be to dismiss unwarranted allegations as paranoid, but to recognize that all such beliefs operate in a highly charged atmosphere of folk explanation and suspicion whose formal adaptations have a long history. Instead of a token-gesture mention of Tuskegee and FBI surveillance of King, a far more detailed and compelling account of the ill treatment of black Americans might help explain why so many start from the assumption that the authorities are at least partly to blame for criminal neglect, if not for deliberate plotting. In *Whiteout: The CIA, Drugs and the Press*, Alexander Cockburn and Jeffrey St. Clair present an account of "the one thing that was conspicuously ignored" in the explanations of "black paranoia," namely "the long history of the racist application of U.S. drug laws."[24] It is important to remember that the Webb story did not induce an epidemic of "paranoia" in the black community, but confirmed what many already suspected. These beliefs were based less on detailed knowledge of the complex concatenations of power and intrigue during the 1980s, than a living knowledge of how drugs affect black communities. This ranges from the heavy-handed paramilitary invasions of the inner cities under Reagan's War on Drugs campaign, to the lop-sided sentencing for crack dealing (by a factor of one hundred compared to cocaine offences), a legal disparity which has played its part in the appalling rise of incarceration rates among young black men since the mid-1980s.[25] As Turner discovered in her study of conspiracy allegations in black America, these rumors do not appear out of nowhere, but instead form displaced and often symbolic expressions of deep-rooted anxieties about sex, money, and power, which are nonetheless rooted in reality. Though there is a long history of misdealing and misdemeanor by the authorities, it is the *continuing* daily experience of many black Americans that makes conspiracy theories so popular. The by now well-known, but no less shocking, statistics seem to speak for themselves: more young black men are in prison than in college; half of all black children live in poverty; life expectancy rates for blacks are falling; black unemployment rates are double those for the rest of America, and so on. The possibility that the forces of government and big business could be so callous to treat African Americans as less than fully human likewise resonates with a daily awareness of neglect and prejudice in healthcare, education, welfare, and the judicial system.

In his analysis of conspiracy rumors about genocide circulating on Black Liberation Radio, John Fiske presents a powerful version of this argument. Before replaying the snippets of "stolen" information the "knowledge gangsters" at BLR splice together into a charge of genocide, Fiske lays out in detail the statistics of black hardship and inequality. This preface functions as an initial, sociological explanation of why black Americans might be willing to believe in theories that are for most people beyond the pale, given how excluded African Americans are from the economic and social mainstream (Fiske characterizes this kind of alternative public sphere of common sense as the "blackstream"). But the statistics of inequality, from housing to healthcare, also lay the groundwork for taking the charge of genocide seriously. The implicit challenge is: how else could we account for the vast disparities in life chances if there isn't a conspiracy against black people, whether through intention or by default? Having rehearsed in considerable detail the conspiracy theory about AIDS as a biowarfare weapon made to reduce the black (and gay) population, Fiske remains unsure what to believe, and wonders "which of two possible 'wrong' beliefs would have the worse effects—not to believe AIDS-as-genocide if it were true or to believe it if it were not."[26] Though Fiske is right to ponder whether such beliefs are harmful or helpful, there is something troubling about the idea of wilfully choosing what to believe because of the political effects it will have. His conclusion is that because this "counterknowledge" offers a resistance to racism and homophobia it is worth taking seriously. There is the danger, however, that Fiske's faith in the political usefulness of these alternative, populist beliefs would lead him to endorse these rumors even if he didn't believe in them himself. There is something disturbingly patronizing about championing other people's paranoia in the hope that it might serve one's own political agenda, no matter how worthy that objective might be. To argue that there are many good reasons why black Americans might express their grievances in the shape of conspiracy theories is not necessarily to endorse those beliefs. Though black conspiracy theories about genocide might well offer a popular and provocative challenge to unexamined assumptions held by the mainstream, that does not make them inherently transgressive and politically useful.[27]

But neither does "black paranoia" *necessarily* end up diverting otherwise well-intentioned protopolitical fervor from the real struggle for decent education, jobs, and healthcare. This, however, is a popular accusation.

Robert Robins and Jerrold Post, for example, argue that "such beliefs, although psychologically reassuring, even flattering, will divert the sufferer from dealing with genuine problems and will lead him to tilt at the imaginary windmills of conspiracy."[28] In a similar fashion but from a very different institutional location, David Gilbert (a former underground student revolutionary serving a life sentence) argues in *Covert Action Quarterly* that black Americans are doing themselves a disservice by believing in conspiracy theories about AIDS as a genocidal weapon against people of color. Gilbert warns that believing in such theories—giving in to paranoia, in his eyes—can only lead to more people catching the disease. "After more than nine years doing AIDS education in prison," Gilbert writes, "I have found these conspiracy myths to be the main internal obstacle in terms of prisoners' consciousness to implementing risk reduction strategies."[29] As Chapter 5 discusses in more detail, there is substance to Gilbert's warnings. Convinced by accounts of the dangerous contamination of vaccines by unknown or possibly man-made viruses (all caught up in a tale of the genocidal proclivities of governments and pharmaceutical companies), the Nation of Islam recommended that the black community should boycott all compulsory vaccination programs for children in the U.S.[30]

While "black paranoia" can indeed lead to political and personal apathy (not to mention the avoidance of vaccinations), conspiracy theories can also galvanize believers into action. For an article on the sociology of conspiracy theories in African American communities, Theodore Sassoon conducted interviews with several black neighborhood groups in Boston. He discovered that many people believed in the major conspiracy theories about crack and AIDS in the ghetto, but, far from making them quiescent, their suspicions made them more aware of these problems and more determined than ever to do something about them.[31] Contrary to the claim that a willingness to blame sinister, outside influences prevents a community from trying to pull itself up by its bootstraps, education consultant Jawanza Kunfuju's book series *Countering the Conspiracy to Destroy Black Boys* offers a program of resistance. Kunfuju begins by outlining the contours of the conspiracy of white supremacy, but then goes on to enumerate a whole series of educational and social policies which the black community, led by the Nation of Islam, should be implementing for itself—not least because they cannot trust the duplicitous white mainstream to keep to their political promises. Recommending the creation of black male classrooms led by dedicated, Afrocentric male teachers, Kunfuju warns that "you are a member of the conspiracy if you allow a child to sit in a classroom one extra day with an unconcerned teacher."[32] Leaving aside the question of whether this particular educational policy is for the best (it was not surprisingly challenged in the courts by the NOW and ACLU), it must still be acknowledged that Kunfuju's prescriptions for black self-help social and educational policies are inextricably tied to his analysis of a society-wide conspiracy. As we saw with the feminist movement, the possibility of naming and blaming, from government policies to corporate mismanagement, can actually serve to bring the question of agency and responsibility back in, helping coalesce community-based forms of opposition and self-help—even if the ultimate product of this rethinking of social responsibility is not one that you would personally welcome. Conspiracy theories are neither innately radical nor inevitably harmful.

Some political observers have argued, however, that conspiracy theories in black America are damaging not because they divert attention from the real issues of social injustice, but because they blame other people for what are homegrown problems. Instead of taking responsibility for the rise in drugs, disease and crime in their neighborhoods, the argument goes, African Americans latch on to conspiracy theories which put the blame on racism and white supremacism. In *The End of Racism*, for example, Dinesh D'Souza attacks black Americans for their "pathological" predilection for "racial paranoia," which he defines as the "reflexive tendency to blame racism for every failure."[33] D'Souza cites the prominent statements and opinion polls quoted above, and many more extreme ones in addition, arguing that since racism no longer exists in any meaningful sense in America, then such views are signs of a social pathology.

D'Souza is not alone in attacking conspiracy theories as not just psychologically damaging but also politically inexpedient. Several black intellectuals, mainly of a conservative bent, have also suggested that African Americans should spend less time seeking to blame others and more time trying to sort out their problems themselves. Hugh Price, President of the Urban League, advised that "we must not let ourselves and especially our children fall into the paranoid trap of thinking that racism accounts for all that plagues us."[34] *Washington Post* columnist William Raspberry likewise wondered, even if there was a conspiracy to flood the ghetto with crack, then wasn't it the black community's responsibility to reject it?[35] Writing in the *New York Times*, Shelby Steele argued in a similar vein that, "If you actually believe that the society in which you live is feeding AIDS and drugs to you, to eliminate you, you're not going to see your own possibilities in that society ... It's a profoundly destructive belief."[36] In an e-zine editorial, black journalist Earl Ofari Hutchinson also warns that "the issue of black culpability, personal responsibility, and punishment of black drug dealers was buried in the rush to pump the conspiracy line."[37]

Attacks on "racial paranoia" stem from the conservative insistence that instead of finding a scapegoat for their troubles, people must take responsibility for their own lives. These dismissals ensure any appeal to larger, institutional forces as an explanation for injustice gets tarred with the same brush of extremism. In this climate it becomes virtually impossible to discuss the idea of coordinated patterns of prejudice without being labeled "paranoid." The very definition of a conspiracy theory and the diagnosis of paranoia itself become vital in determining which views are to count as legitimate ones in the social arena, and which ones are to be dismissed as deluded.

There is, however, something paradoxical about these right-wing condemnations of black conspiracy thinking. As we have seen, the traditional complaint against conspiracy theorists is that they fail to understand that history is not the product of powerful and ruthless men, but rather the slow cumulative shift of vast, impersonal economic and social forces. This critique is usually made by commentators of a progressive bent, taking right-wing conspiracy nuts to task for their outmoded Carlylian faith in the power of individual agency (orchestrated into a small cabal) to shape history. But for conservative critics of "racial paranoia," it is precisely the tendency to explain things in terms of vast social, psychological and economic forces such as racism that is dismissed as paranoid. As we saw in D'Souza's case, the charge now is that African Americans suffer from a pathological need to blame their plight on institutional racism. "Racism itself," D'Souza remarks, "becomes a scapegoat."[38] In effect, then, the kind of African American conspiracy theories I've been looking at in this chapter reverse the usual expectations. A view of history as the product of the complex interaction of social and economic forces is thus no longer seen as the cure for the delusions of conspiracy thinking but as one of its manifestations. It's a no-win situation: you're accused of being paranoid if you blame everything on a small cabal of sinister agents, and you're accused of being paranoid if you don't. In the case of feminism and black activism, conspiracy theory has become a rough and ready appropriation of the language and logic of the social sciences, a do-it-yourself sociology in an age that finds any discussion of social causation deeply suspicious. Always blaming other people is undoubtedly misguided, but it is perhaps far more damaging always to ignore the role that external forces play, whether malicious or not.

A Conspiracy by any Other Name

One reason for this surprising reversal lies in the *naming* of certain beliefs as paranoid or conspiracy minded. From the perspective of most critics discussing African American rumors about genocide, the labeling of a viewpoint as a conspiracy theory or as paranoid is sufficient to dismiss it. On this logic, it is not that a rumor is wrong because it is conspiratorial, but that it is classed as conspiratorial because it is deemed to be inaccurate—or merely not in line with one's own theory of causation and agency. But the media attention on conspiracy theories in the black community over the past decade has produced an escalating self-consciousness in the terminology, upping the political stakes in an already tense debate. On the one

side, conservative critics are quick to accuse the black community of succumbing to what they see as the dysfunctional logic of *paranoia*, which in
itself is a loaded term which only serves to polarize discussion further. On
the other side, many African Americans employ the language of conspiracy
expressly, only too aware of the incendiary charge such rhetoric carries.
For example, Kunfuju opens *Countering the Conspiracy to Destroy Young Black
Boys* with a dictionary definition of the word "genocide," followed by a discussion of his provocative title:

> To use the word *conspiracy* to describe certain aspects of our society
> is a strong indictment against the social fabric of this country. I
> have been challenged hundreds of times in debates and by the
> media with the use of the word *conspiracy*. Many of the challengers
> want me to document who were the plotters of this conspiracy,
> where was the meeting and when did it take place?

In reply to this challenge, Kunfuju asks a series of his own questions: "Can
you explain how less than 10 percent of the world's population which is
White own over 70 percent of the world's wealth?" And, "Is it an
accident that African American males comprise six percent of the US population, but represent 35 percent of the special education children and
50 percent of the inmates?" He continues with a stream of similar statistics
and observations, and asks, "could the above be happenstance, irony,
luck, or a conspiracy?"[39] For Kunfuju there is only one logical conclusion
to the overwhelming mass of evidence, namely that there is a conspiracy
to commit genocide against black men. But after such a provocative
opening, the rest of the book is comparatively moderate in its language
and conclusions. The "conspiracy" gets a mention now and again, but the
main emphasis is on the problem of encouraging young black boys to
take more interest in school. In many ways, then, Kunfuju does not use
the word "conspiracy" merely as a simple declaration of belief. Instead he
uses it as a strategically useful and deliberately provocative term in his
struggle—however misguided in practice—to improve education for
inner-city black children. He collapses the distinction between a consciously
planned conspiracy, the operation of institutional racism as a "more
subtle" version of conspiracy, and the witting or unwitting complicity of
both whites and blacks in allowing an unjust situation to continue. It
might be argued that Kunfuju is merely misusing the term, but it is
important to recognize that the definition of the term is for him as much
part of the struggle as the promotion of African American teachers or the
provision of an Afrocentrist curriculum.

The key issue again and again is whether there is literally a conspiracy, or
merely something that is like a conspiracy. With the "Dark Alliance"
article, Webb was repeatedly called to account for claiming conspiratorial

causation where none existed. The *Los Angeles Times*, for example, insisted that "the explosion of cheap smokeable cocaine in the 1980s was a uniquely egalitarian phenomenon, one that lent itself more to makeshift mom-and-pop operations than to the sinister hand of a government-sanctioned plot."[40] But Webb, sensitive to the importance of the terminology, insists that he never produced a conspiracy theory: "I never believed, and I never wrote, that there was a grand CIA conspiracy behind the crack plague." Indeed, Webb continues, "the more I learned about the agency, the more certain of that I became. The CIA couldn't even mine a harbor without getting its trenchcoat stuck in its fly."[41] Yet many of Webb's readers and critics understood that even if he hadn't actually used the word "conspiracy," he meant it.

In her account of popular rumors, Turner makes what is for many a common sense distinction between theories which involve "malicious intent" and those that merely point to "benign neglect."[42] But in her analysis of drug rumors she discovers that often the two positions begin to elide, as her respondents frequently hold beliefs that hover between the two. A comment by Jesse Jackson demonstrates this elision. In what at first sight seemed like a return to the worst days of the civil rights struggle in the 1960s, in 1996 a series of arson attacks on black churches in the South attracted much attention from the media and politicians. Jackson argued that it wasn't just a few individuals who were responsible for the church burnings, but that there exists "a 'cultural conspiracy' " which creates an atmosphere conducive to violence. In giving the vocabulary of conspiracy a metaphorical twist, it might be argued that Jackson is stirring up an already tense situation with emotive language (not least when further investigations failed to reveal any coordinated racial motive). But Jackson's designation of a cultural conspiracy emphasizes the difficulty of distinguishing between individual and social responsibility. Just how far is anyone ever entirely in control of their own actions in a complex and interconnected global era? How much blame or credit should individuals take for their successes and failures? How far can we make history under conditions not of our own choosing? These ideological conundra are, of course, far from new, but the point here is that important political and moral discussion now takes place partly through arguments about whether a particular event is "literally" a conspiracy or not. Furthermore, the extension of the figurative use of conspiracy makes it harder to maintain a firm distinction between the two positions. The heated public exchanges over the aptness of the terms "conspiracy" or "genocide" suggest less a pathological tendency to paranoia than a far wider uncertainty of long-held ethical distinctions between deliberate action and criminal negligence—between conspiracy and collusion, in effect.

In contrast to the conservative condemnations of "racial paranoia," Henry Louis Gates takes black conspiracy thinking to task not so much because it is delusional or too quick to blame external factors, but because it simplifies complex problems:

> The manifold ambiguities of black masculinity and its social valence have led, inevitably, to an outpouring of books with titles like *The Conspiracy to Destroy Black Men*. Talk of conspiracy is a nearly irresistible labor-saving device in the face of recalcitrant complexity. One of the reassuring things about talk of conspiracy is that it posits a bright line between victims and victimizers. Of course, it is all too simple.[43]

In many cases Gates is correct that conspiracy talk reduces the intractable complexity of social issues to a simple Them and Us scenario. But in some instances the rhetoric of conspiracy is itself highly ambiguous, wavering between the literal and the metaphorical, as it circles around the problems of agency, responsibility, and blame. Far from being reassuring, the ambiguous rhetoric of conspiracy muddies the bright line between victim and victimizer. Even as it provides a superficially clear answer to the question of why things are like they are, the provisional and half-unbelieving faith with which conspiracy rumors are passed on can undermine the certainties they seem to embody. Often theories about white supremacist genocide, for example, are no more than a collection of well-known statistics and wild speculations which fail to coalesce into a coherent theory. Conspiracy thinking can thus end up promoting uncertainty, casting once routine common sense beliefs into doubt.

In the play of accusation and counteraccusation of "racial paranoia," a great deal of confusion arises over the status of conspiracy beliefs. The question of exactly what it means to believe in a conspiracy theory is far from clear, despite the seemingly lucid statistics of opinion polls. Indeed, opinion polls are perhaps less an indication of actual belief, than a vehicle—albeit a crude and constrained one—for the public expression of political views which all too often are ignored by the mainstream. They do not necessarily represent the true belief of a certain statistical percentage of those polled; instead they allow respondents a preformatted expression of ideas which in reality are often quite confused. Assenting to a conspiratorial statement in an opinion poll allows some people ready-made stories in which to express feelings—about prejudice, suffering, fear, distrust—that might be difficult to give voice to in other ways. The clarity of percentages belies the often contradictory nature of respondents' beliefs.

In his detailed analysis based on peer-group interviews, Sassoon discovered that people often expressed views that shifted fluidly between seemingly contradictory positions. Contrary to the usual portrait of conspiracy theorists as excessively rigid in their beliefs, Turner likewise learned that her respondents were frequently quite vague or noncommittal about the exact identity of the conspirators or the precise mechanism of the plot. Often Turner's respondents would pass on theories and rumors without necessarily fully believing in them themselves (although, conversely, those who did firmly believe in the rumors were often unpersuaded when Turner presented evidence to the contrary, as if the authority of experience counted for more than any other evidence). This form of uncommitted but highly expressive belief—or belief that is more akin to faith—might go some way towards explaining the high percentage of "black paranoia" found in the opinion polls. A whole crowd of attitudes are straightjacketed into the emotive and unstable language of conspiracy, and the issue quickly becomes polarized. It is crucial to remember, therefore, that we are dealing with more than just mere facts. As we saw in feminist writings, the question of figuration can never be forgotten: deciding what counts as a conspiracy theory and as paranoia is not so much a solution to the problem as part of the debate.

Conspiracy Voodoo

We have seen how part of the confusion surrounding the words *conspiracy* and *genocide* is due to a slipperiness in their everyday use. It is also a result of their deliberately confrontational use by black commentators, often with the aim of insisting on a high degree of official moral culpability for what is usually dismissed as "accidental" or "unfortunate," or "your own fault." But some black thinkers and artists use the ambiguities of conspiracy as a positive feature of their formal aesthetic experiments, producing a distinctive black conspiracy culture. This final section will look at three examples: Ishmael Reed's novel *Mumbo Jumbo* (1972), the complicated belief system of the Nation of Islam, and rap artists such as Public Enemy, Tupac Shakur and the Wu-Tang Clan.

Reed's novel is one of the classic postmodernist conspiracy novels, alongside Thomas Pynchon's and William Burroughs's fictions of paranoia. *Mumbo Jumbo* shares with Burroughs's novels a desire to investigate the transhistorical conspiracy to enslave creative consciousness. And like Pynchon's trio of conspiracy novels, it assesses with satirical panache the possibilities and pitfalls of conspiracy theory as an aesthetic and political mode. Though ostensibly a story about the rise and fall of a black cultural explosion centering on the Harlem Renaissance in the 1920s, it is also, like Pynchon's historical novel *Gravity's Rainbow*, written after the tail end of the countercultural adventures of the 1960s, and offers an allegorical examination of the fortunes of the black movements of that decade. As Reed explained in an interview, he tries to use "all the patterns of the time," which includes "the great conspiratorial thing of the sixties—there was always a conspiracy seen behind political events."[44]

Through a collage of detective fiction narrative, vaudeville routines, re-workings of myths, literary parodies, photos, and quotations from numerous historical sources, *Mumbo Jumbo* tells the story of the "Jes Grew" epidemic, which seems to originate in New Orleans and eventually threatens to engulf New York. The name of the epidemic refers to a James Weldon Johnson comment about the origins of the ragtime craze at the turn of the century, which "jes' grew." On one level the plot concerns the spread of "African" culture in the 1920s, from jazz dance crazes to voodoo rituals. But it is also a symbolic story of an epic, trans-historical Manichaean struggle between, on the one hand, the forces of black cultural and spiritual freedom and, on the other, the ongoing, clandestine endeavors of the white establishment ("the Atonists"), led by a fictional secret society, the Wallflower Order of the Knights Templar. *Mumbo Jumbo* follows the investigations of Papa LaBas, a voodoo church elder, who attempts first to uncover the plots of the Wallflower Order to sabotage the epidemic, and then to reveal the mystery of the ancient missing Book which will give Jes Grew its textual fulfilment as mystical force.

The narrator explains that "behind or beneath all political and cultural warfare lies a struggle between secret societies," and in many ways *Mumbo Jumbo* offers a vast, Masonic "conspiratorial hypothesis about some secret society molding the consciousness of the West," in the words of one character.[45] The novel purports to explain not only why the Harlem Renaissance failed (the Atonists caused the Depression in order to stop the epidemic), but also how the whole of Western civilization has involved the suppression of its perpetual, carnivalesque antagonist. But in telling this conspiracy-minded revisionist history, Reed deliberately mixes into his hybrid narrative elements of factual history (for example, the virtual news blackout on the American invasion of Haiti in the 1920s), fictionalized versions of the gray areas of history (President Harding's collaboration in the suppression of Negro culture), and a thoroughly mythical history (the struggle between the Egyptian gods Set and Osiris as a "white" killjoy in opposition to "black" cultural expression). In this eclectic novel, the "evidence" of the various components of the conspiracy is presented through a welter of references to scholarly and alternative histories, as if the reader is meant to take all of its propositions seriously by following up all the footnotes. Yet the erudition is taken to parodic excess, not least in the novel's version of the classic detective fiction revelation scene, when Papa LaBas threatens to blow the cover off the behind-the-scenes dealings of the establishment's secret societies, but ends up producing a sprawling, soporific monologue about Egyptian mythology. "You're supposed to laugh," Reed admits, "when the detective goes all the way back to Egypt and works up to himself in reconstructing the crime."[46] The revelations likewise come not from rational detective inquiry and induction, but from dreams and intuition. Accused of having no evidence to prove his "conspiratorial hypothesis," Papa LaBas replies, "Evidence? Woman, I dream about it, I feel it, I use my 2 heads."[47] For Reed the task is not so much to produce a rational and coherent counterhistory as to "sabotage history" altogether.[48] The novel operates between the factual and the fictional, and between the serious and the satiric. "Always keep them guessing," Reed advises, so that "they won't know whether we're serious or whether we are writing fiction."[49]

Mumbo Jumbo always keeps its readers guessing how literally to take its conspiratorial variations. Like the jazz musician Sun Ra, who expounded a mythology of his own alien abduction so complete that critics could never decide whether he meant it seriously or not, Reed inhabits the territory between the literal and the figural, in a realm beyond simple irony.[50] He deliberately blurs the distinction between the factual and the symbolic, not least with the central motif of the Jes Grew epidemic. It is a metaphor of black African cultural influence that becomes fully materialized, an explanatory figure that develops a life and a history of its own. In the novel, Jes Grew is both a literal epidemic, and a metaphor of cultural transmission. *Mumbo Jumbo* also features the wilful formation of the Mutafikah, a counter-cultural secret society dedicated to the liberation of imprisoned ethnic art in the museums of America. This counterconspiracy in effect constitutes a materialization of the white establishment's worst fears. In a similar fashion the notion of voodoo offers a thoroughly materialized model of psychic infiltration. With the physical possession of an individual's mind and spirit, zombies form both a symbol and an actual causal explanation of the cultural transmission of ideas through the power of ideology. Possibly the most intriguing materialization effect in the novel, however, is the use (on p. 69 in the Avon edition) of a photo of three government figures looking at some Yippies dancing in the street. Though submitted to the publishers in April 1971, long before the Watergate scandal broke, the photo shows future Watergate "conspirators" John Mitchell, Richard Kleindienst and John Dean together. "It's necromancy," Reed explains.[51]

More disturbing than the prophetic photo of the Watergate conspirators, however, is the ghastly and ironic literalization of *Mumbo Jumbo*'s central metaphor. The novel's fiction of a plague centered on black communities that spreads from Haiti to the USA conjures up the AIDS epidemic more than a decade in advance—an epidemic that was, as Chapter 5 discusses in more detail, repeatedly narrated through the logic of conspiracy theory. But in Reed's novel Jes Grew figures as both an epidemic and the blueprint for a counterconspiracy against "Their" secret societies. In combining the two elements it forms a metaphor of the productive and inevitable commingling of African and American culture. "Contagion," as Barbara Browning writes in her analysis of metaphors of infection during the AIDS crisis, "can be recuperated as a positive figure for cultural mixing."[52] For all its plotting of a Manichaean, paranoid separation of opposing traditions, secret societies and racial communities, *Mumbo Jumbo* also enacts a continual aesthetic of infiltration and contamination, both in terms of the story of a contagion of black influence on American culture, and at the textual level of its hybrid literary forms.

If we were meant to take the epidemic and the transhistorical struggle of secret societies quite literally, it would be tempting to dismiss the novel as an offbeat version of popular exposés of Masonic secret histories such as *Holy Blood, Holy Grail*. Or if the Jes Grew epidemic and its attendant conspiracies were merely an extended allegory for cultural influence, the novel would be easier to read as high-minded satire. But with its continual shuttling back and forth between literal accusations and figurative analogies, *Mumbo Jumbo* prevents either escape route into a simple reading. It plays productively on the ambiguities in the popular culture of paranoia, suggesting how it is possible to both believe in a literal conspiracy theory while at the same time holding a skeptical and semi-ironic distance from one's own belief.

The Original Conspiracy

Reed's novel presents a conspiracy-minded and Afrocentric reworking of history, only to undermine that paranoid logic by insisting on not only the impossibility but also the undesirability of a Manichaean cultural quarantine. With its focus on revisionist accounts of Egyptology and its conspiratorial history of the twentieth century, *Mumbo Jumbo* has a lot in common with the Nation of Islam and other black nationalists. Unlike Reed's dialectical approach to the question of cultural and national identity, however, in recent years black nationalism has adopted an increasingly entrenched stance on these issues. From the publication of Martin Bernal's *Black Athena* (1987) to the lawsuit by Leonard Jeffries against his employers, the City University of New York, over the issue of academic freedom, Afrocentrism has become a perplexing battlefront in the ongoing and messy Culture Wars during the 1990s. Bernal, drawing on George G. M. James's *Stolen Legacy* (1954), has been soundly criticized for producing false and conspiratorial revisions of history, with his claims that the Greeks had stolen their ideas from the Egyptians, who were in fact black—and hence that there has been a massive cover-up to deny that black Africa is at the root of civilization.[53] Like the O. J. trial and the Webb story, the Jeffries case has shown the gulf between two different versions of what each side describes as common sense, with seemingly no hope of finding a common ground. There are many good reasons why Afrocentric ideas should be so appealing (not least as a response in kind to the *Bell Curve* debate about innate African American mental inferiority), but that is not to say that the particular conclusions should be left undisputed. To engage with Afrocentric claims is better than to dismiss them wholesale as paranoid mumbo jumbo, not least, as Stephen Howe points out in his powerful critique, because the history of Africa is too important to ignore or distort. It is vital that current Afrocentric ideas are recognized as part of a longer tradition of black nationalist endeavor, even if that historicised view reveals the origin of many Afrocentric ideas in eighteenth-century Masonic misinterpretations of classical history. In many ways *Mumbo Jumbo* shows how these cabalistic ideas can be taken both seriously and skeptically at the same time, since the history of the black Atlantic is a story of contagion and contamination, a tale of myths and fantasies which end up creating a history of their own.

The Afrocentrism debate remains largely within academia, but other aspects of black nationalism have attracted more vitriolic attention. The Nation of Islam (NoI) has come to be the public face of an unacceptable kind of racist paranoia, with speeches of Louis Farrakhan and Khalid Muhammad being reported again and again as manifestations of African American demonology.[54] NoI spokesmen have proposed an increasingly rigid and literal-minded doctrine of racial purity and separation, fueled by demonological attacks on other groups. In particular there have been a series of polarizing standoffs with the Jewish community, sparked by incidents such as the accidental killing in 1991 of a black child by a Hasidic motorist in the racially divided community of Crown Heights in Brooklyn. The tense situation has been made worse with the publication by the Nation of Islam of *The Secret Relationship Between Blacks and Jews* (1991), alleging that the slave trade was organized by Jews. Fears of a rise in black nationalist anti-Semitism have likewise been fueled by a speech made by Khalid Muhammad at Kean College in 1993, excerpts from which were included in an advert in the *New York Times* placed by the Anti-Defamation League.[55] He suggested that "the so-called Jew" was the slumlord of the blacks, and that Jews are as "wickedly great" as Hitler.

While such scapegoating attacks are unconscionable, it is important to recognize how both sides have been quick to exacerbate the mutual fear and loathing, and how the whole issue has been whipped into a moral panic by the mainstream media.[56] Over four hundred editorials and articles instantly condemned Muhammad's speech, as did a host of black leaders, and the entire U.S. Senate. Demonstrating the tendency for the politics of paranoia to spiral out of control, the more Jewish defense organizations have joined in the attack on the Nation of Islam, the more the group has focused its conspiratorial rhetoric on a specifically Jewish target. Though far from mitigating his comments, it must be acknowledged that Khalid Muhammad's attack on Jewish slumlords was part of a longer tirade against a host of other "white slumlords." Though it is of little comfort, the anti-Semitism of black nationalism is at heart more against whiteness than Jewishness, though by now the two have become inseparable in NoI rhetoric. What is perhaps most significant about this admittedly marginal conspiracy discourse in the black community is that it signals a weakening of the rainbow coalition between African Americans and their supporters fostered during the civil rights era. The logic of conspiracy divides as much as it unites.

The rise of the Nation of Islam in inner cities has seemed even more worrying to many observers because of its increasing and at first sight paradoxical affinities with white supremacist groups. In 1990, for example, Gary Gallo of the neo-Nazi-influenced U.S. Third Positionist National Democratic Front wrote an article putting forward their views on racial separatism in the NoI newspaper *Final Call*, while Farrakhan gave an interview for the far-right Liberty Lobby's *Spotlight* magazine.[57] During the Gulf War, the NoI likewise joined the LaRouchites in a loose, conspiracy-fueled opposition to the war. In many ways, of course, it makes no sense for a group dedicated to promoting a version of black cultural and religious heritage to consort with white supremacist organizations committed to eliminating "inferior" races, even if, for the present, the latter are paying lip service to an equal opportunity doctrine of racial purism for all races. Yet a traditionally white conspiratorial version of history which traces the secret society ruling the world back from the Trilateral Commission through the Illuminati and the Masons to ancient Egypt does make some sense if this cabalistic tradition is read as a figure for the ongoing dominance of an oligarchy of white, moneyed power. It would be no exaggeration to claim that the main institutions of American society have traditionally been and are still in the hands of a mainly white, professionally educated upper-middle-class elite (though, as Michael Lind points out in his depiction of this overclass, it would be a mistake to call this clique a conspiracy in the traditional sense, notwithstanding his analysis of practices such as legacy preferences in Ivy League colleges which perpetuate the group's dominance).[58] The adoption by black nationalists of all-encompassing, reactionary militia-style conspiracy theories of the New World Order is, on the one hand, a quite bizarre development in recent conspiracy culture, with, for example, Farrakhan drawing on a passage from *Turner Diaries* almost word for word in one of his speeches.[59] On the other hand, however, this tendency is very much in tune with ghetto conspiracy theories which try to account for the persistence of appalling medical, educational and legal prospects for inner-city blacks despite the successes of the civil rights era. This dark alliance is also the flipside of militia-style revivals of white supremacism, which, as we have seen, are more concerned with the erosion of the traditional economic security of average white folk in a "multicultural" (read: globalized) society. Through the shared but suspect language of racial conspiracies, the black underclass and poor white trash each manage to gesture towards an analysis that is based less on race and more on class inequalities.

Though the Nation of Islam has over the last decade become embroiled in increasingly dogmatic and untenable paranoid assertions of racial purity in opposition to what they see as a persistent white power conspiracy, its core theology remains an intriguing and complicated mixture of faith and doctrine, myth and history. Its founding mythology tells the story of a Supreme Being aided by twenty-four elders or black scientists who together constitute a secret brotherhood, guardians of the sacred knowledge. One rebellious scientist broke away and created the white man to bedevil the original man, the black man. Only the Masons, a white supremacist perversion of ancient Islamic sacred wisdom, are aware of the true devilishness of whites and their conspiratorial plan to rule the world.[60] In its core doctrines, then, the Nation of Islam develops a conspiratorial theology. It provides a fundamental understanding of human and divine interaction in terms of secrecy and brotherhood, justifying the formation of the Nation of Islam as a necessary counterconspiracy to white treachery. It mixes together apocalyptic fervor with confident prophecies based on secret numerological and etymological decodings. Like other religious faiths, it is full of inconsistencies and confusions; Adam, for example, is sometimes identified as Yacub, the evil scientist who fathered the Devil, and at other times as the original black man.[61] But, like other religious faiths, the Nation of Islam operates in the gap between the literal and the figural, insisting at times that the story is merely a metaphor, and at others that this is an accurate historical account. Sometimes the conspiracy-infused story of the creation of a white devil to pervert the true course of black destiny is told literally, including precise dates; for example, the evil scientist Yacub is said to have been born in 8400, according to the Original calendar. But at other times the drama of a secret struggle between black and white secret societies is presented more as a metaphor for the struggle over evil and over unwanted cultural domination within communities and even within individual minds. More than anything, the Nation of Islam shares with other faiths an insistence that nothing is as it seems, and that there is a deeper mystery to events, available to those able to read the secret signs and clues. This world view can easily become solidified into the rigid logic of anti-Semitism, but its wildly eclectic conspiratorial theology can also lend itself to a fluid and powerful commentary on racial history.

America's Nightmare

If the Nation of Islam has produced a theology of conspiracy, then gangsta rap has taken many of its constitutive elements and created an aesthetic of conspiracy.[62] Both the NoI and gangsta are extremely influential in the inner cities (not least because many of the latter are supporters of the former), and both have equally been the subject of moral panics generated by middle America.[63] In each case critics are far too quick to take a quotation out of context and read as quite literal what is often an elaborate (albeit problematic) figural gesture.[64] Despite the many real-life instances of violence in the world of gangsta rap (a cycle of violence that has been hyped out of all proportions by both the moral majority critics and the protagonists), it is crucial to recognize that gangsta as a cultural form works through the elaboration of outlandish boasts whose declaimants insist ever more hyperbolically—and ever more rhetorically—on the visceral literalness of their rhymes. It might be argued, then, that the genre of gangsta relies on a continual erosion and refortification of the boundary between the literal and the metaphorical, and this is no more true than its reliance on the culture of conspiracy.

The title of Public Enemy's seminal 1990 album *Fear of a Black Planet* plays semi-ironically on white fears about black power. The back cover features a photo of the group dressed in paramilitary style ("Gear I wear got 'em going in fear"), with uniformed men from the Fruit of Islam (the inner guard of the Nation of Islam), exaggeratedly conspiring over a map of the world.[65] The militant personae and rhetoric are as ambiguous as the group's logo: with the knowledge of armed FBI attacks on the Black Panther Party, what might at first be taken as the silhouette of a black power activist framed by the crosshairs of a white soldier's rifle might instead be seen as the opposite: a white supremacist targeted by the pinpoint accuracy of the group's rhyming prowess.[66] As a declaration in the liner notes explains, the only way to counter a conspiracy is to form your own one: "Black Power 1990 is a collective means of self-defense against the worldwide conspiracy to destroy the black race. It's a movement that puts fear in those that have a vested interest in the conspiracy." The aim is to conjure up a "counterattack on world supremacy," as the telegraphic news strip on the front cover announces. Public Enemy perform a complicated double bluff of taking seriously the projections of "black paranoia" by reprojecting outwards the specter of a conspiracy that they had already been internalized. If "They" are dumb enough to get seriously paranoid about our paranoia about "Their" conspiratorial plans for white supremacy, the logic goes, then we'll signify on "Their" panic by pretending to take seriously our own counterconspiratorial performance—right down to the stylized military uniforms and see-through inflatable globe in the back-cover photo. Instead of merely mirroring their oppressors in the creation of a counterconspiracy, they return a distorted and satiric image. In effect, by identifying themselves as the "Public Enemy," Chuck D. and Co. are strategically turning the panicked attacks back against their critics as a form of empowerment (albeit a very constrained one), parodically acknowledging that they will materialize into what white fantasy has made them. As rap legend and paranoid spokesman Tupac Shakur declared in a defiant reappropriation of white hostility (what Eithne Quinn calls a "self-demonologizing move"), he is "America's nightmare."[67]

166

Arguably the most creative use of conspiracy culture comes from the Wu-Tang Clan. This ever-shifting cluster of talent emerged from Staten Island in 1993 with *Enter the Wu-Tang (36 Chambers)*, a heady mixture of Five Percent doctrine (a Nation of Islam offshoot), conspiracy theory, ufology, martial arts lore, Mafia aggrandisement, and gangsta bravado. They combine numerology with esoteric etymologies which "prove" their conspiracy routines; for example, when asked by an interviewer what Islam means to him, Ol' Dirty Bastard replies "I Sincerely Love Allah Mathematics."[68] The pronouncements consistently waver between the wildly rhetorical and the all too literal. Like many self-mythologizing rappers, they have had many encounters with the law, creating, if not actually proving, their street reputation. But also, like Public Enemy, they form their ever-shifting group identity around the creation of a counter-conspiracy. They each maintain numerous comic-book hero personae and kung-fu styles, defying any attempt to solidify their aesthetic into a rigid doctrine. Though seemingly immersed in the arcane conspiratorial complexities of Five Percenter theology and not shy of claiming that vaccinations lead to "babies being born with disfigurations," they are also capable, for example, of warning in a song of the danger that conspiracy theories of AIDS will discourage safe sex. They satirically air the thoughts of a loser who believes that AIDS is a "germ warfare product" that is "government made" in order to "keep niggaz afraid," so that "they won't get laid, no babies be made," with the result that the "black population will decrease within a decade."[69] The Wu-Tang take to new heights the use of conspiratorial rhetoric in a trickster aesthetic, at times destructive and narrow minded, but at others comic and expansive. They make conspiracy culture work for them, not by seeking to fix the distinction between what is literally a conspiracy and what is merely like a conspiracy, but by deliberately confounding the opposition through a series of deft and exuberant rhetorical jujitsu maneuvers. Many conspiracy theories circulating among African American communities are undoubtedly misguided and malicious. Yet some forms of black conspiracy culture manage with wit and ironic exaggeration to keep the complex questions of causality and responsibility on the agenda by hijacking and retooling the terminology of conspiracy.

5

BODY PANIC

I can no longer sit back and allow Communist infiltration, Communist indoctrination, Communist subversion, and the international Communist conspiracy to sap and impurify all of our precious bodily fluids.

(Dr Strangelove)

Does the body still exist at all, in any but its most mundane sense? Its role has steadily diminished, so that it seems little more than a ghostly shadow on the X-ray plate of our moral disapproval. We are now entering the colonialist phase in our attitudes to the body, full of paternalistic notions that conceal a ruthless exploitation carried out for its own good. This brutish creature must be housed, sparingly nourished, restricted to the minimum of sexual activity needed to reproduce itself and submitted to every manner of enlightened and improving patronage. Will the body at last rebel, tip all those vitamins, douches and aerobic schedules into the Boston harbor and throw off the colonialist oppressor?

(J. G. Ballard, "Project for a Glossary of the Twentieth Century")

Metaphoricity is the contamination of logic and the logic of contamination.

(Jacques Derrida, *Dissemination*)

In recent years the body has become one of the most prominent subjects of paranoid fantasies. From horror movies in which bodies are spectacularly mutilated by unseen forces, to tales of abductions by small gray aliens— possibly in collusion with the government—who perform disconcerting medical experiments; and from the sight of police officers wearing latex gloves at an AIDS rally, to reports of corrosive sperm by the wives of men claiming to suffer from Gulf War Syndrome: American culture teems with the traces of body panic. Fear of invasion by body snatchers of one kind or another has reared its head throughout American history, most prominently in the 1950s.[1] Indeed, with the reemergence of a paranoid rhetoric of contamination and infiltration, it can begin to seem that the 1980s and 1990s staged a rerun of the 1950s. In a literal sense the 1950s were remade in films such as John Carpenter's *The Thing* (1982) and David Cronenberg's *The Fly* (1986), a process of mutation and proliferation of earlier horror/sci-fi imagery which reaches an epidemic level in *The X-Files*.[2] The last decades of the century also brought with them a return to a depressingly familiar political culture of demonology. Just when you thought it was safe, the monstrous rhetoric of quarantine, exclusion and scapegoating of the undesirable is back: economic segregation, white flight, gated communities, restricted immigration, disproportionate blaming of minorities for social ills of which they are more usually the victims, fears about domestic terrorists and evil dictators used to justify a repressive, racist backlash, and, most ominously, a return to the public visibility of homophobia which marked the red-baiting era, captured no more insidiously than in William F. Buckley's suggestion that the HIV positive should be tattooed on the buttocks.[3]

Bodies of Evidence

Although it can seem that in many ways the 1980s and 1990s replicated the worst excess of the 1950s, there are also crucial differences. In the 1950s, the language of bodily invasion provided a ready source of metaphors about the imagined threat to the American body politic. Hysterical fears about bugs, germs, microbes, monsters, aliens and all manner of scapegoated Others dominated the political and popular culture of the McCarthy years. For example, in his famous "containment" doctrine, George Kennan pronounced that "world communism is like a malignant parasite, which feeds only on diseased tissue," while J. Howard McGrath, the Attorney General, warned that the Communist is "everywhere—in factories, offices, butcher shops, on street corners, in private businesses—each carries with him the germs of death." Popular health scares blurred into hysterical concerns about un-American influences ("Is fluoridation a Communist plot? Is your washroom breeding Bolsheviks?").[4] The language of immunology lent itself readily to suspicion that the danger lay as much in the compromised "health and vigor of our own society" (as Kennan put it) as in the contaminating influence of the "alien" ideology of Communism. If in the 1950s germophobia functioned principally as a figure for anxieties about attacks on the body politic and the failure of the national immune system, then more recent dramas of immunological paranoia speak only of fears about the body itself. In Stanley Kubrick's satire on 1950s paranoia, *Dr Strangelove* (1964), the mad General Jack D. Ripper fulminates against Communist contamination of his "precious bodily fluids" by the fluoridation of the water supply. Whereas, in Kubrick's film, the rhetoric of polluted bodily fluids was little more than a parodic symbol of a previous generation's paranoid fears, be they Communism or conformity, in the 1980s and 1990s anxiety about precious bodily fluids became quite literal.[5]

The gap between the figurative uses of body panic in the 1950s and its current more literal embodiment can be measured by three examples: drug panics, alien abductions, and mind control. As cybertheorists Arthur and Marilouise Kroker aptly observe, the last decade or two have witnessed the rise of what might be termed "body McCarthyism," a return to the hysterical discourse of covert invasions and loyalty oaths associated with the House Un-American Committee's persecution of alleged radicals and homosexuals who supposedly offered a threat to the integrity of the United States.[6] This time around, however, the fears and investigations are fixated on the body itself. In many ways the War on Drugs in the last two decades functions in much the same way as the McCarthyite campaign against "The Enemy Within."[7] The loyalty oaths of the 1950s demanded a public demonstration of compliance and purity that now takes place at the corporeal level: the Reagan administration's Executive Order 12564 of 1986 made drug testing mandatory in federal agencies for employees in "sensitive positions," those for whom a "reasonable suspicion" of drug consumption exists, and any applicant for employment in those agencies. The Drug-Free Workplace Act of 1988 extended this policy to cover anyone awarded a federal contract and grant in the private sector, and many companies have voluntarily initiated their own drug testing. As David Campbell points out, "drug tests [are] more widespread in the early 1990s than security tests were in the early 1950s."[8] Purity of bodily essence now becomes not a parodic metaphor but a literal matter of patriotic duty. As Cory Servaas of Reagan's Presidential AIDS Commission commented, "It is patriotic to have the AIDS test and be negative."[9] Body politics has replaced the body politic as the occasion for conspiracy-infused fears.

If widespread drug testing represents the literal-minded fears of the authorities about corporeal sedition, then concern about alien abductions and mind control speaks of the populist emergence of body panic for a technological era. In the case of ufology, it is highly significant that the typical reports of UFOs in the 1950s involved the sighting of an unidentified craft from afar (so-called encounters of the first kind), but the most publicized cases from the last decade or so involve close encounters of the fourth kind: the abduction of people from their bedrooms or cars by aliens and, typically, the performance of sinister medical experiments upon the victims.[10] In such narratives the physical body itself is now the perceived target of invasive forces: contact with aliens has turned intimate. Far from the optimism of early contactee accounts of the benevolent ambassadorial role of alien "Space Brothers," more recent testimonies insist that the aliens' motives are far more obscure, if not outright malevolent, and—more disturbing still—that the government might well be in cahoots with the extraterrestrial invaders. The most frequent, and the most notorious, of these stories involve disturbing pseudomedical episodes such as egg collecting, rectal examinations, and the placing of a small implant in the nose. In Whitley Strieber's *Communion*, for example, the author recounts the following episode without the faintest hint of irony:

> Two of the stocky ones drew my legs apart. The next thing I knew I was being shown an enormous and extremely ugly object, gray and scaly, with a sort of network of wires on the end. It was at least a foot long, narrow, and triangular in structure. They inserted this thing into my rectum. It seemed to swarm in me as if it had a life of its own.[11]

Budd Hopkins, the master-collector of abduction tales, calculates that 19 percent or more of his correspondents reported the "insertion of what seem to be tiny implants into their bodies"; some recall a "thin probe of some sort with a tiny ball on the end having been inserted into a nostril"; in other cases the insertion is made through the eye socket or the ear.[12]

The Internet in particular and popular culture in general abound with conspiratorial tales of the body under threat from invasive alien technology, and it is tempting to dismiss much of this new ufology as the hysterical symptom of a collective paranoia, the somatic expression of concerns which ultimately have little to do with the physical body.[13] But to translate out the physical into the psychic would ignore how the besieged body has itself become a crucial player in the scene of contemporary politics. For example, the concentration of fears on rectal penetration must be seen in the context of a hyperbolic focus on the anus as the source and site of medical as well as moral anxiety in discussions of AIDS. Likewise, the prevalence of alien abduction stories which feature invasive gynecological procedures speaks to concerns about rapidly changing reproductive technology, in a decade whose political terrain has been scarred by battles over abortion, and fertility treatments such as surrogacy and cloning. Unlike body-snatching invasions of the 1950s when scientists (often in collaboration with the military) saved the day, alien abduction narratives in the 1990s express fears about medical science's invasion of the body as the source of danger. It comes as little surprise, moreover, that the most frequent visitor, the so-called small gray alien, is typically represented in both personal accounts and Hollywood film as a creature with a disproportionately large head, huge enigmatic eyes, a tiny body and delicate hands

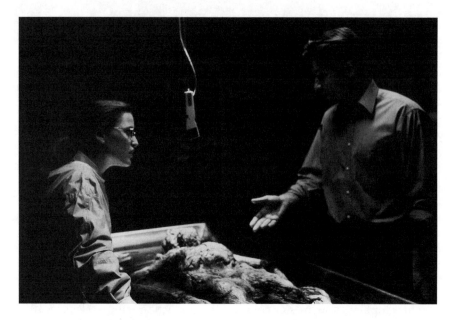

Figure 5.1 In *The X-Files*, Scully and Mulder encounter a small gray alien. Courtesy of the Kobal Collection.

(Figure 5.1). It forms an icon which recalls pictures of fetuses in the womb, a striking and uncanny image of the "alien within" that has only become available through new imaging technology in the last quarter century. The conspiracy-inflected dramas of alien experimentation thus say less about the particular psychic makeup of the individuals telling the stories than they do about a society in which people's (and especially women's) relationship to their own body is so often mediated through technical expertise, be it medical, judicial, or ethical.[14]

In the accounts of many abductees, their lives—and sometimes even their thoughts—are periodically controlled by alien visitors. Hopkins, for instance, speculates that the purpose of the implants runs to "any or all of three unappetizing possibilities":

> They could function as "locators," in the mode of the small radio transmitters zoologists attach to the ears of hapless, tranquillized elk to trace their wanderings. Or they could be monitors of some sort, relaying the thoughts, emotions or even the visual and sensory impressions of the host. Or, and perhaps least palatable, they could have a controlling function as receivers, suggesting the possibility that abductees could be made to act as surrogates for their abductors.[15]

Though Hopkins chooses not to dwell on "these paranoia-inducing theories," others have suggested that alien abductions are in fact cover stories for the real abductions that are taking place under the auspices of top secret government mind control projects. *The X-Files*, for example, plays with this idea, continually instating, overturning and reversing this interpretive possibility.[16] In addition to this particular possibility, there is a long tradition of conspiratorial allegations of mind control experiments. These fears focused on the Soviets as perpetrators in the height of the Cold War, and, in the wake of revelations about the activities of the intelligence agencies in the 1970s, on the American government's covert programs of mind control such as MK-ULTRA (the so-called "Manchurian Candidate" program).[17]

It is significant, however, that in the past the most commonly detailed mechanism was some form of psychological brainwashing, but in the present the stories feature invasive technology, whether in the form of microwaves or the actual implantation of microchips. Tales of discovered implants regularly do the rounds on mind control discussion groups on the Internet, complete with instructions on how to avoid psychic infiltration by wearing a hat lined with baking foil. One of the most frequently cross-posted implant images on the Net is a photo of tiny metallic objects removed by Dr Roger Leir of Southern California from the big toe of a female patient who claims to have been an abductee. The photos and X-rays are usually also accompanied by gory photos of the operation itself.[18] There is also the rumor that Timothy McVeigh, the Oklahoma bomber, claimed that as a member of the covert armed forces he had been implanted with a chip in his buttocks which controlled his actions. Although the location of McVeigh's alleged implant is obviously highly symbolic (though not in its own way implausible), what needs to be emphasized here is that his claim of being controlled by shadowy outside forces takes the literal form of a physical implant in his body.[19] As with drug testing and alien abduction narratives, conspiratorial fears about being controlled by external forces are now regularly located in the body.

Invasion of the Body Snatchers

Some more flesh can be added to the initial claim that body panic has taken a turn to the literal by examining the changing genre of sci-fi horror films since the 1950s. The standard interpretation of a classic "invasion narrative" such as Don Siegel's 1956 *Invasion of the Body Snatchers* is that the zombified pod-people represent the dangers of the faceless conformity of totalitarianism in general and Communism in particular. More recent readings view the film as a warning about the perils of conformity, not to an alien doctrine, but to the dehumanizing dogma of McCarthyism. Other interpretations see the body-snatching invasion as a critique of technocratic rationality which was feared to be turning the postwar American individual into an "Organization Man." Some of these films (such as *Them!* and *Invaders from Mars*) can likewise be seen as expressions of anxiety less about Soviet nuclear attack than about the military–industrial complex which had turned the U.S. into a permanently militarized state. Some have argued that the monstrous invading force in these films is a coded presentation of America's demonologized Others (principally women, blacks and homosexuals) who were taken to constitute a threat to straight, white male hegemony. The alien invasions in these films have thus come to be understood not so much as threats from without as unperceived dangers of "un-American" influences *within* the nation.[20]

Although these assessments vary in detail, they all view American culture of the 1950s as beset by a paranoid concern to forge and police a division between self and other, between what was reliably American and what was intolerably alien to its idealized self-image, even if the distinction between Them and Us was at times hard to maintain. Whether we interpret this popular subgenre as the expression of genuine fears or as the cynical manipulation of a demonological intolerance of difference, the films are nevertheless insistent that there is (in the words of the HUAC accusation) a "clear and present danger" to the American way of life. More recent paranoid scenarios, however, are often quite unspecific or contradictory about the source of imagined harm. The 1956 *Invasion of the Body Snatchers* clearly operates as an admonitory allegory, even if its demonologized object is in dispute. Likewise, in the second version of the film, made in 1976 and set in San Francisco among a group of ex-1960s radicals, the pods can be viewed as representing the dangers of the counterculture "falling asleep" into the complacency of self-absorption in the 1970s. But in *Bodysnatchers!*, Abel Ferrara's 1990s remake, it is extremely hard to discern where the allegorical force of the tale might reside. One critical interpretation, for example, can offer nothing more concrete than the suspicion that the film is about growing up, the generation gap, and the possibility that "age itself is a bodysnatcher."[21] The action focuses on a family of four, the father of which has been called to a military base to investigate environmental contamination. One by one the family are transformed by the pods, until only the angstful teen daughter is left to make her escape. In this version the pods, somehow linked to the medical–military–industrial complex, constitute a vague but nonetheless viscerally present and literal threat to the protagonists. Unlike the other two versions, the 1990s remake shows in vivid detail the process of body snatching, first with the scene of the mother's body suddenly deflating and decomposing into a putrefying mess, and then with the attack by slimy tentacles on the daughter—one of which begins to slide into her throat—as she falls asleep in the bath. Ferrara's film creates a disturbing and graphic sense of the ominous presence of danger without a clear indication what the source or nature of that danger might be. The film produces in effect an impression of conspiracy without conspiring, a generalized and at times paralysing atmosphere of undifferentiated alarm which leaves unclear who or what might be behind it. The only thing we know for sure is that "They" are after the protagonists' bodies.

Unlike the sudden invasion (whether from outer space or from the id) by demonized monsters in the horror films of the 1950s, the nightmares of turn-of-the-millennium America—urban crime, random violence, economic insecurity, drugs, pollution, and viral contamination—create an omnipresent environment of risk which is centered on the individual body. In his introduction to *The Politics of Everyday Fear*, Brian Massumi offers an astute and acerbic commentary on this situation (which in his view is as cynically exploited as the former Cold War terror):

> The cold war in foreign policy has mutated into a state of generalized deterrence against an enemy without qualities. An unspecified enemy threatens to rise up at any time at any point in social or geographical space. From the welfare state to the warfare state: a permanent state of emergency against a multifarious threat as much in us as outside.[22]

The superpower face-off has given way to a policy of "low intensity conflict," producing a continuous but often unspecific sense of threat that is now located everywhere but nowhere in particular. The secure paranoia of the tense yet clear geopolitical division between self and other has given way to the troubling confusions that have emerged since the late 1960s, with uncertainty about the distinction between friend and foe, from American military intervention in Vietnam to the peace-keeping mission in Somalia. After the revival of Cold War demonology during the Reagan years, the "New World Order" of the 1990s has introduced an insecure paranoia in which there is no longer a single recognizable enemy or indeed a clear sense of national identity.[23]

Given the close link between the rhetoric of germophobia and national politics, it comes as no surprise that here has been a corresponding shift in the vocabulary of immunology during this period. Since its emergence as a discipline towards the end of the last century, immunology has primarily been concerned with identifying the mechanisms by which bodies defend themselves from attack by foreign antigens. Its fundamental principle has been the distinction between self and non-self. In immunological discourse in the last three decades the frontline of the battle against disease has shifted from the surfaces of the body (the skin as a protective barrier and personal hygiene as one's best defense) to the complex mechanisms of the immune system as a regulatory process at work within the body in the blood and lymph systems. More recently immunologists have been concerned with the complicated and troubling erosion of the supposedly bedrock distinction between self and other, provoked by an interest in auto-immune diseases in general and HIV/AIDS in particular. The focus of attention is now "The Wars Within," in the words of the subtitle of a famous article by Peter Jaret (with photographs by Lennart Nilsson) in *National Geographic*. The article offers dramatic pictures and accounts of the struggles waged in "inner space," with, for example, macrophagocytes enveloping a bacterium in a scene that looks like nothing so much as an episode from *Star Wars*.[24] The text uses a militarized language of enemies and invasion, but when it comes to discussing HIV, the body-as-battlefield becomes fused with elements from an espionage tale:

> Many of these enemies have evolved devious methods to escape detection. The viruses that cause influenza and the common cold, for example, constantly mutate, changing their fingerprints. The AIDS virus, most insidious of all, employs a range of strategies, including hiding out in healthy cells. What makes it fatal is its ability to invade and kill helper T cells, thereby short-circuiting the entire immune response.[25]

The inert virus is imbued with malicious agency, while the self is repeatedly metonymized into ever more microscopic particles of defense, forming immunological homunculi which are figured as miniaturized special agents. Though its metaphors are still mainly militaristic, immunology now draws on images of messy wars, civil unrest, domestic terrorism, and so on, precisely the kind of troubled, low intensity conflict that has come to dominate the post-Cold War world.[26]

If the origin of the palpable threat can be located anywhere in contemporary sci-fi/horror films it is no longer from the outside but from within. Though the earlier horror movies might equally be concerned that the source of danger was internal to the American body politic, the difference is that films now portray anxiety not so much about the body under threat as the body itself constituting the threat. This transition is captured tellingly by David Cronenberg's ironic reversal of the title of the 1953 classic horror movie, *It Came From Outer Space*, in his pioneering 1974 film *They Came From Within*. In Cronenberg's version the danger comes not from an alien spaceship which crashes into the desert but from blood parasites which turn their victims into sex-crazed zombies. The alien parasites transform the victims' corporeal identities, with the resulting creatures being neither wholly alien nor entirely human. Likewise, leaving aside other differences between the 1958 original of *The Fly* and Cronenberg's 1986 remake, most immediately apparent is the film's heightened depiction of the putrefying and rebellious flesh in Jeff Goldblum's metamorphosis into Brundle-fly. What is significant about Cronenberg's film is not just that the scientist's identity is conceptually broken down, but that his body literally dissolves on screen, effecting a remorseless conspiracy of the flesh against what remains of the self.

What began in the 1970s as an avant-garde preoccupation for directors such as Cronenberg has now become commonplace. Microelectron photographs or schematic diagrams of the "treacherous" human immuno-deficiency virus at work infiltrating a cell are perhaps the most prominent of many similar popular representations of the body as an alien battle zone. As the Manhattan Project gives way to the Human Genome Project, the Virus displaces the Bomb as the subterranean source of popular paranoia. It has even been claimed that the virus has become the new number one public enemy with the collapse of the Cold War.[27] New medical imaging technology helps ensure that inner space replaces outer space in the popular imagination as both the utopian final frontier of tech-noscientific endeavor, and the source of conspiratorial scenarios of enemy invasion, an attack in which the body is simultaneously an uncontrollable mutineer and a vulnerable victim. William Burroughs, pioneer cosmonaut of inner space and creator of some of the most graphic and influential images of body panic, makes the case with sardonic and prophetic under-statement. "The realization," he advises, "that something as familiar to you as the movement of your intestines the sound of your breathing the beat of your heart is also alien and hostile does make one feel a bit insecure at first."[28] When the flesh rebels and the "soft machine" of the body conspires against the self (or whatever is left of that concept), vigilant immunological self-surveillance becomes a vital but ultimately futile necessity. In *The X-Files*, Assistant Director Skinner is infected by a renegade government agent with a biological disease which turns out to be mechanical in origin. It consists of a nanotechnology infiltration of microscopic machines which build up barriers in his arteries, such that "his blood has become a weapon against his body."[29] If popular wisdom in the 1950s warned that there was a red under the bed, then in the 1990s the paranoid motto is to trust no one—least of all one's embodied self.

Indeed, in *The X-Files*, Agent Scully comes to suspect that she has been the victim of an abduction (either by aliens or the government, or the one in collusion with the other) which leaves her with an implant in her neck. To her horror, the implanted chip sends a supermarket register berserk when she scans it through. The removal of the chip causes a virulent cancer to metastasize in her body, which is only reversed when a similar chip is reimplanted. The chip, however, seems to be dictating Scully's actions when she gravitates towards what turns out to be a mass staging for a prospective abduction. At an even deeper level, the fundamental de-marcation of self and non-self is eroded at a molecular level. Investigating an ice-core sample taken from a block of ice containing what turns out to be a faked alien corpse, she discovers not only that the ice contains an extraterrestrial viral culture, but that it matches the DNA from her own contaminated blood.[30] In effect her blood contains unrecognizable—and possibly quite literally alien—genetic material, which in turn, she believes, caused her cancer. Scully's DNA—that most intimate but inhuman location of a unique self—has fused and hybridized with alien genetic viral codes. In the same way that the identity of the forces responsible for Scully's implantation remain hazy and constantly shifting, so too, on the outside, her body begins to dissolve its boundaries with her frequent nose-bleeds. By the sixth series, the Special Agents have come to suspect that the alien virus found in Scully's blood, and also in the blood of Gibson Praise, the child chess prodigy, is present in everyone's DNA:

> SCULLY: Mulder, these are the results. DNA from the claw nail we found [seemingly from an alien creature that has hatched from a lab technician's body]—matching exactly the DNA in the virus you believe is extraterrestrial—
> MULDER: That's the connection.
> SCULLY: —which matches exactly the DNA I found in Gibson Praise.
> MULDER: Wait a minute. I don't understand what you're saying. You're saying that Gibson Praise is infected with the virus?
> SCULLY: No, it's part of his DNA. It's called a genetic remnant. Inactive junk DNA. Except in Gibson it's turned on.
> MULDER: So if that were true it would mean that the boy is in some part extraterrestrial.
> SCULLY: It would mean that all of us are.[31]

Having searched everywhere for confirmation of the feared and desired conviction that "they're here," in other words, that extraterrestrial life exists, Mulder finds that he himself is partly alien to the very core of his being. In the *X-Files* mythology, the dividing line between the human and the alien begins to blur, and in fact (as the show has begun to suggest towards the end of the sixth series) the distinction between the two has always been blurred from the very beginning of life on Earth. We have met the alien enemy, and it is us.[32]

As *The X-Files* scenarios of DNA panic suggest, the paranoid imagination of conspiring enemies no longer serves to guarantee a stable sense of self, whether national or personal. The unspecific but pervasive environment of bodily risk fails to produce a clear enemy against which the identity of the imperiled self might be forged, not least because these contaminatory risks can bring about an erosion of the distinction between self and other at a cellular level. In his account of American horror films since the 1930s, Andrew Tudor argues that since the 1960s the genre has undergone a shift from "secure" to "paranoid" horror, broadly characterized by the transition from external, recognizable threats successfully repelled by effective experts and trustworthy authorities, to internal, unconscious or diffuse threats which escalate out of control.[33] Recasting Tudor's account slightly, it might be argued that the more secure paranoid style of the 1950s, which served to bolster a sense of individual or collective identity, has given way to a paranoia which *results from* the dissolution of the physical body as the stable ground of identity.

Frenzy of the Visible

In contemporary body horror films the privileged figure of a paranoia-inducing erasure of bodily difference is the excess of slime and bodily fluids. Since the pioneering explorations by Cronenberg and other directors in the 1970s into what might be termed the aesthetics of abjection, "gloopy" special effects have become commonplace in the slasher gorefests that are the staple fare of video stores. A great deal of critical attention has been given to the politics of slime in these graphic horror films. Barbara Creed, for example, argues convincingly that the focus in films like the *Alien* trilogy on oozing orifices betrays a complex fear of and desire for the "monstrous-feminine," namely those aspects of maternity and femininity that society finds so hard to accept. Creed draws on Julia Kristeva's study of abjection, which in turn derives some of its arguments from Mary Douglas's seminal work on notions of purity and danger. Kristeva adds a psychoanalytic twist to Douglas's anthropological observations, arguing that the horror of slime results not from its inherently repellent viscosity, but from the cultural and psychological association with femininity of the borderline, the marginal and the contaminatory.[34]

Though these symbolic readings of abjection go a long way to explain the source of bodily paranoia in contemporary horror films, they fail to give an account of why, if the fear of the monstrous-feminine is so constant a feature of our society, the genre should suddenly turn to the graphic representation of the "cultural unrepresentability of fluids" in the 1980s and 1990s.[35] What is perhaps most striking about recent body horror movies is the intensity of their gut-wrenching special effects. The dramatic, visual presence on the screen of the mutilated body in all its pustular mayhem must be understood as a highly significant development in itself, over and above any symbolic interpretations. With the heightened realism of special effects, however, it is a figurative trope which paradoxically insists on its visceral literalism. But why has this visual excess of body horror become so widespread?

In part the answer undoubtedly is to be found in the history of the increasing technical competence of special effects, even before the advent of computer-generated digital animation. Horror movies now show exploding heads, technicolor disembowelments and the appearance of parasites crawling beneath the skin simply because they *can*: Cronenberg, for instance, describes in an interview how *They Came From Within* featured the latter scene, created by a series of sequentially inflated balloons beneath a latex fake skin (an effect which the makers of *The Exorcist* were coincidentally developing at the same time). As Cronenberg comments, "the very purpose was to show the unshowable."[36] In many horror films today special effects become not an enhancement of the main action but its replacement. The graphic nature of such episodes is caught up in the inflationary logic of the spectacle, a process of repetition and innovation which is perhaps the inevitable outcome of a successful but ever more saturated market.

The gruesome realism of the pioneering body horror films of the 1970s, with their emphasis on the specifics of mutilation, might also be understood as at first a countercultural reaction to the ubiquitous but sanitized footage of the Vietnam War in American living rooms in the late 1960s and early 1970s. It must be remembered, however, that the increasing explicitness of body horror films is only part of a larger, "liberatory" movement away from censorship towards an aesthetic of corporeal hyperrealism in both cinema and society at large. The tendency towards the "frenzy of the visible" structures both hardcore pornography and other cultural artefacts.[37] As we saw in Chapter 2, in the 1960s the fatal head wound shown in the Zapruder footage of the Kennedy assassination was only publicly available in the mismatched sequence of black and white stills published in the Warren Commission Report. By the early 1970s bootlegged versions began to circulate in the underground art scene of New York, often intercut with hardcore porn, connecting the exploding head shot to pornography's ejaculatory money shot. In the mid-1970s the footage was shown on national television for the first time on the *Geraldo* show. In the 1980s there appeared full-color coffee-table books of assassination imagery, including the notorious (and previously unshown) full-color autopsy photos. The 1990s witnessed Oliver Stone's *JFK* which featured both a reshooting and a computer-enhanced, slow-motion version of the Zapruder footage. And, most recently, the Zapruder family has released an even more enhanced (read: graphic) version on video. The compulsion and ability to show everything (albeit often in the stylized form of choreographed violence or sexuality) operates across a wide range of contemporary American culture, making the body's terrors (and passions) one of its principal subject matters.[38]

The obsessively literal insistence on the brute materiality of the body—as much in its visceral, mutinous incarnation as in its glossy silicone-enhanced perfection—works strenuously to cover up its own figurative function, but in so doing it cannot help but call attention to its rhetorical excess. The special effects of body horror movies, for example, operate in a similar fashion to Naomi Wolf's ever more figurative insistence on the literal (discussed in Chapter 3): the hyperreal but nevertheless stylized aesthetics of slime and gore are optical illusions, hyperbolic figurations of the revolting body's promotion to principal signifier of the inescapable materiality of the real. The more viscerally realistic the representation of slime, the more it becomes a metonymic substitute for the unrepresent-ability of brute reality. The mutilated, abject body in effect constitutes a metaphor for the body's resistance to metaphor, an allegory of the limits of allegory.[39]

Bodies of Knowledge

It is therefore not difficult to see that scenarios of bodily horror have become more literal and more explicit because the body has become more prominent in the contemporary American cultural imaginary. But explain-ing why the body and its horrors have become increasingly important over the last two decades is, however, far from easy.

One increasingly popular explanation for the proliferation of germo-phobic body imagery is the emergence of new diseases, from AIDS to Ebola. It is no wonder we are beset by nightmare scenarios of bodily infil-tration, the argument goes, because these diseases are indeed scary. While there is undoubtedly a lot of truth in this common-sense claim, it tends to distort the larger picture. HIV did not so much create fantasmatic fears of contamination as arrive on a social scene already structured by endemic homophobia and racism.[40] Furthermore, the emergence of new diseases (and the persistence of older ones) must be read against the backdrop of a manifest failure of the techno-utopian promise of antibiotics to rid the world of serious infectious diseases, and the failure of campaigns such as Nixon's War on Cancer.[41] Moreover, the increasing visibility of disease is in part an effect of new medical imaging technologies, which make manifest in striking ways the uncanny, alienating horror of previously hidden bodily processes.

The prominence of body panic is not merely a reflection of new diseases emerging, or existing ones becoming more visible. It is also the creation—whether through negligence or cynical misinformation—of new anxieties by an enormous health industry and New Age movement anxious to sell new products, from radon home-testing kits to cholesterol-measuring devices. Although America indeed has a long history of snake-oil merchants profiting from popular fears which they helped create in the first place, recent years have seen a revival of this tradition on an unprece-dented scale in the realm of health and body maintenance.[42]

Though much could be said about the failings of the contemporary American diet, the rise over the past decade of the dietary supplement indus-try—much of it unregulated—has been spectacular: you know you've got to worry when there's a Vitamin Shoppe on every street corner. Recalling an earlier era of patent medicines, health claims for foods became common in the mid-1980s, with the food industry undergoing a process of deregulation, following the landmark Kellogg's All-Bran case in 1984, which allowed the cereal manufacturer to promote its product's supposed health benefits.[43] Another example of the reflection and (almost conspiratorial) creation of new anxieties about body image and health is the sudden emergence and success of men's lifestyle magazines. Though it might be conceded that they have served to break the conspiracy of silence around "men's problems" such as impotence or prostate cancer, it must also be recognized that they are the logical extension of the saturated market in women's glossies. Likewise the phenomenal growth of the bottled water industry (sales in the United States increased 144 per cent in the decade to 1997) can only partly be explained by reference to particular episodes of contaminated public water supply (such as the Milwaukee incident in 1993 when 69 people died and more than 400,000 suffered the effects of *Cryptosporidium* in the water), or by an account of a general change in taste preference for unchlorinated water. The ads for bottled water focus on desires for purity and fears of contamination, even though tap water, in safety terms alone, still beats bottled water. A lot of money is being made—and now Pepsi and Coca-Cola are muscling in on the highly profitable act—from the exploitation of consumer fears about the pervasive pollution of life's most essential commodity.[44]

Significantly, in the last decade or so there has been an exponential increase in the amount of coverage the media gives to health issues. It is hard to tell whether this is merely a reflection of the audience's increasing interest in health or an exploitative maneuver by the media (and their healthcare product advertisers) in the knowledge that nothing sells like body panic. Hardly a week goes by without the uncritical reporting of a new half-baked medical "discovery," which is silently contradicted by later "revolutionary" and "important" findings: salt is good for you, salt is bad for you; HRT prevents cervical cancer, HRT can cause breast cancer; oat bran prevents heart disease, oat bran has negligible effects; and so on. Even if the dystopian prospect of general "information overload" in the cyberfuture has been exaggerated by conservative critics, in the case of healthcare it seems particularly plausible. Paranoia about the body now seems to arise less from a lack of medical knowledge about the body and its processes (as might have been the case in the past), than an excess of contradictory and often highly technical information.

Another explanation, which has been expounded recently in a manner only half-joking, is that there is a growing fear of the vulnerabilities of the body in direct proportion to the ageing of the self-obsessed and media-dominating boomer generation. As disease and infirmity come to preoccupy a cohort whose identity was forged by an ethic of bodily pleasure, it is no wonder, so the argument goes, that images of the body conspiring against the self have come to the fore. Behind this zeitgeisty observation,

however, lies the more convincing—though perhaps no less clichéd—
account of the transition of the communal politics of 1960s counterculture
radicals into the individualism of the 1980s and 1990s. Despite the story
of yippie to yuppie frequently being used metonymically as a demonstration
of the "failure" of the 1960s, it nevertheless helps to capture emblematically
how the public sphere of community action has been replaced by the
private, commodified realm of health, fitness and self-improvement. As
personal rather than public health issues become of prime concern, it is no
surprise that the language of health is now insistently moralizing. As
Barbara Ehrenreich so cuttingly observes, "as virtue drained out of our
public lives, it reappeared in our cereal bowls ... and our exercise
regimens ... and our militant responses to cigarette smoke, strong drink,
and greasy foods."[45] It might be more accurate to say that the obsession
with bodily processes is less a substitution of the political by the personal
than the internalization of social fears of surveillance and contamination.

It is important to note, however, that the "culture of narcissism" (as
Christopher Lasch prophetically dubbed it a quarter of a century ago)
now involves not merely a concentration on the self instead of the community, but an obsessive focus on the *body itself*. From a gym-cultivated
physique of ripped abs and buns of steel to New Age health fads such as
colonic irrigation, the body in its idealized perfection and its feared decay
is of prime concern in the contemporary United States. Americans now
spend more on fitness and cosmetics than they do on education or social
services.[46] It might well be argued that the obsessive attention on bodily appearance is not necessarily a sign of self-indulgent moral weakness—Lasch's
attack on "narcissism" is often insistently moralistic. It is instead an effect
of the shift towards a service and information economy in which image is
everything, from the advertising of products to the selling of oneself in
the job market.

The changing nature of the American economy—from a fordist pattern
of heavy industry and (comparative) job security to a postfordist restructuring of business in the name of flexibility and the exporting of manufacturing
jobs—also helps explain the otherwise perhaps surprising increase in the
display of the *male* body in advertising, films and magazines. The pumped-
up bodies of action heroes like Schwarzenegger and Stallone are not the
epitome of manhood, but the excessive performances of masculinity in an
era when it no longer comes naturally. The insistent yet stylized symbolic
presence of the perfected and dissected body in general—and the hypermas-
culine hardbody in particular—speaks to a situation in which the laboring
body has begun to be redundant in the American economy of the information age.[47] As the actual physical body becomes less important, so in com-
pensation its symbolic representations become more vital. Likewise, the
irony of the avant-garde cyberpunk dream to leave behind the fallible
"meat" or "wetware" of the body by entering the datasphere is that this

process is already happening for many blue-collar Americans, though not in the utopian fashion imagined by technovisionaries.

It has long been noted that capitalism works to colonize the body. But in recent years this process has intensified, with the body itself becoming the ultimate commodity. Exercise machines that work on a single body part and new cosmetic surgeries like pectoral implants produce a twisted form of commodity fetishism, in which body parts are alienated from the self that produces them. The creation of what might thus be termed "organs without a body" (to reverse Deleuze and Guattari's utopian prescription for a postmodern embodiment) reaches a new, grotesquely literal level with the persistent urban legends about a medical black market in organs for transplants, and the scientific trade in body parts. "Only a few years ago," Andrew Kimbrell writes, "the biological materials of the human body had little or no value." Now, he continues, "a whirlwind of advances in various biological technologies has created a boom market in the body." In response, "more and more people are selling themselves," selling their "blood, organs, and reproductive elements."[48] Body horror does not only take place in the fantasmatic realm of cinema: the insistent realism of the horror genre's special effects is always outdone by the brutal literalism of the contemporary economy of the body.

As we saw in Chapter 3, it is therefore significant that Naomi Wolf's analysis of the "Beauty Myth" focuses on eating disorders in her critique of the corporate colonization of the corporeal. Though her analysis of the manipulative force of media imagery is at times compelling, what Wolf's conspiracy theory of mass culture leaves out is how illnesses such as anorexia and bulimia have more to do with issues of rebellious control (both *of* the body and *by* the body) than conformity to idealized types. The alimentary body comes to be seen as the sole remaining location of agency, the only thing left over which a woman feels herself to have precarious but tenacious control. As Susan Bordo argues, these illnesses need to be understood in terms of "deeper psycho-cultural anxieties ... about internal processes out of control—uncontained desire, unrestrained hunger, uncontrolled impulse," with the bulimic embodying the "incompatible directions of consumerism, contradictions that make self-management a continual and virtually impossible task."[49] In a similar vein, the contemporary fascination with practices of body decoration (such as tattooing, piercing, scarification, and techniques of body modification like cosmetic surgery, gender reassignment surgery and the performances of avant-garde body-artists like Stellarc and Orlan) also needs to be understood as an attempt to dramatically reclaim the body as perhaps the only possession in one's power. Moreover, as the ever expanding culture of addiction suggests, the revolting body is out of control, and only the inner-panopticism of twelve-step programs can discipline and punish it back into line.[50]

It might begin to seem, then, that the Foucauldian insistence on replacing talk of interior subjectivity with the materiality of the body has become commonplace in everyday culture. But what was for Foucault and other theorists a strategically radical move in the rejection of humanism has become a matter of anxious necessity for many Americans today. The material body is often all that matters, but only in its buffed or brutalized hypervisibility. Indeed, as Terry Eagleton puts it pithily, "from Bakhtin to the Body Shop, Lyotard to leotards, the body has become one of the most recurrent preoccupations of postmodern thought"—and, it might be added, popular culture.[51] In an unstable world, the biological body comes to represent the ultimate ground of solid realism, simultaneously the only thing that can be trusted, and the source of our worst nightmares; the well-spring of new modes of identity, but also the opportunity for new forms of surveillance.

From a situation in which the physical body and physical sciences provided the rhetorical source for political allegories, there is now often a circularity and a confusion between vehicle and tenor in the metaphorical contract. The sci-fi/horror films of the 1950s used the metaphor of the body controlled by alien forces in their conspiratorial scenarios of national paranoia. By contrast, in contemporary American culture the insistent atten-tion on the brute (and brutalized) body as the substitute for politics serves to erase the distinction between the tangible metaphorical vehicle of the body and the symbolic tenor of the body politic. As the Monica Lewinsky scandal demonstrated, intimate body politics has come to dominate the body politic. What makes this realignment between figure and ground more complicated is the paranoia-producing, virally-induced confusion over what is to count as the body and the self. With the contemporary materialization of once figurative body panic, it is hard to know whether images of conspiracy are meant to be taken literally or figuratively. The body can no longer, for example, offer a stable source of metaphors for national politics because the body itself is no longer a stable entity. But in an era of rapid globalization with its erosion and reformation of national loyalties, neither can the body politic offer a fixed source of metaphors for the individual body. The rhetoric of corporeal conspiracy is insistently literal, even as it gives rise to ever more elaborate figurations. As the boundaries of the national and personal immune system begin to erode, so too does the boundary between the literal and the metaphorical. Drawing on Derrida's discussion of the nature of metaphor, it might be concluded that the contemporary paranoid metaphoricity of bodily contamination produces a contamination of metaphoricity itself.[52]

Safe Haven for Troubled Times

The contamination of metaphoricity is endemic in contemporary body panic. Paranoid scenarios of the erosion of clearly demarked boundaries between self, disease, and environment at a molecular level sit uneasily alongside more general conspiracy theories about the institutional responsibility for events in the global realm. The increasing awareness of the imbrication of the individual body and the body politic into ever wider circuits of exchange is often expressed in a paranoid-inflected rhetoric that is simultaneously attuned to the corporeal *and* the corporate. The stylized materiality of paranoia-inducing body panic rubs up against the insistently literal-minded accusations of clandestine corporate malfeasance as the source of intimate infiltrations of the body. From environmental allergies to food scares, the language of conspiracy is put to work in both a literal and a figurative capacity which serves to undermine the distinction between the two.

The recognition in some newer theories of immunology of a continuously shifting interface between individuals and their environment suggests that the conspiratorial language of defense and invasion is beginning to be replaced by a vocabulary drawn from systems theory and post-fordist management studies.[53] But these newer models based on flexibility and fluidity have produced their own scenarios of paranoia, no more so than in the popular reaction to autoimmune diseases. Multiple chemical sensitivity—popularly known as being allergic to the twentieth century—is (along with HIV/AIDS) the limit case of what was once known as *horror autotoxicus*, the frightening fusion between self and non-self, friend and foe, inside and outside. The exact nature of the disease is very much in dispute, but victims seem to find themselves allergic to a wide and often shifting array of everyday products and foodstuffs, at first largely synthetic (such as hairspray and car exhaust), but often gradually expanding to include much of their surrounding environment. These products, however, are only the initial stimulus for an allergic reaction: the violent symptoms are in effect the body attacking itself, as the immune system goes into overdrive. Everything—including one's own body and home—is potentially hazardous, and sufferers become understandably paranoid at the lack of a safe haven.

Todd Haynes's film, *Safe* (1995), dramatizes some of the problematic aspects of multiple chemical sensitivity, while also exploring the twilight zone between the literal and the metaphorical. It tells the story of Carole White, an affluent "homemaker" in an oppressively bland Los Angeles suburb, who begins to suffer severe allergic reactions to everyday chemicals and pesticides. At first she tries to pass off her attacks as stress related, and even begins to agree with her doctor that the cause of her suffering is more psychological than physiological. At this stage, Haynes's film threatens to follow the double bluff of *The Stepford Wives* (1975), in which a bored housewife suspects that she is either going mad, or that her own paranoid anxiety about the zombified behavior of the commuter town's womenfolk is the result of pesticides in the water supply, only for it to emerge that the men are conspiring literally to turn their wives into automata. But *Safe* rejects both the psychological and the literal-minded conspiracy explanations for Carole's illness, and seems to drift into the generic territory of made-for-television illness movies which plot a course from sickness to recovery. After a particularly bad reaction that is (almost) conclusively sparked off by garden pesticides, Carole decides to check into Wrenwood, an isolated New Mexico detox retreat that promises a chemical-free environment, "a safe haven for troubled times." But then *Safe* performs its own double take, and it emerges that this safe haven is, if not exactly the haunted mansion of gothic horror, then certainly a disquieting place, more cult than clinic. Wrenwood encourages its patients to stop blaming the environment and start taking responsibility for their own illness, a doctrine of voluntarism that Carole readily embraces, for all along she has seen her illness as somehow a result of her personal failings. Moreover, the obsessive desire for immunity and safety brings its own dangerous state of social and personal isolation, as visible in Carole's antiseptic suburban enclave as in the white ceramic igloo that becomes her virtual prison at Wrenwood.

Haynes's unnerving film offers an interesting commentary on the politics of body paranoia, in the way that it maintains contradictory explanations side by side. *Safe* gives the viewer good reason to think that Carole's illness is purely psychological, with her nosebleeds and asphyxia as violent hysterical reactions to her claustrophobic middle-class environment. But the film also strongly suggests that her allergic reactions are indeed caused by external factors, and that to take on responsibility for such illness is a dangerous mistake.[54] In this way *Safe* presents Carole's body panic as both metaphorical and literal at the same time, without claiming that this hermeneutic tension can—or should—be resolved.

In contrast, most analyses of body panic, from accounts of alien abduction to cultural studies of eating disorders, insist on either a strictly literal or a metaphorical reading. As we saw in the Introduction, Elaine Showalter contends in *Hystories* that the graphic physiological symptoms of disputed illnesses such as Gulf War Syndrome (GWS) are in effect metaphors for psychic troubles. In each case she insists that the allergic reactions are the hysterical symptoms of a mind pushed out of kilter (in the case of GWS, by the trauma of a war whose messy reality was far from its clean media image of surgical precision). Showalter argues that the frequently conspiratorial popular explanations for the syndrome—that soldiers were exposed either by accident or on purpose to pesticides or cocktails of antinerve gas drugs, details of which the government is now covering up—only serve to prevent sufferers from confronting the real source of their problems, namely their own troubled minds. Though Showalter is quick to point out that their suffering is very real even if it is psychological, like the cult leader at Wrenwood she counsels that victims must take responsibility for their illness (though not, obviously, for its causes), and stop blaming external sources for what are internal problems. It makes more sense, however, to recognize that both the conspiracy theories and the bodily symptoms are a metaphorical expression (though not necessarily a result of) unacceptable aspects of the social rather than the personal landscape, at the same time as being insistently literal. In effect, instead of instantly dismissing conspiracy theories and body panic as the hysterical products of an unbalanced mind, it is important to find a way of simultaneously understanding the symptoms and the conspiracy talk both literally and metaphorically in the kind of hermeneutic limbo at work in *Safe*. The lesson from revisionist immunology and Haynes's film is that it is no longer possible or even desirable to make a morally or scientifically clear distinction between the internal and the external, the psychological and the physiological, the individual and the environmental, or the literal and the metaphorical. As Gaye Naismith suggests in her astute discussion of *Safe*: "it is possible to see Carole's reactions as both symptoms of hysteria *and* of environmental illness if we take hysteria to be a form of environmental illness, instead of regarding environmental illness as a form of hysteria."[55] Like *The X-Files*, *Safe* plays one explanatory framework off against another, always leaving open the possibility that seemingly definitive explanations can be reframed. Though many conspiratorial scenarios about Gulf War Syndrome or multiple chemical sensitivity, for example, are undoubtedly inaccurate as they stand, in their hermeneutic oscillation between the literal and the metaphorical, and between the physiological and the psychological, they cannot be dismissed merely as simplifications of complex issues. At the very least, they take seriously the notion that the immunological body is inextricably enmeshed in its social and physical environment, such that there is no possibility of total immunity any longer.

Risky Business

It might be argued, then, that the impossibility of ever being free from contamination might no longer necessarily be the sign of paranoiacally delusional thinking—even if in certain cases the particular accusations do not stand up to scrutiny. With the proliferation of biological, nuclear and chemical hazards forming a globalized economy of risk, no one can be certain any longer that they are ever entirely immune. There is now a growing body of theory about the role that notions of risk and security play in contemporary Western societies. Ulrich Beck's pioneering work makes the case that the concept of risk is now central to the workings of multinational capitalism, with freedom from risk (often in the form of environmental hazard) replacing the traditional forms of class division based on wealth.[56] The growing dependence in postfordist economies on strategies of risk assessment ensures that an awareness and a tacit acceptance of ever-present but statistically low-level threats becomes the norm.

Indeed, it might even be argued that risk is just paranoia quantified and routinized, and no more so than in the calculus of threat associated with the vulnerable body.

The final chapter explores in more detail the role of conspiracy theories in accounting for agency and responsibility in a risk-dominated society whose motto might well be that everything is connected. But for the moment it is worth concentrating specifically on those perceived risks to the body which often take on a conspiratorial air, and which bring together the corporeal and the corporate. Anxieties about food in particular frequently operate with this double logic. Although there is a long history of fears about food safety in the USA (most famously dramatized in Upton Sinclair's *The Jungle*), in the last decade public panics about food safety have become particularly prominent, often fueled by the assumption that the wonders of modern technology had cured what is often taken as a sign of underdevelopment.

A great many of these concerns are expressed in terms of threats to the individual body. For example, Olestra, the synthetic fat substitute developed by Proctor and Gamble, has been the subject of very public discussions about its effects on the digestive system. At first, products such as Pringle crisps made from Olestra carried an FDA health warning that they might cause "abdominal cramping and loose stools," or, in a term used in some medical reports which became widely circulated, "anal leakage." There were many reports of people suffering from these potential side-effects, and the stories quickly entered the realm of urban legend. There is now even an entire website dedicated to haikus about the unpleasant side-effects of Olestra. On the one hand, it is not difficult to see that these tales of the leaking, abject body speak to homophobic fears about one's anus being out of control, and recall, for example, the pseudomedical hysteria in the early years of the AIDS epidemic about the dangers of sharing locker rooms with gay men because of their leaky anuses.[57] On the other hand, the stories also draw attention to perhaps quite reasonable concerns that the FDA might have granted approval to this new miracle product too hastily, overlooking not so much its laxative properties as its tendency to leech out of the digestive system what remaining vitamins those locked into a junk-food diet still possess. It does not take much for these urban legends to link up with wider, and wilder, conspiracy theories about Proctor and Gamble, which has long been the subject of unfounded rumors that it is a Satanic organization. Moreover, panic stories which focus on abjection and the "alien" nature of Olestra's synthetic polymers that cannot be assimilated into the body need to be set alongside the altogether more widespread and often unquestioned representation of regular, nutritional fat as an evil, alien substance which must be expunged from the body, in the form of "fat-free" diets and the extreme procedure of liposuction. What might be taken as "paranoid" fears in the case of Olestra are only too normal in the discourse of fat in contemporary American culture. Products made with Olestra may have occasioned body panic among some consumers, but for many others the promise of fat-free snacks is the stuff of technological utopia, allowing one, as it were, to have one's cake and eat it.

As well as paranoiacally-inflected stories about certain "lifestyle" non-nutritional products like Olestra and NutraSweet, there has been much concern recently (though more in the UK than in the USA) about genetically altered crops such as Monsanto's tomato. There are also many urban legends about specific foodstuffs or outlets, particularly in black communities.[58] But as well as these product-specific anxieties, there is an increasing number of reports about food safety in general. The last decade or so has seen public scares about the safety of eggs, meat, fruit and vegetables, and tap water in connection with incidents of E. coli and salmonella poisoning, not to mention BSE, so-called mad-cow disease.[59] Spoiled, Nicols Fox's best-selling exposé on food safety, follows the pattern of books on newly emerging diseases such as Richard Preston's The Hot Zone, by offering graphic descriptions of the effects of severe food poisoning. "Lauren's stools seemed more like pure blood and tissue," Fox informs her readers matter of factly, going on to announce that Lauren's body "continued to be wracked by excruciatingly painful cramps."[60] Alongside her forays into the genre of body horror, however, Fox presents the case that food contamination is now endemic as a result of current systems of transnational food production and distribution. The danger of food poisoning, according to Fox, is now less likely to come from poor storage and cooking, than from the foods themselves, and their methods of production and transportation.

At times the account in Spoiled verges on the conspiratorial, with suggestions that, in the case of BSE for example, governments have been deliberately slow to acknowledge the extent of the problem. Whereas conspiracy theories in American culture have traditionally made claims about the sudden corruption of the normal order of things, in the case of contemporary food fears they suggest that the normal order of agribusiness is itself endemically corrupt. In Oprah Winfrey's 1998 court trial as a result of her public remarks about the dangers of American beef, the jury found in favor of the chat show star, suggesting not only that the perception of endemic risk in the most ordinary of commodities is becoming widespread, but that the public believes the industry is covering up what it knows.

An episode of The X-Files captures some of these tensions nicely. In "Our Town," Scully and Mulder investigate the disappearance of an inspector at Chaco Chicken's processing factory which coincides with the appearance of scorch marks in the surrounding fields and rumors of fire spirits.[61] The local sheriff suspects that the inspector has merely run off with a woman, but investigation reveals that he was about to recommend the closure of the plant on health and safety grounds. After a young worker at the plant is shot when she goes crazy on the factory floor, Scully's autopsy reveals that, like the inspector, she had developed Creutzfeldt-Jakob Disease (CJD), and that she was far older than she looked. It eventually turns out that the boss of the poultry plant, Walter Chaco, along with innumerable townsfolk, have been practising cannibalism for years, and the skeletal remains of the victims are discovered in a nearby lake. The episode thus pits the possibility of a paranormal explanation (of ritual cannibalism providing the secret of eternal life) against Scully's rational hypothesis that the scorch marks are merely bonfires and that the unnatural youthfulness of some of the townsfolk can be explained by a genetic mutation. The mode of small-town American gothic likewise comes up against the different generic expectations of body horror with graphic scenes from the autopsy and subsequent discovery of mutilated bodies. The seemingly literal (and conspiratorial) explanation of the mysterious happenings in the small town in terms of an outbreak of CJD covered up by the Chaco company is then trumped by a new revelation. The real explanation is the seemingly fantastical one of cannibalism—only for the episode to provide a further twist with its final shot revealing that the Chaco chickens are being fed on the remains of previously slaughtered birds. The public's fear of "cannibalism" in meat production (revelations about BSE in the UK were beginning to appear when the episode was broadcast) are first literalized with the cannibalism story, and then brought up against the even more literal evidence of the original fear. Like *Safe*, this *X-Files* episode teasingly but deftly keeps aloft several different explanatory possibilities at the same time, refusing to let any one element of the paranormal, the paranoid, and the conspiratorial claim the final ground of stability.

In a similar fashion both urban legends and investigative journalism about food safety combine in an uneasy tension the individualized language of body horror with a more general analysis of the elaborate and often covert systems of industrial food production. Both offer a representation of the vulnerable body of the consumer (who has in many respects replaced the citizen as prime location of political subjectivity) caught up in unfathomably complex circuits of multinational trade, from the microbial to the financial. However, anxieties about the source and safety of everyday items are perhaps only the flipside of the fetishization of commodities. The desire *not* to know where the hygienically packaged products in our supermarkets come from or how they are made is as strong as the concern to discover the conspiratorial links between the transnational corporations and the government regulation agencies that dominate agribusiness.

The "Plague of Paranoia"

If fears about food form one pole of the paranoia-inducing insertion of the body into globalized networks of exchange, then the other is occupied by

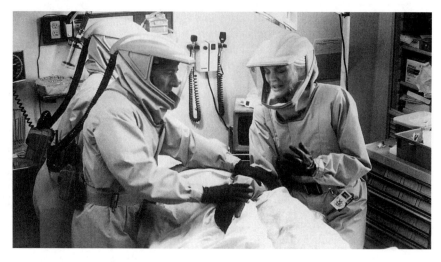

Figure 5.2 In *Outbreak* (dir. Wolfgang Petersen), Rene Russo fears that her level-4 biohazard protection suit has been breached. Courtesy of the Kobal Collection.

popular representations of epidemiology. It might be argued that the graphic nonfictional accounts of the abject body ravaged by newly emerging diseases now provide the same terrors and excitements that the fictional explorations of film directors like Cronenberg once afforded. Indeed, the coincidental alarm in 1995 about the Ebola virus in the former Zaire and the release of the film *Outbreak* suggested, for some commentators, a far more sinister link between the fictional and the factual than most of us would like to consider. *Outbreak* features moments of individualized body paranoia, most notably in the scene where the scientist played by Dustin Hoffman fears that the Level 4 biohazard suit of his colleague (Rene Russo) has been breached (Figure 5.2). But the film also sustains a wider conspiracy theory plot, drawing on the tradition of *The Andromeda Strain* (1971), with suggestions of high level government collusion in the clandestine creation of newly emerging diseases as biowarfare weapons.[62]

Whether on CNN or in the cinema, the sight of Center for Disease Control (CDC) scientists in biohazard protection suits in Africa provides a dramatically paranoiac image of the dangers lurking in the jungle which now, thanks to international air travel, are close at hand, as *The Hot Zone* insistently reminds us: "A hot virus from the rain forest lives within a twenty-four hour plane flight from every city on earth."[63] It might be argued that the overblown media focus on alarming but extremely rare and "exotic" diseases like Ebola, Lassa Fever, Hanta Virus and Necrotizing Fasciitis (the so-called flesh-eating bacteria) is merely a coded representation of AIDS, which might be equally horrifying, but whose public acknowledgement is often deeply problematic. It might also be said that these spectacular scenes merely serve to deflect attention from the more pressing but far less glamorous diseases that plague America today—the return of tuberculosis in poor urban areas being a prime example. The new subgenre of virus hunting, with its swashbuckling tales of lone epidemiologist-detectives locating the unique source of a mystery illness, offers a compensatory fantasy of the heroic achievements of medical science in an age when once vanquished diseases are returning and complex syndromes prevent easy diagnosis.[64] It might even be claimed that the image of American CDC officials bravely leading the way in the Congo functions as an ideological rewriting of the failures of recent U.S. foreign policy in Africa, most conspicuously in the UN "peace-keeping" effort in Somalia which ended in defeated chaos. But the heroic promise and scary threat of the sci-fi protection suits (favorite items in *The X-Files*, for example) has been brought back home in a series of simulated terrorist biowarfare exercises, most notably in New York City. Emergency personnel in "haz-mat" suits roaming around Broadway provide a paranoiac image of zero immunity for the "zero tolerance" city.[65] In the New World Order of global disease, there's nowhere left to hide.

Plotting AIDS

Narratives about newly emerging diseases often bring together visceral descriptions of clinical symptoms with speculative accounts of their origin and epidemiology. They also readily lend themselves to more "literal" conspiracy theories. Nowhere is this dual emphasis more apparent than in the case of the AIDS epidemic, whose representation is often at one and the same time insistently literal and fantasmatically symbolic. So much has been written on AIDS over nearly two decades of public alarm that it would be impossible in this chapter to do justice to the breadth and passion of responses the epidemic has provoked. But the paranoid rhetoric of body panic, as well as more literal conspiracy theories, have never been far from the surface in much of that outpouring. Katie Roiphe, in the preface to her second book on the sexual mores of the "postfeminist" Generation X, suggests that remembering where they were when they heard the news that Magic Johnson had tested HIV positive is for her peers the equivalent of the Kennedy assassination in a previous era.[66] While Roiphe's claim is more than a little exaggerated, it does capture the way in which the AIDS epidemic has provided some of the most generation-defining moments of the 1980s and 1990s. It also reminds us that, like the Kennedy assassination, conspiracy theories are one of the major ways in which the AIDS epidemic has been interpreted by diverse communities.

There have been many different conspiracy-minded stories surrounding the AIDS epidemic, which construct varying scenarios about the origin of the disease and the purposes of those deemed responsible. These accounts have been produced in, and taken up by, a broad spectrum of constituencies, and they fulfill an equally diverse range of functions for each group. In short, there is not one essential characteristic of conspiracy theories about AIDS that would help us recognize and condemn them in advance; instead it is necessary to understand each in its specific historical and political context. It is possible, however, to divide the various conspiratorial narratives into two broad (but not always exclusive) camps: those told *about* the principal victims of AIDS, and those told about hegemonic sources of power mainly *by* those most affected.

Throughout Western history diseases associated with sex have provoked strongly moralized reactions, which, by equating sexuality with sin, have tended to hold responsible those suffering from the illness.[67] The AIDS epidemic has produced a particularly extreme form of this rhetoric, with the widespread belief promoted by New Right politicians and echoed implicitly by the media that this "plague" is the result of—if not the punishment for—the unclean and deviant behavior of gay men, IV drug users and black people of Haitian extraction (three of the original four so-called 4H risk groups—the fourth was hemophiliacs). As Jerry Falwell notoriously pronounced: "AIDS is God's judgement of a society that does not live by His rules."[68] During the 1980s, some right-wing commentators claimed that the AIDS epidemic was a plot by the USSR to weaken America, reviving the old McCarthyite equation between "Commies" and "queers" as un-American influences. Appropriate to the hotting up of the Cold War in the Reagan years, the Soviet press carried reports (which apparently first surfaced in India and were then taken up by two East German doctors) that HIV had been manufactured as a biowarfare weapon by the American army at its Fort Detrick labs.[69]

Somewhat bizarrely, allegations of Communist involvement still circulate today, with the continued influence of William Campbell Douglass's 1992 treatise, *AIDS: The End of Civilization*. The book, in one of those moments of complicated and uneasy alliance which attend the culture of conspiracy, is influential in both the black community and on the extreme right. The book alleges that the World Health Organization (WHO) is a Communist front whose ultimate aim is the end of Western civilization—or, at any rate, the white, straight, god-fearing community that Douglass takes for civilization. As well as Communists, Douglass blames gay men for spreading the disease in America; he explained in an article in *The Spotlight* how he feels "resentful of the homosexuals because of the holocaust they have brought upon us."[70]

In addition to these more explicit conspiracy theories which blame those most affected by the epidemic, AIDS has occasioned an extraordinary level of moral panic. For two decades the media, popular culture and Congressional hearings have been full of scaremongering reports. There is, for example, the case of Ryan White, a 13-year-old boy who tested HIV positive and was excluded from his school; or reports about the attack on a young schoolgirl in Brooklyn in 1995 allegedly by a man with a hypodermic needle; or the 1998 trial in New York City of Nushawn Williams, a black man accused of murdering young women by sleeping with them when he knew he was HIV positive. These stories frequently focus on unusual incidents which play upon people's worst fears (principally about blacks and gays), and are often used emblematically in place of a more considered analysis of the larger picture. The death of Rock Hudson, for example, was widely taken as a sign that the disease (or perhaps homosexuality itself) could now affect anyone.[71] The tone of these stories regularly appeals to a sense of shared panic, which serves to create an exclusionary model of the "public sphere" in the name of paranoia.

In tune with the wider social and political trend noted earlier, much of the panicked discussion of AIDS has revolved around the questions of risk. Government health campaigns and media warnings which talk of the "exchange of bodily fluids" are at once too specific, with their fixated evocation of horror film excess, and too vague, in their euphemistic refusal to specify which bodily fluids and which practices are risky and for what reasons. Many early media accounts latched on to scare stories of accidental needle pricks amongst medical staff, or fears about sharing communion cups or kissing, or, in the case of Magic Johnson's colleagues, worries about being infected by his blood on court.[72] These stories conjure up all sorts of nightmare scenarios about the "exchange of bodily fluids" in gruesome detail, with little suggestion that some routes of transmission are extremely unlikely. In this logic, all bodily fluids become inherently "polluted." It comes as no surprise, then, that sexual practices which involve little or no "exchange of bodily fluids," no matter how safe, are becoming more prominent. Sadomasochism, for instance, might be interpreted as a form of controlled sexual danger and excitement, but without the exchange of bodily fluids. Likewise, phone sex has become one of the boom industries of the quarantined mentality of the "Just Say No" 1980s and 1990s: a licensed form of electronic intercourse that keeps bodily fluids well apart.[73]

Whether there is good cause for panic—whether, in effect, a certain degree of paranoia is justified—has been at issue in complex ways throughout the epidemic. In the early 1980s there were tense debates within the gay community about whether to play down or play up the apocalyptic scenarios that epidemiologists were beginning to present. In a 1983 article, Larry Kramer, one of the most influential pioneer activists, notoriously insisted that "if this article doesn't scare the shit out of you we're in real trouble," since, in his view, that was the only way that gay men would change what he saw as their dangerous lifestyles, and in particular their dedication to the bathhouses.[74] Others warned, however, that to promote a sense of doomsday panic and accede to across-the-board closure of bathhouses was to give in to the New Right's reactionary agenda. A parallel debate has continued in the ensuing years, about whether it should be strenuously denied that AIDS is a "gay" (or "black") disease by placing the emphasis on sexual acts rather than identities, or whether, since AIDS still afflicts those "risk groups" at a vastly disproportionate rate, AIDS should be regarded as a special problem for those particular constituencies.[75]

The flipside of this difficult dilemma within gay activism is the story of how "mainstream" society has chosen to acknowledge the disease as a threat. In the first few years AIDS was seen as primarily a gay problem, and comparatively little was done to investigate the causes of the deaths or promote ways of preventing further ones. It was not until Thanksgiving 1987—some six years and 25,644 known deaths into the epidemic in America—that President Reagan ordered the Department of Health and Human Services, as he so tellingly put it, "to determine as soon as possible the extent to which the AIDS virus has penetrated our society."[76] This comment expresses the logic of containment that equates the human immunodeficiency virus with a promiscuous sexuality which threatens to violate the clean body of the American populace. AIDS thus became inscribed into a rhetoric which divides society into "*our* population" (read: white, straight, monogamous, non-drug-using, family-centered), and the so-called four-H risk groups. These classifications came under strain, however, first when it emerged around 1983 that women and babies were HIV positive (that is, it could be amongst "us"), and then in the summer of 1985 when it was disclosed that Rock Hudson was being treated for AIDS-related illnesses. The revelations about Hudson were popularly taken to mean either that one of "us" could turn out to be "one of them," or that the disease could spread to the "general population."[77] The cover story of *U.S. News and World Report* in January 1987, for example, announced that "suddenly the disease of *them* is the disease of *us*."[78]

These confusions over "safe"/"at risk" categories contributed to a crisis of recognition as the strategy of containment came under stress. Senator Jesse Helms, for example, insisted that "the logical outcome of testing is a quarantine of those infected."[79] By 1987, the official policy, promoted in health literature, then shifted to the idea that everyone was potentially at risk, and this is when the rhetoric of panic escalated. But some writers (primarily on the right) began to question the epidemiological statistics and concluded that the possibility of a widespread "heterosexual plague" was just a myth.[80] Such accounts often took on the iconoclastic rhetoric of conspiracy theory exposés, as they simultaneously offered a false sense of security to those in "normal" society merely by their identity as heterosexual (rather than what practices they actually engaged in or not). These stories also heightened the scaremongering about the "unnatural" behavior of homosexuals who, in the moral majority's eyes, had brought the illness upon themselves.

More recently, however, the question of whether the frightening epidemiological scenarios of HIV infection have been conspiratorially exaggerated has taken a new twist. A growing number of writers have started to challenge the consensus that there are twenty million HIV-positive people in the AIDS belt of central Africa, and that the rate of infection is set to continue. For example, Charles Geshekter, a professor of African American history at UC Berkeley, argues that the rate of HIV infection in Africa has been wildly exaggerated since there is a different method of classifying what is to count as AIDS in the continent. As in other parts of the world, in Africa the definition of AIDS requires a positive HIV test in conjunction with the symptoms of one of a number of illnesses. But in Africa, Geshekter argues, the HIV test is unreliable. Furthermore, the list of illnesses includes not just the rare opportunistic infections usually associated with AIDS in the West, but also conditions such as diarrhea, weight loss and tuberculosis. Immune deficiency caused by malnutrition is common in Africa, so the argument goes, and thus many cases of what are everyday—but no less deadly—illnesses are being redefined as cases of AIDS.[81]

What for Geshekter is a matter of Western medicine inappropriately imposing its framework in colonialist fashion on Africa, is for other investigators a more deliberate, almost conspiratorial, attempt to boost figures. A breakaway AIDS activist group called HEAL (Health Education AIDS Liaison) argues that AIDS statistics in Africa are exaggerated through misdiagnosis in order to receive more Western research and aid money, which would be unavailable for other more "mundane" but equally fatal problems like chronic malnutrition. Western pharmaceutical companies and international agencies such as the WHO actively collude in this process, the argument continues, because it is in their vested interests to supply expensive drugs to and test vaccines on vast numbers of Africans.[82] Though HEAL's uncovered "facts" may turn out to be misleading, and though their position too easily feeds into reactionary arguments that AIDS in the West is nothing to worry about, it is harder to dismiss their underlying rationale as the work of rabid conspiracy theorists. By seeing the larger story of medical science, their stance, for all its flaws, at least begins to consider whether the interests of the patient are always best served by the multinational pharmaceutical companies.

Queer Fear

Although AIDS is certainly a horrifying and perplexing disease, it can easily seem that the reaction to it has been at times excessively panicked.[83] As we saw earlier, there has developed a widespread paranoiac concern about the body and its vulnerabilities over the last two decades, but this general explanation seems insufficient to account for the specific culture of body panic surrounding the AIDS epidemic. One explanation is that the flames of panic have been fanned by reactionary forces who have worked to combine fear of the disease with fear of (homo)sexuality through scaremongering about the dangers of promiscuity in general and anal sex in particular. Susan Sontag, for instance, argues that panic about AIDS, marshaled in the language of conspiracy, has been used by the New Right to attack not just homosexuality, but the entire project of sexual liberation of the 1960s.[84] Moreover, the incitement of fear and prejudice works to forge an uneasy consensus, as a quarantined individualism comes to represent both medical wisdom and common sense about personal and social relations.

Listening to pronouncements by LaRouche or Falwell, for instance, we might wonder whether the New Right is indeed cynically and fully in control of its own rhetoric. At times it seems their paranoid denunciation of anal sex is heartfelt (to the point of being phobic) rather than merely cynically contrived in the manner of a manipulated moral panic. In his compelling analysis of media representations of AIDS, Simon Watney argues that a "moral panic theory" about the hysterical rhetoric surrounding the epidemic fails to "address questions concerning the operation of fantasy and the unconscious."[85] Only an analysis which takes into account psychic mechanisms such as projection, disidentification, disavowal, repression and so on, Watney argues, can begin to understand why the response of the media and the New Right should be so insistently homophobic. With his psychoanalytic terminology it might seem that Watney is in danger of diagnosing panicked responses to AIDS as pathologically paranoid, thereby foreclosing on further analysis. Moreover, it might appear that his linking of paranoia and homosexuality merely replicates Freud's classic analysis in the Schreber case of paranoia as a consequence of disavowed homosexuality. But there are crucial differences. First, Watney's analysis applies less to the idiosyncratic psychic life of individuals than to the psychic formation of an entire culture, in which the threat of homosexual contamination works to police the border between the normal and the deviant. Second, *Policing Desire* argues that the reaction to AIDS did not so much create new fears as rely on existing ones, such that the hysterical response to the epidemic was not a sudden and unusual outburst but the normal—and at times conspiratorially systematic—workings of an institutionalized homophobia which governs sexual and social relations in society. In effect Watney contributes to what Eve Kosofsky Sedgwick identifies as a "chain of powerful, against-the-grain responses to Freud's argument," which "has [recently] established the paranoid stance as a uniquely privileged one for understanding not—as in the Freudian tradition—homosexuality itself, but rather precisely the mechanisms of homophobic and heterosexist enforcement against it."[86]

Impressive though Watney's account is, it still does not quite give us the entire picture. We also need to factor in an account of the role that a conspiratorial account of homosexuality in general and the AIDS epidemic in particular have played in shaping the New Right. Cindy Patton, for example, describes how a camp parody produced by gay activists of New Right paranoia about homosexuals was then taken quite literally by the New Right. The New Right latched on to this spoof as evidence—in its very frankness—of a now far more dangerous "conspiracy" against the American way of life, which no longer needs to hide itself. Patton deftly unpacks the discursive logic by which the New Right uses a conspiratorial interpretation of the AIDS epidemic to whip up homophobia in order to shape and strengthen their own identity—white, straight, and conservative—as itself an embattled minority.[87] The language of conspiracy, on this model, is less a sign of a quasi-clinical paranoia than a discursive structure which performs powerful cultural work for the group espousing those beliefs. Patton's analysis of this case provides a model for thinking about the panicked, paranoid reaction of the homophobic right that is in danger neither of collapsing into individual psychopathologizing, nor of producing an intentional, quasi-conspiratorial account of the cunning manipulation of those fears by the cynical master strategists of the New Right, as Susan Sontag's account, for example, is liable to. In this way it is possible to talk of body panic, using the full range of analysis of mechanisms of projection, disavowal, and so on, but without being committed to a psychoanalytic theory of the troubled minds of the proponents.

Conspiracy of Science

In contrast to the paranoid rhetoric of the tabloid media and the New Right which tends to view the epidemiological connection between victims in conspiratorial terms, there are accounts of the AIDS epidemic which focus on the collusion of powerful vested interests in the "medical–military–industrial complex." One strand of these conspiratorial accounts takes its starting point from the work of Peter Duesberg, a Nobel Prize-winning biochemist and authority on retroviruses. In a series of books and articles Duesberg draws attention to seeming anomalies in the scientific account, arguing that AIDS is not necessarily caused by HIV, and that many other factors of immunological weakening need to be taken into account. Duesberg's views can be understood as a claim about the complexity of AIDS as an immunological syndrome which necessitates understanding the vast array of influences that make up a person's interaction with his or her environment.[88] It is an argument which claims, in effect, that there is always a complex and overdetermined connection between cause and effect. But his challenge to mainstream scientific accounts of HIV/AIDS can as easily feed into accounts which blame the epidemic on the "fast lifestyle" of the urban gay population.

The questioning of the link between HIV and AIDS has also been taken up by several investigative journalists, whose challenges to orthodox scientific accounts start from the position—favored by countercultural conspiracy theorists—that "everything you know is wrong." Jad Adams, John Lauritsen and Jon Rappoport have all latched on to the inconsistencies in the way HIV was discovered, how AIDS is diagnosed, and how it is treated.[89] Rappoport, for instance, tells the convoluted story of Robert Gallo's isolation of HIV in 1984, and points out how it either seems a case of fraudulent industrial espionage (with Gallo stealing the discovery from Luc Montagnier at the Institut Pasteur) or a conclusion too hastily reached that has since determined the entire course of the multibillion dollar AIDS research industry. Rappoport and others single out pharmaceutical companies (and behind them the vast government-funded research network) as the real culprits in the AIDS story. Beginning from the position that AIDS is a result of immunological weakening that can come from many sources, these writers claim that since AZT (one of the first major anti-AIDS drugs) is so poisonous it is more likely to be the cause of AIDS than its cure.

While such investigations have many damning things to say about the dishonesty of scientists and the profiteering of pharmaceutical companies, they suggest only that the collusion of interwoven vested interests *might as well be* a conspiracy. Other accounts, however, make a much more explicit claim about the conspiratorial origin of AIDS. As we have already seen, writers like William Campbell Douglass have put together a story about army biowarfare experiments at Fort Detrick and vaccine experiments by the WHO. Others have started from much the same "facts," but draw very different conclusions. All these accounts latch on to an item in the record for 9 June 1969 of the House of Representatives Subcommittee on Department of Defense Appropriations which appears to discuss the feasibility of the U.S. Army developing a biowarfare agent that would outwit the body's immune system. Dr Donald MacArthur, Deputy Director of the DOD's Research and Technology testified that "molecular biology is a field that is advancing very rapidly, and eminent biologists believe that within a period of five to ten years it would be possible to produce a synthetic biological agent that does not naturally exist and for which no natural immunity could have been acquired," a disease which, he later added, "might be refractory to the immunological and therapeutic process upon which we depend to maintain our relative freedom from infectious disease."[90] This is taken as direct evidence that the American government was planning to develop as a biowarfare weapon exactly the kind of disease that AIDS turned out to be.

Those inclined to conspiracy theories add this seemingly prophetic testimony to the fact that AIDS was first detected amongst sexually active gay men in New York and Los Angeles, with the first appearances of the disease being traced back to 1979—a year after just over a thousand "non-monogamous" gay men from New York were involved in a test program for a new hepatitis vaccine. By 1984 nearly two-thirds of that cohort had died from AIDS-related illnesses; similar tests had been carried out in other major American cities, with similar "coincidental" mortality rates. A connection is also made between the fact that seroprevalence of HIV was initially highest in those parts of Africa which had been the subject of a smallpox vaccination program administered by the WHO.

Since the early years of the AIDS epidemic many conspiracy theories have circulated in the gay community that the outbreak of the disease in one of the most reviled groups in society was not a coincidence but rather evidence that the genocidal rhetoric of homophobic hatemongers was finally coming true.[91] Alan Cantwell, a gay medical doctor, has written several books and articles which formulate these suspicions into a fully fledged conspiracy theory. He asks in conclusion, "Are millions of deaths required for the New World Order? ... How many more AIDS deaths are required before people speak about this secret genocide?"[92]

Like Cantwell, Leonard Horowitz takes as his starting point the 1969 biowarfare hearings in his monumental 600-page investigation, *Emerging Viruses: AIDS and Ebola—Nature, Accident or Intentional?*[93] Horowitz slowly develops a case about the specific science of HIV—the text is complete with diagrams of virus molecules and copious extracts from and references to scientific papers. He alleges that Gallo's discovery of HIV in 1983 was no such thing, not least because the latter had been at the center of a long process of experimentation with new retroviruses, seemingly in the multibillion dollar red herring to prove that cancer was caused by a virus, but which in fact served to create new and incurable diseases as bio-warfare weapons. Horowitz then mounts an equally detailed account of the "deep politics" behind the development of a biowarfare program which, after President Nixon's supposed canceling of the project in 1972, continued in covert fashion at Henry Kissinger's behest. In fact, it turns out in Horowitz's enormously detailed saga that Kissinger is the linchpin in a vast concerted effort to curb world population growth, which the latter deemed to be the number one threat to world security and hence America's continued prosperity. Like HIV, Ebola is also claimed to be a man-made virus, produced either by accident (as a result of cross-contamination of vaccinations tested in lab monkeys) or on purpose.

Like many conspiracy theories about AIDS, the issue of malign intentionality is taken for granted, instead of being proved. Given the long history of anti-gay prejudice, Cantwell is convinced that homophobic elements of society must be behind the current atrocity. In a similar fashion, the question of conspiratorial intentionality emerges in an incremental, cumulative fashion in Horowitz's account, and though he produces pages of documents as evidence, he is unable to come up with a single smoking gun. But he is convinced that he has shown that both the scientific capability and political will existed to produce such weapons, and it matters little whether it all turned out as planned or it was an experiment that got out of control. Resonance can count for more than evidence.

Though he has his own limited political agenda, Horowitz's account of the genocidal proclivities of governments and pharmaceutical companies has been taken up by the Nation of Islam. As Horowitz relates in the epilogue to the "expanded Reference Edition" published in 1998, he was invited by Alim Muhammad, health minister of the Nation of Islam, to address a meeting headed by Louis Farrakhan. Convinced by Horowitz's account of the dangerous contamination of vaccines by unknown or possibly man-made viruses, the Nation of Islam recommended that the black community should boycott all compulsory vaccination programs for children in the U.S.. As we saw in Chapter 4, conspiracy theories about AIDS have been immensely popular within black communities. One reason conspiracy theories are so popular among African Americans is not an imputed, innate propensity to paranoia, but their awareness that the possibility of a disease targeted at black people—whether through genocidal intent or criminal negligence in the administration of vaccination trials that amounted to much the same thing—makes only too much sense. The rhetorical stance is that it *might as well* be true.

In many ways, then, the AIDS epidemic provides the logical but chilling culmination of the increasing wave of body horror this chapter has documented. It has, as we have seen, provided some of the most telling elisions of the boundary between the individual body and the body politic. Its viral processes have also caused great anxiety about the blurring of more literal boundaries both between and within individuals. On the one hand, scientific and popular accounts of HIV draw readily on the rhetoric of conspiracy in their descriptions of the autoimmune breakdown of self and non-self. On the other, the origin of the disease has been inserted into numerous existing patterns of blame, many of which, as we have seen, have a conspiratorial flavor.

Many people have argued that it is more important to counter the "conspiracy of silence" (about the lack of public healthcare, for example) in the present than trying to establish the conspiratorial origins of HIV in the past. Finding someone to blame for what is ultimately an inexplicable disease might make emotional sense, the argument goes, but it provides false comfort. Others have warned that pursuing unprovable and irrelevant conspiracy theories is not merely a distraction but is positively harmful, if it discourages people from safe sexual practices, for example.

These arguments are compelling, not least when the conspiracy theories blame those already victimized by the epidemic. But some of these narratives of conspiracy can also serve the laudable purpose of drawing attention to the usually unthinkable topic of U.S. involvement in biowarfare, and, more importantly, to the sometimes scandalous practices of the pharmaceutical industry, biomedical research and regulatory agencies such as the FDA. They can also point to the fact that the official stories of origin—most notoriously the African green monkey theory, but also the Richard Preston line that AIDS is the eco-revenge of the rain forest—are as equally implausible as the alternative, conspiratorial versions. Conspiracy theories about AIDS might be misleading and misguided, but they can also gesture towards an understanding of the interpenetration of individual bodies and the global body politic. Horowitz's account of the collusion between Kissinger and Gallo for Malthusian ends is in both its conclusion and many of its details undoubtedly way off the mark. But his accumulated glimpses of the collusion between government, the military, and corporate science points towards the kind of analysis that few others are prepared to make. Plotting the connections—whether epidemiological or conspiratorial—between individual and national immune systems has become a frighteningly difficult task in the era of AIDS, not least because the formerly secure paranoid division between self and other has begun to erode. Some conspiratorial accounts simplify the complex interconnections by blaming a single evil conspirator and locating a single moment of origin for the human immunodeficiency virus. But other forms of more insecure paranoia tap into the scary interpenetration of the corporeal and the corporate, offering explanations which float somewhere between the literal and the metaphorical, and even undermine the distinction between the two. Scenarios of body panic can therefore provide a highly charged if distorted way of representing forms of connectedness, of both the individual body and the body politic, for which there are as yet no adequate maps.

6

EVERYTHING IS CONNECTED

> Paranoia is nothing less than the onset, the leading edge of the
> discovery that *everything is connected*, everything in Creation, a
> secondary illumination.
>
> (Thomas Pynchon, *Gravity's Rainbow*)

> Everything connected at some undisclosed point down the
> systems line. This caused a certain disquiet. But it was a
> splendid mystery in a way, a source of wonder, how a brief
> equation that you tentatively enter on your screen might
> alter the course of many lives, might cause the blood to rush
> through the body of a woman on a tram many thousands of
> miles away, and how do you define this kind of relationship?
>
> (Don DeLillo, *Underworld*)

The assumption that everything is connected has been one of the guiding
principles of conspiracy theory. The hope—but also the fear—is that
every seemingly insignificant fact or detail might turn out to be a clue to a
larger plot, if only one could see the hidden connections. Over the last
few decades conspiracy theories have shown signs of increasing complexity
and inclusiveness, as once separate suspicions are welded into Grand
Unified Theories of Everything. For example, A. Ralph Epperson's *The
Unseen Hand: An Introduction to the Conspiratorial Theory of History* brings
together conspiracy theories about the American Revolution, the Civil
War, the Cuban Revolution, the Trilateral Commission, the Federal
Reserve, population control, abortion, education, and so on for 488 pages.
The author insists that "a conspiracy does indeed exist, and that it is extremely large, deeply entrenched, and therefore extremely powerful." It is
working, Epperson continues, "to achieve absolute and brutal rule over
the entire human race by using wars, depressions, inflations and revolutions
to further its aims."[1]

The conviction that everything is ultimately connected is also precisely
what the critics of conspiracy thinking see as its major logical and factual

mistake. Richard Hofstadter, as we have seen, allows that conspiracy theories have from time to time affected the course of events, but takes issue with the belief that "conspiracies are *the motive force* in history."[2] Both academic and popular commentators concur that seeing hidden connections is itself not necessarily a problem—indeed, some of our most sophisticated scientific and social–theoretical thought consists in spelling out the links between previously separate ideas and realms.[3] But again and again the warning is that there is a sensible limit to how far the operation of paranoid thinking should go. Some argue on empirical grounds that the claim of a vast conspiracy is unfounded, either because, quite simply, the United Nations or the Trilateral Commission is not plotting to take over the world, or, more resignedly, as one pundit asserts, that "our government just isn't smart enough, efficient enough, motivated enough or organized enough to undertake conspiracies on the scale it's currently credited with."[4] Contemporary conspiracy culture, however, tends to keep pushing beyond the limit. It seems that there is nothing to stop the process of interpretation and connecting.

The suspicion that everything is connected in a sinister but as yet undiscovered way is thus taken to be one of the tell-tale signs of paranoid thinking, a sign that the boundaries of logic and common sense have been exceeded. But a faith in—and at times a fear of—the fundamental connectedness of everything is also taken for granted in a host of other ways of making sense of the contemporary world that are seen as quite sane. Everything Is Connected could function as the operating principle not just for conspiracy theory, but also for epidemiology, ecology, risk theory, systems theory, complexity theory, theories of globalization, boosterism for the Internet, and even poststructuralist literary theories about intertextuality. What is the connection between these discourses and the way conspiracy theory views the world? Is the conspiracy theorist's insistence on a hidden cause and connection behind seemingly random events a sign of a narrow-minded inability to understand the challenge of these new paradigms to traditional notions of agency and causality? Or is the conspiracy theorist's paranoia, as the suspiciously omniscient narrator of *Gravity's Rainbow* suggests, the "leading edge" of a discovery that seems to be changing the way we think about the world, from ecology to economics? This final chapter explores what happens to conspiracy theory in a world of global connectedness.

Six Degrees of Separation

After a series of experiments in the 1960s involving sending a parcel to a randomly chosen recipient using only chains of mutual acquaintances, sociologists claimed that people (in the USA, and possibly in the world as a whole) are all connected by no more than six degrees of separation.[5] This statistical endorsement of connectedness was a fitting discovery for an era optimistically believing itself to be on the verge of becoming a global village. The insight has now filtered into popular wisdom, typified by the film *Six Degrees of Separation*:

> I read somewhere that everybody on this planet is separated by only six other people. Six degrees of separation. Between us and everybody else on this planet. The President of the United States. A gondolier in Venice. Fill in the names ... every person is a new door, opening up other worlds.[6]

The idea of endless connectedness has also found semi-ironic expression in the popular campus film-buff game, Six Degrees of Kevin Bacon, which involves finding a link between the B-list actor and any other named Hollywood star via chains of mutual co-stars. There is now even a Web-based email provider called sixdegrees.com, premised on the theory of finding new customers through existing customers' friends.[7]

This benign sense of interpersonal connectedness is in tune with the rise of ecology since the 1960s. According to Barry Commoner's *The Closing Circle*, a seminal analysis of the environmental crisis published in 1973, "Everything Is Connected to Everything Else" is the "First Law of Ecology."[8] The science of ecology has made visible the previously unimagined and unrepresentable complex interaction of natural (and industrial) forces in both small scale and global systems. For some people in the ecology movement, the principle of interconnectedness harmonizes with a near mystical faith that everything in creation is part of a coherent and coordinated whole. Taking this faith to its extreme limit, some ecologists have interpreted James Lovelock's Gaia hypothesis (that Earth is a complex, self-regulating system) as proof that the planet is capable of taking care of itself, with each part carefully held in delicate balance by all the others.

The reassuring belief in universal harmony has as its flipside ecological and epidemiological fears about the connexity of the modern world. In addition to its affinity with Eastern forms of spirituality based on a sense of oneness, the ecological movement also has a more pessimistic lineage. This can be traced back to works such as Rachel Carson's *Silent Spring* (1962), the classic account of the harmful and largely unanticipated consequences for both humans and the natural world resulting from the use of pesticides such as DDT. Warnings about impending eco-catastrophe argue that interfering with nature is also likely to harm people, because in the modern world the natural and the artificial are inextricably entwined in complex causal patterns that can't be predicted or controlled.

More recently "risk society" theorists such as Anthony Giddens and Ulrich Beck have argued that the threat of ecological disaster is the unintended but nevertheless inevitable consequence of modernity itself. The seemingly unstoppable tide of global industrialization brings with it unfore-seen—and perhaps unforeseeable—risks that are only now becoming apparent. For example, there is a growing consensus among scientists that the complex interaction of, amongst many other factors, greenhouse gasses, ozone depletion, and increasing industrial production does indeed lead to global warming. In many countries, at any rate, there is a popular heightened awareness that strange weather patterns might be attributable to a host of factors associated with the rise of global industrialization that can be traced back decades—if not centuries—ago. With no firm agreement over the scientific projections of the phenomenon (it was, after all, not long ago that scientists were warning about the coming of the next ice age), it is virtually impossible for people to pinpoint a specific source for the looming catastrophe, or with certainty come up with an appropriate response to it. Not only is the location of blame in the past becoming harder, but the time scale of the "boomerang effect" of cause and result in the future is likewise indefinite. As Beck puts it pithily, "the injured of Chernobyl are today, years after the catastrophe, not even born yet."[9] It is precisely because everything is connected that it becomes impossible to separate out the contributory factors in locating causes and apportioning blame. Fears about genetically modified (GM) food, for example, link together concerns about the unpredictable long term effects of contamina-tion of the gene pool, with suspicions about the sinister plans of biotech conglomerates to monopolize the world supply of seed. As we saw in the case of alarms about the New World Order and food safety, it comes as little surprise that people have expressed their fears about the unfathomably complex causal connections in conspiratorial terms.

If the idea of six degrees of separation represents a 1960s faith in social harmony, then a more apt slogan for the 1980s and 1990s would be the de-liberately scaremongering epidemiological advice that in sleeping with someone you were in effect sleeping with everyone s/he'd slept with. In a witty but poignant adaptation of Noam Chomsky's quasi-conspiratorial diagrams of corporate collusions, the Argentinean-Canadian performance artist Guillermo Verdecchia has a routine in which he draws a chart of the complex sexual interconnections in his own life.[10] Paranoia-inducing forms of interconnectedness now appear far closer to home. As we saw in Chapter 5, the epidemiology of HIV/AIDS revealed what for many people was a frightening permeability of both the individual body and the body politic. In the former case, the human immunodeficiency virus can confuse the body's ability to distinguish between self and non-self. Only with the paranoiacally vigilant use of latex, the public health wisdom insisted, could sex become comparatively safe again—though without the transmission of bodily fluids. In the latter case, as long as the epidemic seemed to be confined to the four original "risk groups," many people were confirmed in their prejudice that society as a whole was not really connected, while nevertheless suspecting that *within* the shadowy worlds of homosexuals, heroin addicts and Haitians there was a dangerously promiscuous commingling. But by the mid-1980s the epidemic began to confound the American public's confidence in the natural barriers between social groups, as the divisions began to collapse between straight and gay, between them and us, and, in the telling phrase of health officials (echoed by President Reagan), between the so-called "general population" and the designated "at risk" groups.[11] The disease also brought home just how permeable the borders of the national body politic had become. From the knee-jerk assumption that the disease must have come from Africa and then been introduced into the American public by Haitians, to the more realistic scenario of sex tourists from the USA spreading HIV infection in their Third World destinations, the epidemic has forced people to think about the complicated and often unequal routes of transmission in a globalized society. Much of this scapegoating "geography of blame" has been shaped by the language of conspiracy.[12]

In the age of globalization, some forms of connectedness are paranoiacally discouraged, while others are feverishly promoted. Stern warnings against the free flow of libidinal desire are issued by the very same voices calling for the unfettered circulation of consumer desire (in the form of capital and information rather than individual workers) in the global market. The motto for the turn of the millennium might well be "free trade but safe sex." In both cases the assumption is that, for better or for worse, everything is connected: we are all hooked into global circuits of consumption and production, whether we like it or not. In an account of the "universe of communication," Jean Baudrillard captures the scary but also exhilarating sense of immersion in a vast, fluid network of exchange. He suggests we are living in a new, "'proteinic' era of networks," a "narcissistic and protean era of connections, contact, contiguity, feedback and generalized interface." With the "immanent promiscuity of all these networks, with their continual connections," Baudrillard fears that there is "too great a proximity of everything, the unclean promiscuity of everything which touches, invests and penetrates without resistance, with no halo of private protection."[13] In a world in which everything is connected, individual and national boundaries begin to blur, and an older, more comforting form of paranoia which dealt with rigid certainties and organizations in effect gives way to a schizophrenia of immediacy. For some theorists and cultural practitioners this cyborg fluidity opens up the possibility of escape from constricting forms of identity. For example, in an episode of *The X-Files* written by William Gibson, a goth computer genius wants to be uploaded onto the Internet so as to achieve disembodied unity with her boyfriend. "Imagine being mingled so completely with another," Esther muses, "you no longer need your physical self. You are one."[14] But for others it means that threatening forces are perpetually invading the last remnants of the private space of the self, and, more worryingly, that the very idea of a separate and autonomous self has itself begun to collapse.[15]

The dialectic of connectedness is made more complicated by the circularity of the metaphors used to describe it. Is the flow of information and capital in the global market like the operation of the immune system, or vice versa? Is the threat of viral contamination and infiltration literal or metaphorical? Is the economy merely like an ecosystem, or has it actually become one? Baudrillard's account of the ecstasy of communication, for example, mixes metaphors taken from biology ("'proteinic' era of connections"), social hygiene ("unclean promiscuity"), and cybernetics ("switching center"). With projects like the decoding of the human genome, the biological and the informational become not merely like one another but at a fundamental level one and the same thing. In his study of the possibilities and pitfalls of connectedness, Kevin Kelly uses the word "vivisystems" to describe the increasing equivalence between machines that are alive and living creatures that behave like machines. He explores examples ranging from manufactured ecosystems like Biosphere II to the structures of global corporations, and from telephone networks to the hive mind of ants. At a fundamental level they operate in the same way. However, it is not just that seemingly distinct realms of biological, social and economic life are becoming locked into larger and larger interconnecting systems. The very conceptual tools for analysing the connections are also beginning to merge, or, more accurately, it is becoming more difficult to distinguish between formerly discrete areas of life. The challenge for many of these new scientific endeavors is to find a language in which to capture the increasing connectedness beneath the surface diversity. Metaphors of conspiracy lend themselves readily to such a project. But in doing so they are themselves transformed.

Virtual Paranoia

Computer viruses also inhabit this in-between world where the literal and the metaphorical fuse. "Real" viruses are now being redescribed by biologists as inert strings of code (software) waiting for a suitable host (the hardware) in which to operate. In the same way that the AIDS epidemic brought home the phenomenal interconnectedness of the social world, so too have some of the more famous computer viruses highlighted the alarming interdependence of the digital world. For example, in March 1999 the Melissa virus caused consternation across cyberspace, making the headlines like many viral threats before it. It worked by making a host computer running Microsoft Word automatically email an infected document to the first fifty names in the user's address book once an hour. The sudden overload from the chain reaction of emailing caused some servers to crash. The only thing that spread more quickly than the virus itself, however, was the wave of alarmist stories about the apocalyptic damage the virus could inflict, rumors which turned out to be wildly over-stated. There have been numerous moral panics about hackers infiltrating sensitive computer systems, and releasing computer viruses into the data-sphere. Many of these paranoid scares turn out to be unfounded, either cynically spread, so the argument goes, in order to legitimate increasing government control of the comparative anarchy of the Internet, or, so the rumor has it, deliberately fomented by software security companies to drum up business.[16] The specter of a digital viral plague has captured the public imagination, not least in Hollywood thrillers such as *Sneakers* (1992), *Hackers* (1995) and *The Net* (1995). Even if the terminal meltdown never seems to come in the real world, the speed with which the hoax warnings ricochet around cyberspace ironically ends up demonstrating the dizzying interconnectedness of the Internet in any case. The sense of a paranoid lack of immunity seems impossible to quarantine, as we each become an unwitting node in a chain reaction of suspicion and contagion.

Panic about the unstoppable viral connectedness of the Net is the specter stalking the inflationary promotion of the digital and new media world. Soon, we are promised, everything will be connected: newspapers, books, television, music and videos will all be available through one integrated interface. Soon, we are told, everyone will be connected. At the current rate of growth, the cyberpundit Nicholas Negroponte informed his readers in 1995, there will be more Internet users than people on the planet by 2003.[17] And though this statistic remains a fantasy (given that most people in the world are not even connected to running water or elec-tricity, let alone a computer), it is nevertheless scarcely an exaggeration that on the World Wide Web everything—if not everybody—is ultimately connected. Every page is linked to at least one other, and so, in theory if rarely in practice, it is possible to click endlessly from one site to any other at will.

Some commentators have complained that it is the insatiable connectivity of the Web that makes it the ideal breeding ground for conspiracy thinking. In particular, so the argument goes, the architecture of the Net en-courages the most paranoid of cross-references. There are frequent laments that cyberspace is becoming less the idealized town hall that the digerati have idealized, and more an infinite shopping mall of porn and kooky, con-spiratorial obsessions.[18] These two dizzyingly popular passions of the Internet operate on a shared logic of concealment and revelation, and in-creasingly access to the hidden realms of both involves a credit card. The involvement for the spectator in each case is a process of uncovering.

Other commentators have lambasted the way in which the Net breeds the dangerous virus of false information, as rumors are circulated and cross-posted around the world, until they reach a critical mass of acceptance. The fear is that if paranoid hearsay is posted on enough sites it soon becomes taken as fact. Pierre Salinger's conspiratorial claim about a cover-up in the case of downed airliner TWA 800 in 1996 pushed these fears into new prominence. Likewise, the popular discovery in the wake of the Oklahoma bombing that the formerly technophobic militia used bulletin boards, email and websites to promote their ideas brought a wave of moralizing editorials about the dangerously seductive and pervasive power of the Internet. Though these alarmist reactions are exaggerated, it is nevertheless true that the Web in particular and new media in general allow conspiracy thinking to flourish. The user-friendly Web permits a widespread and virtually free netcast of alternative ideas that is potentially untraceable and uncensored. Unlike previous forms of conspiracy culture, the Web allows anyone to put forward to a potentially huge audience whatever views they like, crackpot or otherwise, with no overheads, no quality control, and usually no legal comeback. Since it is easy to cut and paste from other pages and documents, conspiracy sites can quickly take on a baroque complexity, as each minor conspiracy theory is linked to all the others. More than anything, the Web encourages viewers to make links and trace the hidden connections.

In numerous pulp thrillers and films the infinite labyrinth of the infosphere has spawned conspiratorial tales of evil cabals and corporations taking over satellites and computer networks. It comes as no surprise, then, that the plot of William Gibson's *Neuromancer* (1984), the first literary imagining of the networked world of information, should revolve around Case, a console cowboy, who is hired to hack into and destroy Tessier-Ashpool S.A., a hive-like sinister conglomerate with world domination plans that has been devolved into an organization controlled by artificial intelligence. In hindsight it seems almost inevitable that the novel which helped imagine the Internet into being should be narrated through the conspiracy logic of a thriller. In the same way that the thriller offers the vicarious pleasures of a lone hero decoding clues of corporate and government wrongdoing, so conspiracy theory on the Web provides surfers with a substitute sense of empowerment of being an active participant in the process of discovery and detection.

In tandem with fears of corporate misuse, the development of the Internet as we know it today has also been fueled by a populist, hacker ethic of "liberating" information from wherever it happens to be stored in cyberspace. Information, the hackers and cyber-gurus proclaim, wants to be free, and there are many adepts who are only too keen to liberate data, clandestine or otherwise. The hacker ethic encourages conspiracy theorists to make public the hidden information which is out there somewhere.

The truth is out there, as *The X-Files* promises, but it takes some finding amid the excess of information on the Net. For every netizen who celebrates the utopian possibilities of nothing remaining secret in the endless connexity of free-flowing information, there are others who dwell on the potential for paranoia in integrated computer networks controlling more and more of daily life in cyberia. Many people worry that the increasing ubiquity of the Internet in everyday personal and business transactions will lead to universal state surveillance—not least with the U.S. government's plans (now apparently shelved) to introduce a back-door entry for the intelligence agencies into any public encryption system. Far from becoming the all-seeing electronic eye of state surveillance, however, the Internet looks much more likely to promote the corporate invasion of privacy through the continual and coordinated gathering of data about individuals from every website visit and online transaction. In the New World Order of e-commerce, our desires are endlessly predictable and instantly connected, no longer wholly our own. It's enough to make you paranoid.

Out of Control

In some ways, then, the highly interconnected Net attracts conspiracy thinking, both in its form and in its content. The origins of the Internet in Cold War defense strategy also lend it an aura of secrecy and concealment. But it might be argued that its architecture also works against the logic of conspiracy. The Internet developed from the ARPANET, a project of the Defense Advanced Research Projects Agency (DARPA) begun in practice in 1969, and was based on a design by the Rand Corporation conceived at the height of the atomic arms race. The idea was to link lines of communication by computer such that if a nuclear attack wiped out part of the system, the messages could still be rerouted around the problem. In essence the design was for a decentered network, in which every node is connected to multiple other nodes, thus avoiding a centralized channel of communication. That structure—albeit unimaginably more complicated, remains the guiding principle of the Internet today. Despite attempts by various governments to impose some form of top-down control, the Net remains to a large extent devoid of central authority. In the eyes of its most utopian advocates this is precisely its greatest advantage. For many cybervisionaries the decentered anarchy of the Net is not only uncontrolled but also uncontrollable, whether by heavy-handed government interference, or by covert, conspiratorial stealth. If conspiracy theorists seek to find the hidden hand and the hidden center of the Net they will be disappointed, the argument goes, quite simply because the network of networks has no central control, hidden or otherwise. As much as the very structure of the Net seems to encourage paranoia, then, at a more fundamental level it offers a radical alternative to the traditional conspiracy theorist's fear of and faith in an invisible hand controlling our lives.

The ecological understanding of connectedness offers a similar challenge to the standard way of conspiracy thinking. Ecological claims of connectedness have leant themselves easily to versions of benign mysticism, from the narrator of *Gravity's Rainbow*'s drug-inspired sense of a "secondary illumination," to the optimism (often derived from popular understandings of the Gaia hypothesis) that the planet can take care of itself. Other accounts of the interface between technology and ecology, however, have presented a more disturbing, posthumanist vision of the consequences of connectedness. This new thinking has been spurred on by the development of chaos and complexity theory. The idea is that the more elements that are connected into a system—be it an ecosystem or a computer system—the more likely that it will begin to organize itself into new and unexpected patterns of complex behavior. Simple examples include beehives, ant nests, and bird flocks. The unthinking, individual creatures go about their business without any sense of the larger unit, but out of the endless chains of communication and continual feedback within the group there emerges a sophisticated and coordinated whole that seems to have a sense of purpose and identity. Individual bees have a memory of only a few days, it is believed, but a swarm appears to "remember" the location, say, of a potential place for a new hive in terms of months—more than the lifespan of any single bee. "What emerges from the collective," Kevin Kelly sums up in his survey of these kinds of systems, "is not a series of critical individual actions but a multitude of simultaneous actions whose collective pattern is far more important. This is the swarm model."[19] Whole ecosystems are thought to operate in this way, with the chains of mutual feedback ensuring surprising levels of complexity and stability.

Scientists have begun to discover the emergence of organized complexity out of seemingly random connectedness in a wide range of natural and artificial systems (if that distinction can be said to hold any more). It is now theorized, for example, that human intelligence emerges from the low-level and unthinking interaction of neurons endlessly connected to one another in the brain. Computer programs likewise have simulated the emergence of artificial life in replica ecosystems which evolve their own forms of complex behavior out of the continual interaction and adaptation of comparatively simple ground rules. Examples range from digital simulations of the flocking behavior of birds to the computer program Polyworld, which sets running an artificial ecology of mathematical shapes which adapt and evolve over time. Some proponents of artificial life (A-life) have claimed that these experiments are not just simulations of life, but are forms of life itself, *in silico*. Encouraged by the new mathematics of chaos theory, some economists have likewise begun to consider the global economy as a form of self-organizing complex system, that is both unpredictable and uncontrollable. In a cross-pollination of ideas that seems to bear out the theory that all these systems eventually connect, cultural theorists have speculated that human culture itself has all the qualities of a vast interconnected vivisystem. And in the ultimate fantasy of the new biology, techno-shamans of the Internet have wondered if something entirely new and of a wholly different magnitude of self-organizing complexity—a global-hive mind, in effect—will suddenly emerge from the continual entanglement of computer systems on a world-wide scale.

These new areas of theoretical inquiry suggest two important conclusions. The first is that traditional models of causality do not hold true for these systems. There is no longer an obvious correlation between cause and effect: small causes can produce large effects, and, conversely, large causes can have little effect on the overall system at all. This idea is encapsulated in the now commonplace adage that a butterfly flapping its wings in one place can cause a tornado on the other side of the planet. Though the two events are in theory connected, there is no hope in practice of ever being able to plot the causal chain. Furthermore, the entanglement of indirect feedback mechanisms at work in global systems, from the weather to the world economy, means that everything influences everything else in a continual process that cannot be separated into single links in a chain of causation. Precisely because everything is connected it is impossible to work out how one thing leads to another. In a similar fashion, in medicine there is currently a lot of interest in syndromes, such as Gulf War Syndrome and AIDS. Unlike simple diseases, the diagnosis of a syndrome allows for an oblique and nonnecessary causal connection between the underlying cause and the symptom. These new understandings of causation are at first sight the very opposite of traditional conspiracy theories, which supply a strongly plotted story of how, in Senator McCarthy's words, we arrived at the Present Situation. Yet, as the previous chapters have demonstrated, some recent forms of conspiracy culture have played a part in rethinking how everything is connected causally—and how we can imagine and represent those connections. It comes as little surprise that conspiracy theories about, for example, the origins of HIV which hover between the literal and the metaphorical should coincide with uncertain and shifting medical definitions of what it is to count as the syndrome of acquired immune deficiency.

The second distinctive feature of complex systems is that they are not just out of control but are to a great extent uncontrollable. There is no hidden intelligence behind the behavior, for example, of a beehive—even the queen bee is a mindless supplier of eggs and not in charge of orchestrating the whole swarm. Likewise in the brain there is no conscious homunculus providing the real intelligence behind the electrochemical interactions of neurons. As Kelly explains, one of the distinguishing features of complex, coevolutionary systems is an "absence of imposed centralized control."[20] Because everything is connected horizontally across a network (instead of in a top-down chain of command), there is little chance of imposing a firm control on an ecosystem, without running the risk of unexpected and unintended chain reactions spiraling out of control. Some theorists have argued that this is true not just of nature (and artificial nature), but also of cultural systems. In his account of contemporary media culture, Douglas Rushkoff argues that conspiracy theories about shadowy cabals controlling the global information and entertainment industry from the top down are no longer convincing. "Except for the most primitive of conservatives and fundamentalists," he insists, "we no longer blame a group of humans like the 'cultural elite' or 'Jewish conspiracy' for the media's obvious societal influence."[21] The media has a "life of its own," Rushkoff continues, and it "behaves like a living thing, in spite of our efforts to restrain it." Though it is quite literally out of control, Rushkoff warns, it nevertheless has enormous power over us. This situation is potentially as paranoia inducing as the older suspicion that the media was indeed manipulated by a de facto conspiracy of establishment interests. But the lack of control allows the mechanism of influence to be used against the grain. Ideas and images spread like viruses (known as "memes") through the mediascape, and it is therefore possible, Rushkoff believes, to release Trojan horse memes to harness the power of the media for subversive ends—though with no guarantee of results. The argument can be pushed further. If there is no way of asserting authority on the relatively restricted terrain of the media, then there is even less chance of rationally and ruthlessly controlling the broad sweep of history—whether through official or clandestine means, for good or for ill. On this model, history, like the wayward force of mass media, has a life of its own. It is a vivisystem that is beyond the control of any single agency, beyond even the control of a secret cabal.[22]

At the end of the day these chaos-theory-inspired challenges to paranoid thinking are likely to be no more effective in stemming the tide of gullibility than other stern warnings that conspiracy theorists have misunderstood how history works. But for all the insistence that these new paradigms consign conspiracy thinking to the intellectual scrap heap, in other ways the rhetoric of conspiracy seems more attractive than ever. The remarkable thing about distributed systems is not so much that no one is in charge as that they act *as if* there were a plotting intelligence behind their behavior. The consequences of increasing connectedness defy logic and defy description. The causal pattern of these complex systems is fundamentally counterintuitive, and in many ways there is as yet no satisfying way to explain or represent how highly organized events emerge out of lower-level random activity. If control is a spectrum, Kelly argues, at one extreme there is the model of top-down domination; at the other end there is the possibility that things are totally out of control. In between, he suggests, "are varieties of control we don't have words for."[23] Some versions of conspiracy culture, I've been arguing in this study, attempt to supply the words for these new varieties of control. In doing so they reconfigure both the traditional notion of control and the traditional logic of conspiracy talk.

Without really intending to, these kinds of everyday paranoia in effect offer a continual challenge to skeptics: if there isn't a conspiracy, then how do you explain why it looks as if there is one? As we saw in Chapter 3 with Judith Butler's exasperation at popular misunderstandings of Foucauldian forms of social constructionism, unless you are a lifelong card-carrying post-structuralist, how do you explain how there can be control without a controller? How else do you account for the paradoxes of causation and control in a world in which everything is connected, without sounding paranoid? Conspiracy theories may be misleading and misguided, but their residual attraction—half-serious, half-ironic—suggests that for many people the respectable, nonconspiratorial accounts are as yet equally inadequate. We are caught between two modes of representation, neither of which is fully convincing. The popular rhetoric of paranoia offers a temporary solution—albeit inevitably flawed—to this dilemma by placing its conclusions, as it were, *sous rature*. Complexity theory revives Adam Smith's metaphor about an invisible hand controlling the everyday economic interactions of unwitting agents. As Kelly puts it, "hidden in the Net is the mystery of the Invisible Hand—control without authority."[24] But the logic of paranoia tempts us to take that metaphor literally. Again and again in this study we have come across examples of conspiracy thinking which float the suspicion that there is a sinister force controlling events, only for that knowledge itself to be cast into doubt. In its most creative and disturbing forms, conspiracy culture can leave us stranded in the epistemological quicksand between the literal and the figurative, between certainty and doubt—between, in effect, an older faith in humanism and an as yet unconvincing and scary posthumanist future.

The Truth is in Here

If some Net-heads and ecovisionaries have found hope in the idea that everything is becoming connected, for many others the vision of total connectedness brings with it nothing but fear and cynicism. As we saw in Chapter 1, in the world of *Vineland* soon there will be no realm of secrecy—for good or bad—because there is scarcely any place outside the endless hypervisibility of commodity culture. Eventually everything will be connected into a media conglomerate, it is feared, and everything will be on display and available—at a price (as I write this AOL and Time/Warner have just announced their record-breaking merger). In this vision of total saturation the last enclaves of mystery and nonconformity will finally disappear, as everything comes under the control of the media–military–industrial complex that no longer even has to hide its power-crazed domination.

The only hope of escaping total control is in the last few remaining spaces beyond its iron grip. Like Pynchon's dystopic novel and the surreal mysteries of *Twin Peaks*, *The X-Files* has (until the most recent two series) been rooted in the backwoods of the Pacific Northwest. The show's episodes

216

can broadly be divided between the paranormal (the monster of the week) and the paranoid (the ongoing conspiracy arc). The paranormal episodes usually take place in the dark forests and small towns of the gothic imagination. They represent the anachronistic remnants of an older world that has somehow escaped the inexorable process of modernity and rationalization. Beasts of the paranormal such as the Flukeman (half-man, half-worm), "Big Blue" (a version of the Loch Ness monster) and the red-eyed spirit of an endangered primeval forest, it might be concluded, have temporarily escaped from what Max Weber termed the "iron cage" of modernity.[25]

Yet the strange creatures and occurrences that Mulder and Scully investigate in the standalone tales of the unexplained and monster-of-the-week episodes quite often turn out to have some link to sinister government experiments gone wrong, and therefore possibly to the vast interconnecting conspiracy arc. The unexplained monsters and psychic events are not so much escapees from modernization as by-products of one hyperbolic part of it. For example, the Flukeman, in a witty turn on a popular urban legend, is a monster found in the New Jersey sewer system. It turns out that it is a genetic mutation born in "primordial soup of radioactive sewage," as Scully puts it, transferred to America by a Russian ship removing radioactive waste from Chernobyl. Likewise when the FBI agents are sent to investigate several unexplained murders in a high-tech firm they discover not only that the building's central computer is displaying uncanny signs of artificial life, but also that clandestine elements elsewhere in the government are extremely interested and will do anything to protect the discovery.[26] In another variation on the same idea, the audience is shown the possibility that some unexplained events and strange phenomena might be deliberately concocted as cover stories to hide the more sinister machinations of the conspiracy. For example, a Man in Black from the notorious top secret Area 51 of UFO lore, who has accidentally been transposed into Mulder's body, reveals that several of the headlines in the Lone Gunmen's newspaper were deliberate disinformation items invented by himself.[27] The paranormal, in both cases, is inexorably swallowed up by the insatiable connectivity of the paranoid.

The UFO poster in Mulder's office announces that "I want to believe." It expresses his atavistic desire for something beyond the logical strictures of orthodox science initially represented by Agent Scully—and beyond even the long tentacles of the conspiracy. The poster in effect evinces a desire for something that is outside the confines of the normal and the controlled. "I see hope in such a possibility," Mulder confesses to Scully.[28] The conspiracy episodes in *The X-Files* suggest, however, that the unknown is to be found as often as not *within* the very centers of power. It is to be found, for example, in the impossibly vast archives in the Pentagon basement in which the archconspirator the Cigarette Smoking Man is seen to deposit purloined evidence of alien existence, and into which Mulder gains access on his quest to find a cure for Scully's cancer. Mulder and Scully also come across unfathomably vast government-gathered archives stored in a disused mine under a mountain, which seem to contain clandestine medical information on every American citizen. The digitally multiplied vista of endless filing cabinets within a government bureaucracy is one of the key images in *The X-Files*, whose very title points to the idea of the FBI's unnameable and unacknowledged archive.[29]

For all its scenes of shadowy cabals, *The X-Files* often suggests that the conspiracy emerges not outside the proper rule of law but out of the everyday operation of a labyrinthine government bureaucracy. Evidence of conspiracy is as often as not to be found *within* the corridors of power, and the show has focused repeatedly on the iconography and rhetoric of a labyrinthine bureaucracy, with endless scenes of briefings, the presentation of official reports, and high-level committee meetings and hearings. In the cliff-hanger between Seasons Four and Five, during a tense disciplinary hearing Scully announces that the plot "designed to lead to Agent Mulder's demise, and my own" was "planned and executed by someone *in this room*."[30]

The power of the unexplained is even to be found within the agents' minds and bodies. Arguing that he be allowed to undergo a dangerous procedure to help him recover lost memories of the abduction of his sister, Mulder insists that "the truth is in there, recorded, and I've gotten access to it."[31] The conspiracy even appears to have infiltrated Agent Scully's own body, with her discovery of a sinister alien chip in her neck, and alien genetic material within her own DNA. When the newly disillusioned Mulder is trying to convince Scully that the answers to the mysteries lie not in tales of extraterrestrials but with clandestine government experiments, he declares that "your cancer, your cure, everything that's been happening to you now: it all points to that chip. The truth you've been searching for?" Mulder asks rhetorically, "the truth is in you."[32] As much as the conspiratorial truth is "out there," as the show's trademarked slogan affirms, it is also to be found "in here," within the circuits of power in Washington, within one's own mind—even within one's own body.

The Truth Is Elsewhere

In this way *The X-Files* provides an allegory of how the very machinery of state power and bureaucratic knowledge generates from within itself a pervasive climate of conspiracy—almost by accident. But the show does, of course, also present increasingly obvious glimpses of a sinister and ruthless puppet master pulling the strings, a series of stereotyped vignettes of hidden hands behind historical events. But in offering an excess of possible conspirators within a circuit of endlessly displaced power, *The*

X-Files slowly begins to undermine the orthodox notion of agency which underpins traditional conspiracy theories. The chain of subservience, duplicity and command built up over seven series is an extremely long one. Agent Scully, as a scientist, is initially instructed by two high-level officials to monitor—and possibly debunk—Agent Mulder's investigations into the paranormal. But soon Scully finds *herself* under surveillance, with the discovery, for example, of a sinister surveillance device in her pen.[33] Assistant Director Skinner, Mulder and Scully's immediate boss, at first seems to be merely overseeing the agents' activities, but as the story has unfolded Skinner's loyalties have become increasingly conflicted, leading the Special Agents to suspect that he has been "working with" the mysterious Cigarette Smoking Man "all along."[34] First Deep Throat and then the more ambiguous X have provided Mulder with inside information seemingly at the very highest levels, but, as even X is forced to admit, "there are limits to my knowledge."[35] In a similar fashion, with a comic variation on the Area 51 mythology, it turns out ironically that even the project commander of the ground zero of UFO activity doesn't really know what's going on: they just fly the UFOs, which are engineered somewhere up in Utah. When Mulder gains unrestricted access to this inner sanctum of classified knowledge, the base commander uses the opportunity to ask the FBI Special Agent whether "aliens *really* exist."[36] In the compartmentalized epistemology based on a need-to-know policy, no one ever has the full picture.

If anyone would be likely to hold such an overview, it would be the Cigarette Smoking Man. "Cancer Man" (as Mulder calls him) is a blueprint of the archconspirator pulling the strings of history. He works within the bureaucracy of the government's intelligence agencies, but his power extends beyond their control. We even see him individually directing the major events as well as the minutiae of history. He personally fires the shot that kills President Kennedy, in addition to ordering the assassinations of Martin Luther King and Robert Kennedy; in the recent past, we see him giving instructions regarding the Anita Hill hearings, the Rodney King trial, and even ordering that the Buffalo Bills never make it to the Superbowl. (It is at this point that we remember that the stunning revelations we see on screen are in fact narrated by Frohike, one of the nerdish Lone Gunmen trio, who has found the life story of the Cigarette Smoking Man in an obscure mail order magazine.)[37] Yet at other times the CSM is merely a henchman for the Syndicate, taking his orders from the ultimate portrait of a shadow world government ("a consortium representing global interests"), and finding himself at times left out of the loop on key decisions.[38] In a dramatic turn of events at the beginning of the fifth series, the Cigarette Smoking Man is himself shot, presumably by the Syndicate.[39]

The Syndicate, like the Council on Foreign Relations on which it is modeled, meets in secret in mid-town Manhattan. It seems to be the major player in the global conspiracy involving alien colonization and human DNA experiments. At first the chief player in the Syndicate appears to be the Well-Manicured Man, but even he is unceremoniously killed off by a car bomb in *The X-Files: Fight the Future* (1998), a murder presumably orchestrated by his erstwhile coconspirators. Later in the same season the possibility opens up that the Syndicate itself is merely one more player in an international game that also features the ambiguous loyalties and powers of the mysterious female Russian-speaking UN agent. We even begin to suspect that both sides in this post-Cold War order are mere pawns in the ultimate scenario of extraterrestrial domination. In "One Son" in the sixth series, for example, the Syndicate themselves are wiped out almost entirely by a group of the featureless alien rebels. The longer the show runs, the more it seems that there is one more layer to the mystery of ultimate power (and responsibility). As Skinner puts it, "we all take our orders from someone."[40] Scully has reason to remind Skinner of this when the latter promises to do all in his power to bring the murderer of Mulder's father to justice. "With all due respect, sir," Scully informs Skinner, "I think you overestimate your position in the chain of command."[41] Learning at the beginning of Season Five that all the evidence of aliens has been faked, Scully is herself forced to confront the possibility that "for four years we've been nothing more than pawns in a game."[42] In the end, everyone is controlled by someone else.

Time after time Scully and Mulder and the audience learn that "it goes much higher" than we ever expected, as X, the substitute for Deep Throat, warns Mulder. Every time we think we know who is in control, it turns out that they are merely unwitting agents in someone else's plot. In this way, the real center of power is continually displaced, just as the final revelation of the ultimate conspiracy is always deferred. "You've never been closer," Deep Throat encourages Mulder in "The Erlenmeyer Flask" at the end of the first series, but, six series further on, we can begin to wonder whether he is indeed any closer to the final truth. Evidence of secret manipulation is found everywhere, and yet nowhere is there a final location of control. "There are groups within groups," Deep Throat warns in "The Erlenmeyer Flask", that are "conducting covert activity unknown at the highest levels." A complicated and shifting network of clandestine domination thus bootstraps itself into existence. The final location of authority and agency is endlessly postponed, like the lap-sitting game in which a circle of people simultaneously sit down on the knees of the person behind at exactly the same moment, with the (metaphorical) seat of power always seeming to be one person further on. Paradoxically, then, the more *The X-Files* promises to reveal a traditional humanist conspiracy of top-down control, the more it seems to paint a Foucauldian portrait of decentered power which is everywhere in the system but in no particular location. In a tone of increasing despair and frustration at never getting to the bottom of things, Mulder declares to a UFO convention that there is "a conspiracy wrapped in a plot inside a government agenda."[43]

Even the dauntingly complicated connectedness of the *X-Files* plot is perhaps not what it seems. As the seven series have proceeded, slowly but surely the audience is led to suppose that more or less everything in the conspiracy episodes—and even a fair proportion of the paranormal shows—is connected. The abduction of Mulder's sister is linked to the secret medical experiments in which his father was involved after the war, which are connected with the clandestine accommodation of Nazi scientists in Operation Paperclip, which have something to do with the cloning experiments, which are associated with the alien abductions, which are part of the DNA experiments, which are related to the sinister black-oil cancer, which is an integral part of the plans for alien colonization, and so endlessly on. Doing some investigations of his own, Skinner finds out in "Redux II" that the FBI mole, Section Chief Blevins, was on the payroll of a biotech company which is "somehow connected to all of this." Likewise when Scully finds that the blood of the child chess prodigy with second sight contains the same virus which was found in her own blood, Mulder asks what it means. "I don't know," she replies, "I don't know. But I think we're onto something huge. A link." Mulder replies deadpan, "I'll call that bet and raise."[44] Later in the episode Scully discovers that the DNA from the nail claw of a mysterious and murderous creature matches the DNA of what Mulder believes is an extraterrestrial, which in turn matches Scully's own mutated DNA, and so on.

The X-Files thus teases its audience with the promise that eventually everything will be revealed to be part of a huge, interconnecting plot. But in the same way that the ultimate source of power is never revealed, so too is the final truth of the murky past and eerie present never fully exposed. As the program has developed, the audience has seen tantalizing evidence that seems to confirm the existence of both the aliens and the paranormal. But the revelations always present more questions than they answer. Chasing what he thinks is the captured body of a crashed alien pilot in the first series episode "E.B.E.," for example, Mulder is given repeated glimpses of incontrovertible evidence that always just eludes him. He begins to suspect that most of the events (for instance, what seems to be a dramatic rescue mission from above of the captured alien) have been hoaxes deliberately planned to lead him astray from whatever the real story is. Reporting on the faked death of her partner in "Gethsemane," Scully informs the hearing that in investigating an alien corpse found buried in an ice core, Mulder "was fooled by an act of scientific sleight of hand calculated to perpetuate false truths," namely "the larger lie." Given the endless proliferation of false clues, "I'm wondering," Mulder confesses in "E.B.E.," "which lie to believe."

Though still surprising every time, we have come to expect the plot twist at the end of each episode which ensures that the crucial evidence either disappears or turns out not to be what it seemed. Every certainty is eventually cast into doubt, and the clinching evidence always remains elusive. At the end of the second series, for example, Mulder receives an encrypted computer file obtained by a hacker, which seems to contain all the Defense Department's dealings with aliens since the crash at Roswell. But, having come so tantalizingly close to the MJ-12 documents, the Holy Grail of ufology, Mulder's father is shot and then Mulder himself is nearly killed. The digital tape is forcibly snatched from Skinner, and Scully's printout of the files is stolen when her car is stopped by government soldiers. In another second series episode, having uncovered signs of a government-sponsored experiment to test a newly discovered rainforest disease on unwitting prisoners, Mulder and Scully once again become exasperated as all the physical evidence disappears—the prisoners' bodies are incinerated, and the whole incident can be explained away by the powers that be as a case of a mistaken address (the package from the rainforest went to a prisoner with the same name as the scientist who was supposedly the intended recipient). "We can't prove a thing," Scully laments, "they made sure of it."[45]

Over the course of the show's history, even the fundamental poles of belief and cynicism have been reversed time and again. If, by the time of the "Gethsemane/Redux/Redux II" trilogy at the end of Season Four and the beginning of Season Five, Scully now begins to suspect that there might be more "out there" than she previously suspected (not least because she has to account for the fact of her own abduction), then Mulder has come to doubt his previous conviction that the government is engaged in a conspiracy to hide the existence of aliens, believing instead that the extraterrestrial story is a deliberate lie to cover up a program of sinister medical experiments. "The lie that you believe, that they have cleverly led you to believe," a Defense Department employee informs Mulder in "Gethsemane," is that "there is intelligent life other than our own," leaving Mulder to face the possibility that "this has all been orchestrated, a hoax." In "Patient X" he tells a UFO convention that his belief in ETs, and even his memories of his own sister's abduction, have been mistaken. "The conspiracy is not to hide the existence of extraterrestrials," he explains, "it's to make people believe in it so completely that they question nothing."[46] But by "Two Fathers" in Season Six, Mulder has come to believe that the revelation about the disinformation campaign is itself an orchestrated act of disinformation designed to cover up the real truth that there is indeed extraterrestrial existence.

Any seemingly incontrovertible revelation can therefore always be reframed and reinterpreted, cast into a spiral of suspicion. Having in the second series at last found his long-lost sister (she was abducted as a child), Mulder is forced to trade her for Scully, who herself has been abducted by an alien bounty hunter. It then turns out that the person Mulder believed to be his sister is just one of many identical clones: everything turns out not to be the final discovery but possible evidence of deliberately planted false trails, and hence clues to something much larger.[47] No answer is ever final; no truth sacred; no interpretation set in cement. Even the X-Files themselves have been closed and reopened, burnt to oblivion, resurrected, closed down again—and reopened once more in the sixth series after the Syndicate seems to have been destroyed.

The X-Files, we might conclude, operates on a principle of *différance*, an endless deferral of the ultimate signifier which would ground the whole chain of meaning. As much as the show hints that everything is connected, it also perpetually withholds the keystone that will lock everything into place. At the end of the fifth series, for example, the likeliest candidate seemed to be Gibson Praise, the bespectacled chess prodigy with second sight whose DNA might offer evidence of a prehistorical connection between humans and aliens. But the boy, needless to say, is kidnapped from Mulder and Scully's custody before they can establish conclusive proof. Without that final clue, without the moment of ultimate revelation, the show remains in epistemological free fall, permanently floating between revealing everything and coming up with nothing.[48]

This liminal zone is arguably where much recent conspiracy culture hovers. Thomas Pynchon, as we saw in Chapters 1 and 2, anticipated this mode of postmodern paranoia in *The Crying of Lot 49*. The endless deferral of ultimate revelation in *The X-Files* might well be dismissed as merely a necessary plot device to keep the show running for seven series that has nothing to do with the nature of contemporary conspiracy culture. In a literal sense, the show's producers are making it up as they go along, with key plot episodes like Scully's abduction being dictated more by having to work around the actress Gillian Anderson's pregnancy than any deeper narrative rationale. "The truth is," Chris Carter admits, "as much as we had planned, there are still so many things that we didn't foresee."[49] In a similar vein, Pynchon's elaborate striptease of paranoid illumination might be pigeonholed as mere poststructuralist game playing that in the final analysis has little to do with the social culture of conspiracy.

The same logic of an endlessly deferred revelation, however, structures some of the most prominent examples of "real world" conspiracy theories in recent decades. "The Gemstone File" and "the Octopus" are two of the more intriguing examples whose claim that everything is connected has attracted widespread attention in the conspiracy world. "The Gemstone File" was allegedly a collection of letters written by Bruce Roberts, rumored to be a one-time player with the intelligence agencies. The letters, apparently written to one person (possibly Roberts's mother) ended up with Mae Brussell, the renowned housewife-turned-conspiracy-theorist from California.[50] Stephanie Caruana, a reporter living with Brussell in the mid-1970s, read some of the letters, and, in order to help her sort out their confusing allegations, she jotted down a "skeleton key." This brief, annotated chronology was then duplicated and circulated by hand, its revelations becoming part of conspiracy lore. The letters have never been published, but the skeleton key has appeared in various guises around the world in printed form. "The Gemstone File" outlines in compressed and fragmented form an all-encompassing plot that has dominated twentieth-century history. The conspiracy involves Onassis, the Mafia and elite power brokers in America, and has been behind every major event imaginable, from the Kennedy assassination to Watergate, and from the disappearance of Howard Hughes to Chappaquiddick.

At first sight, then, "The Gemstone File" lives up to the identikit picture of a conspiracy theory insatiably including everything within its paranoid orbit, and in the process turning unfounded rumors into dogmatic assertions of fact. But the form and the content of "The Gemstone File" are far more intriguing. Apart from Brussell and Caruana, no one has ever seen the letters, and there is a dispute as to their number. For her part, Caruana claims there were "over a thousand" and that they were written in the prose style of *Finnegan's Wake*. In comparison the entries in the "Skeleton Key" are often cryptically terse, and they merely suggest ultimate connectedness rather than actually documenting it. They proceed by association rather than causal and logical links—sometimes in quite a surreal fashion. For example, the entry for January 1973 reads as follows: "Tisseront [head of the College of Cardinals at the Vatican] was dead—but as the Church rushed to destroy every copy of his papers, Roberts received one—and wrote a few of his own ...: (1) 'The Cover-up of the Murder of Jesus Christ'; (2) 'The Yellow Race Is Not in China—The Yellow Race Dead-Fucks Mary-Jo Kopechne'; (3) 'Mrs Gianni's Bank of America financed the death of JFK at Dallas via Alioto's Frattiano, Brading and Roselli,'" and so on.[51] The same names crop up in different places, and there is the presiding assumption that each coincidental association is a clue to the larger, hidden whole that remains endlessly displaced. "The Gemstone File" concludes after the death of Roberts in March 1975, but the file takes on a life of its own even after the death of its author, as Caruana continues Roberts's speculations into April with information about the Howard Hughes-sponsored endeavor to recover the bodies of Russian sailors drowned in a nuclear submarine. Moreover, there is also in existence "The Kiwi Gemstone," an anonymous version of the original that takes Roberts's story further, and concentrates mainly on New Zealand affairs. Finally, the fact that some people have doubted that the letters themselves really exist—and even that there was a Bruce Roberts—conjures up the Borgesian possibility that Caruana's text is a commentary on a nonexistent and potentially infinite library of revelation. The possibility of doubt multiplies exponentially with each new link and each new version that is made. The more that everything is connected, the more uncertain things become.

The investigative reporter Danny Casolaro's theory of an interlocking conspiracy he dubbed "the Octopus" functions in a similar fashion to "The Gemstone File." Before he died in suspicious circumstances, Casolaro was working on a story about connections between the so-called October Surprise, the arms-for-Iraq and supergun episode, the drugs trade, the collapse of BCCI (Bank of Credit and Commerce International), and the Promis legal-case software program. The latter was supposedly pirated by a friend of Attorney General Edwin Meese for use in clandestine government surveillance and encryption operations, and its theft protected by the Justice Department. The journalist was found dead apparently from suicide in a motel room in Virginia in 1991, his body embalmed before an autopsy could be performed, and his notes missing. Except for the suspicious circumstances of his death counting as evidence that he was on the right track, all that remains is Casolaro's tantalizingly brief and inconclusive book proposal. The pitch for "Behold, a Pale Horse: A True Crime Narrative" promises that ultimately each arm of the "Octopus" is linked to a central body, but, like "The Gemstone File," it perpetually withholds what it promises to reveal. It necessarily remains a suggestive and prematurely terminated outline.[52]

At first sight these examples of recent conspiracy culture bear out Fredric Jameson's analysis of conspiracy theory as "a degraded figure of the total logic of late capital," and "a desperate attempt to represent the latter's system."[53] From "The Gemstone File" to *The X-Files*, these popular imaginings of conspiracy maintain a faith that the heroic detectives might one day uncover the "total logic" of the all-encompassing conspiracy, and hence, in Jameson's allegorical reading, the total logic of global capitalism itself. But with its reliance on an endless displacement of power and an endless deferral of revelation, the contemporary culture of paranoia undermines the faith that there is an ultimate totality to the power dynamics of late capitalism—or, at the very least, that there is any one form of representation that will capture the complexity. The conviction that there is a hidden unity behind all the coincidences and connections keeps the search going, but the fact that the search never comes to a definitive resolution undermines that original conviction. In recent forms of conspiracy culture, the suspicion that beneath the surface confusion everything is connected into one vast system is therefore held in tension by the structural denial of that resolution.

Post-Paranoia

The examples of all-inclusive paranoia I have been investigating in this chapter suggest not that conspiracy theory is now hopelessly outdated in the light of new ways of thinking about causality and agency, but that it is itself being transformed in line with these newer scientific and geopolitical paradigms of connectedness. The career of Don DeLillo in general, and in particular his most recent novel, *Underworld*, provide a compelling example of this subterranean shift in the style and function of popular paranoia towards an uncertain vertigo of interpretation. DeLillo has long been hailed as the "chief shaman of the paranoid school of fiction," a prime exponent of postmodern conspiracy fiction.[54] His novels have dramatized the conspiracy-infused postwar period in America, the time when, as DeLillo claims, "paranoia replaced history in American life."[55]

As we saw in Chapter 2, DeLillo's Kennedy assassination novel, *Libra*, retrospectively posits the origin of this cultural dislocation in those seven seconds of mayhem in Dallas. Some reviewers of *Underworld* argued that that period was now over, presumably with the end of the Cold War. Writing in the *London Review of Books*, Michael Wood suggested that Pynchon's *Mason and Dixon* and DeLillo's *Underworld* are "post-paranoid" epics. DeLillo's *Libra*, Wood pronounced, was "perhaps the last really good novel of the great age of American paranoia," an age that "faded away somewhere in the early nineties."[56] But other critics accused *Underworld* of having an unnecessarily paranoid structure, of hinting at connections where none exist; for instance, James Wood, writing in the *New Republic*, declared that *Underworld* "proves, once and for all, the incompatibility of paranoid history with great fiction."[57] So, just when we might expect paranoia to have gone beyond its sell-by date in that six-floor book depository of postwar American literature containing (amongst others) Pynchon, Burroughs, Norman Mailer, Ismael Reed and DeLillo, it seems that for some commentators *Underworld* has brought the topic out of storage and back onto the shelves. The solution to this conundrum, the remainder of this chapter will argue, is that *Underworld* plots a secret history of conspiracy culture, tracing how it has shifted from the comparatively secure paranoia of the Cold War years, through the countercultural hopes of the 1960s and after, and into the as yet unconfigured world of insecure paranoia beyond the end of the Cold War.

As we saw in the discussion of *Libra* in Chapter 2, there is a strong element of nostalgia in DeLillo's retrospective plotting of the Kennedy assassination as an inaugural event in the society of the spectacle, the limit case of modernist solidity before politics finally gave way to postmodern simulation. According to this logic, the horrifying spectacle of the President's head exploding might once have had the power to shock, but, by the mid-1970s underground artworld screening of looped tapes of the Zapruder footage in *Underworld*, it too becomes endlessly repeated and decomposed, subsumed into the routinized cynicism of a paranoia that has turned a political trauma into an avant-garde artwork. Through a parallel mechanism of nostalgia, the recreation in *Underworld* of the 1951

Giants/Dodgers baseball game confirms and extends DeLillo's argument that the Kennedy assassination marks the watershed between an older faith in the communal "sense of manageable reality" that has been missing since November 1963, and a feeling of uncontrolled suspicion towards events that are entirely subsumed within the logic of the commodified image.[58] Brian Glassic, waste manager and amateur pundit, counterpoises Thompson's home run against the Kennedy assassination, another "shot that was heard around the world":

> When JFK was shot, people went inside. We watched TV in dark rooms and talked on the phone with friends and relatives. We were all separate and alone. But when Thompson hit the homer, people rushed outside. People wanted to be together. Maybe it was the last time people spontaneously went out of their houses for something.[59]

If the Thompson homer was an event experienced together in public, then the Kennedy assassination marked the emergence of the substitute and isolated community of a national (and global) television audience—compare, for example, the scene in *Libra* with Beryl Parmenter, the CIA operative's wife, endlessly watching the reruns of the "live" death of Lee Harvey Oswald. In comparison, the unrepeatable and more distant memory of the Thompson home run takes on a far greater stability and solidity than the Kennedy assassination, which by now has dissolved into endless repetitions, not of the raw event itself, but of its mediated and commodified versions.

In *Underworld* the division between a before and after is not something that is immediately recognized by the characters at the time, but is strategically projected backwards through the lens of nostalgia. The novel does not evoke nostalgia for a Norman Rockwellesque version of the 1950s—a view that is thoroughly satirized in the Jell-O section, which links together the domestic innocence of suburbia with the military economy that underpins it. Rather, it calls up an earlier, more traditional form of paranoia that in retrospect can seem oddly comforting. For example, visiting a nuclear test site in Kazakhstan, Nick Shay feels a "kind of home-sickness" (*U*, 793) for the 1950s brand-name products left on the shelf of a recreated American home destined for destruction. This is a homesickness not so much for the "safe" domesticity of the 1950s as for the paranoia of the atomic age. The obsessive dedication to murderous detail can almost seem touching in a time when, with the privatization of public responsibility, the paranoiacally intimate interest of the State in the daily lives of its citizens—even for sinister purposes—has begun to disappear. In a similar fashion, when they meet again after four decades, the artist Klara Sax voices her suspicion to Nick, her one-time lover, that "life [took] an unreal turn at some point" (*U*, 73), an echo of DeLillo's long-running pre-occupation with the post-1960s "aberration in the heartland of the real." She goes on to explain how as a young woman during the 1960s she used to watch mysterious lights in the sky and wanted to believe that they were from B-52 bombers carrying their nuclear cargo:

> War scared me alright but those lights, I have to tell you those lights were a complex sensation. Those planes on permanent alert, ever present you know, sweeping the Soviet borders, and I remember sitting out there rocking lightly at anchor in some deserted cove and feeling a sense of awe, a child's sleepy feeling of mystery and danger and beauty.
>
> (*U*, 76)

Looking back from beyond the end of the Cold War (she is now turning those decommissioned planes into an artwork), her past fear comes to seem paradoxically appealing:

> Now that power is in shatters or tatters and now that those Soviet borders don't even exist in the same way, I think we understand, we look back, we see ourselves more clearly, and them as well. Power meant something thirty, forty years ago. It was stable, it was focused, it was a tangible thing. It was greatness, danger, terror, all those things. And it held us together, the Soviets and us. Maybe it held the world together. You could measure things. You could measure hope and you could measure destruction. Not that I want to bring it back. It's gone, good riddance. But the fact is.
>
> (*U*, 76)

In an age when power has become unstable, unfocused and intangible, Klara expresses a fondness for the certainties of four decades ago, while also recognizing the misery of living under the shadow of such terror. Marvin Lundy, the baseball collector, likewise argues that "the Cold War is your friend":

> It's the one constant thing. It's honest, it's dependable. Because when the tension and the rivalry come to an end, that's when your worst nightmares begin. All the power and the intimidation of the state will seep out of your personal bloodstream.
>
> (*U*, 170)

These characters express what has now become a widespread nostalgic yearning, which is less for the constrictions of the containment culture of the 1950s than for the more manageable certainties of Cold War anxiety. In comparison with the insecure paranoia that DeLillo presents as an effect of the Kennedy assassination's effects, the secure paranoia of the Cold War years takes on a comforting solidity.

Where DeLillo's previous novels give narrative shape to the shifting, spiraling paranoia of "the age of conspiracy, the age of connections, links, secret relations," by contrast *Underworld* presents an outline of an earlier notion of paranoia as a source of stability.[60] The novel characterizes atomic-age fear as paradoxically a form of security, a psychic strategy for maintaining a stable sense of personal and national identity. During the opening ballgame, for example, we hear J. Edgar Hoover speculate that a form of national consensus is not so much a result of a natural unity as a product of there being a definite and coherent enemy:

> Edgar looks at the faces around him, open and hopeful. He wants to feel a compatriot's nearness and affinity. All these people formed by language and climate and popular songs and breakfast foods and the jokes they tell and the cars they drive have never had anything in common so much as this, that they are sitting in the furrow of destruction.
>
> (*U*, 28)

In this version of the Cold War, paranoia "displaces religious faith" with "radioactivity, the power of alpha particles and the all-knowing systems that shape them, the endless fitted links" (*U*, 241, 251). Paranoia in effect becomes the glue that cements the nation together.

Underworld suggests that paranoia is not merely a strategic belief (whether spontaneously emerging from the people or cynically imposed on them from above) which serves to forge a sense of national consensus at precisely the time when it was beginning to come under internal threat from the collapse of the traditional white middle-class male hegemony. DeLillo's novel also devotes many pages to the psychic damage inflicted by the nuclear age, to the "hundred plots [that] go underground, to spawn and skein" (*U*, 51). Even though the presentation of Cold War paranoia is suffused with nostalgia, there is still a recognition that this mentality was at best a defense mechanism which exacted a high price in both individual and national terms. In his drug-enhanced state of paranoia at a "bombhead" party in the mid-1970s, Matt Shay hears a colleague intone in a cartoon Prussian accent that "You can never underestimate the willing-ness of the state to act out its own massive fantasies" (*U*, 421), though later, when Matt looks at a photograph of Nixon, he wonders whether "the state had taken on the paranoia of the individual or was it the other way around" (*U*, 465). In *Underworld* Cold War paranoia comes to represent a genuine psychic disturbance of the state whose "power and intimidation" have seeped their way into the "personal bloodstream" of its citizens, from Lenny Bruce's mantra of "We're all gonna die!" during the Cuban missile crisis to Sister Edgar's obsessive use of latex gloves to protect her from the "submicroscopic parasites in their soviet socialist protein coats" (U, 241).

Dietrology

In addition to *Underworld*'s straightforward portrait of paranoia in the 1950s as a national pathology, the novel sketches an intriguing and suggestive picture of more recent modes of conspiracy thinking. Despite the fixation on the Bomb, throughout its 827 pages and its half-century span *Underworld* maintains a texture of everyday fear that exceeds the rigid, bipolar logic of the Cold War and its accompanying Manichaean anxieties. Many characters in the novel experience moments of low-level paranoia that are not directly connected to the overt concern with the monomania of the anti-Communist nuclear threat (and which might instead be seen as more in tune with a more complex foreign policy of "low intensity conflict" and concerns about domestic unrest). For example, Ismael Muñoz, aka the graffiti artist Moonman 157, worries that the gallery world's sudden desire to buy his art is merely a plot by the authorities to trap him (U, 436). An old man on a street corner in Harlem rants about the pyramid on the dollar bill (U, 354, 365). Marvin Lundy speculates that Greenland either doesn't exist at all or is being kept secret for a reason (U, 316). Sims, Nick Shay's colleague, floats the possibility that the government is altering the census reports on the number of black people in America (U, 98, 334). Sister Edgar dismisses popular suspicions that the government spread HIV into the ghetto, believing instead—in a throwback to the mid-1980s Reaganite revival of paranoia about the "Evil Empire"—that "the KGB was behind this particular piece of disinformation" (U, 243). Albert Bronzini is tempted by the rumor that the moon landings were faked in a Hollywood studio. In addition, many characters feel the pull of numerology, and the number thirteen in particular. This collection of quirky fears speaks of a bewildering and strangely connected world shaped by forces beyond anyone's control. It has more to do with ongoing anxieties about race, class, gender and sexuality than with ideological struggle between two superpowers. Everyday tactics such as conspiratorial forms of numerology can perversely come to make sense in a society in which numbers are always the bottom line for the dispossessed, and in which "voodoo economics" forms official policy. As with previous DeLillo novels, conspiracy theory becomes a routinized defense strategy, a provisional but ever-present way of making sense of the world and giving narrative shape to fears that are more a reflection of the society at large than one's own personal psychopathology.

In *Underworld* many forms of paranoid thinking work outside the conventional modes of conspiracy theory. On one of his trips to track down the missing link in the Thompson home-run saga, Marvin Lundy visits the Conspiracy Theory Café in San Francisco, a place filled with "books, film reels, sound tapes, official government reports in blue binders." Given Marvin's predilection for wild conspiratorial theories, it is perhaps surprising that he "waved the place off" as a "series of sterile exercises" (*U*, 319). He does so because he believes that "the well-springs were deeper and less detectable, deeper and shallower both, look at billboards and matchbooks, trademarks on products, birthmarks on bodies, look at the behavior of your pets" (*U*, 319). For both Marvin and the novel as a whole, the hidden story of recent history is not to be found buried in government files, waiting to be pieced together into a coherent story of shadowy conspirators. Instead the secret signs of power are to be found in the daily ephemera and vast entanglement of multinational consumer capitalism, both more obvious because they are omnipresent, and less detectable because they are so much taken for granted.

The exchanges between Sims and Nick about the real story of the mysterious garbage boat likewise offer a revealing contrast between a straightforward version of conspiracy theory, and a more provisional, uncertain mode of paranoid belief. Sims suggests to Nick that their theories about the underworld involvement of the Mafia and the CIA are part of a recognizable conspiratorial world view:

> "There's a word in Italian. *Dietrologia*. It means the science of what is behind something. A suspicious event. The science of what is behind an event."
>
> "They need this science. I don't need it."
>
> "I don't need it either. I'm just telling you."
>
> "I'm an American. I go to ball games," he said.
>
> "The science of dark forces. Evidently they feel this science is legitimate enough to require a name."
>
> "People who need this science, I would make an effort to tell them we have real sciences, hard sciences, we don't need imaginary ones."
>
> "I'm just telling you the word. I agree with you, Sims. But the word exists."
>
> "There's always a word. There's probably a museum too. The Museum of Dark Forces. They have ten thousand blurry photographs. Or did the Mafia blow it up?"
>
> (*U*, 280)

There are several revealing touches in this exchange. On the one hand, Nick resolutely dismisses this kind of post-Watergate explanation as somehow inappropriate for America (he insists that "History was not a matter of missing minutes on the tape" [U, 82]), yet he alone maintains a conspiracy theory about his father's disappearance. On the other hand, though Sims seems to be trying to give his conspiratorial speculations the weight and precision of an exact science, it is noticeable that he seems uncommitted to his belief:

> He liked saying this even more. Not that he believed it. He didn't believe it for half a second but he wanted me to believe it, or entertain the thought, so he could ridicule me. He had a hard grin that mocked whatever facile sentiments you might be tempted to shelter in the name of your personal conspiracy credo.
>
> (U, 280)

If Sims takes the idea of dietrology only half seriously here, then later in the novel he presents in earnest his theory that the census reports have been doctored, with the result that Nick reminds him that: "We're not, remember, we don't have a word, you and I, for the science of dark forces. For what is behind an event. We don't accept the validity of this word or this science" (U, 335). Sims floats dietrological possibilities and then retracts them, hiding behind layers of irony too complex to unmask. In his world there is no longer a stable, monolithic "personal conspiracy credo" which one can adhere to unswervingly, only a temporary and strategic form of self-reflexive paranoia.

Sims's theories are presented as both undeniably plausible and yet probably false, in the same way that Matt's bombhead colleague makes out a convincing case about the unwitting use of "downwinders" in nuclear tests, only to deny the claims at the end of the conversation. In both the former Soviet Union and the Nevada desert such experiments are presented as an "open secret," paradoxically something that everyone knows but which is officially kept hidden. The paranoid beliefs of Sims and Matt's colleague hover between the gullible and the jaded, and between the serious and the ironic, never quite coalescing into the rigid logic of a dietrological world view. When Detwiler tries to persuade Nick and Sims that the garbage boat might be carrying CIA heroin, it is not because of any particular facts he knows, but because "it's stupid not to believe it" (U, 289), or, as DeLillo puts it in the 1983 Rolling Stone article, "paranoia in some contexts is the only intelligent response."[61] After all the revelations about government and corporate malfeasance ("Knowing what we know," says Jesse Detwiler, that "everything's connected" [U, 289]), a self-conscious and sophisticated expectation of a conspiracy comes both to be taken for granted, and yet held at arm's length. The suggestion is that one can never be paranoid enough, but a secure, single-minded faith in paranoia—either in the form of a McCarthyite political expediency or a countercultural reaction against such abuses of power—is no longer an option. In a similar fashion, one of the young volunteers on Klara's project to paint decommissioned bombers in the desert tells Nick of the joke about the end of the Cold War that is making the rounds of the camp: "the whole thing is a plot to trick the West" (*U*, 81). She laughs at the joke, but admits that "no one seems sure that it's a joke." In *Underworld* conspiracy theories become not so much items of irrefragable faith as tentative gestures toward understanding the unknown, provisional forms of representation that can only approximate the "deeper and less detectable" wellsprings of power. The novel tunes in to the transition in American paranoia over the last four decades from an inflexible and monolithic belief structure in a personalized cabal, to a contradictory, ironic, and self-reflexive appropriation of the language of conspiracy theory as a populist way of making sense of larger social and political changes. This newer paranoia, as Chapter 1 argued, is both cynical and sincere. The characters recognize how bankrupt conspiracy theory has become, but nevertheless continue to propose the theories anyway.

In many ways these shifting, subterranean beliefs operate in precisely the opposite way to conventional explanations of what I have been calling secure paranoia. They can hardly be said to maintain a stable sense of self, whether personal or national, since they conjure up at best a blurred outline of a shadowy and fragmented force that offers no coherent sense of a nameable enemy—and hence little possibility of an integral personal or national identity under threat. In Sims's discussion, he hints at connections between CIA heroin smuggling, nuclear-waste management and the Mafia, but, unlike the traditional painting-by-numbers conspiracy theorist, Sims doesn't develop an extended and documented narrative of how "They" might link together, or what "Their" purpose might be. Nor does he attribute ruthlessly efficient agency to the supposed conspirators. *Underworld* creates a sense that there are larger forces in our lives over which we have no control, but this suspicion refuses to coalesce for more than a moment into a recognizable conspiracy theory—and only then merely as a half-serious approximation of those unthinkably complex and hence unrepresentable forces. In effect the novel develops a vision of conspiracy without conspiring. Its reconfiguration of paranoia is an appropriate response to the bewildering complexities of the current world in which everything is connected but nothing adds up.

The Whole Thing Is a Plot to Trick the West

How are we to account for this broad shift from secure to insecure paranoia? If the need to plot such a division is an effect of the nostalgia of the present, then what is it about the present that creates such a need? The obvious answer is the end of the Cold War. In publicity interviews for the novel DeLillo reinforced the explicit emphasis of *Underworld* on the Cold War and its uncertain aftermath, using many of the same formulations as Klara Sax within the novel. "I don't think there's any clear sense," DeLillo comments, "of what the ending of the Cold War meant, and what it's going to mean":

> We're in between two historical periods, the Cold War and whatever it is that follows it. I'm not sure that this is what follows it. This may just be the interim. I think we're just beginning to wonder what happened, and what didn't happen.[62]

DeLillo goes on to discuss how the nuclear threat paradoxically produced, for all its restrictiveness, a "sense of limits we don't have any more," a "kind of ceiling against which other things were measured." But *Underworld* also contains clues to a less visible but ultimately more convincing account of the disorienting instabilities of the New World Order. The spectacular end of the Cold War and its attendant reconfiguration of national boundaries, the novel suggests, are but an effect of the far more significant—and ongoing—underground reshaping of the global economy. The end of the Cold War presents itself as a belated, convenient and dramatic explanation for what is documented in subterranean ways throughout the novel. It is in many ways a red herring, a distraction from What Is Really Going On, the flipside of the joke making the rounds at Klara's art project in the desert, that "the whole thing [the fall of the Soviet empire] is merely a plot to trick the West" (U, 81).

We can make more sense of the shift from secure to unstable paranoia if we read it as a way of making sense of and giving expression to changes in American society which are the result of, not so much the sudden collapse of the Berlin Wall, as the gradual transition from a fordist to a post-fordist, global order. In *Underworld*, Nick expounds upon the changes in the world's economy, borrowing phrases from Viktor Maltsev, the executive of a toxic-waste trading company in the former Soviet Union:

> Foreign investment, global markets, corporate acquisitions, the flow of information through transnational media, the attenuating influence of money that's electronic and sex that's cyberspaced ... Some things fade and wane, states disintegrate, assembly lines shorten their runs and interact with lines in other countries. This is what desire seems to demand. A method of production that will custom-cater to cultural and personal needs, not to cold war ideologies of massive uniformity. And the system pretends to go along, to become more supple and resourceful, less dependent on rigid categories.
>
> (U, 786)

At first sight the postfordist mode of production Maltsev describes would seem to promote a fluidity of desire and identity that is commendable in comparison with the "rigid categories" and "massive uniformity" of "cold war ideologies." But the globalized economy as it appears in *Underworld* is not only uncontrolled in practice but also uncontrollable in theory, producing a system that can only "pretend to go along" with the desires of its participants, with its specialization of production leading paradoxically to a transnational "planing away of particulars" (as Nick puts it). The flipside of the loss of "rigid categories" and "massive uniformity" of the Cold War period is the loss of a sense of control over national (not to mention individual) economic destiny that previously allowed governments to guarantee the social contract between the state, capital, and labor. The absence of a fordist sense of stability and security now manifests itself, as we have seen, in reconfigured forms of traditional right-wing conspiracy culture, such as the increasingly common accusations of UN-controlled black helicopters flying in secret over the USA. These popular narratives of world conspiracy and suspicion that the government is betraying its people to alien forces begin to make sense in the age of NAFTA, downsizing, job insecurity and the erosion of the welfare state. The nostalgia many characters in *Underworld* feel for the stable paranoia of the Cold War might therefore be read instead as a displaced and timely nostalgia for the older—though no less scary—secure paranoia of fordism.

The real secret history of paranoia in *Underworld*, then, is not the simple story of the replacement of bomb-induced fears by newer anxieties resulting from the fragmentation of those former geopolitical certainties. It is instead an underground current of increasing awareness and consternation that slowly everything is becoming connected in a global marketplace. In the architecture of the novel there is far more continuity than the end-of-the-Cold-War hypothesis would suggest. It is for example noteworthy that, if the beginnings of the Cold War nuclear terror are present in the novel through the dramatic simultaneity of the two "shots that are heard around the world" (the Soviet bomb and the Thompson homer), then the fall of the Berlin Wall—the equally symbolic end of the Cold War—is almost entirely absent from *Underworld*. Instead DeLillo offers glimpses, sometimes metaphorical, at other times literal, of the increasing interconnectedness of social and economic relationships within a global economy.

Underworld thus repeatedly explores how "all technology refers to the bomb" (*U*, 467) in the postwar period, tapping into the underground currents that link civilian and military hardware. The "October 8, 1957" section dwells not just on the shared futuristic language of brand names and weaponry, but also on the unsettling physical resemblance between domestic and military products: young Eric masturbates into a condom "because it had a sleek metallic shimmer, like his favorite weapons system" (*U*, 514); his mother doesn't like one of her Jell-O molds because it was "sort of guided missile-like" (*U*, 515); her loaf of bread is "strontium white" (*U*, 516); and the vacuum cleaner is "satellite-shaped" (*U*, 520).

Matt Shay, a systems analyst involved in bomb production, has a moment of insight into those interlocking systems of production and consumption:

> He was thinking about his paranoid episode at the bombhead party the night before. He felt he'd glimpsed some horrific system of connections in which you can't tell the difference between one thing and another, between a soup can and a car bomb, because they are made by the same people in the same way and ultimately refer to the same thing.
>
> (*U*, 446)

In Vietnam Matt experiences another sudden flash of insight, when he notices that "the drums [of agent orange] resembled cans of frozen Minute Maid enlarged by crazed strains of DNA" (*U*, 463). What at first appears to be merely a visual resemblance, the product of a bombed-out mind, years later becomes a troubling ethical question as Matt waits for the sun to rise in the desert whilst he contemplates leaving his bomb-related job: "how can you tell the difference between orange juice and agent orange if the same massive system connects them at levels outside your comprehension?" (*U*, 465). Matt comes to sense that "everything connects in the end, or only seems to, or seems to only because it does" (*U*, 465). His access to the deep-forged linkages between seemingly uncon-nected areas of the economy that are "outside your level of comprehension" is through a series of verbal and visual associations. Matt's subliminal awareness that "everything connected at some undisclosed point down the line" (*U*, 408) is a long way from a hyperbolically conspiratorial exposé of the misdealings and hidden mutual interests of the wartime and peacetime economies. It is also a long way from the traditional form of systems analysis in which he was trained, since, with the interpenetration of the logic of the market into every last enclave of social life, there is no way to separate out self-contained systems.[63]

Although the force field of the military–industrial complex is not mapped in detail in *Underworld*, its metaphoric convergences offer an alterna-tive and subtextual history of the emergence of a globalized economy, in contrast to the novel's manifest interest in the end of the Cold War. The catalog of brand names and intersecting vested business interests runs from the set piece about "simonizing" the car in the breezeway during the 1950s, to the complicated transnational operation run by Viktor Maltsev to dispose of toxic waste using converted nuclear weapons in the 1990s ("Tchaika is connected to the commonwealth arms complex, to

bomb-design laboratories and the shipping industry" [*U*, 788]). The continuity of these forms of interconnectedness throughout the time span of
the novel suggests that the overt ideological struggle of the Cold War was
merely a sideshow for what was—and still is—literally business as usual.

Minute Maid Orange Juice

Though some of the connections in *Underworld* can be inserted into a
coherent narrative of the quasi-conspiratorial collusion of vested interests
in the globalized economy, there are many others that refuse to be assimilated so easily. Take the example of the Minute Maid drums. In the
passages quoted above, the link between weapons and domestic goods,
though operating more at an emblematic than a factual level, nevertheless
taps into the plausible suggestion that both are part of a larger system of
production. But what are we to make of the other references to orange
juice in the novel? In passing we learn that Chuckie Wainwright's ad
agency father is daydreaming about the Minute Maid account on the day
he decides to give the baseball to his ungrateful son—who later ends up
in Vietnam. And in the novel's transcendent ending, the image of the
street kid Esmeralda appears on a billboard underneath a poster for—what
else?—Minute Maid orange juice.

It is precisely these forms of strange connection, however, which led
some reviewers to attack the novel for being unnecessarily paranoid.
James Wood argues that the novel ends up replicating the paranoid world
view of a figure like Hoover, such that "*Underworld* surrenders fiction to
the mysticism it should repel."[64] In a similar vein, Michael Dibdin concludes that DeLillo's novel "ultimately offers a hollow confirmation of the
paranoid fears it addresses by being overtly manipulated from start to
finish."[65] In many ways these criticisms repeat the longstanding objection
to conspiracy fictions for "hiding the obvious behind a veil of obscurity."[66]

In a certain sense, then, the bewildering connectedness of *Underworld* can
indeed be read as paranoiacally mystifying real social and economic relations.
Yet the novel is full of many different instances of interconnectedness, only
some of which intimate vast threatening forces beyond our control. Taken
together, they cannot be dismissed as simple conspiracy theories. In this
labyrinth of a novel, the list of uncanny convergences is a long one. There
are strange parallels, some of which are appropriately thematic. Sister Edgar
and Marvin Lundy echo Hoover's germophobia with their latex gloves
(Erica the 1950s housewife similarly has a passion for her "rubberoid"
gloves). Hoover and Albert Bronzini both have an interest in Bruegel.
There is Pafko at the wall in the baseball game, in addition to the Berlin
Wall, and the Wall in the Bronx with its commemorative mural of fallen
residents. Nick and Klara are both involved, though in different ways, with
the recycling of waste, and both visit at different times the Watts Towers in

LA. Nick's betrayal of Klara's marriage in the 1950s is repeated with a difference when it is Nick as a married man who engages in infidelity with the woman at the swingers' convention, and reversed when Nick's wife has an affair with his friend Brian Glassic. And in their respective son's homes there is Albert's dying mother and much later Nick's dying mother.

Examples of quirky doublings that are harder to classify include the references to the Fred F. French building, noticed by Klara from a rooftop in the 1970s, which reminds her of the punchline in a tale about double-dating in a car with her friend Rochelle back in her adolescence, and it is—of course—the building where ad executive Charles Wainwright works. Then there is the blackout of the North-Eastern seaboard, experienced by Nick when he returns to New York after many years' absence, and referred to by Sims as his comparison point when talking about the underreporting of the numbers of black people in the USA.

There are subtle synchronicities, with the main armature of the book provided by the front-page pairing of the Thompson home run and the Soviet nuclear bomb test, the two shots that were heard around the world. There is also, for instance, the scene where Marvin and his wife, chasing a lead in the story of the baseball in San Francisco, are waiting for the arrival of Chuckie Wainwright's ship from Alaska, but instead all they find is the infamous shit-filled garbage boat. There are also odd repetitions and coincidental allusions. The taxi-driving volunteer on the desert art project mentions the Texas Highway Killer, the home movie video of whose murderous activities is watched at different times by Nick, Matt and old Albert Bronzini, while Nick's teenage son develops a belated obsession for the Highway Killer through a website (he also incidentally later becomes hooked on the Esmeralda website). Similarly, the issue of *Time* magazine featuring Klara crops up in several of the characters' homes. Finally, heroin features in the lives of George the waiter, Nick's wife Marian and Lenny Bruce.

Despite the novel's sprawling form, there is an unsettling economy of characters, coupled with an intertwining of many different lives. For example, the 1960s garbage guerrilla Detwiler, who orchestrates the raid on Hoover's trash can, later shows up as a waste consultant and colleague of Nick Shay in the 1990s; Klara was also at Truman Capote's Black and White ball which is interrupted by the garbage guerrillas. Or, for instance, we learn in passing that the next project of Jane Farish, a BBC producer working on a project about waste for which she is interviewing Nick, is making a documentary about Klara. We also learn that Moonman 157, the young graffiti artist sought by Klara's agent, turns out to be Ismael, the leader of a scrap-metal gang in the Bronx whom Sister Edgar relies upon for protection.

More than anything, however, in a series of virtuosic developments there is the central strand of uncanny coincidences and convergences, with one part of the novel's fictional world intruding upon another. Klara is the organizer of an art project in the 1990s which involves painting decommissioned bombers in the desert. The project is called Long Tall Sally (the name, incidentally, of an erotic goods store in San Francisco that Marvin the baseball collector passes), and it takes its title from the nose painting on a particular plane, which turns out to have been the one in which Chuckie Wainwright flew during the Vietnam war. Nick visits Klara in the desert, some four decades after their brief affair in the Bronx; he is now also the owner of the legendary baseball. Meanwhile, his brother, Matt, who worked on bomb systems in the desert, was an image analyst for bombing missions in Vietnam like those flown by Chuckie. And, just to complete the complex system of connections, Matt's chess coach as a child was none other than Albert Bronzini, Klara's first husband.

Taken individually, many of these connections are perhaps no more than the usual thematic concentration of a well-composed work of fiction; in publicity interviews DeLillo talked about the well-crafted construction of the text.[67] But taken together they amount to an extended demonstration of the hypothesis—at times even the faith—that everything is connected. *Underworld*'s revised version of paranoia is concerned to represent not just the conspiratorial concatenations of power and influence made visible in a dietrological account, but the deeper linkages that refuse to yield their hidden import so easily. It suggests that what is wrong with the usual forms of conspiracy theory is not that they connect too many factors but that they don't connect enough.

The structure of *Underworld* takes to a new level DeLillo's struggle to find a form of representation commensurate to the impossibly complex interactions in the age of globalization between individuals and the larger determining forces that resemble but nevertheless exceed the logic of conspiracy. Though *Libra* is explicitly concerned with conspiracies and secrets at a political level, it also evinces, as we saw in Chapter 2, a fascination with all the coincidences that are in some way connected with the assassination, but which cannot be subsumed into a simple plot, whether fictional or conspiratorial. In a parallel fashion, the labyrinthine path of the Bobby Thompson baseball in *Underworld* offers DeLillo a way of shedding light on vast areas of American culture normally omitted in other inquiries. Some of the most remarkable passages in the novel consist merely of lists of the hands through which the home run baseball has passed, forming an evocative litany of desires and frustrations that cannot be reduced to a socioeconomic analysis. In this way DeLillo's quasi-conspiratorial presentation of coincidences and connections is not so much a failed attempt to cognitively map the totality of late capitalism as an attempt to capture some of the intricacies which might well be left out of what Jameson considers the real hidden agenda, namely the "single vast unfinished plot" of class struggle, which is to be uncovered through rigorous, scientific socioeconomic analysis.[68] The novel elegantly represents the unrepresentable concatenations of the personal and the global, but without subsuming them into a totalized plot.

Sometimes the subterranean connections are indeed sinister, combining with other facts and rumors to suggest malign though decentered and impersonal forces conspiring to control people's lives. But these connections also exceed the inexorable stranglehold of power and surveillance. The proliferation of small-scale rhizomatic entanglements of meaning are part of "some curious neuron web of lonely-chrome America" (U, 84), which operates not outside of but emerges from the interstices between the binary gridwork of power that dominated the Cold War years.[69] In the novel's final pages, for example, Sister Edgar experiences not only the claustrophobic, paranoia-inducing horror of finding the nuclear holocaust endlessly repeated on a website, but also a quasi-spiritual transcendence through the ultimate connectivity of the Internet (she too comes to understand that "everything is connected in the end" [U, 826]).

Although *Underworld* is structured by the principle that everything is connected, what is striking about the novel is how confusing and fragmented its narrative is. We learn about connections belatedly, haphazardly, in passing, since the different strands of the novel's converging plots are not presented in a linear, chronological fashion. Causes are presented long after their relevant effects, out of sequence, such that part of the frustration—and the reward—in reading the novel is piecing together the complex relations between its many different parts. That everything is connected remains, for the reader as much as for the novel's characters, both a subliminal suspicion and an act of discovery, rather than a tritely proved observation. If chaos theorists are right that causal linkages in vast distributed systems are fundamentally counterintuitive and nonpredictable, then our discovery of these unexpected patterns and connections in the novel will invariably come with a frisson of surprise, of mystery, of wonder—and not infrequently of paranoia. DeLillo seems to be experimenting with different ways to represent connectedness, trying to find a narrative grammar that can do justice to the kind of question that troubles Matt when he begins to realize that his neat mathematical equations of systems analysis fail to capture the fissiparous multiplying of effects:

> Everything connected at some undisclosed point down the systems line. This caused a certain disquiet. But it was a splendid mystery in a way, a source of wonder, how a brief equation that you tentatively enter on your screen might alter the course of many lives, might cause the blood to rush through the body of a woman on a tram many thousands of miles away, and how do you define this kind of relationship?
>
> (U, 409)

Underworld is an attempt to define this kind of relationship through an exploration of the dialectic of connectedness, both the disquiet and the wonder. Its narrative structure gestures towards the complex connections and convergences that operate underneath the heavy-handed conspiratorial coagulations of the military–industrial–media complex.

In this way DeLillo's new novel can be read alongside the other contemporary discourses of interconnectedness explored in this chapter. With its cast of conspiracy-minded characters and its plot about waste management, *Underworld* revives and rethinks the logic of paranoia, fusing a conspiratorial sense that everything is connected to an ecological one. It is both a product of and a creative response to the New World Order of connectedness that has reshaped the history of the last half-century. A "post-paranoid epic," it calls up traditional specters of humanist agency and causality, only to call both into question with its paradoxical posthumanist drama of conspiracy without conspiring. Its mutation of the rigid armature of conspiracy theory into a decentered circuit of interplotted relationships is in tune with the larger cultural shift from secure to insecure paranoia. Although operating within the field of conspiracy theory, it also goes beyond the confines of any simple notion of plotting or paranoia, reaching for new expressive possibilities commensurate to a world in which everything is becoming connected.

241

AFTERWORD

The bulk of this book was completed before the turn of the millennium. If any event seemed tailor made to excite the fevered mind of American paranoia, it was the rollover into the year 2000. End-times predictions fused together apocalyptic religious fervor and high-tech doomsday scenarios of global computer systems failure. The Millennium Bug was predicted to bring about the end of the world as we know it: TEOTWAWKI, in the acronym-laden lingua franca of the Internet. Or, in one conspiracy rumor, the prospect of a terminal computer meltdown would allow the Federal Emergency Management Agency (FEMA) to start implementing martial law, just one step away from the institution of the New World Order's global government.

In the end, of course, not much happened. The major millennial news story was that there was nothing to report. In a New Year's color supplement article on the passing of an earlier era of American conspiracy culture with the deaths of David Belin (Kennedy assassination lawyer) and Leonard Lewin (author of *Report from Iron Mountain*), Andrew Sullivan acknowledged that the year 1999 was not a "vintage year for paranoia." We were, he suggests, "prepared for all manner of hysteria: survivalist panics, religious retreats, cultic chaos." And yet "none of it materialized."[1] But the failure of Y2K panic to live up to the hype should have come as little surprise. As early as 1985, Jean Baudrillard was declaring in his usual rhetoric of hyperbole that the year 2000 wouldn't happen, because the idea of the end of history was an illusion that had already imploded on itself. Way before its time, the year 2000 had already happened (as the English translation of Baudrillard's article put it).[2] Given the saturation of end-times hype that left most spectators exhausted before we even got close to the date, it was little wonder that the genuine millennial anxieties failed to match up to the alarmist anticipation of an outburst of popular paranoia. In the event, it began to seem that there were more armchair sociologists holed up metaphorically in log cabins awaiting the first signs of crackpot hysteria than there were actual survivalists camped out in the backwoods.

This notably self-conscious and self-ironizing lack of genuine millennial panic bears out the increasing tendency of conspiracy culture to collapse in on itself that I outlined in my reading of Pynchon's *Vineland* in Chapter 1. In a climate of insatiable exposure coupled with a routinized cynicism, conspiracy theory becomes a machine for imagining in advance every worst possible scenario of apocalyptic paranoia. Anything that does come to pass is then merely confirmation of what was already suspected long ago—even when nothing happens. With Y2K, everyone was on the lookout for signs of a naïve and fanatical paranoia that is becoming less common. Though there was much talk of conspiracy in the air, few people fully believed in the rumors that were circulating. Nor, in many cases, did they fully disbelieve them either. Perhaps the most convincing conspiracy theory surrounding Y2K was the suggestion that the panic about computer mayhem had been deliberately and cynically hyped up for the benefit of the data-protection industry. The only genuine conspiratorial fear left, then, was the very knowing suspicion that the alarmist specter of popular paranoia was itself nothing but a cunning fabrication.

In the run-up to the millennium, the success of *The X-Files* and its clones seemed to suggest that there was a tidal wave of populist paranoia about to crest with the turn of the century. It turned out, however, that the culture of conspiracy had entered its own labyrinth of mirrors, as everyone began to mistake the kind of self-conscious cultural diagnosis that *The X-Files* performs for a genuine symptom of a widespread cultural malaise. The conspiracy, Mulder and Scully had been told again and again, always goes much higher, producing an inflationary logic of endlessly deferred revelation that can never be cashed in. At some stage it was inevitable that viewers would begin to think that the show is crying wolf. Fittingly, even in the eyes of some dedicated fans *The X-Files* began to collapse into exhaustion in its seventh series that spanned the turn of the millennium, with accusations in online forums that the show's writers and actors are now merely going through the motions.

It might begin to seem, then, that conspiracy culture has had its day. The zeitgeist-sampling essay in the *New York Times* magazine article, for example, comes to the conclusion that American paranoia is merely a subculture now, the domain of a core of increasingly marginal fanatics whose heyday of public prominence and acceptability in the 1970s has waned. In a similar vein, the studies by Daniel Pipes and Robert Robins and Jerrold Post both suggest (as I outlined in the Introduction) that conspiracy theories have ceased to be a worrying or influential ideological force in the United States, because they have become merely cultural. In contrast, I have been arguing in the foregoing chapters that conspiracy theory has become more influential precisely because it has become taken for granted as a cultural phenomenon, and as an everyday explanation for how the world works. There might well be a subculture of hard-core genuine believers, but for many more people in the mainstream the possibility of conspiracy thinking is always hovering in the background, more a process of endless self-ironizing suspicion than a fixed, ideological product. In effect, the rhetoric of conspiracy now hovers somewhere between the literal and the metaphorical, neither merely a symptom of the zeitgeist, nor fully a diagnosis of it.

If it is tempting to conclude a book on conspiracy theory with dire predictions about the imminent dangers of mass paranoia (or even complacent declarations that the danger has now passed), then it is also tempting to dismiss it as irrelevant in the twenty-first century. From the hyperbolic (and frequently apocalyptic) perspective of posthumanist theory, for example, conspiracy theory might be said to have outlived its utility. The accusation is that it relies on a traditional liberal humanist faith in the power of individual agency, even in the case when that agency is amplified into the megamachinations of powerful corporations, syndicates and cabals. But, as we have seen, in the very act of imagining the ruggedly individual self under threat from a frightening cluster of infiltrating forces, the culture of conspiracy ends up making visible and therefore intelligible exactly what it fears. By imagining a self immersed in a global environment of risk, or caught in a vast web of anonymous interconnecting forces, popular paranoia in effect undermines the logical coherence of the very thing it was seeking to defend. In a world bereft of immunity from risk and in which conspiracies seem to emerge without evidence of actual conspiring, the idea of a fully autonomous self (or secret society of selves) in control of its actions begins to erode, even if the nostalgic yearning for it doesn't fully disappear. Since the symbolic watershed of the Kennedy assassination, the rhetoric of conspiracy has given voice to a world in which the notions of self-sufficient agency, self-contained bodily identity and straightforward causality are no longer convincing, but which has not yet come to terms with or come up with terms for a posthumanist alternative.

NOTES

INTRODUCTION (pp. 1–22)

1. Hillary Rodham Clinton, interview with Matt Lauer, '*Today*,' NBC network, 27 January 1998.
2. See, for example, the professional-looking spoof website belonging to the self-declared Vast Right-Wing Conspiracy (VRWC) at <http://home.att.net/~joserojas/conspiracy.html>. There is also an entire web ring of sites proudly proclaiming that they belong to the VRWC: <http://www.world-net.net/home/mdtcmt/vrwc.htm>.
3. Bernard Bailyn, *The Origins of American Politics* (New York: Knopf, 1968), 13.
4. David Brion Davis, ed., *The Fear of Conspiracy: Images of Un-American Subversion from the Revolution to the Present* (Ithaca: Cornell University Press, 1972), 23.
5. In addition to Davis's anthology and the work of Richard Hofstadter (discussed more fully later in the Introduction) on the American history of countersubversive fears, see Eric Mottram, "Out of Sight but Never Out of Mind: Fears of Invasion in American Culture," *Blood on the Nash Ambassador: Investigations in American Culture* (London: Hutchinson Radius, 1989), 138–80. In *Conspiracy and Romance: Studies in Brockden Brown, Cooper, Hawthorne and Melville* (Cambridge: Cambridge University Press, 1989), Robert S. Levine provides an astute analysis of conspiratorial structures in the American romance novel of the nineteenth century. He argues that the imagination of sinister forces in these novels was part of the larger "romantic" act of imagining a cohesive sense of American national identity into being through the nativist rhetoric of conspiring enemies.
6. For an overview of this position, see Davis's introduction to *The Fear of Conspiracy*; and the essays collected in Richard O. Curry and Thomas M. Brown, eds, *Conspiracy: The Fear of Subversion in American History* (New York: Holt, Rinehart and Winston, 1972).
7. According to the National Election Study annual survey, in 1958 73 percent of respondents answered that they trusted the government in Washington to do what is right just about always or most of the time; in 1994 (the lowest point), only 21 percent fell into these categories (in 1998 it was up to 34 percent).
8. A few of the many examples include: Alexander Cockburn, "The Kooks Have It," *New Statesman & Society*, 17 January 1992, 14; Paul Gray, "The Spores of Paranoia," *Time*, 15 January 1990, 69–70; Christopher Hitchens,

"On the Imagination of Conspiracy," in *For the Sake of Argument: Essays and Minority Reports* (London: Verso, 1993), 12–24; George Johnson, "The Conspiracy That Never Ends," *New York Times*, 30 April 1995, D5; John Yemma, "A Penchant for Plots: Conspiracy Theories Are All the Rage in the US," *Boston Globe*, 25 September 1996, A1. In "Injections and Truth Serums: AIDS Conspiracy Theories and the Politics of Articulation," in *Conspiracy Nation*, ed. Peter Knight (New York: New York University Press, forthcoming), Jack Bratich reports that the *Reader's Guide to Periodicals* cites twenty articles on conspiracy theory in 1990–94, and eighty-eight in the period 1995–99.

9. Daniel Pipes, *Conspiracy: How the Paranoid Style Flourishes and Where It Comes From* (New York: Free Press, 1997), xi.

10. Richard Hofstadter, "The Paranoid Style and Other Essays" (London: Jonathan Cape, 1966), 36. Further references are abbreviated in the text as PS.

11. Pipes, *Conspiracy*, 49.

12. Chip Berlet, "Conspiracism," <http://www.igc.apc.org/pra/tooclose/conspiracism.htm>.

13. Elaine Showalter, *Hystories: Hysterical Epidemics and Modern Culture* (New York: Columbia University Press, 1997), 8.

14. Pipes, *Conspiracy*, 49.

15. Showalter, *Hystories: Hysterical Epidemics and Modern Culture*, rev. ed. (London: Picador, 1998), xii.

16. Carl Sagan, *The Demon-Haunted World: Science as a Candle in the Dark* (New York: Random House, 1995), and Michael Shermer, *Why People Believe Weird Things: Pseudoscience, Superstition, and Other Confusions of Our Time* (New York: W. H. Freeman, 1997).

17. For a perceptive discussion of the conspiratorial overtones of masscult theory, see Andrew Ross, "Containing Culture in the Cold War," in *No Respect: Intellectuals and Popular Culture* (London: Routledge, 1989), 42–64.

18. Karl Popper, "Prediction and Prophecy in the Social Sciences," *Conjectures and Refutations* (London: Routledge & Kegan Paul, 1963), 341; first published in *Library of the 10th International Congress of Philosophy* 1 (1948): 336–46. Popper makes a similar argument in "Towards a Rational Theory of Tradition," *Conjectures*, 120–35; first published in *The Rationalist Annual* 1 (1949). In "Popper Revisited, or What Is Wrong with Conspiracy Theories," *Philosophy of the Social Sciences* 25 (1995): 3–34, Charles Pidgen refutes Popper's own refutation of conspiracy theories, arguing that it is neither factually nor logically correct to assert that conspiracy theories have played no role in shaping the history of the USA and other countries.

19. Popper, *Conjectures*, 342.

20. Gordon S. Wood, "Conspiracy and the Paranoid Style: Causality and Deceit in the Eighteenth Century," *The William and Mary Quarterly* 39 (1982): 441.

21. Wood, "Conspiracy," 441.

22. Robert S. Robins and Jerrold M. Post, *Political Paranoia: The Psychopolitics of Hatred* (New Haven: Yale University Press, 1997), 18–19.

23. Pipes argues that real conspiracy theories (i.e. "world" conspiracy theories) only emerged at the time of the French Revolution. Though Pipes makes this point only in the context of developing a particular pedigree for his narrow conception of the paranoid style, it nevertheless opens up the useful suggestion that a certain kind of global conspiracy thinking arises with fears and fantasies about the emergence of an international (more

accurately, a colonial) market that operates in previously unimaginable ways. As much at the end of the eighteenth century as at the end of the twentieth, conspiracy theories mount an attack on the idea of a world system of trade that is still coming into being, while at the same time helping make that process conceptually possible through their proleptic imagination of a vast interconnected system.

24. In keeping with this shift to a broader and more nebulous form of conspiracy culture, this study employs various terms interchangeably to describe the phenomenon, in order not to limit the definition in advance: conspiracy talk, the discourse of conspiracy, dietrological assumptions, the rhetoric of paranoia, and so on. Although I take issue with the psychologizing assumptions behind the use of the term "paranoid" by critics like Hofstadter and Pipes, I employ the word "paranoia" not as part of a technical (or even metaphorical) psychoanalytical vocabulary, but as a reflection of everyday usage that often is meant to signify nothing more than "conspiracy-minded."

25. Showalter, *Hystories*, 206.

26. Gregory S. Camp, *Selling Fear: Conspiracy Theories and End-Times Paranoia* (Grand Rapids, MI: Baker Books, 1997). A similar approach is taken by Paul T. Coughlin, *Secrets, Plots and Hidden Agendas: What You Don't Know About Conspiracy Theories* (Downers Grove, IL: InterVarsity Press, 1999).

27. For an account of the reception of Showalter's book see, for example, Wray Herbert, "The Hysteria over *Hystories*," *U.S. News & World Report*, 1 May 1997, 14.

28. Patricia A. Turner, *I Heard It through the Grapevine: Rumor in African-American Culture* (Berkeley and Los Angeles: University of California Press, 1993).

29. Robins and Post, *Political Paranoia*, 64.

30. Somewhat disturbingly, Robins and Post observe, almost without comment, that Prozac has been shown to alter the dominance hierarchies in monkeys (and hence lessen aggressive paranoiac tendencies). The implication seems to be that paranoia in humans is a sickness that might also be amenable to such treatment.

31. Robins and Post, *Political Paranoia*, 64.

32. For a more explicitly psychoanalytical approach, see, for example, Erich Wulff, "Paranoiac Conspiracy Delusion," in *Changing Conceptions of Conspiracy*, ed. Carl F. Graumann and Serge Moscovici (New York: Springer-Verlag, 1987), 172–89.

33. Pipes, *Conspiracy*, 14, 145, 49.

34. The circumstances of Meir's retort to Henry Kissinger are discussed in Joseph H. Berke et al., eds, *Even Paranoids Have Enemies: New Perspectives on Paranoia and Persecution* (London: Routledge, 1998), 1.

35. Pynchon, *Gravity's Rainbow* (New York: Viking, 1973), 581.

36. Showalter, *Hystories*, 207.

37. For further discussion of this kind of approach, see Michael Rogin, *"Ronald Reagan, The Movie"; and Other Episodes in Political Demonology* (Berkeley and Los Angeles: University of California Press, 1988); and Eric Goode and Nachman Ben-Yehuda, *Moral Panics: The Social Construction of Deviance* (Oxford: Blackwell, 1994).

38. Rogin himself took this revisionist line in *The Intellectuals and McCarthy: The Radical Specter* (Cambridge: MIT Press, 1967).

39. Fredric Jameson, "Cognitive Mapping," in *Marxism and the Interpretation of Culture*, ed. Cary Nelson and Lawrence Grossberg (Basingstoke: Macmillan, 1988), 356.

40. Jameson, *Postmodernism, or, The Cultural Logic of Late Capitalism* (London: Verso, 1991), 38.

41. Jameson, *The Political Unconscious: Narrative as a Socially Symbolic Act* (London: Methuen, 1981), 20.

42. Mark Fenster, *Conspiracy Theories: Secrecy and Power in American Culture* (Minneapolis: University of Minnesota Press, 1999), 225–26.

43. Jodi Dean, *Aliens in America: Conspiracy Cultures from Outerspace to Cyberspace* (Ithaca, NY: Cornell University Press, 1998). Negative reviews of Dean include Alexander Star, "The Truth Is Out There," *New York Times Book Review*, 9 August 1998, 10–11; Norman Levitt, "Why Professors Believe Weird Things," *Skeptic Magazine* 6, no. 3 (1998): 28–35; Christopher Hitchens, "Invasion of the Body-snatchers," *TLS*, 15 May 1998, 18–19; and Frederick Crews, "The Mindsnatchers," *New York Review of Books*, 25 June 1998, 14–19.

CHAPTER 1 (pp. 23–75)

1. Daniel Pipes, *Conspiracy: How the Paranoid Style Flourishes and Where It Comes From* (New York, Free Press, 1997).

2. Richard Hofstadter, *The Paranoid Style in American Politics and Other Essays* (London: Jonathan Cape, 1966), 7 (emphasis in original). Further references are abbreviated in the text as PS.

3. As with conspiracy theories about the Kennedy assassination, the details of the prime event are very much in dispute. For a summary of the six different versions of the Roswell story that circulate in ufological circles, see Benson Saler, Charles A. Zeigler and Charles B. Moore, *UFO Crash at Roswell: Genesis of a Modern Myth* (Washington, DC: Smithsonian Institute Press, 1997).

4. The story of how a UFO crash-landing at Roswell came to be part of the national mythology is a long and complicated one. The story was quickly forgotten at the time, and by the time it was revived in the late 1970s by the ufologist Stanton Freidman, it had been transformed into a much richer story involving rescued aliens being stored in a hangar at an Air Force base, the details of which had been partly transposed from *Behind the Flying Saucers*, Frank Scully's 1952 hoax investigation of another crash.

5. Gerald K. Haines, "CIA's Role in the Study of UFOs, 1947–1990," *Studies in Intelligence* 1, no. 2 (1997), available at <http://www.odci.gov/csi/studies/97/unclas/ufo.http>.

6. James McAndrew, *The Roswell Report: Case Closed* (Washington, DC: Headquarters United States Air Force, 1997).

7. Bruce Handy, "Roswell or Bust," *Time*, 23 June 1997, available at <http://www.pathfinder.com/time/magazine/1997/dom/970623/society.roswel_or_bus.html>.

8. For a consideration of the significance of the DNA evidence in the trial, see Andrew Ross, "If the Genes Fit, How Do You Acquit?: O.J. and Science," in *Birth of a Nation'hood: Gaze, Script, and Spectacle in the O. J. Simpson Case*, ed. Toni Morrison and Claudia Brodsky Latour (London: Vintage, 1997), 241–72.

9. David C. Martin, *Wilderness of Mirrors* (New York: Harper & Row, 1980).

10. *The X-Files*, "Patient X" (5X13), first broadcast 1 March 1998.
11. David Wise and Thomas B. Ross, *Invisible Government* (New York: Random House, 1964), 1–2.
12. Richard Gid Powers, Introduction to Daniel Patrick Moynihan, *Secrecy: The American Experience* (New Haven: Yale University Press, 1998), 41. Powers and Moynihan both argue that the routinization of secrecy in Washington has resulted in more harm than good. The self-serving bureaucratic guarding and trading of secrets led to many bad decisions being made on the basis of information that would have been disputed had it been debated in the public arena. Their prime example is how CIA overestimates of the military and economic strength of the Soviet Union blinded government decision makers to the reality of that country's incipient breakup, thereby perpetuating a vastly increased military and nuclear budget in the United States. The irony, however, is that the release of secret documents from the Cold War in fact confirmed what had long been dismissed as McCarthyite paranoia, namely that there was a successful Soviet program to infiltrate the US government and steal its atomic secrets. As Powers and Moynihan argue, the threat was never as large as feared, and was soon discovered and contained, but the maintenance of secrecy over the events for decades meant that both left and right held unnecessarily conspiratorial views about Soviet subversion and American countersubversion.
13. Jodi Dean, "Declarations of Independence," in *Political Theory: The Cultural Turn*, ed. Dean (Ithaca: Cornell University Press, forthcoming).
14. Michael Rogin, "'Make My Day!': Spectacle as Amnesia in Imperial Politics," in *Cultures of United States Imperialism*, ed. Amy Kaplan and Donald E. Pease (Durham, NC: Duke University Press, 1993), 499–534.
15. Norman Mailer, "Author's Note," in *Harlot's Ghost* (1991; London: Abacus, 1992), 1,375.
16. Mailer, *Harlot's Ghost*, 1,376.
17. *The X-Files*, "Musings of a Cigarette Smoking Man" (4X07), first broadcast 17 November 1996.
18. *Three Days of the Condor*, dir. Sidney Pollack (1975).
19. Carl Oglesby, *The Yankee and Cowboy War: Conspiracies from Dallas to Watergate* (Kansas City: Sheed Andrews and McMeel, 1976), 15.
20. *The X-Files*, "Ascension" (2X06), first broadcast 21 October 1994.
21. "Wake up America! It Can Happen Here! A Post-McCarthy Guide to Twenty-three Conspiracies by Assorted Enemies Within," *Esquire*, May 1966, 165.
22. Ralph Larkin and Daniel Foss, "Lexicon of Folk-Etymology," in *The 60s without Apology*, ed. Sohnya Sayres et al. (Minneapolis: University of Minnesota Press, 1984), 375.
23. Herb Blau, "From '(Re)Sublimating the 60s,'" in *The 60s without Apology*, 318.
24. John Carroll, *Puritan, Paranoid, Remissive: A Sociology of Modern Culture* (London: Routledge & Kegan Paul, 1977), 80.
25. Hendrik Hertzberg and David C. K. McClelland, "Paranoia: An Idée Fixe Whose Time Has Come," *Harper's*, June 1974, 52.
26. Hertzberg and McClelland, "Paranoia," 53.
27. Hertzberg and McClelland, "Paranoia," 52.
28. Ralph Waldo Emerson, "Self-Reliance" (1841), in *Essays and Lectures*, ed. Joel Porte (New York: Library of America, 1983), 261.

29. William Burroughs, *Naked Lunch* (1959; London: Flamingo–HarperCollins, 1993), 33.

30. Sigmund Freud, "Psychoanalytic Notes on an Autobiographical Account of a Case of Paranoia" (1911), in *Standard Edition of the Complete Psychological Works of Sigmund Freud*, trans. James Strachey, vol. 22 (London: Hogarth Press, 1958), 9–82.

31. Don DeLillo, "American Blood: A Journey through the Labyrinth of Dallas and JFK," *Rolling Stone*, 8 December 1983, 24.

32. In addition to the works cited in the introduction by David Brion Davis, the collection of essays edited by Richard O. Curry and Thomas M. Brown, and the work of Chip Berlet, other examples include Seymour Martin Lipset and Earl Raab, *The Politics of Unreason: Right-wing Extremism in America, 1790–1970* (New York: Harper & Row, 1970); George Johnson, *Architects of Fear: Conspiracy Theories and Paranoia in American Politics* (Los Angeles: Jeremy P. Tarcher, 1983); and David H. Bennett, *The Party of Fear: From Nativist Movements to the New Right in American History* (New York: Vintage, 1990).

33. In *"Ronald Reagan, The Movie"; and Other Episodes in Political Demonology* (Berkeley and Los Angeles: University of California Press, 1988) Michael Rogin locates Hofstadter's analysis of provincial status politics in relation to Hofstadter's (and his own) problematic status as a Jewish cosmopolitan intellectual.

34. According to the National Election Study annual survey, in 1958 73 percent of respondents answered that they trusted the government in Washington to do what is right just about always or most of the time; in 1994 (the lowest point), only 21 percent fell into these categories (in 1998 it was up to 34 percent). As with most polls, the significance of these figures is disputed; see, for example, Richard Morin, "Less Than Meets the Eye," *Washington Post*, 16 March 1998, available at <http://washingtonpost.com/wp-srv/politics/polls/wat/archive/wat031698.htm>. For a wider discussion of the loss of faith in government in general, see Joseph S. Nye, Jr, Philip D. Zelikow and David C. King, eds, *Why People Don't Trust Government* (Cambridge: Harvard University Press, 1997).

35. See, for example, Michael Kelley, "The Road to Paranoia," *New Yorker*, 19 June 1995, 60–75.

36. 〈http://www.sss.org/lbh/helos.html〉. Daniel McKiernan provides a useful page of links to black helicopter websites at 〈http://weber.ucsd.edu/~dmckiern/blakchop.htm〉. A hyperbolic extension of black helicopter rumors is offered in Jim Keith, *Black Helicopters over America* (Lilburn, GA: IllumiNet Press, 1994). For a wide-ranging discussion of the function of helicopters in the American imaginary, from Vietnam to South Central, see Alasdair Spark, "Flight Controls: The Social History of the Helicopter as a Symbol of Vietnam," in *Vietnam in Images: War and Representation*, ed. Jeffrey Walsh and James Aulich (Basingstoke: Macmillan, 1987), 86–111.

37. *New York Times*, 18 September 1996, A9.

38. Gary Benoit, editorial, *New American* (Special Report: Conspiracy for Global Control), 16 September 1996, 1.

39. Pat Robertson, *The New World Order* (Dallas: Word Publishing, 1991), 97.

40. Patrick J. Buchanan, "Will the American Nation Survive?" press release, n.d. [1996], available on the 1996 Buchanan for President website: <http: 207.153.218.152/AmeryNet/polysnet/polyforms/survive.htm>.

41. In a review of *The New World Order*, Michael Lind makes a plausible case for the coded nature of Robertson's anti-Semitism. Lind, "Rev. Robertson's Grand International Conspiracy Theory," *New York Review of Books*, 2 February 1995, 21–25

42. For a roundup of estimates of the size of the movement, see Mark Rupert, "A Virtual Guided Tour of Far-Right Anti-Globalist Ideology," <http:// www.maxwell.syr.edu/maxpages/faculty/merupert/Research/far-right /mainstrm.htm>. The Southern Poverty Law Center, for example, provides an annual listing of active Patriot groups, at<http://www.igc.apc.org/pra/>.

43. Richard Barnet and John Cavanagh, *Global Dreams: Imperial Corporations and the New World Order* (New York: Simon & Schuster, 1994), 19.

44. Gary Wills analyzes the popularity of this position across the political divide in "The New Revolutionaries," *New York Review of Books*, 10 August 1995, 50–55.

45. Kristin Dawkins, "NAFTA, GATT, and the World Trade Organization: The New Rules for Corporate Conquest," in *The New American Crisis: Radical Analyses of the Problems Facing America Today*, ed. Greg Ruggiero and Stuart Sahulka (New York: The New Press, 1996), 75.

46. Letter written by Timothy McVeigh to his local newspaper on 11 February 1992, quoted in Mark Hamm, *Apocalypse in Oklahoma: Waco and Ruby Ridge Revenged* (Boston: North Eastern University Press, 1997), 158.

47. For a broad account of the American public's disillusionment with the political process, see Michael J. Sandel, *Democracy's Discontent: America in Search of a Public Philosophy* (Cambridge: Harvard University Press, 1996). Sandel argues that, alongside the erosion of community, the sense that we are "losing control of the forces that govern our lives" defines the "anxiety of the age" (3).

48. Andrew MacDonald [William Pierce], *The Turner Diaries* (1978; New York: Barricade, 1996), 56. Further references are abbreviated in the text as *TD*.

49. For a fascinating discussion of the way the New Right has recreated itself as a besieged minority in the face of a conspiratorial specter of homosexuality that it has itself conjured up, see Cindy Patton, "Tremble, Hetero Swine!" in *Fear of a Queer Planet: Queer Politics and Social Theory*, ed. Michael Warner (Minneapolis: University of Minnesota Press, 1993), 43–77. Patton notes that "in the new right literature [of the 1980s], lesbian and gay men graduated from a covert conspiracy to an open and audacious lobby." She goes on to argue that although this transformation meant in effect that lesbian and gay men had been recognized and accepted as a political force, the New Right could now predicate its identity on its reinterpretation of the proud performativity of coming out as an unwitting confession of perversity. "If coming out says, 'We're queer, we're here, get used to it,'" Patton writes, "new right identity appropriates this to say, 'We knew it,' and to society, 'We told you so'" (146).

50. Robert S. Robins and Jerrold M. Post, *Political Paranoia: The Psychopolitics of Hatred* (New Haven: Yale University Press, 1997), 198.

51. This is not to say, however, that the paranoid style is only to be found in the narrowly political realm in the past. See, for example, Robert S. Levine, *Conspiracy and Romance: Studies in Brockden Brown, Cooper, Hawthorne and Melville* (Cambridge: Cambridge University Press, 1989).

52. [Leonard C. Lewin], *Report from Iron Mountain* (New York: Dial Press, 1967).

53. Given the insatiable operation of paranoid suspicion, it comes as no surprise that the legendary conspiracy text, "The Gemstone File" (explored in

more detail in Chapter 6), insists that the Pentagon Papers are themselves faked revelations, prepared by Ellsburg in order to distract people from the political assassinations of the 1960s and 1970s.

54. See Christopher M. Andrew, *The Mitrokhin Archive: The KGB in Europe and the West* (London: Allen Lane, 1999). Kennedy assassination researchers immediately questioned the authenticity of Mitrokhin's claims, suspecting a deliberate piece of disinformation designed to cover up the truth about the original conspiracy theories—that, for example, a letter supposedly written by Oswald to E. Howard Hunt (later to be one of the Watergate burglars) is in fact quite genuine after all, contrary to the pronouncement in 1978 by the House Select Committee on Assassinations that it is a fake. See, for example, Gary Mack, "RE: Dear Mr Hunt letter/KGB/Joestin," JFK Lancer listserv (online posting), 15 September 1999.

55. Len Bracken, afterword to *NASA, Nazis and JFK: The Torbitt Document and the Kennedy Assassination*, ed. Kenn Thomas (Kempton, IL: Adventures Unlimited, 1996), 229.

56. *The X-Files*, "War of the Coprophages" (3X12), first broadcast 5 January 1996.

57. *The X-Files*, "Small Potatoes" (4X20), first broadcast 20 April 1997.

58. *The X-Files*, "Post-Modern Prometheus" (5X06), first broadcast 30 November 1997.

59. Ritual abuse is dealt with, for example, in *The X-Files*, "Die Hand Die Verletz" (2X14), first broadcast 27 January 1995; and recovered memories of abduction/sexual abuse are covered, for instance, in *The X-Files*, "Demons" (4X23), first broadcast 11 May 1997.

60. *The X-Files*, "731" (3X10), first broadcast 1 December 1995.

61. *The X-Files*, "The Unnatural" (6X20), first broadcast 25 April 1999.

62. *The X-Files*, "Wetwired" (3X23), first broadcast 10 May 1996.

63. *The X-Files*, "Patient X."

64. *The X-Files*, "Nisei" (3X09), first broadcast 24 November 1995.

65. *The X-Files*, "Drive" (6X02), first broadcast 15 November 1998.

66. *The X-Files*, "Pusher" (3X17), first broadcast 23 February 1996.

67. *The X-Files*, "The Beginning" (6X01), first broadcast 8 November 1998.

68. *The X-Files* also played with this idea in an episode developed at roughly the same time. In "El Mundo Gira" (4X11), first broadcast 12 January 1997, the social invisibility of Mexicans is literalized into the idea of an invisible force that kills people.

69. For analyses of the complicated meanings and functions of supermarket tabloids, see, for example, Elizabeth Bird, *For Enquiring Minds: A Cultural Study of Supermarket Tabloids* (Knoxville: University of Tennessee Press, 1992), and John Fiske, *Power Plays, Power Works* (London: Verso, 1993).

70. The quotations are from the film's official promotional website, ⟨www.conspiracytheory.com/cmp/interviews.html⟩.

71. Brian Lowry, *The Truth Is Out There: The Official Guide to "The X-Files"*, vol. 1 (New York: Harper, 1995), 12.

72. *The X-Files*, "José Chung's *From Outer Space*" (3X20), first broadcast 12 April 1996.

73. Lowry, *The Truth*, 12.

74. The Watergate meeting takes place in *The X-Files*, "Little Green Men" (2X01), first broadcast 16 September 1994.

75. Andy Meisler, *I Want to Believe: The Official Guide to "The X-Files"*, vol. 3 (New York: Harper, 1998), 9.

76. Devon Jackson, *Conspiranoia!: The Mother of All Conspiracy Theories* (New York: Plume–Penguin, 1999), xi.
77. Richard Metzger, on "Disinfo Nation," Channel 4 (UK), 17 February 2000.
78. Morris Dickstein, *Gates of Eden: American Culture in the Sixties* (New York: Basic Books, 1977), 125.
79. Thomas Pynchon, *V.* (1963; London: Picador, 1975), 226.
80. Pynchon, *V.*, 153.
81. Pynchon, *The Crying of Lot 49* (1966; London: Picador, 1979), 33. Further references are abbreviated in the text as *CL*.
82. This is a familiar criticism of Pynchon; for example, in *The Minimal Self: Psychic Survival in Troubled Times* (1984; London: Picador, 1985), Christopher Lasch accuses Pynchon's novels of "hiding the obvious behind a veil of obscurity" (159).
83. Pynchon, *Gravity's Rainbow* (New York: Viking, 1973), 638. Further references are abbreviated in the text as *GR*.
84. Dale Carter pieces together this story in *The Final Frontier: The Rise and Fall of the American Rocket State* (London: Verso, 1988).
85. Terence Rafferty, "Long Lost," *New Yorker*, 19 February 1990, 108–12; Christopher Walker, "Thomas Pynchon's Vineland," *London Review of Books*, 8 March 1990, 45.
86. J. Anthony Lukas, "*Vineland* by Thomas Pynchon," *BOMC News*, April 1990, 3; Donna Rifkind, "The Farsighted Virtuoso," *Wall Street Journal*, 2 January 1990, A9.
87. Wendy Steiner, "Pynchon's Progress: Dopeheads Revisited," *Independent* (London), 3 February 1990, 30.
88. Christopher Lehman-Haupt, "*Vineland*, Pynchon's First Novel in 17 Years," *New York Times*, 26 December 1989, C21.
89. Walker, "Pynchon's *Vineland*," 5; Salman Rushdie, "Still Crazy After All These Years," *New York Times Book Review*, 14 January 1990, 1, 36–37; Paul Gray, "The Spores of Paranoia," *Time*, 15 January 1990, 69–70.
90. Frank Kermode, "That Was Another Planet," *London Review of Books*, 8 February 1990, 3–4; Kermode, "Decoding the Tristero," in *Pynchon: A Collection of Critical Essays*, ed. Edward Mendelson (Englewood Cliffs, NJ: Prentice-Hall, 1978), 162–66.
91. J. Kerry Grant, *A Companion to "The Crying of Lot 49"* (Athens, GA: University of Georgia Press, 1994); Steven Weisenburger, *A "Gravity's Rainbow" Companion* (Athens, GA: University of Georgia Press, 1988).
92. Tony Tanner discusses the original choice of title in *Thomas Pynchon* (London: Methuen, 1982), 78.
93. Pynchon, *Vineland* (1990; London: Minerva, 1991), 142. Further references are abbreviated in the text as *VL*.
94. This is not to argue, however, that the modes of conspiracy and romance are in opposition. Levine's *Conspiracy and Romance*, for example, argues that in nineteenth-century American fiction a conspiracy plot, like the romance plot, provides a symbolic resolution to the perceived real contradictions of society. It is also worth noting that the conspiracy mythology of *The X-Files* has increasingly come to hint that not only the ultimate secret of the abduction of Mulder's sister, but also the origin of the alien–human hybrid experiments and the continuation of the X-Files investigation is all caught up with the possibility that the Cigarette Smoking Man is Mulder's father.

95. In *Gravity's Rainbow* there is, for example, the scene in which Pirate Prentice confronts the fact that he might unwittingly have been a double agent for the other side (542); there is also the startling jump-cut forward to an unspecified time when a "spokesman for the Counterforce" admits "in a recent interview with the *Wall Street Journal*" that "We were never that concerned with Slothrop *qua* Slothrop" (738). Roger Mexico likewise daydreams of "the failed Counterforce, the glamorous ex-rebels ... doomed pet freaks," with the suspicion that "They will use us. We will help legitimize Them, though they don't need it really, it's another dividend for Them, nice but not critical" (713).

96. Pynchon himself has commented on the significance of the change from a subculture associated with cannabis, speed and LSD to the rave scene based on Ecstasy: "[with MDMA] the circuits of the brain which mediate alarm, fear, flight, lust, and territorial paranoia are temporarily disconnected. You see everything with total clarity, undistorted by animalistic urges. You have reached a state which the ancients have called nirvana, all seeing bliss." Cited in Douglas Rushkoff, *Cyberia: Life in the Trenches of Hyperspace* (London: Flamingo/HarperCollins, 1994), 110.

97. This fear, however, has come back with a vengeance with *The X-Files* (and the feature film in particular), which has repeatedly hinted that FEMA is involved in coordinating the overall alien–human hybrid project. In *The X-Files: Fight the Future* (1998) Mulder is reminded forcefully that "FEMA allows the White House to suspend constitutional government upon declaration of a national emergency. It allows creation of a non-elected national government." FEMA even went so far as to issue public relations advice to its employees explicitly refuting the show's accusations, a denial which inevitably leaked beyond the Agency and which only seemed to spur the program's more die-hard believers into smelling a disinformation campaign. See FEMA, "Public Affairs Guidance," no. 1 (24 March 1998) and no. 2 (18 June 1998); for a discussion of the whole affair, see Jon Elliston, "FEMA's X-File: Emergency Public Affairs Are 'Not for the Outside World,'" Parascope dossier, ⟨http://www.parascope.com/ds/articles/femaXfile.htm⟩.

98. Some critics have discussed DeLillo in these terms. Pat O'Donnell, for example, explores the disappearance of paranoia into obviousness in DeLillo, in "Obvious Paranoia: The Politics of Don DeLillo's *Running Dog*," *Centennial Review* 34 (1990): 56–72. Likewise, John McClure traces DeLillo's rewriting of the romance genre in an age devoid of secret spaces, in "Postmodern Romance: Don DeLillo and the Age of Conspiracy," *South Atlantic Quarterly* 89 (1990): 337–53.

99. John Dugdale's *Thomas Pynchon: Allusive Parables of Power* (London: Longman, 1990) provides probably the best account of *Lot 49*'s intertexts. Pynchon's first three novels of course contain many engagements with mass culture, but in *Vineland* there are scarcely any references to anything else.

100. The filming of *The Return of the Jedi* in Vineland County was what changed the loggers bar, but movies themselves have been overtaken by the process of yuppification found in the Noir Center movie-theme shopping mall, which "runs to some pitch so desperate that Prairie at least had to hope the whole process was reaching the end of its cycle" (*VL*: 326).

101. Eve Kosofsky Sedgwick, "Introduction: Queerer than Fiction," *Studies in the Novel* 28 (1996): 277.

102. Fredric Jameson warns against a parallel irony in critical theory, when the paranoid outlook becomes so successful that it is in danger of undermining the original critical impulse: "What happens is that the more powerful the vision of some increasingly total system or logic—the Foucault of the prisons book is the obvious example—the more powerless the reader comes to feel. Insofar as the theorist wins, therefore, by constructing an increasingly closed and terrifying machine, to that very degree he loses, since the critical capacity of his work is thereby paralyzed, and the impulses of negation and revolt, not to speak of those of social transformation, are increasingly perceived as vain and trivial in face of the model itself." Jameson, *Postmodernism, or, The Cultural Logic of Late Capitalism* (London: Verso, 1991), 5–6.

103. Peter Sloterdijk, *Critique of Cynical Reason*, trans. Michael Eldred (Minneapolis: University of Minnesota Press, 1987), 5. In *Everybody Knows: Cynicism in America* (Minneapolis: University of Minnesota Press, 1999), William Chaloupka argues that cynicism has become an extremely widespread and diverse phenomenon in contemporary American political and cultural life. It is evident, he argues, in the cynical manipulation by those in power of popular conspiracy thinking as well as in the everyday cynicism of popular distrust of government.

104. Jameson, *Postmodernism*, 36.

105. Jean Baudrillard, *The Ecstasy of Communication*, trans. Bernard Schutze and Caroline Schutze (New York: Semiotext(e), 1988), 22.

106. Terry Eagleton, "Capitalism, Modernism and Postmodernism," in *Against the Grain* (London: Verso, 1986), 132.

107. Eagleton, "Capitalism," 144.

CHAPTER 2 (pp. 76–116)

1. See Stephen E. Ambrose, "Writers on the Grassy Knoll: A Reader's Guide," *New York Times Book Review*, 2 February 1992, 23–25.

2. D. M. Thomas, *Flying in to Love* (London: Bloomsbury, 1992), 3.

3. Hofstadter goes on to claim that "no European, to my knowledge, has matched the ingenuity of Professor Revilo P. Oliver of the University of Illinois," who was eventually dismissed from his post for his far-right allegations that JFK was shot by the International Communist Conspiracy because he was becoming too "American." Hofstadter's basic argument—that the paranoid style is favored only by minority movements in America—is therefore only confirmed by this apparent counterexample. Richard Hofstadter, *The Paranoid Style in American Politics and Other Essays* (London: Jonathan Cape, 1966), 7. For a sociological overview of the immediate reactions to the assassination, see also Bradley S. Greenburg and Edwin B. Parker, eds, *The Kennedy Assassination and the American Public: Social Communication in Crisis* (Stanford: Stanford University Press, 1965).

4. '*48 Hours*' on CBS (5 February 1992) reported 77 percent of respondents believed in a conspiracy, and 75 percent that there was an official cover-up. A 1993 poll by ICR Research Group of Media, Pennsylvania found that only 12 percent of the American public believed that they have been told the whole truth, and that 71 percent think Oswald was part of a larger conspiracy. "Doubts Remain in Shooting: 7 out of 10 Say Killing of JFK a Conspiracy," *Cincinnati Enquirer*, 21 November 1993, A7, cited in Ronald F. White, "Apologists and Critics of the Lone Gunman Theory:

Assassination Science and Post-Modern America," in *Assassination: Experts Speak Out on the Death of JFK*, ed. James H. Fetzer (Chicago: Catfeet Press, 1998), 377. Report about Clinton and Gore in Bob Callahan, *Who Shot JFK?: A Guide to the Major Conspiracy Theories* (New York: Simon & Schuster, 1993), 147.

5. William Manchester, cited in Max Holland, "After Thirty Years: Making Sense of the Assassination," *Reviews in American History* 22 (1994): 192.

6. See, for example, the collection of testaments in Abigail van Buren, ed., *Where Were You When President Kennedy Was Shot?: Memories and Tributes to the Slain President, as Told to "Dear Abby"* (Kansas City: Andrews and McMeel, 1993).

7. Gregory Benford, *Timescape* (London: Victor Gollancz, 1980). In a piece of clever speculation, Mark Lawson's *Idlewild, or, Everything is Subject to Change* (London: Picador, 1995) imagines what if Kennedy had survived and Marilyn Monroe had not committed suicide.

8. Judith A. Eisner, "Mae Brussell: Fears 'Hidden Government' Plans Assassinations," *The Pine Cone* (Carmel-by-the-Sea, CA), 21 September 1972, 43–44. For a biographical profile of Brussell, see Jonathan Vankin, *Conspiracies, Cover-ups and Crimes: Political Manipulation and Mind Control in America* (New York: Paragon House, 1991).

9. Robert J. Groden, "The Killing of a President," *Arena*, Autumn 1993, 120–35. In recent years Groden has eked out a living selling videos of his work in Dealey Plaza, as well as providing "expert" testimony on photographic evidence in the O. J. Simpson trial.

10. Eric Norden, "Jim Garrison: A Candid Conversation with the Embattled District Attorney of New Orleans," *Playboy*, October 1967, 59–60+; available at <http://members.aol.com/Labyrinth13/Main/Garrison.htm>.

11. Gallup opinion polls cited in Max Holland, "After Thirty Years: Making Sense of the Assassination," *Reviews in American History* 22 (1994): 203.

12. For a full account of visual representations surrounding the case, see Art Simon, *Dangerous Knowledge: The JFK Assassination in Art and Film* (Philadelphia: Temple University Press, 1996).

13. Oswald was in fact initially accused of conspiring with Communists to take the life of the President, though these charges were quickly dropped. Reported in the BBC 1 Timewatch documentary, broadcast on 22 November 1993.

14. "Dallas Prosecutor's News Conference," *New York Times*, 26 November 1963, 14.

15. *Report of the President's Commission on the Assassination of President John F. Kennedy* (Washington, DC: United States Government Printing Office, 1964), 21.

16. *Report*, 22.

17. *Report*, 423.

18. Reported in Callahan, *Who Shot JFK*, 35.

19. Dr Renatus Hartogs, *The Two Assassins* (New York: T. Cromwell, 1965).

20. Priscilla Johnson McMillan, *Marina and Lee* (New York: Harper & Row, 1977).

21. Gerald Ford, *Portrait of the Assassin* (New York: Simon & Schuster, 1965).

22. David Swanson, Philip Bohnert and Jackson Smith, *The Paranoid* (Boston: Little, Brown & Co., 1970), 378–94. There have, of course, been many Presidential assassination attempts since 1970: an attempt on Nixon, two on Gerald Ford, one on Reagan, Bush's claim that a group of Iraqis

plotted to kill him, and, more recently, we might include the mysterious light aircraft that crashed into the White House in 1994.

23. This is the angle that Steven Sondheim explores in his musical *Assassins* (New York: Theatre Communications Group, 1991). For example, Leon Czolgosz, who killed William McKinley in 1901, declared in his last words that, "I killed the President because he was an enemy of the good people. I am not sorry for my crime."

24. For accounts of the historiographical turn to psychohistory, see Michael Rogin, "American Political Demonology: A Retrospective," in *"Ronald Reagan, The Movie"; and Other Episodes in Political Demonology* (Berkeley and Los Angeles: University of California Press, 1988), 272–300; and Gordon S. Wood, "Conspiracy and the Paranoid Style: Causality and Deceit in the Eighteenth Century," *The William and Mary Quarterly* 39 (1982): 401–44.

25. The three essays are: Lawrence Zelic Freedman, "Psychopathology of the Assassin"; David A. Rothstein, "Presidential Assassination Syndrome: A Psychiatric Study of the Threat, the Deed, and the Message"; and Thomas Greening, "The Psychological Study of Assassins," in *Assassinations and the Political Order*, ed. William J. Crotty (New York: Harper & Row, 1971), 143–266.

26. See in particular Crotty, "Assassinations and Their Interpretation within the American Context," and Ivo K. Feierabend, Rosalind L. Feierabend, Betty A. Nesvold, and Franz M. Jaggar, "Political Violence and Assassination: A Cross-National Assessment," in Crotty, *Assassinations*, 3–140.

27. Gerald Posner, "It Was Him All Along," *Mail on Sunday* (London), 2 October 1993, 13.

28. Alexander Cockburn, "Propaganda of the Deed," *New Statesman & Society*, 19 November 1993, 30–31. Similarly, in an early article on the assassination, I. F. Stone urged his readers to "ask ourselves honest questions," such as, "how many Americans have not assumed—with approval—that the CIA was probably trying to find a way to assassinate Castro?" Stone recognized that through tacit support of such covert operations, "we all reach for the dagger, or the gun, in our thinking when it suits our political thinking to do so" (I. F. Stone, "We All Had a Finger on That Trigger," *I. F. Stone's Weekly*, 9 December 1963, 12).

29. Norman Mailer, "The Great American Mystery," *Book Week Washington Post*, 28 August 1966, 1, 11–13.

30. Mailer, *Oswald's Tale: An American Mystery* (London: Little, Brown & Co., 1995), 605.

31. Stone, "The Left and the Warren Commission Report," *I. F. Stone's Weekly*, 5 October 1964, 12. Stone was not the only commentator on the critical left to be totally convinced by the Warren Commission's work, and to be relieved that America was not about to be absorbed in an escalating spiral of mutually assured destruction by the assassin's bullet. Herbert L. Packer, writing in *The Nation*, admired the "conscientious and at times brilliant job the commission has done," in the way that it "admirably fulfilled its central objective by producing an account of the circumstances under which President Kennedy was assassinated that is adequate to satisfy all reasonable doubts." Packer, "The Warren Report: A Measure of the Achievement," *The Nation*, 2 November 1964, 295.

32. "The Warren Commission Report," *Time*, 2 October 1964, 19.

33. Loudon Wainwright, "The Book for All to Read," *Life*, 16 October 1964, 35.

34. Most people's access to both the findings and the hearings was through two selective editions put out by the *New York Times*. In *Accessories After the Fact: The Warren Commission, the Authorities and the Report* (New York: Bobbs-Merrill, 1967), Sylvia Meagher pointed out the many ways in which the selections in the edited version avoided many of the inconsistencies which were apparent in the full-length version.

35. Edward Jay Epstein, *Inquest: The Warren Commission and the Establishment of the Truth* (London: Hutchinson, 1966), and Mark Lane, *Rush to Judgement: A Critique of the Warren Commission's Inquiry into the Murders of President John F. Kennedy, Officer J. D. Tippit and Lee Harvey Oswald* (London: The Bodley Head, 1966).

36. Jim Garrison, *On the Trail of the Assassins* (1988; Harmondsworth: Penguin, 1992).

37. US Department of Justice, "1968 Panel Review of Photographs, X-Ray Films, Documents and Other Evidence Pertaining to the Fatal Wounding of President John F. Kennedy on November 22, 1963 in Dallas, Texas," reprinted in Harold Weisberg, *Post Mortem: JFK Cover-Up Smashed* (Frederick, MD: H. Weisberg, 1975).

38. US President's Commission on CIA Activities Within the United States (Rockefeller Commission), *Report to the President* (Washington, DC: Government Printing Office, 1975); US Senate Select Committee to Study Governmental Operations with respect to Intelligence Operations, (Church Committee), *Alleged Assassination Plots Involving Foreign Leaders*, Interim Report (Washington, DC: Government Printing Office, 1975); and *The Investigation of the Assassination of President John F. Kennedy: Performance of the Intelligence Agencies*, Book 5, Final Report (Washington, DC: Government Printing Office, 1976).

39. US House of Representatives, *Report of the Select Committee on Assassinations* (Washington, DC: Government Printing Office, 1979).

40. For an example of a conspiracy-minded account of the fate of witnesses, see, for example, Anthony Summers, *The Kennedy Conspiracy*, rev. ed. (1980; London: Warner, 1992).

41. For a full list of the various official inquiries, see the Assassination Records Review Board, *Final Report of the Assassination Records Review Board* (Washington, DC: Government Printing Office, 1998), ch. 1, sec. B; available at <http://www.fas.org/sgp/advisory/arrb98/part03.htm>.

42. ARRB, "Review Board Recommendations," *Final Report*, <http://www.fas.org/sgp/advisory/arrb98/part12.htm>.

43. For a cogent overview of assassination "critics" over the last four decades, see Simon, *Dangerous Knowledge*, ch. 1.

44. Scott Dikkers, ed., *Our Dumb Century* (London: Boxtree, 1999), 101.

45. Cited in Callahan, *Who Shot JFK?*, 63.

46. The Conspiracy Museum (Dallas), "Welcome to the Great Coalbin Exhibit" (leaflet, 1997).

47. Press release issued by JFK Lancer "November in Dallas" conference, November 1997. For George Michael Evica's expanded position statement, see <http://www.jfklancer.com/Statement.html>.

48. Harrison Edward Livingstone, *Killing the Truth* (New York: Carrol & Graf, 1993), 369, cited in White, "Apologists," 403. In *Conspiracy Theories: Secrecy and Power in American Culture* (Minneapolis: University of Minnesota Press, 1999), Mark Fenster argues that the "community" of assassination

researchers is far from cohesive, and is in any case a very poor substitute for the real community anticipated in the utopian political imagination.

49. Jack White, "Evidence ... or Not?: The Zapruder Film: Can It Be Trusted?" in *Assassination Science*, 211.

50. Posner, *Case Closed: Lee Harvey Oswald and the Assassination of JFK* (New York: Random House, 1993), 318.

51. White, "Apologists," 392–93.

52. Cyril Wecht cited in White, "Apologists," 400–01.

53. For an account of the whole *JAMA* saga, see Fetzer, ed., *Assassination Science*, pt. 1. Needless to say the dissenting doctor has published a book on the subject: Charles A. Crenshaw, *JFK: Conspiracy of Silence* (New York: Penguin, 1992).

54. Bill Drenas, paper given at the JFK-Lancer "November in Dallas" conference, 1997.

55. John Armstrong's ideas have been contested point by point by other researchers and skeptics; see, for example, W. Tracy Parnell, "Harvey & Lee: Polishing the Big Apple and Other Matters," ⟨http://www.madbbs. com/~tracy/lho/h&l2.htm⟩.

56. Armstrong, paper given at "Death of JFK" conference, University of Minnesota (1999), available at <http://enteract.com/~hargrove/ UMinn99.htm>.

57. Baudrillard evokes the "vertigo of interpretation" in a discussion of theories about Deep Throat's role in Watergate, and the problem of interpreting any given bombing in Italy as the work of leftist extremists, or right-wing or centrist provocation. "Simulacra and Simulations," in *Jean Baudrillard: Selected Writings*, ed. Mark Poster (Cambridge: Polity, 1988), 174–75.

58. Don DeLillo, "American Blood: A Journey through the Labyrinth of Dallas and JFK," *Rolling Stone*, 8 December 1983, 28.

59. According to David Perry, by 1995 sixty-one different people had been identified as the shooter or an accomplice (<http://mcadams.posc.mu.edu/ rashomon.htm>).

60. Mailer, *Oswald's Tale*, n.p.

61. A similar recuperation is performed at the end of Condon's *The Manchurian Candidate* (1959). For most of its length the novel is a vicious satire on the kind of right-wing Cold War paranoia represented by Senator McCarthy, but at the end it turns out that the Senator's wife is not part of the ultra-right but is in fact in the pay of the Russians, thereby seeming to justify the very paranoia that has been the target of the novel's satire.

62. Pynchon, *The Crying of Lot 49* (1966; London: Picador, 1979), 36.

63. Pynchon, *The Crying of Lot 49*, 89.

64. For an account of the media coverage of *JFK* see Art Simon, "The Making of Alert Viewers: The Mixing of Fact and Fiction in *JFK*," *Cinéaste* 19 (1992): 14–15. Somewhat surprisingly, two review essays in the *American Historical Review* praised the film for its historical accuracy. Marcus Raskin, "*JFK* and the Culture of Violence," and Robert A. Rosenstone, "*JFK*: Historical Fact/Historical Film," *AHR* 97 (1992): 487–99, and 506–11.

65. Other films have appeared in the last decade which also involve the Kennedy assassination, yet none has provoked anything like the passions which attended the release of Stone's film. The list includes *Love Field* (1992), *In the Line of Fire* (1993), *Ruby* (1992), *Malcolm X* (1993), and a feature-length episode of *Quantum Leap* broadcast on BBC 2 on the assassination's thirtieth anniversary in 1993.

66. Stone's Op-Ed pieces are collected in Oliver Stone and Zachary Sklar, eds, *"JFK": The Book of the Film* (New York: Applause Theatre, 1992).

67. "How can we account for the present situation unless we believe that men high in this government are concerting to deliver us to disaster? This must be the product of a great conspiracy, a conspiracy on a scale so immense as to dwarf any previous such venture in the history of man. A conspiracy of infamy so black that, when it is finally exposed, its principals shall be forever deserving of the maledictions of all honest men ... What can be made of this unbroken series of decisions and acts contributing to the strategy of defeat? They cannot be attributed to incompetence." Senator McCarthy, *Congressional Record*, 82nd Cong., 1st sess. (14 June 1951), 6,602; quoted in Hofstadter, *The Paranoid Style*, 8.

68. Garrison, *On the Trail of the Assassins*, xi.

69. On the teleological narrative drive of detective and other fiction, see Peter Brooks, *Reading for the Plot: Design and Intention in Narrative* (Cambridge: Harvard University Press, 1984).

70. Jonathan Culler, "Story and Discourse in the Analysis of Narrative," in *The Pursuit of Signs* (London: Routledge & Kegan Paul, 1981), 174.

71. Michael Rogin develops a similar argument about the homophobic impulse in *JFK*, in "Body and Soul Murder: *JFK*," in *Media Spectacles*, ed. Marjorie Garber, Jann Matlock and Rebecca L. Walkowitz (London: Routledge, 1993), 3–22. In *Scandals, Scamps and Scoundrels: The Casebook of an Investigative Reporter* (New York: Random House, 1992), James Phelan makes the accusation that Garrison in fact believed the assassination was a "gay thrill kill."

72. Anthony DeCurtis, " 'An Outsider in This Society': An Interview with Don DeLillo," in *Introducing Don DeLillo*, ed. Frank Lentricchia (Durham, NC: Duke University Press, 1991), 47–48.

73. Frank Lentricchia discusses the reception of *Libra* in "The American Writer as Bad Citizen," in *Introducing Don DeLillo*, 1–6.

74. Don DeLillo, *Libra* (1988; Harmondsworth: Penguin, 1989), 178. Further references are abbreviated in the text as *L*.

75. In a very different take on the novel, Skip Willman argues persuasively that *Libra* creates a stance of social critique by pitting conspiracy theories against contingency theories of historical causation. On the one hand, the novel creates a Marxist sense of social necessity in its portrait of Oswald, in contrast to the Warren Commission's "contingency theory" of Oswald as a misfit lone gunman—an aberration, as it were, in the normal functioning of America. Conversely, *Libra* rejects a model of society and history shaped by ruthlessly efficient covert agents by resolutely insisting on the contingency at the heart of the assassination. While I would agree with Willman's account of the novel's dual critique of liberal humanist agency, I would argue, however, that *Libra* also explores the idea of coincidence as a realm between simple conspiracy and contingency, that pushes beyond our normal powers of understanding or representation. Willman, "Traversing the Fantasies of the JFK Assassination: Conspiracy and Contingency in Don DeLillo's *Libra*," *Contemporary Literature 39* (1998): 405–33

76. DeCurtis, "An Outsider," 56.

77. *The X-Files*, "The Red and the Black" (5X14), first broadcast 8 March 1998.

78. DeCurtis, "An Outsider," 48.

79. *The X-Files*, DeLillo, "American Blood," 22.

80. DeLillo quoted in David Remnick, "Exile on Main Street: Don DeLillo's Undisclosed Underworld," *New Yorker*, 15 September 1997, 42–48.
81. Maria Nadotti, "An Interview with Don DeLillo," *Salmagundi* 100 (1993): 94.
82. Pynchon, *Gravity's Rainbow* (New York: Viking, 1973), 521.
83. Frank Lentricchia, "*Libra* as Postmodern Critique," in *Introducing Don DeLillo*, 193–215.
84. DeLillo, "American Blood," 24.
85. DeLillo, "American Blood," 24.
86. DeLillo, "American Blood," 24.
87. See Nick Trujillo, "Interpreting November 22: A Critical Ethnography of an Assassination Site," *Quarterly Journal of Speech* 79 (1993): 447–66.
88. Fredric Jameson, *Postmodernism, or, The Cultural Logic of Late Capitalism* (London: Verso, 1991), 354–55.
89. For an extended discussion of the role of the Zapruder footage (and the *Challenger* disaster) in forging a postmodern identity for Americans based on the logic of the simulacrum, see Marita Sturken, *Tangled Memories: The Vietnam War, the AIDS Epidemic, and the Politics of Remembering* (Berkeley: University of California Press, 1997).
90. DeLillo, "American Blood," 22.
91. Harold Jaffe, "Introduction," in Derek Pell, *Assassination Rhapsody* (New York: Autonomedia/Semiotext(e), 1989), 7–8.
92. DeLillo, "American Blood," 28.
93. White, "Apologists," 407.
94. Jean Baudrillard, from *Simulacra and Simulations*, trans. Paul Foss, Paul Patton and Philip Beitchman, in *Jean Baudrillard: Selected Writings*, ed. Mark Poster (Cambridge: Polity, 1988), 177.

CHAPTER 3 (pp. 117–142)

1. Naomi Wolf, *The Beauty Myth: How Images of Beauty Are Used Against Women* (1990; London: Vintage, 1991), 17–18. Further references are abbreviated in the text as *BM*.
2. Susan Faludi, *Backlash: The Undeclared War Against American Women* (New York: Crown, 1991), xxii.
3. Here "popular" designates not so much the degree of popularity (although the two books this chapter concentrates on, *The Feminine Mystique* and *The Beauty Myth*, were both bestsellers), but rather the way in which a certain tradition of "middlebrow" American feminism is marked out as "popular" precisely because of its modes of address and rhetorical structures, one of which is the trope of conspiracy. In an article on celebrity feminism, Jennifer Wicke argues that "to the extent that academic feminism has an opposite, it is not movement feminism per se, but the celebrity pronouncements made by and about women with high visibility in the various media." Instead of immediately vilifying "celebrity feminism" as "a realm of ideological ruin," counsels Wicke, "we must recognize that the energies of the celebrity imaginary are fuelling feminist discourse and political activity as never before." Wicke, "Celebrity Material: Materialist Feminism and the Culture of Celebrity," *South Atlantic Quarterly* 93 (1994): 753.
4. Betty Friedan has continued to use this idiom and narrative structure for each of her subsequent books. In *The Second Stage* (New York: Summit,

1981), Friedan describes how she began to realize that women in the 1970s were being led astray not by the feminine mystique, but by the *feminist* mystique of career and family. And in *The Fountain of Age* (London: Jonathan Cape, 1993), Friedan's "historical Geiger counter" detects "clues" about the "age mystique" (ix).

5. Friedan, *The Feminine Mystique* (1963; Harmondsworth: Penguin, 1992), 17. Further references are abbreviated in the text as *FM*.

6. On the history of brainwashing, see J. A. C. Brown, *Techniques of Persuasion: From Propaganda to Brainwashing* (Harmondsworth: Penguin, 1963), and David Bromley and James Richardson, eds, *The Brainwashing/ Deprogramming Controversy* (New York: Edwin Mellen, 1980).

7. In her persuasive rereading of *The Feminine Mystique*, Rachel Bowlby makes a similar point: "Friedan is constantly caught in this contradiction, which can be smoothed over only by accepting the arbitrary distinction between true and false dreams—between those that are from within and correspond to the 'human' potential, and those that are from without and are imposed by the manipulators of the 'feminine mystique.'" Bowlby, "'The Problem With No Name': Rereading Friedan's The Feminine Mystique," in *Still Crazy After All These Years: Women, Writing and Psychoanalysis* (London: Routledge, 1992), 87. Bowlby also draws attention to the conspiratorial aspects of the book, but does not elaborate on this observation.

8. Vance Packard, *The Hidden Persuaders* (New York: David McKay, 1957).

9. For an overview of this writing, see Gayle Greene, "Mad Housewives and Closed Circles," in *Changing the Subject: Feminist Fiction and the Tradition* (Bloomington and Indianapolis: Indiana University Press, 1991), 58–85. Greene claims that "Friedan is so accurate a chronicler of white middle-class women's experience in these years that *The Feminine Mystique* provides historical documentary for what the novels portray fictionally." I would argue instead that both the novels and Friedan's nonfictional account rely on metaphors—such as the figuration of conspiracy—that are all the more powerful because they remain unacknowledged. In effect, Friedan taps into the tropes of popular fiction to ground her analysis as much as the mad-housewife novels draw on the "historical documentary" of *The Feminine Mystique*. The concerns and imagery of mad-housewife fiction also emerge in so-called stalker novels, such as Diane Johnson's *The Shadow Knows* (1974), Margaret Atwood's *Bodily Harm* (1981) and Ira Levin's *Sliver* (1991), which portray the persecution of women, in both home and body.

10. Sylvia Plath, *The Bell Jar* (1963; New York: Bantam, 1981), 69.

11. Paulina Palmer, *Contemporary Women's Fiction: Narrative Practice and Feminist Theory* (Hemel Hempstead: Harvester Wheatsheaf, 1989), 69.

12. Ira Levin, *Rosemary's Baby* (New York: Random House, 1967). In "Placing Rosemary's Baby," *Differences* 5 (1993): 121–53, Sharon Marcus provides a compelling analysis of the novel's portrayal of female paranoia in the face of male experts controlling every intimate detail of women's lives—not least in the form of Dr Spock's advice on childrearing.

13. See Chapter 5 for a discussion of a similar double take in *Safe* (1995), Todd Haynes's reworking of the mad-housewife film.

14. The Redstockings, "Manifesto" (1968), reprinted in *Sisterhood Is Powerful*, ed. Robin Morgan (New York: Random House, 1970), 533–36.

15. Interview with Mainardi, cited in Alice Echols, *Daring to Be Bad: Radical Feminism in America, 1967–75* (Minneapolis: University of Minnesota Press, 1989), 99.

16. For an account of these events see Echols, *Daring to Be Bad*, 265–69; and Ellen Willis, "Radical Feminism and Feminist Radicalism," in *The 60s Without Apology*, ed. Sohnya Sayres et al. (Minneapolis: University of Minnesota Press, 1984), 91–118. See also Frank J. Donner, *The Age of Surveillance: The Aims and Methods of America's Political Intelligence System* (New York: Random House, 1981), 150–55 and 268–75; and Carol Hanisch, "The Liberal Takeover of Women's Liberation," in *Feminist Revolution*, ed. Redstockings (New York: Random House, 1979), 163–64. The original article, "Gloria Steinem and the CIA," was included in the 1975 version of the Redstockings' *Feminist Revolution*, but was edited out for legal reasons under publisher influence when Random House produced an abridged version in 1979.

17. Baxandall cited in Echols, *Daring to Be Bad*, 97.

18. Some of WITCH's flyers and "spell poems" are reprinted in Morgan, ed., *Sisterhood is Powerful*, 545–50.

19. Quoted in *Daring to Be Bad*, 214–15. The Congress is also discussed in David Deitcher, ed., *Over the Rainbow: Lesbian and Gay Politics in America Since Stonewall* (London: Boxtree, 1995), 36–38.

20. Susan Faludi, for example, has returned to this rhetorical turning of the tables. Finding that when Op-Ed editors give women column space, they usually turn to a select bunch of conservative commentators, Faludi takes up the advice of a former *New York Times* editor, who suggests that feminists should "start their own think tank with secret sources of funding." Faludi agrees, concluding somewhat ironically that "after all, they already think we're part of a feminist conspiracy. Why not make it true?" Faludi, "Media Matters," *The Nation* (1996), available at <http://www.thenation.com/1996/issue/960429/0429falu.htm>.

21. Mary Daly, *Gyn/Ecology The Metaethics of Radical Feminism* (1978; London: The Women's Press, 1984), 29. Further references are abbreviated in the text as *GE*.

22. Meaghan Morris, "A-Mazing Grace: Notes on Mary Daly's Poetics" in *The Pirate's Fiancée* (London: Verso, 1988), especially 40–43.

23. Susan Brownmiller, *Against Our Will: Men, Women and Rape* (New York: Simon and Schuster, 1975), 14–15

24. Susan Griffin, "Rape: The All-American Crime" (1970) in *Rape: The Power of Consciousness* (San Francisco: Harper & Row, 1979), 322; Brownmiller, *Against Our Will*, 209.

25. Chapter 5 discusses the turn to the literal in fictions of body horror in more detail.

26. Andrea Dworkin, *Pornography: Men Possessing Women* (London: The Women's Press, 1981), 18.

27. The passage comes from Ann Jones's foreword to *Women Who Kill* (New York: Ballantine, 1981), vii–xviii. Noting that "among academic historians and literary historians" it "seems to be incumbent upon the author to say that readers who gain the impression from the book that men as a group have done something unpleasant as a group to women as a group are entirely mistaken," Jones concludes that, "if this book leaves the impression that men have conspired to keep women down, that is exactly the impression I mean to convey; for I believe that men could not have succeeded as well as they have without concerted effort" (xvii).

28. Compare, for example, Faludi's portrayal of the Backlash: "In the last decade, the backlash has moved through the culture's secret chambers,

traveling through passageways of flattery and fear. Along the way it has adopted disguises … It manipulates a system of rewards and punishments … Cornered, it denies its own existence, points an accusatory finger at feminism, and burrows deeper underground … The backlash line blames the women's movement" (Faludi, *Backlash*, xxii).

29. Wolf, *Fire with Fire: The New Female Power and How It Will Change the 21st Century* (London: Chatto & Windus, 1993), 201. As with Friedan's second book, Wolf transfers the charge of conspiracy from patriarchal institutions of the backlash to certain feminists whom (in a telling use of the label with which she had herself been charged) she calls "victim feminists."

30. Lynne Segal, *Is the Future Female?: Troubled Thoughts on Contemporary Feminism* (London: Virago, 1987), 231.

31. Mica Nava, *Changing Cultures: Feminism, Youth and Consumerism* (London: Sage, 1992), 165.

32. Cora Kaplan, "Radical Feminism and Literature: Rethinking Millett's *Sexual Politics*," in *Sea Changes: Essays on Culture and Feminism* (London: Verso, 1986), 21.

33. Jacqueline Rose, "Femininity and its Discontents," in *Sexuality and the Field of Vision* (London: Verso, 1986), 90.

34. For accounts of this argument see Pamela Moore and Devoney Looser, "Theoretical Feminism: Subjectivity, Struggle, and the 'Conspiracy' of Poststructuralisms," *Style* 27 (1993): 530–58, and Patricia Waugh, "Modernism, Postmodernism, Feminism: Gender and Autonomy Theory," in *Practising Postmodernism/Reading Modernism*, ed. Waugh (London: Edward Arnold, 1992).

35. Judith Butler, *Bodies that Matter: On the Discursive Limits of "Sex"* (London: Routledge, 1993), 6.

36. Butler, *Bodies that Matter*, 6–9.

37. Tania Modleski, *Feminism Without Women: Culture and Criticism in a "Postfeminist" Age* (London: Routledge, 1991), 57.

38. Jane Gallop, *Around 1981: Academic Feminist Literary Criticism* (London: Routledge, 1992), 136, 79.

CHAPTER 4 (pp. 143–167)

1. Even Daniel Pipes, who in the main follows Hofstadter's terminology and analysis, lists African Americans alongside the hard right as exemplars of, respectively, "the disaffected" and "the suspicious," in his preliminary sketch of the contemporary scene of the paranoid style. Pipes, *Conspiracy: How the Paranoid Style Flourishes and Where It Comes From* (New York: Free Press, 1997), 1–14.

2. David Brion Davis, ed., *The Fear of Conspiracy: Images of Un-American Subversion from the Revolution to the Present* (Ithaca: Cornell University Press), 362.

3. The significant exception, discussed later in this chapter, is the large volume of often lengthy works putting forward Afrocentric ideas (many of which include conspiratorial accounts of how whites have covered up the knowledge that Western civilization is not Greek in origin but Egyptian and hence African). The Nation of Islam has also distributed pamphlets and books which explain its theories that the Jews were at the heart of the slave trade. There are of course many books on Malcolm X and Martin Luther King which deal in passing with conspiracy theories about their

assassinations, but this is a far cry from the immense outpouring of conspiracy culture surrounding the Kennedy shootings.

4. Jawanza Kunfuju, *Countering the Conspiracy to Destroy Black Boys* (n.p.: African American Images, 1985).

5. Patricia A. Turner, *I Heard It Through the Grapevine: Rumor in African-American Culture* (Berkeley: University of California Press, 1993).

6. Civil Rights Congress, *We Charge Genocide: The Historic Petition to the United Nations for Relief from a Crime of the United States Government Against the Negro People* (New York: Emergency Conference Committee, 1951); quotation from Paul Robeson, "Genocide Stalks the USA," *New World Review*, February 1952, 24–29; reprinted in *Paul Robeson Speaks: Writings, Speeches, Interviews, 1918–1974*, ed. Philip S. Foner (London: Quartet Books, 1978), 308–11.

7. Stokeley Carmichael and Charles V. Hamilton, *Black Power: The Politics of Liberation in America* (New York: Vintage Books, 1967), 22–23; reprinted in Davis, ed., *The Fear of Conspiracy*, 326.

8. On the Church's rumor and other corporate conspiracy theories, see Turner, *Grapevine*, ch. 2–6.

9. Though media interest in the sociology of black beliefs is new, Turner mentions, on a more pragmatic note, rumor clinics established during the Second World War to help quash racially inflected rumors damaging to the communal spirit of the war effort (*Grapevine*, 1).

10. For a discussion of African American conspiracy theories about the O. J. trial, see Jewelle Taylor Gibbs, *Race and Justice: Rodney King and O. J. Simpson in a House Divided* (San Francisco: Jossey-Bass, 1996), 237–38, 241.

11. Jason DeParle, "Talk of Government Being Out to Get Blacks Falls on More Attentive Ears," *New York Times*, 29 October 1990, A12. For a more detailed analysis of the poll, see Anita M. Waters, "Conspiracy Theories as Ethnosociologies: Explanation and Intention in African American Political Culture," *Journal of Black Studies* 28 (1997): 112–25. See also M. Cooper, "The Return of the Paranoid Style in American Politics," *U.S. News and World Report*, 12 March 1990, 30–31.

12. K. Bates, "AIDS: Is It Genocide?" *Essence*, September 1990, 76–117.

13. "Bill Cosby's AIDS Conspiracy," *New York Post*, 12 April 1991, 26; Spike Lee's comment appeared in a Bennetton advertising insert, *Rolling Stone*, 12 November 1992.

14. Associated Press, 29 September 1996.

15. Although this scene has been quoted many times as an example of "black paranoia," it is important to think about how it functions within the larger context of the film. Furious Style's comment about the crack epidemic is placed within the larger exchange on the street corner about who is responsible for the sufferings of the black community: the gangs or the white elite. Likewise, as much as he is concerned to blame other people ("they") for the black community's problems with guns, drink and drugs, he is equally insistent that black people must take responsibility for themselves, by ensuring that everything in the community is black owned, and by refusing to participate in the escalation of gang violence. Furthermore, the scene functions as the hinge between hope and futility: Tre and Ricky have just come from their exam when everything about their future hangs in the balance; the following scene sees the pair becoming embroiled in a gang standoff that leads to the tragic shooting

spree with which the film ends. When quoted in isolation, Furious's pro-nouncements suggest that the film is promoting a rigid conspiracy theory, a message of paranoia. But the overall structure of the film weighs up competing explanations against one another without reaching a firm conclusion.

16. Gary Webb, "Dark Alliance: The Story Behind the Crack Explosion," *San Jose Mercury News*, 18–20 August 1996. These articles formed the basis of Webb, *Dark Alliance: The CIA, the Contras, and the Crack Cocaine Explosion* (New York: Seven Stories Press, 1998). For an extended discussion of the Webb affair, see Alexander Cockburn and Jeffrey St. Clair, *Whiteout: The CIA, Drugs and the Press* (London: Verso, 1998), 1–62.

17. For an account of the black journalist's dilemma, see Jack E. White, "Caught in the Middle: The CIA–Crack Story Put Black Reporters in a Bind," *Time*, 26 May 1997; and Joel Dreyfus and Richard Prince, " 'Dark Alliance': Of Conspiracies, Theory and Silence," *NABJ Journal* 14, no. 7 (1997): 20–23.

18. Tim Golden, "Though Evidence Is Thin, Tale of CIA and Drugs Has Life of Its Own," *New York Times*, 17 October 1996, A14.

19. Eleanor Randolph and John M. Broder, "The Cocaine Trail" (Part 3), *Los Angeles Times*, 22 October 1996, A14. See also the sidebar by black journalists Sam Fulwood and John Mitchell on 24 October 1996.

20. Michael Fletcher, "History Lends Credence to Conspiracy Theories," *Washington Post*, 4 October 1996, A1.

21. "The Story of the Crack Explosion," *Washington Post*, 9 October 1996.

22. John M. Deutch, "A Time to Open Up the CIA," *New York Times*, 18 May 1997, B17.

23. Cited in Golden, "Evidence is Thin," A1.

24. Cockburn and Clair, *Whiteout*, 70.

25. For example, in 1983, 8.8 percent of the total prison population was for drug offences, while a decade later, the proportion was 25.1 percent; from 1986 to 1991, incarceration rates for drug crimes increased 106 percent for whites, but 429 percent for blacks. Figures from Cockburn and Clair, *Whiteout*, 76.

26. John Fiske, "Blackstream Knowledge: Genocide," in *Media Matters: Everyday Culture and Political Change* (Minneapolis: University of Minnesota Press, 1994), 216.

27. In *Conspiracy Theories: Secrecy and Power in American Culture* (Minneapolis: University of Minnesota Press, 1999), Mark Fenster argues that Fiske is wrong to claim that black conspiracy theories are a necessarily resistant form of counterknowledge, because popular practices only take on a political meaning when they are articulated to larger political projects in specific historical contexts. But, as we saw in the Introduction, Fenster goes on to offer the broad damning conclusion that "conspiracy theory ultimately fails as a political and cultural practice" (225–26).

28. Robert S. Robins and Jerrold M. Post, *Political Paranoia: The Psychopolitics of Hatred* (New Haven: Yale University Press, 1997), 62.

29. David Gilbert, "Tracking the Real Genocide: AIDS: Conspiracy or Unnatural Disaster?" *Covert Action Quarterly* 58 (1996), available at <http://caq.com/CAQ/CAQ58TrackGenocide.2.html>.

30. Leonard J. Horowitz, *Emerging Viruses: AIDS and Ebola—Nature, Accident or Intentional?* (1996; Rockport, MA: Tetrahedron, Inc., rev. and expanded ed., 1998), 517–30.

31. Theodore Sassoon, "African American Conspiracy Theories and Social Construction of Crime," *Sociological Inquiry* 65 (1995): 265–85. In a related fashion, the most successful anti-tobacco adverts in recent years are not those that use scare tactics, nor those that give the straight facts of risk and disease, nor even those that tried to make not smoking as cool as its counterpart; instead the most effective ads, particularly in black communities, have been those that play on people's fears that they have been the dupes of unscrupulous tobacco firms.
32. Kunfuju, *Countering*, 15.
33. Dinesh D'Souza, *The End of Racism: Principles for a Multiracial Society* (New York: The Free Press, 1995), 487.
34. Hugh Price, keynote address at National Urban League Convention, Indianapolis, 24 July 1995; cited in D'Souza, *The End of Racism*, 522.
35. Quoted in Dreyfus and Prince, "Dark Alliance."
36. Quoted in DeParle, "Talk of Government."
37. Earl Ofari Hutchinson, "Blacks Should Avoid the Conspiracy Trap," *Jinn Magazine*, <http://www.pacificnews.org/jinn>, 30 October 1996.
38. D'Souza, *The End of Racism*, 487.
39. Kunfuju, *Countering the Conspiracy*, 1–2.
40. Jesse Katz, "Tracking the Genesis of the Cocaine Trade" (Part 1 of "The Cocaine Trail), *Los Angeles Times*, 20 October 1996, A1.
41. Webb, *Dark Alliance*, 438.
42. Turner, *I Heard*, 189–90.
43. Henry Louis Gates, Jr, *Thirteen Ways of Looking at a Black Man* (New York: Random House, 1997), xxi.
44. John O'Brien, "Ishmael Reed," (interview), in *The New Fiction: Interviews with Innovative American Writers*, ed. Joe David Bellamy (Urbana: University of Illinois Press, 1974), 134.
45. Ishmael Reed, *Mumbo Jumbo* (1972; New York: Scribner, 1996), 18, 25. In *Constructing Postmodernism* (London: Routledge, 1993), Brian McHale suggests helpfully that the truly suspicious reader will invert Reed's dictum along the lines of Fredric Jameson's aphorism that conspiracy is the poor person's cognitive mapping. "Beneath or behind all representations, at the content level, of struggles between secret societies," McHale suggests, "lies the reality of political and cultural warfare" (180–81).
46. O'Brien, "Ishmael Reed," 132.
47. Reed, *Mumbo Jumbo*, 25.
48. John Brown, *Interviews with Black Writers* (New York: Liveright, 1973), 179.
49. Brown, *Interviews*, 179.
50. For an account of Sun Ra's complex ironies, see Graham Lock, *Blutopia: Visions of the Future and Revisions of the Past in the Work of Sun Ra, Duke Ellington and Anthony Braxton* (Durham, NC: Duke University Press, 2000).
51. O'Brien, "Ishmael Reed," 134. What makes the story more bizarre is that Reed apparently claims to have lost the original photo, and so in subsequent editions of the novel it is omitted.
52. Barbara Browning, *Infectious Rhythm: Metaphors of Contagion and the Spread of African Culture* (New York: Routledge, 1998), 137.
53. For critiques of Afrocentrism (the second more astutely argued than the first), see Mary Lefkowitz, *Not Out of Africa: How Afrocentrism Became an Excuse to Teach Myth as History* (New York: Basic Books, 1996), and

Stephen Howe, *Afrocentrism: Mythical Pasts and Imagined Homes* (London: Verso, 1998).

54. For a summary of these views, see Robert Singh, *The Farrakhan Phenomenon: Race, Reaction, and the Paranoid Style in American Politics* (Washington: Georgetown University Press, 1997).

55. For a detailed account of the speech, see Mattias Gardell, *Countdown to Armageddon: Louis Farrakhan and the Nation of Islam* (London: Hurst, 1996), 263–66.

56. While NoI anti-Semitism has been widely discussed, less commonly reported, for example, is a "Death to Farrakhan" march organized by the Jewish Defense League (Gardell, *Countdown*, 269).

57. For an overview of alliances between far-right and black nationalist groups see Gardell, *Countdown*, 273–84.

58. Michael Lind, *The Next American Nation: The New Nationalism and the Fourth American Revolution* (New York: Free Press, 1996), 139–80.

59. For details of Farrakhan's speech, see <http://www.nizkor.org/ftp.cgi/orgs/american/adl/uncommon-ground/who-rules-america>.

60. For a sympathetic synthesis of NoI creed, see Gardell, *Countdown*, ch. 7.

61. Gardell, *Countdown*, 165–74.

62. In her perceptive article on Tupac Shakur, Eithne Quinn develops an account of an "aesthetic of conspiracy." Quinn, " 'All Eyez on Me': The Paranoid Style of Tupac Shakur," in *Conspiracy Nation*, ed. Peter Knight (New York: New York University Press, forthcoming).

63. For an example of a "literalist" reading of gangsta, see D'Souza, *The End of Racism*, 511–14. Tricia Rose's *Black Noise: Rap Music and Black Culture in Contemporary America* (Hanover: Wesleyan University Press, 1994) provides an astute account of the performativity of rap. For a case study of the most prominent moral panic surrounding a gangsta record, see Barry Shank, "Fears of the White Unconscious: Music, Race, and Identification in the Censorship of 'Cop Killer,' " *Radical History Review* 66 (1996): 124–45. For an overview of moral panics in general, see John Springhall, *Youth, Popular Culture and Moral Panics: Penny Gaffs to Gangsta-Rap, 1830–1996* (New York: St. Martin's, 1999).

64. For an example of the tendency to take all gangsta pronouncements at face value, see D'Souza, *The End of Racism*, 511–14.

65. Public Enemy, "Welcome to the Terrordome," on *Fear of a Black Planet* (Def Jam Recordings/CBS, 1990).

66. Andrew Ross develops an analysis of the P.E. logo in "Ballots, Bullets, or Batmen: Can Cultural Studies Do the Right Thing?" *Screen* 31 (1990): 26–44.

67. Tupac Shakur, "Words of Wisdom," cited in Quinn, "All Eyez on Me."

68. Andrew Harrison, "Re-Enter the Dragons," *The Face*, May 1997, 93–98. Like Mary Daly's feminist reworkings of the dictionary, it is hard to know how literally to take black nationalist etymological decodings.

69. Wu-Tang Clan, "A Better Tomorrow," on *Wu-Tang Forever* (Loud Records, 1997), and "America," on *A.I.D.S. (America Is Dying Slowly)* (WEA/Elektra Entertainment, 1996).

CHAPTER 5 (pp. 168–203)

1. For an overview of these anxieties, see Eric Mottram, "Fear of Invasion in American Culture," in *Blood on the Nash Ambassador: Investigations in American Culture* (London: Hutchinson Radius, 1989), 138–80.

2. Carpenter's and Cronenberg's films are remakes of, respectively, *The Thing from Another World*, dir. Christian Nyby (1951), and *The Fly*, dir. Kurt Neumann (1958).

3. Buckley proposed that "everyone detected with AIDS should be tattooed in the upper forearm, to protect common needle users, and on the buttocks to protect victimization of other homosexuals," while Senator Jesse Helms insisted that "the logical outcome of testing is a quarantine of those infected." William F. Buckley, Jr, "Crucial Steps in Combating the AIDS Epidemic: Identify All the Carriers," *New York Times*, 18 March 1986, A27; the Jesse Helms comment is cited in Douglas Crimp, ed., *AIDS: Cultural Analysis, Cultural Activism* (Cambridge, MA: MIT Press, 1988), 8.

4. George Kennan, "The Sources of Soviet Conduct" (1947) in *The Cold War: A Study in U.S. Foreign Policy*, ed. Walter Lippmann (New York: Harper & Row, 1972), 73; William Tanner and Robert Griffith, "Legislative Politics and McCarthyism: The Internal Security Act of 1950," in *The Specter: Original Essays on the Cold War and the Origins of McCarthyism*, ed. Robert Griffin and Athan Theoharis (New York: New Viewpoints/Franklin Watts, 1974), 179. Both are cited in Andrew Ross's excellent discussion of the germophobic Cold War logic of containment in *No Respect: Intellectuals and Popular Culture* (New York: Routledge, 1989), 47. In *The End of Victory Culture: Cold War America and the Disillusioning of a Generation* (New York: Basic Books, 1995), Tom Engelhardt provides a similar analysis of the dynamic of inclusion and exclusion which produced an uneasy dialectic of tolerance and purging in both foreign and domestic policy in the postwar years.

5. It might also be noted that suspicions about fluoridation are no longer necessarily a product of right-wing conspiracy scenarios but are part of widespread and quite literal distrust about the unknown long-term effects of hazardous chemicals. For a presentation of this case, see David C. Kennedy, "Fluoridation: A 50 Year Old Blunder and Cover-Up—A Referenced Review of the Fluoridation Issue," <http://emporium.turnpike.net/P/PDHA/fluoride/blunder.htm>. Indeed, it might be argued that the explanation offered for the current vogue for bottled water—it just tastes better than chlorinated tap water—is in part a displaced rationalization of an otherwise socially unacceptable protest against fluoride in the public water supply.

6. Arthur Kroker and Marilouise Kroker, "Panic Sex in America," in *Body Invaders: Panic Sex in America*, ed. Kroker and Kroker (Montreal: New World Perspectives/CultureTexts Series, 1987), 10–19.

7. "Drugs: The Enemy Within" was the title of the 15 September 1986 *Time* cover story; quoted in David Campbell, *Writing Security* (Minneapolis: University of Minnesota Press, 1992), 199.

8. Campbell, *Writing Security*, 208. Though tests may be now be more widespread, it is significant that the same minority groups have been disproportionately targeted in each case: "women, blacks, foreigners, radicals, the 'insane,' and the 'sexually deviant'" (Campbell, *Writing Security*, 205).

9. Cited in Allison Fraiberg, "Of AIDS, Cyborgs, and Other Indiscretions: Resurfacing the Body in the Postmodern," *Postmodern Culture* 1, no. 3 (1991), <http://jefferson.village.virginia.edu/pmc/text-only/issue.591/fraiberg.591>.

10. Perhaps the most influential classification of alien encounters appears in Budd Hopkins, *Intruders: The Incredible Visitations at Copley Woods* (New York: Random House, 1987; London: Sphere Books, 1988). See also Whitley Strieber, *Communion: A True Story* (New York: Beech Tree Books, 1987); John Mack, *Abduction: Human Encounters with Aliens* (New York: Simon & Schuster, 1994); and C. D. B. Bryan, *Close Encounters of the Fourth Kind: Alien Abduction, UFOs, and the Conference at MIT* (New York: Knopf, 1995).

11. Strieber, *Communion*, 30.

12. Hopkins, *Intruders*, 50 (page citations are to the paperback edition). When Budd Hopkins asks one patient who has been describing his forced examination by aliens whether they paid special attention to any particular part of his body, the patient replies that "they had more than a reasonable interest in my genitals" (171). A scene in the 1996 Halloween episode of *The Simpsons* satirizes just how routine the reporting of this "reasonable interest" has become. In the cartoon, candidates Clinton and Dole are replaced by bug-eyed monsters, who in turn abduct Homer for witnessing their electoral switch. On board the aliens' spacecraft, Homer goes to bend over and drop his pants, saying resignedly, "I suppose you want to probe me. Well, might as well get it over with." The green aliens hastily reply: "Stop! We have reached the limits of what rectal probing can teach us" ("Treehouse of Horror VII" [4F02]).

13. This is the line that Elaine Showalter, for example, takes in *Hystories: Hysterical Epidemics and Modern Culture* (New York: Columbia University Press, 1997).

14. Bridget Brown makes a compelling extended argument for this connection; see, for example, "'My Body Is Not My Own': Personalizing Disempowerment in Alien Abduction Narratives," in *Conspiracy Nation*, ed. Peter Knight (New York: New York University Press, forthcoming). It is also interesting to note that a visual connection between the alien and the fetus is increasingly being made within popular culture. *The X-Files*, for example, has repeatedly shown what are understood to be alien–human fetuses being cultured within glass jars, and which are linked to the larger story of an enforced hybrid breeding program. The first glimpse we have of an alien–human fetus, for example, is in "The Erlenmeyer Flask" (1X23), first broadcast 13 May 1993. At the beginning of the second series Agent Scully herself is abducted, and a short-circuiting connection is made between abduction, pregnancy and sinister medical testing—whether by aliens or by the government, we are not sure. The hybrid fetuses appear again in "Emily" (5X07), first broadcast 14 December 1997, and "One Son" (6X12), first broadcast 14 February 1999.

15. Hopkins, *Intruders*, 70.

16. *The X-Files'* hermeneutic slippage is discussed in more detail in Chapter 6. On mind control, see also, for example, Jim Keith, *Mind Control, World Control* (Atlanta, GA: IllumiNet Press, 1998).

17. For an account of the history of the CIA's mind control experiments, see John D. Marks, *The Search for the "Manchurian Candidate": The CIA and Mind Control* (London: Allen Lane, 1979). In addition to Keith's book cited above, for a representative selection of conspiratorial books on mind

control see also Alex Constantine, *Virtual Government: CIA Mind Control Operations in America* (Portland, OR: Feral House, 1997), and Jerry E. Smith, *HAARP: The Ultimate Weapon of Conspiracy* (Kempton, IL: Adventures Unlimited, 1998).

18. For an example of a website including the images, see ⟨http://no-more-secrets.net/firsthomepage.htm⟩. Leir has now published a complete book on alien implants: *The Aliens and the Scalpel: Scientific Proof of Extra Terrestrial Implants in Humans* (Columbus, NC: Granite Publishing, 1999).

19. If the US government supports programs to electronically tag prisoners and plant identification chips in pets, and a (British) scientist has recently been implanted with a chip that communicates with his office management computer, it would come as little surprise that the American military uses implanted chips to keep track of its covert armed forces operating behind enemy lines. McVeigh's flight of fantasy is not so much his claim that he had had a chip implanted as his assertion that he had been a member of the special forces—by all accounts it seems that he was rejected for elite service. For a less-than-skeptical discussion of the various claims, see Jim Keith, "McVeigh and the Controllers," in *OK Bomb!* (Atlanta, GA: IllumiNet Press, 1996).

20. The original alien = Communist interpretation of these films was furnished by Patrick Luciano, *Them or Us: Archetypal Interpretations of Fifties Alien Invasion Narratives* (Bloomington: Indiana University Press, 1987). In order of discussion in the text, revisions of this position have been provided by: Peter Biskind, *Seeing Is Believing: How Hollywood Taught Us to Stop Worrying and Love the Fifties* (London: Pluto, 1983); Mark Jancovich, *Rational Fears: American Horror in the 1950s* (Manchester: University of Manchester Press, 1996); Michael Rogin, *"Independence Day," or How I Learned to Stop Worrying and Love the Enola Gay* (London: BFI Publishing, 1998); Cyndy Hendershot, "The Atomic Scientist, Science Fiction Films, and Paranoia: *The Day the Earth Stood Still*, *This Island Earth*, and *Killers from Space*," *Journal of American Culture* 20 (1997): 31–41; Michael Rogin, "Kiss Me Deadly: Communism, Motherhood, and Cold War Movies," *Representations* 6 (1984): 1–36; Adam Knee, "The American Science Fiction Film and Fifties Culture," unpublished PhD diss., Cinema Studies, New York University, 1997; and Harry M. Benshoff, *Monsters in the Closet: Homosexuality and the Horror Film* (Manchester: Manchester University Press, 1997).

21. Michael J. Collins, "Version/Inversion: Paranoia in Three Cases of Bodysnatching," *Contributions to the Study of Science Fiction and Fantasy* 70 (1997): 195–202.

22. Brian Massumi, "Everywhere You Want to Be: Introduction to Fear," in *The Politics of Everyday Fear*, ed. Massumi (Minneapolis: University of Minnesota Press, 1993), 10–11.

23. In a persuasive reading, Michael Rogin finds a similar logic at work in the film *Independence Day*: "[it] gratifies the wish for apocalyptic triumph aborted when the Cold War ended not with a bang but with a whimper. But post-Cold War anxieties experienced as personal rather than political fuel the retrospective force of the victory wish; from toxic wastes and environmental cancers to epidemic diseases, no evil empire is now their source and no apocalyptic world-ending big bang their culmination. The single giant enemy of *Independence Day*, who can be met in battle and defeated—Ahab's whale—is actually an imaginary defense against the

271

proliferation of multiple, disorganizing, diffuse points of bodily vulnerability" (*Independence Day*: 64).

24. Peter Jaret, "Our Immune System: The Wars Within," *National Geographic*, June 1986, 702–35.

25. Jaret, "Our Immune System," 709.

26. Indeed, international relations readily borrows its terminology from immunological discourse, which in turn draws its militarized metaphors from the world of geopolitics. There is a circularity in their mutual definition: politicians turn to the language of the natural sciences to naturalize and justify their actions, but that scientific discourse is already heavily inflected with the terms and assumptions of military conflict. The rhetoric used to justify Reagan's *Star Wars* fantasy Strategic Defense Initiative (SDI) was full of immunological terminology. On the history of immunology and its metaphors, see Emily Martin, *Flexible Bodies: Tracking Immunology in American Culture—From the Days of Polio to the Age of AIDS* (Boston: Beacon Press, 1994); Donna Haraway, "The Biopolitics of Postmodern Bodies: Constitutions of Self in Immune Systems Discourse," in *Simians, Cyborgs, and Women: The Reinvention of Nature* (London: Free Association Books, 1991), 203–30; Cindy Patton, *Inventing AIDS* (London: Routledge, 1990); Scott L. Montgomery, "Codes and Combat in Biomedical Discourse," *Science as Culture* 12 (1991): 341–90; Catherine Waldby, "Body Wars, Body Victories: AIDS and Homosexuality in Immunological Discourse," *Science as Culture* 5 (1995): 181–98; Alfred I. Tauber, *The Immune Self: Theory or Metaphor?* (Cambridge: Cambridge University Press, 1994); and Arthur M. Silverstein, *A History of Immunology* (London: Academic Press, 1989). For an indication of the shift over the last half-century from a notion of disease as an external threat to disease as inextricably part of the immune system, see, for example, Frederick Eberson, *Microbes Militant: A Challenge to Man: The Story of Modern Preventive Medicine and Control of Infectious Diseases* (New York: The Ronald Press Company, rev. ed. 1948), and William R. Clark *At War Within: The Double-Edged Sword of Immunity* (New York: Oxford University Press, 1995). The latter features an appendix on "Diversity, Tolerance, and Memory: The Politically Correct Immune System."

27. Tim Weiner, "Finding New Reason to Dread the Unknown," *New York Times*, 26 March 1995, D1.

28. William Burroughs, *The Ticket That Exploded* (1962; London: John Calder, 1985), 57.

29. Agent Scully, *The X-Files*, "S.R. 819" (6X10), first broadcast 17 January 1999.

30. *The X-Files*, "Redux" (5X02), first broadcast 2 November 1997.

31. *The X-Files*, "The Beginning" (6X01), first broadcast 8 November 1998. Scully's DNA also features in the sequence of episodes in the fifth series dealing with the mysterious little girl, Emily, who turns out to share Scully's DNA.

32. Plot summaries from *The X-Files* official website (www.thex-files.com) reveal that in the seventh series (which, at the time of writing, has not yet reached terrestrial television in the UK) the show begins to explore the possibility that the very origin of life on Earth comes from outer space. Humans are in effect aliens.

33. Andrew Tudor, *Monsters and Mad Scientists: A Cultural History of the Horror Movie* (Oxford: Blackwell, 1987).

34. Barbara Creed, *The Monstrous–Feminine: Film, Feminism, Psychoanalysis* (London: Routledge, 1993), and "Horror and the Carnivalesque: The Body–Monstrous," in *Fields of Vision: Essays in Film Studies, Visual Anthropology, and Photography*, ed. Leslie Devereaux and Roger Hillman (Berkeley and Los Angeles: University of California Press, 1995), 127–59; Julia Kristeva, *Powers of Horror: An Essay on Abjection*, trans. Leon S. Roudiez (New York: Columbia University Press, 1982); Mary Douglas, *Purity and Danger: An Analysis of Concepts of Pollution and Taboo* (New York: Preager, 1966); Luce Irigaray, "The 'Mechanics' of Fluids," in *This Sex Which Is Not One*, trans. Catherine Porter with Catherine Burke (Ithaca: Cornell University Press, 1985). Elizabeth Grosz provides a stimulating survey of these texts in *Volatile Bodies: Toward a Corporeal Feminism* (Bloomington and Indianapolis: Indiana University Press, 1994).

35. The phrase is from Grosz, *Volatile Bodies*, 195. It is used in connection with her reading of Irigaray's observation that "Fluid—like that other, inside/outside of philosophical discourse—is, by nature, unstable" ("The 'Mechanics' of Fluids," 112).

36. Chris Rodley, ed., *Cronenberg on Cronenberg* (London: Faber and Faber, 1992; rev. ed. 1993), 45, 43.

37. Linda Williams, *Hard Core: Power, Pleasure, and the "Frenzy of the Visible"* (Berkeley and Los Angeles: University of California Press, 1989). Williams, drawing on Foucault's critique of the "repressive hypothesis" about seeming Victorian prudery, argues that the move towards more hard-core pornography since the 1960s is not so much an effect of increasingly liberal sexual attitudes, as a recognition that sexuality is itself extremely political.

38. There is an obvious connection between the increasingly graphic revelation of the body's secrets and the increasingly graphic uncovering of conspiratorial secrets. The Web exploits the spectacle of revelation to the full; for example, the www.theeunderground.com website offers—for a price—access to "forbidden" images ranging from nude pictures of Pamela Anderson to Kennedy assassination autopsy photos.

39. In *Bodies that Matter: On the Discursive Limits of "Sex"* (London: Routledge, 1993), Judith Butler presents a provocative case that the very category of the "material" is itself socially constructed through discourse. A rhetorical insistence on the literal comes to structure not just body-horror films and feminist analysis, but the national political scene. As I write this chapter, the US is awash with the lurid details of the Monica Lewinsky case. Unlike the impeachment proceedings for Nixon which turned on the conspiratorial activities surrounding the Watergate break-in and the extent to which the actions of deputies were an expression of the head of state's will, in Clinton's case the issue revolves around the intimate body politics of the President himself. Clinton has been betrayed not by a leak from Deep Throat, but by his own rebellious, precious bodily fluids—and his DNA in particular—which leaked incriminatingly onto the infamous blue dress. The Starr Report has become the Warren Commission Report for the 1990s. Several recent studies have noted how the President's body has become crucial to the body politic; see, for example, Brian Massumi and Kenneth Dean, "Postmortem on the Presidential Body, or Where the Rest of Him Went," in *Body Politics: Disease, Desire and the Family*, ed. Michael Ryan and Avery Gordon (Boulder, CO: Westview, 1994), 155–71; Michael Rogin, *"Ronald Reagan, The Movie"; and Other Episodes in Political Demonology*

(Berkeley and Los Angeles: University of California Press, 1987); and Maria Demon, "In the Belly of the Beast: Reagan's Body, MIAs, and the Body Politic," in *Mass Culture and Everyday Life*, ed. Peter Gibian (New York: Routledge, 1997), 181–91. Demon offers the following intriguing historical hypothesis: "When an imperial power is embattled, when an economy threatens to collapse, a wild scramble to salvage some kind of certainty ensues, and the physical body emerges as an icon to which ideological significance can be attached. National paranoia and a corollary self-aggrandizement both increase, and questions of boundary play themselves on the fetishized body" (181).

40. Simon Watney makes a powerful case for this view in *Policing Desire: Pornography, Aids and The Media* (London: Methuen/Comedia, 1987).

41. In "The Killers All Around," *Time*, 12 September 1994, 50–57, Michael D. Lemonick reports on how "new viruses and drug resistant bacteria are reversing human victories over infectious disease," with the result that "the age of antibiotics is giving way to an age of anxiety about disease."

42. In *The Gospel of Germs: Men, Women, and the Microbe in American Life* (Cambridge: Harvard University Press, 1998), Nancy Tomes argues that, with the turn to New Age ideas and products such as "air filters, dehumidifiers, vaporizers" and so on, America has returned to the quackery of the nineteenth century (263). This time around, however, it seems far from clear cut whether fears about, say, BSE (so-called mad cow disease) or GMOs (genetically modified organisms) are unnecessarily paranoid or are in fact wisely justified. Without the benefit of historical hindsight, in some cases it is hard to work out which side rationality is on. Indeed, the point about the infinitely complex interactions of risk over indefinitely long time periods is precisely that we don't know how far down the line the surety of hindsight will be granted. This is not to say, however, that "alternative" New Age beliefs are any more reliable. As Andrew Ross points out, the alternative beliefs of what has been called the Age of Aquarius are not necessarily radical or resistant in themselves, not least because their methods, assumptions and protocols are deeply intertwined with the mainstream science they seek to reject. Ross, "New Age—A Kinder, Gentler Science?" in *Strange Weather: Culture, Science, and Technology in the Age of Limits* (London: Verso, 1991), 15–74.

43. See Michelle Stacey, *Consumed: Why Americans Love, Hate, and Fear Food* (New York: Simon & Schuster, 1994).

44. Corby Kummer, "Carried Away," *New York Times Magazine*, 30 August 1998, 38+; Nicols Fox, *Spoiled: Why Our Food Is Making Us Sick and What We Can Do About It* (New York: Basic Books, 1997).

45. Barbara Ehrenreich, "The Morality of Muscle Tone: Are We Confusing Health with Goodness?" *Utne Reader*, May/June 1992, 65–68.

46. Andrew Kimbrell, *The Human Body Shop: The Engineering and Marketing of Life* (San Francisco: Harper, 1993).

47. On the performativity of the male body, see, for example, Mark Simpson, *Male Impersonators: Men Performing Masculinity* (New York: Routledge, 1994). In "Panic Sex," Kroker and Kroker present an interesting Baudrillardian argument about the hypervisibility of the male body in late capitalism.

48. Kimbrell, *The Human Body Shop*, 1.

49. Susan Bordo, "Reading the Slender Body," in *Body/Politics: Women and the Discourses of Science*, ed. Mary Jacobus, Evelyn Fox Keller, and Sally Shuttleworth (New York: Routledge, 1990), 89.

50. Eve Kosofsky Sedgwick, "Epidemics of the Will," in *Incorporations*, ed. Jonathan Crary and Sanford Kwinter (New York: Zone, 1992), 582–95.

51. Terry Eagleton, *The Illusions of Postmodernism* (Oxford, Blackwell, 1996), 69. Eagleton attacks postmodern thought for mistaking the false materiality of the body for the true (dialectical) materialism of Marxist analysis; likewise in "Birth of the Cyber Queer," *PMLA* 110 (1995): 369–81, Donald Morton takes queer theory to task for failing to locate the notion of bodily desire in a fully historicized and materialist account of society.

52. Jacques Derrida, *Dissemination*, trans. Barbara Johnson (Chicago: University of Chicago Press, 1981), 149.

53. For an intelligent summary of recent developments in immunology and their relation to other contemporary discourses, see Martin, *Flexible Bodies*.

54. The film is in part a critique of the vogue for New Age "cures" for AIDS, which involve taking responsibility for one's illness, epitomized by the number of new cookbooks offering recipes for boosting flagging immune systems.

55. Gaye Naismith, "Tales from the Crypt: Contamination and Quarantine in Todd Haynes's *[Safe]*," in *The Visible Woman: Imaging Technologies, Gender, and Science*, ed. Paula A. Treichler, Lisa Cartwright and Constance Penley (New York: New York University Press, 1998), 369.

56. Ulrich Beck, *Risk Society: Towards a New Modernity*, trans. Mark Ritter (London: Sage, 1992).

57. See, for example, the following description: "The weakening of the sphincter through repeated sodomy results in fecal incontinence and the dribbling of blood-stained contaminated stool. The involuntary depositing of the AIDS-virus-infected fecal secretions on the benches in locker rooms, toilet seats and elsewhere also creates a potential for spread by this route." Gene Antonio, *The AIDS Cover-Up? The Real and Alarming Facts About AIDS* (San Francisco: Ignatius Press, 1988), 36.

58. Patricia A. Turner, *I Heard It Through the Grapevine: Rumor in African-American Culture* (Berkeley and Los Angeles: University of California Press, 1993).

59. On aspartame and GM food, see, for example, Alex Constantine, "NutraSweet™, the NutraPoison™," *Prevailing Winds*, 1 (1994), ⟨http://www.prevailingwinds.org/mags/nutras.htm⟩. On anxieties about food safety, see Stacey, *Consumed*; Fox, *Spoiled*; and Sian Griffiths and Jennifer Wallace, eds, *Consuming Passions: Food in the Age of Anxiety* (London: Mandolin, 1998). Sheldon Rampton and John Stauber offer an account of BSE in *Mad Cow USA: Could the Nightmare Happen Here?* (Monroe, MN: Common Courage Press, 1997).

60. Fox, *Spoiled*, 6.

61. *The X-Files*, "Our Town" (2X24), first broadcast 12 May 1995.

62. *The X-Files* has returned repeatedly to gruesome diseases which often turn out to have a conspiratorial dimension. "F. Emasculata" ([2X22], first broadcast 28 April 1995), for example, involves the accidental (or possibly the intentional) release into an American prison population of a rainforest parasitic bug that carries a virus which attacks the immune system. The suspicion by the end of the episode is that the government is secretly testing out possible new biowarfare weapons. The show has drawn

frequently on both the specific details and general iconography of newly emerging diseases, inserting them into a larger story of government conspiracy and public anxiety.

63. Richard Preston, *The Hot Zone* (1994; New York: Anchor–Doubleday, 1995), 16.

64. See, for example, C. J. Peters and Mark Olshaker, *Virus Hunter: Thirty Years of Battling Hot Viruses Around the World* (New York: Anchor, 1997); Peter Radetsky, *The Invisible Invaders: Viruses and the Scientists Who Pursue Them* (New York: Little, Brown & Co., 1991; rev. ed. 1994); Laurie Garrett, *The Coming Plague: Newly Emerging Diseases in a World Out of Balance* (New York: Farrar, Straus & Giroux, 1994); and Ed Regis, *Virus Ground Zero: Stalking the Killer Viruses with the Center for Disease Control* (New York: Pocket Books, 1996).

65. Judith Miller and William J. Broad, "Exercise Finds US Unable to Handle Germ War Threat," *The New York Times*, 26 April 1998, 1. In 1998 there was also a spate of false alarms about germ terrorism, particularly following the FBI's wrongful arrest of two crackpot scientists in Las Vegas for carrying "weapon-grade" anthrax; see Christopher Reed, "Hoax Callers Spread Anthrax Scare," *The Guardian* (London), 29 December 1998, 13. These fears were not calmed by the sight of helicopters spraying the city with the insecticide malathion to combat an infestation of mosquitoes in the summer of 1999. "Blood," an *X-Files* episode from Season Two, featured inhabitants of a small town giving in to violent hallucinations prompted by digital readouts on everyday devices. Further investigation reveals that the town has been the location for the testing of an insecticide sprayed from helicopters, a detail which the episode's writers extrapolated from the real-life use of malathion in Southern California. "Blood" (2X03), first broadcast 30 September 1994.

66. Katie Roiphe, *Last Night in Paradise: Sex and Morals at Century's End* (New York: Little, Brown & Co., 1997).

67. On the moralizing of disease in the context of AIDS, see Sander Gilman, "AIDS and Syphilis: The Iconography of Disease," in Crimp, ed., AIDS, 87–107; and Katharine Park, "Kimberly Bergalis, AIDS, and the Plague Metaphor," in *Media Spectacles*, Marjorie Garber, Jann Matlock and Rebecca L. Walkowitz (London: Routledge, 1993), 232–47.

68. Quoted in Crimp, ed., *AIDS*, 8.

69. For a summary of these allegations see G. L. Krupey, "AIDS: Act of God or the Pentagon?," in *Secret and Suppressed: Banned Ideas and Hidden History*, ed. Jim Keith (Portland, OR: Feral House, 1993), 240–55. Supposedly in the spirit of glasnost, Gorbachev apologized for these reports in 1987.

70. Douglass, quoted in David Gilbert, "Tracking the Real Genocide: AIDS: Conspiracy or Unnatural Disaster?" *Covert Action Quarterly* 58 (Fall 1996), available at ⟨http://caq.com/CAQ/CAQ58TrackGenocide.2.html⟩.

71. For an analysis of the media accounts of Rock Hudson's death, see Richard Meyer, "Rock Hudson's Body," in *Inside/Out: Lesbian Theories, Gay Theories*, ed. Diana Fuss (London: Routledge, 1992), 259–88.

72. The most wide-ranging analysis of AIDS in the media is Watney, *Policing Desire*; on Magic Johnson, see Douglas Crimp, "Accommodating Magic," in Garber et al., eds, *Media Spectacles*, 255–66.

73. It is significant, therefore, that even though Clinton's "relationship" with Monica Lewinsky was in many ways reckless, it took the hygienically "safe" form of phone sex and the exchange of gifts, and, as the visible

proof of the famous stained dress seemed to demonstrate, when it included sexual contact it did not appear to involve the commingling of bodily fluids.

74. Larry Kramer, "1,112 and Counting," *New York Native*, no. 59 (14–27 March 1983), quoted in Watney, *Policing Desire*, 11.

75. For a summary of these arguments, see Patton's section on "Degaying AIDS: The Queer Paradigm" in *Inventing AIDS*, 116–20; see also Watney's rethinking of this position, "Re-gaying AIDS," in *Practices of Freedom: Selected Writings on HIV/AIDS* (London: Rivers Oram, 1994), 153–55.

76. Quoted in Crimp, "AIDS: Cultural Analysis/Cultural Activism," in Crimp, ed., *AIDS*, 11.

77. For a discussion of the gendering of AIDS in the early 1980s see Paula Treichler, "AIDS, Gender, and Biomedical Discourse," in *AIDS: The Burdens of History*, ed. Elizabeth Fee and Daniel M. Fox (Berkeley and Los Angeles: University of California Press, 1988), 200–42, and Cindy Patton, *Sex and Germs: The Politics of AIDS* (Boston: South End Press, 1985). Richard Meyer discusses the reconstruction of Rock Hudson's life and death in "Rock Hudson's Body," in *Inside/Out*, 259–88.

78. Cited in Treichler, "AIDS, Gender and Biomedical Discourse," 193.

79. Both comments are quoted in Crimp, "AIDS," 8.

80. See, for example, Michael Fumento, *Myth of Heterosexual AIDS* (New York: Basic Books, 1990).

81. Charles Geshekter, "Outbreak?: AIDS, Africa, and the Medicalization of Poverty," *Transition* 57 (1995): 4–14.

82. Christine Maggiore, *What If Everything You Thought You Knew About AIDS Was Wrong?* (Studio City, CA: HEAL, 1997).

83. In contrast to most cultural theory work on AIDS, in *The Gospel of Germs: Men, Women, and the Microbe in American Life* (Cambridge: Harvard University Press, 1998), Nancy Tomes argues that the panics about AIDS have less to do with "gestures of separation and classification" than with genuine fear at a truly scary disease that recalls earlier fears of germs.

84. Susan Sontag, *Illness as Metaphor* (Harmondsworth, UK: Penguin, 1989).

85. Watney, *Policing Desire*, 2nd ed., ix.

86. Sedgwick, "Introduction: Queerer than Fiction." *Studies in the Novel* 28 (1996): 277.

87. Patton, "Tremble, Hetero Swine!" in *Fear of a Queer Planet: Queer Politics and Social Theory*, ed. Michael Warner (Minneapolis: University of Minnesota Press, 1993), 143–77.

88. Peter Duesberg, *Inventing the AIDS Virus* (Washington, DC: Regnery Publishing, 1996).

89. Jad Adams, *AIDS: The HIV Myth* (London: Macmillan, 1989); John Lauritsen, *The AIDS War: Propaganda, Profiteering and Genocide from the Medical Industrial Complex* (New York: Asklepios, 1993); Jon Rappoport, *AIDS Inc.: Scandal of the Century* (San Bruno, CA: Human Energy Press, 1988).

90. Quoted for example in G. L. Krupey, "AIDS," 240–55.

91. Dennis Altman, *AIDS in the Mind of America* (Garden City, NY: Anchor Press/Doubleday, 1986), 43–53.

92. Alan Cantwell, Jr, *Queer Blood: The Secret AIDS Genocide Plot* (Los Angeles: Aries Rising Press, 1993), 130.

93. Leonard J. Horowitz, *Emerging Viruses: AIDS and Ebola—Nature, Accident or Intentional?* (1996; Rockport, MA: Tetrahedron, Inc., rev. and expanded ed., 1998). Intriguingly, Horowitz is convinced that Peter Duesberg, source of many conspiracy theories about AIDS, is himself part of the cabal.

CHAPTER 6 (pp. 204–241)

1. A. Ralph Epperson, *The Unseen Hand: An Introduction to the Conspiratorial View of History* (Tuscon, AZ: Publius Press, 1985), 8.
2. Richard Hofstadter, *The Paranoid Style and Other Essays* (London: Jonathan Cape, 1966), 29.
3. In *Paranoia: A Study in Diagnosis* (Dordrecht, Holland: Reidel, 1976), Yehuda Fried and Joseph Agassi argue that in many ways the operation of paranoia is indistiguishable from the operating procedures of scientific thought. They conclude that the two differ not in kind, but in degree and in context.
4. Dan Gearino, sidebar, *News & Observer* (Raleigh, NC), 17 August 1997, available at <http://www.news-observer.com/daily/1997/08/17/qq00_side2.html>.
5. The original results are written up in Stanley Milgram, "The Small World Problem," *Psychology Today*, May 1967, 60–67.
6. *Six Degrees of Separation*, dir. Fred Shepisi (1993).
7. The introductory statement for www.sixdegrees.com reads as follows: "Inspired by the theory of six degrees of separation, sixdegrees is your personal on-line community where you have the ability to interact, communicate and share information and experiences with millions of other members from around the world, all of whom are connected to you."
8. Barry Commoner, *The Closing Circle: Nature, Man, and Technology* (New York: Knopf, 1971), 13.
9. Ulrich Beck, "World Risk Society as Cosmopolitan Society? Ecological Questions in a Framework of Manufactured Uncertainties," *Theory, Culture & Society* 13 (1996): 31.
10. It must be remembered, however, that despite what other people call him, Chomsky insists that he is definitely not a conspiracy theorist, and that real conspiracies are far less significant than the ongoing story of institutional collusion and implicit collaboration for reactionary ends.
11. In her analysis of the discourse of AIDS, Paula Treichler provides an extended list of the many categories whose previously clear boundaries have been eroded in discussions about the epidemic. She argues that the discourse of AIDS plays itself out on the arena of these already entrenched "discursive dichotomies," such as contagion and containment, life and death, knowledge and ignorance, and so on. Treichler, "AIDS, Homophobia, and Biomedical Discourse: An Epidemic of Signification," in *AIDS: Cultural Analysis, Cultural Activism*, ed. Douglas Crimp (Cambridge: MIT Press, 1988), 32–70.
12. The phrase is taken from Paul Farmer, *AIDS and Accusation: Haiti and the Geography of Blame* (Berkeley and Los Angeles: University of California Press, 1992).
13. Jean Baudrillard, "The Ecstasy of Communication," in *Postmodern Culture*, ed. Hal Foster (London: Pluto Press, 1985), 127, 132.
14. *The X-Files*, "Kill Switch" (5X11), first broadcast 15 February 1998.
15. It is worth remembering here that Tony Tanner identified the fear of invasion of the self by external forces as the principal concern of postwar American literature and culture as long ago as 1971 (Tanner, *City of Words: American Fiction 1950–1970* [London: Jonathan Cape, 1971]). However, an important shift has begun to emerge since Tanner's prescient survey. While many literary and popular texts are still concerned with the threat to a humanist sense of autonomy and agency, others have begun to explore

the possibility that the strict logical separation between self and nonself which grounds a humanist ideology is no longer tenable. The conspiracy-minded fear of being taken over by the enemy thus mutates into the viral fear that you have become the enemy of your own self. Drawing on Donna Haraway's work, Allison Fraiberg, for example, argues the need to keep bodily fluids apart in the age of safe sex should not mean giving up on the project of celebrating a posthuman, cyborg networking of bodies and desires. Fraiberg, "Of AIDS, Cyborgs, and Other Discretions: Resurfacing the Body in the Postmodern," *Postmodern Culture* 1 (1991), ⟨http://jefferson.village.virginia.edu/pmc/text-only/issue.591/fraiberg.591⟩.

16. In his essay on the panic surrounding computer viruses and hackers, Andrew Ross argues that it produces two effects. The first is a boost in business for purveyors of security software and systems. The second is a more general ideological contribution to the "paranoid climate of privatiza-tion that increasingly defines social identities in the new post-Fordist order," and which runs counter to both the architecture of the information network, and the communitarian spirit of the hackers. Ross, "Hacking Away at the Counterculture," *Strange Weather: Culture, Science, and Technology in the Age of Limits* (London: Verso, 1991), 80.

17. Nicholas Negroponte, *Being Digital* (New York: Knopf, 1995), 5–6.

18. For a more detailed discussion of the yoking of fears about conspiracy to fears about the Internet, see Jodi Dean, "Webs of Conspiracy," in *The World Wide Web: Magic, Metaphor, and Power* (New York: Routledge, forthcoming).

19. Kevin Kelly, *Out of Control: The New Biology of Machines* (London: Fourth Estate, 1994), 27.

20. Kelly, *Out of Control*, 28.

21. Douglas Rushkoff, *Media Virus!: Hidden Agendas in Popular Culture* (New York: Ballantine, 1994; rev. ed. 1996), ix.

22. In many ways, the idea of memes functions as a form of upmarket mind-control theory. Making up your mind is not a question of autonomous will, in effect, because your mind is merely a node through which the self-organizing memes pass.

23. Kelly, *Out of Control*, 424.

24. Kelly, *Out of Control*, 33.

25. The monsters are shown in, respectively, *The X-Files*, "The Host" (2X02), first broadcast 23 September 1994; "Quagmire" (3X22), first broadcast 3 May 1996; and "Detour" (5X04), first broadcast 23 November 1997.

26. *The X-Files*, "Ghost in the Machine" (1X06), first broadcast 29 October 1993.

27. *The X-Files*, "Dreamland II" (6X05), first broadcast 6 December 1998.

28. *The X-Files*, "Quagmire."

29. The Cigarette Smoking Man is shown entering the Pentagon storage vaults in *The X-Files*, "Pilot" and the first series cliff-hanger, "The Erlenmeyer Flask" (1X23), first broadcast 13 May 1994. Mulder accesses the archives in "Redux II" (5X03), first broadcast 9 November 1997. The underground medical archives are seen in "Paper Clip" (3X02), first broadcast 29 September 1995.

30. *The X-Files*, "Gethsemane" (4X24), first broadcast 18 May 1997; "Redux" (5X02), first broadcast 2 November 1997.

31. *The X-Files*, "Demons" (4X23), first broadcast 11 May 1997.

32. *The X-Files*, "The Red and the Black" (5X14), first broadcast 8 March 1998.

33. *The X-Files*, "Pilot" (1X79), first broadcast 10 September 1993, and "E.B.E" (1X16), first broadcast February 18 1994.
34. *The X-Files*, "Zero Sum" (4X21), first broadcast 27 April 1997.
35. *The X-Files*, "731" (3X10), first broadcast 1 December 1995.
36. *The X-Files*, "Dreamland II."
37. *The X-Files*, "Musings of a Cigarette Smoking Man" (4X07), first broadcast 17 November 1996.
38. *The X-Files*, "The Blessing Way" (3X01), first broadcast 22 September 1995.
39. *The X-Files*, "Redux II."
40. *The X-Files*, "The Host" (2X02), first broadcast 23 September 1994.
41. *The X-Files*, "The Blessing Way."
42. *The X-Files*, "Redux" (5X02), first broadcast 2 November 1997.
43. *The X-Files*, "Patient X" (5X13), first broadcast 1 March 1998.
44. *The X-Files*, "The Beginning" (6X01), first broadcast 8 November 1998.
45. *The X-Files*, "*F. Emasculata*" (2X22), first broadcast 28 April 1995.
46. *The X-Files*, "Patient X."
47. *The X-Files*, "End Game" (2X17), first broadcast 17 February 1995.
48. Since I first wrote this chapter, the sixth series has aired in the UK, including the seemingly all-revealing episodes "Two Fathers" and "One Son," which in part tie together many of the loose strands that the feature film promised to but never quite succeeded in doing. The two-parter reveals that the Syndicate has been working since Roswell in 1947 to strike a deal with the grey aliens to produce a hybrid alien–human race that will make the colonization on Earth possible—and which will save their own selves, of a fashion. They have also been secretly trying to create a vaccination against the alien virus. Their plans have been thwarted, however, by the activities of a group of rebels, the featureless, shape-shifting aliens who succeed in wiping out virtually all the Syndicate and their families as the latter wait for the colonization to begin. Although these episodes seem to provide answers to many of the open-ended puzzles the show has created, they also create their own new mysteries. Although some of the mysteries have been explained, the point about the show's cultivation of boundless suspicion is that nothing is immune from reevaluation and reinterpretation. Trust no one, and trust nothing, six years of viewing have taught us.
49. Andy Meisler, *I Want to Believe: The Official Guide to "The X-Files"*, vol. 3 (New York: Harper, 1998), 16. Here we might contrast the ill-fated rival series, *Dark Skies*, which supposedly had its entire conspiracy arc, from Roswell through to the Kennedy assassination and right up to the present, plotted in detail in advance. Although its lack of subtlety in comparison with *The X-Files* might well have been the main reason for the show's lack of popularity (it was axed after the first series), it is also in part due to its rigid and programmatic unfolding of the plot. It is also without doubt a result of the show's insistence on revealing to the audience more or less its whole box of surprises early on in the series, in contrast to *The X-Files*' tantalizing glimpses of an alien conspiracy, the evidence of which disappears, and the story arc of which is interspersed amid numerous standalone paranormal episodes.
50. By all accounts, Mae Brussell's own library of files, notes, and clippings amounted to a veritable hypertext—in analogue form—of infinite cross-references and associations. The legacy and location of Brussell's library after her death has itself become the subject of much dispute in conspiracy

theory circles. Brussell's dense and meandering essays put forward the theory that the US has been clandestinely taken over by a powerful group of vested interests which bring together Fascist and Mafia forces.

51. Jim Keith, ed., *The Gemstone File* (Atlanta, GA: IllumiNet Press, 1992), 30–31.

52. Casolaro's proposal is reprinted in Kenn Thomas, "Behold, A Pale Horse: A Draft of Danny Casolaro's Octopus Manuscript Proposal," in *Secret and Suppressed: Banned Ideas and Hidden History*, ed. Jim Keith (Portland, OR: Feral House, 1993), 166–73. For a more extended discussion of the case, see Mark Fenster, *Conspiracy Theories: Secrecy and Power in American Culture* (Minneapolis: University of Minnesota Press, 1999), 188–98.

53. Jameson, "Cognitive Mapping," in *Marxism and the Interpretation of Culture*, ed. Cary Nelson and Lawrence Grossberg (Basingstoke, UK: Macmillan, 1988), 356.

54. Robert Towers, "From the Grassy Knoll," review of *Libra*, by Don DeLillo, *New York Review of Books*, 18 August 1988, 6.

55. Fintan O'Toole, "And Quiet Writes the Don," *Irish Times*, 10 January 1998, available at <http://www.irish-times.com/irish-times/papr/1998/0110/fea3.html>.

56. Michael Wood, "Post-Paranoid," *London Review of Books*, 5 February 1998, 3.

57. James Wood, "Black Noise," *New Republic*, 10 November 1997, available at <http://magazines.enews.com/magazines/tnr/archive/11/111097/wood111097.html>.

58. DeCurtis, "An Outsider in This Society," in *Introducing Don DeLillo*, ed. Frank Lentricchia (Durham: Duke University Press, 1992), 48.

59. DeLillo, *Underworld* (New York: Scribner, 1997) 94. Further references are abbreviated in the text as *U*.

60. DeLillo, *Running Dog* (New York: Knopf, 1978), 111.

61. DeLillo, "American Blood: A Journey through the Labyrinth of Dallas and JFK," *Rolling Stone*, 8 December 1983, 24.

62. Richard Williams, "Everything under the Bomb" (interview with DeLillo), *The Guardian* (London), 10 January 1998, Weekend section, 32–37.

63. The fictional treatment of systems theory and cybernetics in contemporary American literature in general and DeLillo in particular has been explored in detail by Tom LeClair, *In the Loop: Don DeLillo and the Systems Novel* (Urbana, IL: University of Illinois Press, 1987), and John Johnston, *Information Multiplicity: American Fiction in the Age of Media Saturation* (Baltimore: Johns Hopkins University Press, 1998).

64. Wood, "Black Noise."

65. Michael Dibdin, "Out to Get Us," *Sunday Times* (London), 4 January 1998.

66. Christopher Lasch, *The Minimal Self: Psychic Survival in Troubled Times* (New York: Norton, 1984), 159.

67. In the *Guardian* interview with Richard Williams, DeLillo contests that "there wasn't a great deal of manipulation," though he does concede that "there are some links, more or less buried, that one doesn't expect will be very easily spotted." He goes on to discuss how, in addition to the "technological connections," there are "curious connections between the characters that I would say are bits of artistic stitching more than anything else." DeLillo talks about the coincidence of Klara and Nick both visiting the Watts Towers, and admits that "it doesn't really mean very much; it's just "part of the book's pattern of repetition, which gives it a certain

structural unity." But then he confesses that "it becomes, to me, fairly important." (Williams, "Everything under the Bomb.")

68. Jameson, *The Political Unconscious: Narrative as a Socially Symbolic Act* (Ithaca, NY: Cornell University Press, 1981), 19.

69. In *Late Imperial Romance* (London: Verso, 1994), John McClure argues persuasively that DeLillo's fiction exhibits a fascination with secrets and mystery which, no longer available in the spaces of romance outside the rationalizing systems of modernity, are now to be found "*within* the intricate fabric woven by a now global economic order, in the mysterious zones produced by the system itself" (119).

AFTERWORD (pp. 242–244)

1. Andrew Sullivan, "The Paranoia Gap," *New York Times*, 2 January 2000, Magazine, 32.

2. Jean Baudrillard, "L'an 2000 ne passera pas," *Traverses* 33/34 (1985): 8–16; reprinted in English as "The Year 2000 Has Already Happened," in *Body Invaders: Panic Sex In America*, ed. Arthur Kroker and Marilouise Kroker (New York: St. Martin's, 1987), 35–44.

INDEX

African American conspiracy theories: as aesthetic 159–67; attacks on 154–55; and civil rights 145–47, 164; of crack in ghetto 148–50, 156–57; in gangsta rap 165–67; and institutional racism 146–47, 154–57; Nation of Islam 162–65; political function of 152–55, 157–59; plausibility of 150–53; prominence in media of 147–55; as rumor 147; and white supremacism 144, 147, 164

Afrocentrism 162–63, 264 n3

AIDS 161, 167, 169–70, 176, 181, 189, 192–203, 207–208; *see also* HIV

alien abduction 170–73, 177, 221–23

Aliens in America (Dean) 21–22

American Tabloid (Ellroy) 106

Anorexia 133–34, 141, 184

Armstrong, John 97–98

assassinations: Martin Luther King and Malcolm X 145; President Kennedy 76–116; other presidential 113–15, 257 n22; *see also* Kennedy assassination

Baudrillard, Jean 74, 99, 115–16, 208, 242

Beauty Myth, The (Wolf) 118, 132–37, 140–41

Beck, Ulrich 188, 206–207

Bell Jar, The (Plath) 124

Berlet, Chip 6

body panic: addiction 184; bodily fluids 195, 273 n39; focus on body itself 182–85; food safety 181–83, 189–91, 207; horror films 169, 173–75, 179–80; new diseases 181,

190–91, 192–93, 197; in 1950s 169–70, 173–74, 194; implants 172–73, 177, 218; immunology 175–79, 188, 199–201; and right wing 198–99; self/non-self distinction 177–79, 185–86, 188, 202, 207–208; visual excess 179–81; *see also* HIV/AIDS

Bodysnatchers! (Ferrara) 174–75

Boyz 'N the Hood (Singleton) 148, 265 n15

brainwashing 119–21, 127

Browning, Barbara 161

Brownmiller, Susan 131

Brussell, Mae 79–80, 223–24, 280 n50

Burroughs, William 17, 34, 159, 177

Butler, Judith 139–40, 216, 273 n39

Camp, Gregory 12

Cantwell, Alan 201–202

Carmichael, Stokeley 146

Carson, Rachel 206

Carter, Chris 53–54, 223

Caruana, Stephanie 224

Casolaro, Danny 225

causality 31, 80, 85, 100, 102–11, 214

CIA 27–28, 30, 70, 86, 88, 127, 149–50, 157

Cigarette Smoking Man (*The X-Files*) 30, 218–20

City of Words (Tanner) 278 n15

Clinton, Hillary Rodham 1

Clinton, President 1, 44, 78, 79

Closing Circle, The (Commoner) 206

Commoner, Barry 206

Condon, Richard: *The Manchurian*

283

Candidate 120, 259 n61; *Winter Kills* 100–101

Conspiracy (Pipes) 5–9, 11, 14, 15, 23, 243

Conspiracy and Romance (Levine) 245 n5, 253 n94

conspiracy theories: African Americans 13, 143–67; body panic 168–203; changes in function of 3–4, 11, 24–55, 74–75, 80–81, 178–79, 215–16, 230–33, 239–41; and connectedness 204–41; and counterculture 32–34, 54, 57–59, 70, 73, 159; of crack in ghetto 148–51, 156–57; and cynicism 19, 55, 73–75, 79, 222, 226; and decentered systems 212–216, 218–23, 236–37; definitions of 10–11, 247 n24; dismissals of 5–9, 9–10, 12–13, 16–17, 123, 154–55, 183, 205, 287; and feminism 117–42; and figuration 49–55, 121–22, 125–26, 129–37, 156–57, 158–59, 161–62, 185, 188, 191, 193, 209; of HIV/ AIDS 161, 167, 169–70, 176, 181, 189, 192–203, 207–208; hoaxes 46–51; history of 2, 9–10, 245 n5; history of term 16; as entertainment 6, 43–45; and Internet 209–14, 242, 273 n38; narrative structure of 103–105, 237–41; and obviousness 70–75; political meaning of 8, 21–22, 32, 152–55, 157–59, 165–67, 202–203, 243–44; and paranoia 14–18; plausibility of 24–25, 31–32, 68-69, 150–53; as popular sociology 9–10, 19–21, 32, 138–40, 154–55, 239–40; and postmodernism 74–75, 112–16, 159; right-wing 37–43, 251 n49; self-reflexivity of 16–18, 34, 49–51, 55, 59–60; and uncertainty 158–59; *see also* body panic; connectedness; globalization; Kennedy assassination; paranoia

Conspiracy Theories (Fenster) 20–21, 259 n48, 266 n27

Conspiracy Theory (Donner) 16, 52–53

Countering the Conspiracy to Destroy Black Boys (Kunfuju) 153–54, 156–57

crack cocaine 148–51, 156–57

Creed, Barbara 179

Cronenberg, David 169, 176, 179–80

Crying of Lot 49, The (Pynchon) 58–59,

62, 63–64, 65–67, 69, 71, 77, 100–102, 223

cynicism 19, 55, 73–75, 79, 222, 226

Daly, Mary 129–31

Dark Alliance (Webb) 148, 156–57

Dark Skies 280 n49

Davis, David Brion 2, 54, 144

Dean, Jodi 21–22, 29

DeLillo, Don 3, 35, 99, 106–107, 114, 116, 226; *Libra* 107–12, 226–27; *Underworld* 226–41

Derrida, Jacques 185

Dietrology 231–32

disinfo.com 45, 55–56

distrust: of experts 27, 94–96, 171–72, 182, 199–200; of government 3, 27, 33–34, 250 n34

Douglass, William Campbell 194, 200

Dr Strangelove (Kubrick) 170

D'Souza, Dinesh 154–55

Duesberg, Peter 199–200

Dworkin, Andrea 132

Eagleton, Terry 75

Ellroy, James 106

Emerging Viruses (Horowitz) 153, 201–202

End of Racism, The (D'Souza) 154–55

Epperson, A. Ralph 204

Faludi, Susan 118, 263 n20, 264 n28

Farrakhan, Louis 163–64, 202

Fear of a Black Planet (Public Enemy) 166

Feminine Mystique, The (Friedan) 118–24, 141

feminism 117–42; antipornography 131–32; mad housewife fiction 124–25; and metaphors of conspiracy 129–36; popular 140–42, 261 n3; poststructuralist 138–40; radical 126–29; victim 132–37

Fenster, Mark 20–21, 259 n48, 266 n27

Fire with Fire (Wolf) 137

Fiske, John 152

fluoridation 269 n5

Fox, Nicols 190

Friedan, Betty 118–24, 129, 141

gangsta rap 165–67
Garrison, Jim 103, 104–105
Gates, Henry Louis 157–58
"Gemstone File, The" (Roberts/ Caruana) 223–25, 252 n53
Geshekter, Charles 197
Gibson, William 201
globalization 20, 37–40, 42, 207–209, 214, 225, 234–35, 239–41, 246 n23
Gravity's Rainbow (Pynchon) 17–18, 59–60, 62, 111, 159, 205, 213, 254 n95
gullibility 7–8
Gyn/Ecology (Daly) 129–32

Harlot's Ghost (Mailer) 30, 106
HEAL (Health Education AIDS Liaison) 197
hermeneutic of suspicion 73–75
Hidden Persuaders, The (Packard) 122
HIV: theories about origin of 199–202, 230; *see also* AIDS
Hofstadter, Richard 5–6, 11, 12, 14, 18, 19, 24, 31, 34, 36–37, 42, 43, 57–58, 77–78, 143, 205
Hopkins, Budd 171–72
Horowitz, Leonard 153, 201–203
horror films 169, 173–75, 179–80
Hot Zone, The (Preston) 192
hysteria 6
Hystories (Showalter) 6, 7, 12–13, 15, 18, 187

I Heard It Through the Grapevine (Turner) 13, 145, 157
immunology 175–79, 188, 199–201
interconnectedness: and chaos theory 209, 213; and computer viruses 209–10; and ecology 206, 212–13; and endless deferral 218–23, 224–25; and epidemiology 207–209; and other discourses 205; of Internet 208–12; six degrees of separation 205
Invasion of the Body Snatchers (Siegel) 173
Invisible Government (Ross and Wise) 28

Jackson, Jesse 150, 157
Jameson, Fredric 19–21, 74, 114, 225, 239–40, 255 n102
JFK (Stone) 76, 102–105

Kelly, Kevin 209, 214–16
Kennedy assassination: and agency 110; and coincidences 96–98, 107–108; conspiracy theories of 87–91; disagreement about 91–97; and experts 94–96; in *JFK* (Stone)102–105; in *Libra* (DeLillo) 107–12; lone gunman theories of 81–87; and narrative structure 103–105; official investigations of 82–84, 87, 88–89; political theories of 86–87; and popular culture 76–79; and postmodernism 112–16, 227; psychological theories of 83–84; sociological theories of 84–85; as watershed 78–81, 226–27
Kimbrell, Andrew 184
Kramer, Larry 195
Kristeva, Julia 179
Kunfuju, Jawanza 153–54, 156–57

Lasch, Christopher 183, 237, 253 n82
Lavender Menace 129
Levin, Ira 125–26
Levine, Robert S. 245 n5, 253 n94
Lewin, Leonard 46, 242
Libra (DeLillo) 107–12, 226–27
Liddy, G. Gordon 30

mad-housewife fiction 124–25
Mailer, Norman 30, 85–86, 99, 106
Mainardi, Patricia 127
Manchester, William 78
Manchurian Candidate, The (Condon) 120, 259 n61
McVeigh, Timothy 39–40, 173
Men in Black (Sonnenfeld) 51
Metzger, Richard 45, 55–56
millennium bug 242–43
mind control 161, 173
moral panic theory 18–19, 165, 198
Muhammad, Khalid 163–64
Mumbo Jumbo (Reed) 159–62

Naismith, Gaye 188
Nation of Islam 162–65, 202
national security state 28–31
narrative structure 103–105, 237–41
Nava, Mica 138–39
Neuromancer (Gibson) 211

"Octopus, The" (Casolaro) 223, 225
Oglesby, Carl 31
Olestra 189–90
On the Trail of the Assassins (Garrison)
   103, 104–105
Oswald, Lee Harvey 81–87
Oswald's Tale (Mailer) 85–86, 99, 106
Outbreak (Petersen) 192

Packard, Vance 122
Palmer, Pauline 124–25
Parallax View (Pakula) 52
paranoia 14–17; Cold War 227–29,
   233–37; definition of 247 n24;
   Freudian theory of 15, 17, 34, 247
   n32; and Kennedy assassination 84;
   and schizophrenia 208; shift to
   insecure 229–33
Paranoid Style (Hofstadter) 5–6, 11, 12,
   14, 18, 19, 24, 31, 34, 36–37, 42, 43,
   57–58, 77–78, 143, 205
Patton, Cindy 199
Pentagon Papers 46
Pierce, William 40–43, 164
Pipes, Daniel 5–9, 11, 14, 15, 23, 243
Plath, Sylvia 124
Political Paranoia (Robins and Post)
   6–9, 11, 12–13, 14, 15, 243
Popper, Karl 9
Posner, Gerald 85
Preston, Richard 192
Public Enemy 166
Pynchon, Thomas 34, 44, 57, 159, 223;
   The Crying of Lot 49 58–59, 62, 63–64,
   65–67, 69, 71, 77, 100–102, 223;
   Gravity's Rainbow 17–18, 59–60, 62,
   111, 159, 205, 213, 254 n95; *V.* 57,
   62; *Vineland* 60–72, 216

Rappoport, Jon 200
Reed, Ishmael 159–62
Report from Iron Mountain (Lewin) 46,
   242
right wing 37–43, 189–99, 251 n49
risk 178, 188, 191–93, 196, 206–208
Robeson, Paul 145–46
Robins, Robert and Jerrold Post 6–9,
   11, 12–13, 14, 15, 243
Rogin, Michael 29, 271 n29
Roiphe, Katie 193

Ross, Andrew 279 n16
Roswell 25–26
Rushkoff, Douglas 215

Safe (Haynes) 186–88
secrecy 28–32, 232, 249 n12
Sedgwick, Eve Kosofsky 73–74,
   198
Segal, Lynne 137–38
Selling Fear (Camp) 12
Shakur, Tupac 166
Simpson, O. J. 27, 147–48
Singleton, John 148
Six Degrees of Separation (Shepisi) 206
Sloterdijk, Peter 74
Sontag, Susan 198–99
Stepford Wives, The (Levin) 125–26,
   186–87
Stone, I. F. 87
Stone, Oliver 8, 33, 76, 102–106
Strieber, Whitley 171
supermarket tabloids 51

Tanner, Tony 278 n15
Thoreau, David 34–35
Three Days of the Condor (Pollack) 30
Tudor, Andrew 178–79
Turner, Patricia 13, 145, 151, 157
Turner Diaries (Pierce) 40–43, 164

UFOs 170–73, 221; Roswell and 25–26,
   222
Underworld (DeLillo) 226–41
Unseen Hand, The (Epperson) 144,
   204

V. (Pynchon) 57, 62
Verdecchia, Guillermo 207
vertigo of interpretation 21, 98–102,
   109, 218–23, 224–25
Vineland (Pynchon) 60–72, 216

Warren Commission Report 82–84, 87,
   111–12, 114
Watney, Simon 198–99
We Charge Genocide (Robeson et al.)
   145–46

Webb, Gary 148, 156–57
Willman, Skip 260 n75
Winter Kills (Condon) 100
WITCH (Women's International
  Terrorist Conspiracy from Hell)
  128–29
Wolf, Naomi 118, 132–37, 140–41,
  180, 184
Wood, Gordon 9
Wu-Tang Clan 167

X-Files, The 27–28, 30, 31, 47, 48–51,
  53–54, 169, 172, 173, 177–78,
  190–91, 216–23, 243, 270 n14, 276
  n65; endless deferral of truth in
  218–23; paranormal vs. paranoia in
  217–18

Y2K see millennium bug

Zapruder footage 89–90, 180, 226